Collins

Cambridge IGCSE®

Geography

STUDENT'S BOOK

Also for Cambridge O Level and Cambridge IGCSE® (9–1)

John Belfield,
Jack and Meg Gillett, John Rutter

William Collins's dream of knowledge for all began with the publication of his first book in 1819. A self-educated mill worker, he not only enriched millions of lives but also founded a flourishing publishing house. Today, staying true to this spirit, Collins books are packed with inspiration, innovation and practical expertise. They place you at the centre of a world of possibility and give you exactly what you need to explore it.

Collins. Freedom to teach.

The News Building
1 London Bridge Street
London
SE1 9GF

© HarperCollins*Publishers*Limited 2018

First published 2012
Second edition 2014
Third Edition 2018

10 9 8 7 6 5 4 3 2 1

ISBN 978-0-00-826015-6

John Belfield, Jack and Meg Gillett and John Rutter assert their moral rights to be identified as the authors of this work.

® IGCSE is a registered trademark of Cambridge Assessment International Education

Exam questions on pages 283–372 are reproduced by permission of Cambridge Assessment International Education. Cambridge International Examinations bears no responsibility for the example answers to questions taken from its past question papers which are contained in this publication.

The questions, example answers, marks awarded and comments that appear in this book were written by the authors. In examination, the way marks would be awarded to answers like these may be different.

All rights reserved. No part of this publication may be reproduced, stored in a retrieval system, or transmitted in any form or by any means, electronic, mechanical, photocopying, recording or otherwise, without the prior written permission of the Publisher or a licence permitting restricted copying in the United Kingdom issued by the Copyright Licensing Agency Ltd, 90 Tottenham Court Road, London W1T 4LP.

British Library Cataloguing in Publication Data.
A Catalogue record for this publication is available from the British Library.

Publisher Celia Wigley
Originally commissioned by Andrew Campbell
Project management by Sheena Shanks
Picture research by Caroline Green and Sheena Shanks
Design and typesetting by Jouve India Private Limited
Cover design by Kevin Robbins
Printed in Italy by Grafica Veneta S.p.A.

With thanks to the reviewers of the first edition: Alex Cook (Sri Lanka), Annabel Hoareau (Seychelles), Pallavi Jha (India), Penelope Law (Antwerp).

Special thanks to Alan Parkinson and the Geographical Association.

MIX
Paper from responsible sources
FSC C007454

This book is produced from independently certified FSC paper to ensure responsible forest management.

For more information visit:
www.harpercollins.co.uk/green

Contents

Introduction   v

World map: locations of case studies   1

Section 1: Population and settlement   2
    Topic 1.1 Population dynamics   2
    Topic 1.2 Migration   21
    Topic 1.3 Population structure   27
    Topic 1.4 Population density and distribution   32
    Topic 1.5 Settlements and service provision   39
    Topic 1.6 Urban settlements   50
    Topic 1.7 Urbanisation   64

Section 2: The natural environment   73
    Topic 2.1 Earthquakes and volcanoes   73
    Topic 2.2 Rivers   82
    Topic 2.3 Coasts   92
    Topic 2.4 Weather   106
    Topic 2.5 Climate and natural vegetation   115

Section 3: Economic development   136
    Topic 3.1 Development   136
    Topic 3.2 Food production   153
    Topic 3.3 Industry   171
    Topic 3.4 Tourism   181
    Topic 3.5 Energy   189
    Topic 3.6 Water   205
    Topic 3.7 Environmental risks of economic development   213

Section 4: Geographical skills   235
    Topic 4.1 Map skills   235
    Topic 4.2 Using maps   245
    Topic 4.3 Graphing and mapping numerical data   251
    Topic 4.4 Using illustrations   263
    Topic 4.5 Fieldwork skills   269
    Topic 4.6 GIS and satellite images   279

Section 5: Exam preparation — 283
- 5.1 Geographical themes — 283
- 5.2 Geographical skills — 301
- 5.3 Coursework — 328
- 5.4 The alternative to coursework examination — 348

Glossary — 373

Index — 382

Acknowledgements — 393

Introduction

Welcome to your new textbook for Cambridge IGCSE Geography. This book has been written to provide support for all students taking Cambridge IGCSE Geography (0460) and Cambridge O Level Geography (2217). The book is also now closely connected with IGCSE (9–1) specifications.

Living geography

Geography literally means 'writing the earth', and this book tells stories from many fascinating places, cities, people, ecosystems and cultures at different levels of development. It will show you places that may be familiar and unfamiliar, and support you through the next stage of your own educational journey.

The book aims to provide you with the skills and knowledge to be able to 'write the earth' in your own words, and be confident that you can take your place as a **global citizen**. This includes a special focus on the mathematical skills that help explain the world, and the tools that geographers use to map it, including Geographical Information Systems (GIS). It will also explore some of the big decisions that lie ahead for young people:

- Where will I live?
- What will I do as a job?
- How big will my family be?
- How will the world change over the coming decades?
- Where will my food, water and energy come from?
- Why do people continue to live in dangerous places?
- How do places change over time?

Geography is the subject that best explains the present, with an eye to the future.

About this book

The topics and activities in this book will take you on a journey. Each topic starts with some key questions which ask you to think about how geography is relevant to your own life. It includes a wide range of information in the form of maps, graphics, data, reportage facts and opinions for you to use, and sets out a range of tasks which will challenge you to think like a geographer.

Cambridge IGCSE and O Level Geography are qualifications which expect quite a lot of you as a student, and also of your teachers. There is an expectation that by the end of the course you will have:

- An understanding of location on a local, national and regional scale.
- An awareness of the characteristics, distribution and processes affecting contrasting physical environments.
- An understanding of the ways in which people interact with each other, and with their environment.
- An awareness of the contrasting opportunities and constraints presented by different environments.
- An appreciation of and concern for the environment.
- An appreciation of the earth.

This book will guide you through all of these areas and will help you build the skills needed for success in exams.

How to use this book

Sections of the book

This Student Book covers all the content and the different assessment models from the updated Cambridge IGCSE Geography and O Level Geography syllabuses. It is divided into five sections and a glossary.

Sections 1, 2 and 3 match the three key topics which make up the syllabus (Section 1: Population and Settlement; Section 2: The Natural Environment; Section 3: Economic Development).

Topics within each section follow the order of contents within the syllabus.

Section 4 covers Geographical Skills. It looks at using maps, graphs, illustrations and numerical data with an expanded section on the latter. It also covers a range of fieldwork skills, including conducting questionnaires and surveys and measuring natural processes and human impacts.

Section 5 will help you to prepare for examinations for IGCSE and O Level Geography. Here you will find advice to help you achieve success in examinations, how to interpret the 'command words' (instruction words) used in exam papers and how to answer different types of exam questions. You can also see example questions and answers written by the author as well as comments on why some answers are stronger than others.

Investigative geography

You'll notice that most double pages start with a big question which will be explored in depth. This develops the idea of 'geographical enquiry': a structured way of exploring the world, using a range of resources and reaching conclusions which need to be explained and then reflected on. The activities in the book will support your thinking, and help you work through these enquiries.

Case studies

The book includes a number of case studies from many locations, each of which is mapped. These focus on particular areas of the world: sometimes a region, sometimes a city. Remember that no matter where you live, there are global connections that exist across the continents and oceans to all of these places. Take the time to explore further and find out more about these places, so that you appreciate how the world fits together, and can write about them effectively.

Glossary

The key terms are highlighted in the text *like this*, and are explained in the glossary. These are words and phrases which have specific meanings in Geography, and which it would be helpful for you to know.

Now Investigate

Answers to these questions can be found at www.collins.co.uk/IGCSEanswers

Best wishes for the course.

Locations of case studies used in the book

1 Liberia: p. 9
2 Canada and Tanzania: pp. 11–12
3 China: pp. 16–17, 151, 192
4 Senegal: p. 25
5 Singapore: p. 35
6 Sahel: pp. 36–37
7 England: pp. 48–49, 61–63, 233–234
8 India: pp. 67, 210
9 Japan: pp. 30, 78–79
10 Monserrat: pp. 80–81
11 Vietnam: pp. 87–88
12 USA: pp. 89–91, 150–151
13 Australia: pp. 103–105, 229–231
14 Borneo: pp. 119–120, 225–226
15 Namibia: pp. 126–128
16 Malaysia: pp. 158–160
17 Bangladesh: pp. 161–162, 176–177
18 Bolivia: pp. 168–170
19 France: pp. 184–185
20 Kenya: p. 187–188
21 Kazakhstan and Uzbekistan: pp. 215–217
22 Greenland: pp. 218–219
23 Papua New Guinea and Carteret Islands: p. 224

Section 1 . Topic 1

Population dynamics

Learning objectives:
- describe and give reasons for the rapid increase in the world's population
- show an understanding of over-population and under-population
- understand the main causes of a change in population size
- give reasons for the contrasting rates of natural population change
- describe and evaluate population policies

Why are some families larger than others?

Population growth

In the last 50 years, the world's population has grown faster than ever before. This happened so quickly, it is known as the **population explosion**. Graph **C** shows how the world's population has changed over the last 150 years. It also shows that most of this increase took place in poorer countries. For a long time the graph line is almost level and then it suddenly becomes much steeper. This is the point when the population explosion took place. Graph **D** shows the points when global population increased by another billion (one thousand million).

> Halbi! My name is Kadlin. I live in Svelvik, a small town not far from the capital city, Oslo. I live with my parents and my grandmother. Like many children in Scandinavia, I'm an only child. I often wonder what it would be like to have even one brother or sister. When I asked Mum about this, she told me, 'Your father and I wanted you to have the best – and a chance to go to university. That's very expensive, so we decided not to have any more children.' Mum also said she needed to get a good start to her career before she settled down – she was 31 before she and Dad got married.

A Kadlin and her family live in Norway, one of the richest countries in the world

B Daksh's family live in India, which has many poor people

> Namaste! I'm Daksh and I live in Nindar, Jaipur. My father wanted to follow the local tradition of having sons to help him on the farm. After I was born, though, my four sisters arrived before a brother came along – so now there are six of us. I used to dream of going to university and becoming a doctor, but I left school at 14 and now do much of the work in the fields because father is getting older and isn't well.

Skills link

Graphs **C** and **D** are different types of line graph. Learn more about line graphs in Topic 4.3 page 251.

Fantastic fact

Every minute of every day, the world's population increases by at least 150 people!

Topic link

You can learn more about over-population in Topic 1.1 pages 8–12.

C World population change, 1900–2050

- Less economically developed countries (LEDCs)
- More economically developed countries (MEDCs)
- — Actual population
- --- Predicted population

2   Population and settlement

Effects of population growth on people

Population increase affects people and places in different ways. A population can grow so rapidly that there are no longer enough essential resources such as food and water. This is called **over-population**.

An increasing population can also have economic benefits:

- There are more customers to buy locally made goods. This creates jobs close to where people live.
- Manufacturing large quantities means goods can be made more cheaply, so more people can afford to buy them.
- Cheaper goods means they are easier to sell abroad, which earns extra money for the country.
- More jobs means less unemployment, which enables more parents to provide their children with a better standard of living.

D World population 1800–2011: the 'billion-person points'. World population reached 7.5 billion on 24th April 2017.

More people ⟶ more workers ⟶ increased output ⟶ more to sell ⟶ greater wealth

Now Investigate

1. What are some factors that influence family size? How many people are there in your own family?

2. The world's population increases by at least 150 people every minute. Use a calculator to work out how many million extra people there are in a year.

3. a) Copy and complete the table below, using information on graph **D**.
   b) What does your table tell you about how quickly the world's population increased after the year 1900?

Billion-people points		Number of years between these two points
First	Second	
Second	Third	
Third	Fourth	
Fourth	Fifth	
Fifth	Sixth	
Sixth	Seventh	

4. Referring to graphs **C** and **D**, select the correct number from those shown in brackets.
   a) The world's population in 1800 was about (*10/100/1 000/10 000*) million people.
   b) The world's population in 2010 was about (*6/7/8/9*) billion people.
   c) In 2000, most people lived in (*developed/developing*) countries.
   d) With low or medium fertility, the rate of world population growth is (*slowing down/speeding up/staying about the same*).
   e) Using the high fertility prediction, the global population in 2050 is predicted to be about (*7.5/8.5/9.5/10.5*) billion people.

Section 1.1: Population dynamics

Why did the population explosion happen?

The 'population explosion' took place in two stages. The first was in the earliest industrialised countries like the UK. The second was much later, in poorer, mainly agricultural countries (map/graphs **A**). This later stage is continuing in some parts of the world.

There were four main reasons for the population explosion:

- **Economic** Children can be an important source of income. In the poorest communities, every contribution, however small, is vital to the family budget. A child's income can mean the difference between starvation and survival for a family (photo **B**).

- **Care of the elderly** Older children can support the family by looking after elderly parents, or parents whose working lives are cut short by illness or accidents. Children may be the only support in countries that don't provide pensions or care facilities for the sick and elderly.

- **Infant mortality** Parents want to make sure that at least some of their children will survive and become adults. In poor societies, where medical facilities are limited, there is a high **infant mortality rate**. Having a large family provides security against the problems of old age.

- **Life expectancy** People are now living longer because of improved medical knowledge and treatment. Better farming methods have increased crop yields so there

A *The population explosion happened in different places at different times*

B *Children at work*

C *Modern machinery helped to increase global cereal production by over 250% in the late 20th century*

4 Population and settlement

is more food and a more nutritious diet (photo **C**). At school, children learn how to stay healthy for longer. The average life expectancy of the world's population is now approximately 70 years, compared with only 40 years two centuries ago.

Stages of the population explosion

- **Stage one** In the 18th and 19th centuries, the development of industry led to rapid population growth, especially in Europe. The new factories needed large numbers of workers. Many people moved into the towns from surrounding rural areas. More children survived infancy, so the **fertility rate** increased.

- **Stage two** In the 20th century, improved medical facilities worldwide increased the life expectancy of ordinary working people. There was now a much greater difference between the **death rate** and the **birth rate**.

Diagram **D** explains why the rate of population growth has slowed down in recent years. In fact the world's fertility rate is now 2.4 children, half what it was in 1950.

> **Fantastic fact**
>
> In the UK, it can cost over £200 000 to bring up one child from birth to age 21. This is an increase of 63% since 2003!

- Birth control – allows people to choose how many children they will have
- National population control policies – lead to a lower birth rate, e.g. in China
- Lower fertility rate – parents know that most of their children will survive
- Higher cost of living – so families in the richest countries tend to be smaller
- Career decisions – more women take up a career rather than having several children

Why has the population explosion slowed down?

D Declining rate of population growth

Now Investigate

1 a) One way of remembering facts is to use letters that stand for key words. These words can then be joined to make a simple phrase that is easy to remember. Try doing this with the four reasons for the population explosion (E C I L). You can put them in a different order, if this helps!

b) Now think of another way to remember facts, and use this to help you remember the information in diagram **D**.

2 Match each of the following key terms with the correct definition:

Key term	Definition
1 Birth rate	a the average number of children women have in their lifetime
2 Death rate	b the average number of deaths in a year (for every 1000 people)
3 Fertility rate	c the average number of live births in a year (for every 1000 people)
4 Growth rate	d the average number of years people can expect to live
5 Infant mortality rate	e the difference between the birth rate and the death rate
6 Life expectancy	f the proportion of children dying at birth or before their first birthday

Section 1.1: Population dynamics

3. **a)** Name the continent that was most affected by the first stage of the population explosion.
   b) Name three continents that experienced the second stage of the population explosion.
   c) Which of these three continents was most affected by the second stage of the population explosion?
   d) Write a few sentences about how quickly population has increased in the continents you have named.

Why do populations grow at different rates?

As in any country, the rate of population growth in your country is due to changes in three variables:

- birth rate
- death rate (including the infant mortality rate)
- international migration.

The infant mortality rate is usually the most important of these. Parents may be aware that some of their children are likely to die before they reach adulthood, because of a lack of a good diet or poor healthcare, and they may have this in mind when deciding how big their family should be. This topic explains why children's survival is so important to the future of many families in less economically developed countries. Apart from old age, the main causes of death are:

- diseases and infections such as cholera and typhoid

Topic link

- Look back at Topic 1.1 pages 2–5 to remind yourself about population growth.
- You will learn more about international migration in Topic 1.2 pages 21–26.

Fantastic fact

Locusts can make famines much worse. A swarm of 80 million locusts can eat 160 tonnes of cereal and fresh fruit *every day*!

CHINA
1907	24 million
1911	100 000
1923	234 000
1928-30	3 million
1931	1 million
1935	145 000
1936	5 million
1941	3 million
1976	300 000

ITALY
| 1908 | 123 000 |

HAITI
| 2010 | 223 000 |

ETHIOPIA
| 1978 | 100 000 |
| 1984 | 300 000 |

INDIA
1901-02	19 million
1943	2 million
1967	1.5 million

BANGLADESH
1943	2 million
1970	500 000
1991	138 000

MYANMAR
| 2008 | 138 000 |

JAPAN
| 1923 | 142 000 |

VIETNAM
| 1945 | 2 million |
| 1971 | 100 000 |

INDONESIA
| 2004 | 166 000 |

Legend: Cyclone/Hurricane, Earthquake, Tsunami, Drought, Famine, Flood, River flood

Year	Fatalities
2010	223 000

A Natural hazard events since 1900 that killed over 100 000 people

Bar chart — Millions of fatalities:
- Africa: ~3.9 (11 events)
- Asia: ~1.5 (10 events)
- Europe: ~0.05 (1 event)

The number on each column represents the number of events involved.

B Conflict events since 2000

Population and settlement

- natural hazards, especially earthquakes and floods
- human conflict.

Human conflicts and natural hazards can have a serious impact on a country's population (map **A** and graph **B**). However, there can be significant differences in their long-term effects on population change.

For example, a natural hazard such as a tsunami or powerful earthquake may sweep away almost everything and everybody in the area (photo **C**). That place may be abandoned, or be re-populated. The main impact of such events is on the *total* population; they do not differentiate between individual age and gender groups.

C The Japanese tsunami, 2011, which devastated the nuclear plant at Fukushima

Human conflict has a similar effect. It can involve the death and injury of hundreds and even thousands of people, as for example in Bosnia-Herzegovina in Europe (1992–95), Darfur in Sudan (2003–06) and Syria (2011 onwards).

Armed fighters in the 20–45 year age range are most likely to die in such conflicts. However, modern warfare can affect people of any age, and can have a long-lasting effect on a country's total population (photo **D**).

D When there is conflict in a country, people often lose their homes and their land

Topic link
You can learn more about famines – a widespread shortage of food – in Topic 3.2 pages 163–170.

Topic link
To learn more about the 2011 Japanese earthquake, look at Topic 2.1 on pages 77–79.

Topic link
Look at Topic 2.5 pages 128–135 to learn more about how people are affected by natural hazards.

Further research
Find out what events may have influenced the death rate in your own country or continent in recent times.

Section 1.1: Population dynamics

> **Now Investigate**

1 a) Describe the global distribution of each type of natural hazard shown on map **A**.

   b) Try to identify any world regions where there appear to be 'clusters' of similar events.

2 a) Draw a scatter graph to plot the numbers of fatalities in the six famines shown on map **A**, then add a best-fit line to highlight the trend it shows.

   b) What trend in the number of famine casualties does your line graph show?

   c) Suggest possible reasons for the trend.

3 Study graph **B**.

   a) Which continent has been most affected by human conflict during the 21st century, in terms of:

   i) the number of events

   ii) the total number of fatalities?

   b) Using your answers to question (a), suggest the long-term effects of conflict on the populations of continents.

How are population growth and resources linked?

Over-population

If the number of people living in an area cannot be supported by the resources in that area and enjoy a reasonable standard of living, it is **over-populated**. Regions like the African deserts may be over-populated, even though very few people live there (they are **sparsely populated**), because the land cannot support the number of people who live there.

However, just because many people live in an area (that is, it is **densely populated**), that does not always mean a place is over-populated. Some of the most densely populated places on Earth are well resourced. For example, Japan is not over-populated, because it has many profitable industries which provide jobs and income through the country's exports. Those items that cannot be produced in their own country can be bought from abroad using money earned from these exports.

Under-population

If the number of people living in an area is fewer than the number that can be supported by the resources in that area, then it is **under-populated**. For example, Canada has many resources which are under-used. Many more people could live there and enjoy a high standard of living.

> **Fantastic fact**
>
> Just 29% of the world's surface is land, but only about 40% of this is suitable for food production.

Population and settlement

1.1

Resources and population

There are two questions to ask when deciding whether a country is over-populated or under-populated:

- Do people have what they need in order to stay alive and to provide for their families (diagram **C**)?
- Are the country's resources sufficient to support its population?

CASE STUDY

Liberia – a country with a high rate of natural population growth

Table **A** shows that Africa is predicted to have the greatest natural population growth (NPG) of all the continents for the foreseeable future. Liberia is one of Africa's smallest countries, with only 4.3 million people; it once had the continent's highest NPG rate (over 4.5%); but, by 2017, this had fallen to 2.4%. It remains one of the world's poorest countries, mainly due to its recent civil wars which killed over 250 000 people and ruined the economy. Unemployment remains very high (85%) and almost three-quarters of its workers depend on agriculture for a living. Diagram **B** provides more information about Liberia.

FACTS ABOUT LIBERIA'S PEOPLE

- The infant mortality rate is one of the world's 20 highest
- Contraceptives are used by only 20% of adults
- 61% of all Liberians are below 25 years of age
- Life expectancy is 59.0 years
- The birth rate is 34 per 1000 people
- The literacy rate is only 47.6%
- 64% of Liberians live in poverty, down from 80%
- The fertility rate is the world's 26th highest; it used to be the 5th

B *Facts about Liberia's people*

Years	Africa	The Americas	Asia	Europe	Oceania	World
1950–2000 (Actual)	253	148	137	33	139	143
2000–2050 (Prediction)	204	45	42	–3	84	59
2050–2100 (Prediction)	77	0	–7	–9	25	15

A *Global percentage population changes, 1950–2100*

Section 1.1: Population dynamics

Too many people, too few resources

There are a number of reasons why a place may not be able to support a large number of people – that is, why it may be over-populated. For example:

- **A lack of clean water** may force people to use polluted sources and possibly fall ill with diseases, many of which are life-threatening, especially for the very young and old.
- **Droughts** are becoming more frequent and severe due to climate change. They increase the risk of starvation in already over-populated countries.
- **Loss of jobs** – when valuable natural resources become exhausted, workers are no longer needed and will not be able to support their families.
- **Population growth** – when there is rapid population growth, or an increase in immigrants, a country may be less able to provide for its people.
- **Clearing of forested areas** can result in families not having the fuel they need for cooking, heating and washing.
- **Natural disasters** such as earthquakes and floods often deprive local communities of the resources they need, for example water, food and shelter.

WATER – Most important of all – without it, people die after 3–4 days

SHELTER – Protects people from hazardous elements of weather and climate

CLOTHING – Protects the body against extreme temperatures

FOOD – Most people need 1500–3000 calories every day. A balanced, healthy diet includes:
- fats, e.g. from meat, cheese, milk, fish – provide energy to fuel the body's activities
- carbohydrates, e.g. from rice, potatoes – provide warmth and aid body tissue growth and repair
- proteins, e.g. from meat, fish – provide immunity to disease and infection
- minerals, e.g. iron from red meat – helps blood to circulate oxygen to all parts of the body
- vitamins, from fruit, vegetables, nuts, cereals, fish – keep body in good working order

C *People's basic needs*

Now Investigate

1 a) Do you think your country is sparsely populated or densely populated?

b) Is it over-populated or under-populated?

2 a) Use Table **A** to compare Africa's natural population growth (NPG) trends with those of the other continents and the world as a whole.

b) Suggest reasons why Europe's NPG rate is predicted to decline – and at an increasing rate.

3 Write all the information in Diagram **B**, and the data in the paragraph about Liberia in a table. Use the headings: Information about Liberia's population change rates; Reasons for these rates of population change; Other information about Liberia.

- Lowlands
- Deserts
- Dense coniferous forest
- Polar regions (tundra)
- Mountains

D *Environments of the world's land areas*

Population and settlement

1.1

Over-population and under-population

Both large and small countries can be under-populated and over-populated. On these pages we look at one very large country, in terms of area, which has a relatively small population and another which has one of the largest and fastest growing populations in Africa. Canada is under-populated because it has an advanced industrialised economy and so many valuable natural resources that it could easily provide extra people with a high standard of living. Tanzania is an over-populated country; the information on these two pages will allow you to understand why and how Tanzania differs from Canada.

CASE STUDY

Canada – an under-populated country and Tanzania – an over-populated county

Canada is a huge country – the second largest in the world after Russia. Vast stretches of the nation are almost totally uninhabited (photo **B**). Significantly, though, GDP per capita for the country is high.

Table **A** summarises information about the populations of Canada and Tanzania. Figure **C** looks at Canada's resources of which its greatest natural assets are its mineral resources such as oil and gas. Many of these are found in remote, wilderness areas.

Fact	Canada	Tanzania
Area (km²)	9 984 670 (2)	947 300 (31)
Population (millions)	35.4 (32)	52.5 (27)
Average population density (people per km²)	4.0 (232)	62.0 (153)
Annual population growth rate (%)	0.7 (146)	2.8 (11)
Net migration (per 1000 inhabitants)	5.7 (20)	−0.5 (128)
Infant mortality rate (per 1000 live births)	4.6 (179)	41.2 (48)
Fertility rate (average number of children per woman)	1.6 (183)	4.8 (17)
Life expectancy (years)	81.9 (19)	62.2 (193)
Literacy (% of population)	99 (36)	67.8 (179)
GDP per capita ($)	46 200 (32)	3 100 (190)
GDP annual growth rate (%)	1.2 (169)	7.2 (9)
Access to safe drinking water (%)	99.8 (40)	55.6 (178)
Human Development Index	0.92 (10)	0.5 (151)
Population in poverty (%)	9.4 (143)	67.9 (50)
Value of exports ($ billion)	402.4 (12)	6.0 (108)
Value of imports ($ billion)	419 (9)	10.0 (96)

A *Factfile for Canada and Tanzania – the figures in brackets indicate the world rankings of both countries*

Fantastic fact

Canada has a land area 14 325 times larger than Singapore, one of the smallest countries in the world, but its population is only 6 times bigger!

Topic link

Topic 3.1, pages 136–40 explains how GDP, the Where-to-be-born Index and the Human Development Index are calculated.

Section 1.1: Population dynamics   11

B Canada occupies most of the North American continent above latitude 41°North

Topic link

This topic has links with Topic 3.2 pages 163–164

The figures in factfile **A** and photograph **B** clearly show that Canada is under-populated:

- The infant mortality rate is very low and life expectancy is high – this suggests that there is adequate medical care.

- Literacy rates are high – this shows that education facilities are well funded and effective.

- Unemployment rates are very low – which means that most people are able to find suitable paid work.

- The Where-to-be-born Index rating of 9, is high by global standards, showing that most people in Canada are generally content with their standard of living.

In many ways, Tanzania is similar to several other African countries. It has high youth unemployment and most of its families depend on agriculture for their survival; also, AIDS and under-nourishment mean that few people live beyond 65 years of age. Tanzania is certainly a country with great potential, but rapid population growth makes it very difficult to improve its people's standard of living.

Natural resources
- Longest coastline in the world – so fish are plentiful
- Huge coniferous forests in the north, producing large amounts of timber
- One of the world's five largest producers of aluminium, gold, nickel, uranium and zinc

Farm produce
- Huge country, so has a range of climate types, which allows production of many different crops
- Major global exporter of wheat

Water resources
- More lakes than any other country, holding much of the world's fresh water reserves

Main industries
- Aircraft and car manufacturing
- Timber industries
- Oil refining
- Aluminium smelting

Support services
- Healthcare is paid for by the state

Energy resources
- Huge deposits of oil and natural gas
- A net exporter of energy

International migration
- Encourages over 250 000 new residents every year; this is to increase the workforce and compensate for its aging population

Trade
- One of the world's top ten trading nations – most of trade is with the USA, EU and China
- The St Lawrence Seaway is a vital inland shipping route
- Major ports on both Atlantic and Pacific Ocean coasts

C Canada's resources

Now Investigate

1 What evidence in table **A** and figure **C** proves that Canada is *under*-populated? Include reasons for your answer.

2 a) Write full sentences to discuss the significance of at least six of the data comparisons in Table **A**.

b) Use the information in Table **A** to explain why Tanzania is over-populated. You could discuss this information under sub-headings such as Access to safe drinking water, Education and The economy.

3 Suggest reasons why rapid population growth makes it difficult to improve people's standard of living.

Diseases are deadly!

Death rates across the world have decreased significantly over the last 50 years, largely due to improvements in healthcare, although the cause of death is noticeably different in different parts of the world (graphs **A** on page 14). Reasons for this decline include:

- increased medical knowledge
- more effective medicines and healthcare
- education about the importance of a balanced, nutritious diet.

However, many diseases are still major killers. For example, malaria kills at least 1 million people every year. Most deaths from malaria occur in tropical countries, where breeding conditions for mosquitoes are ideal. Even now, one in every five childhood deaths in Africa is due to this disease. Diagram **B** on page 14 explains how people are infected with malaria.

A **pandemic** is an outbreak of an infectious disease so widespread that it kills millions of people in a very short time. There have been several pandemics in the past, for example:

- The so-called 'Black Death' of the mid-14th century, which we now know was spread by rat-born fleas, killed over 75 million people in Europe. It had a significant impact on the global population at that time.
- The 'Spanish Flu' pandemic of 1918–20 that killed a similar number of people. It was probably so deadly because many people had already been weakened by the effects of the First World War (1914–18).

HIV/AIDS is the most recent pandemic. It is particularly widespread among people under 60 years of age. Since it was first identified in 1981, it has caused an estimated 36 million deaths – equivalent to the population of Canada, Morocco or Uganda. HIV and AIDS are very closely linked, but are not the same! HIV (human immunodeficiency virus) is a *virus infection*, transmitted by the exchange of bodily fluids, usually through sexual activity. It reduces the body's resistance to illness and other infections and, so far, has no known cure. AIDS (acquired immune deficiency syndrome) is the *medical condition* of a person in the later stages of HIV, when victims become weak, lose weight and develop flu-like symptoms which can prove fatal.

Further research

Use the internet to create table **A** and figure **C** for your country. (If you live in Canada, investigate another country.) Use the information to decide whether your country is over-populated or under-populated.

Further research

Use information from the internet to create a factfile on a widespread disease like cholera or typhoid. Include details about:

- what causes it, and how its spreads
- what medicines are available to treat it
- those parts of the world where it is still a common cause of death
- especially serious outbreaks: when and where they took place, and how many people died.

Section 1.1: Population dynamics

Less economically developed countries (LEDC)

More economically developed countries (MEDC)

- HIV/AIDS
- Bronchitis & other breathing problems
- Heart attacks
- 'Childhood diseases', e.g. chickenpox, measles, scarlet fever, whooping cough
- Cholera and dysentery
- Strokes
- Malaria
- Tuberculosis

- Heart attacks, incl. stress-induced attacks
- Lung cancer, bronchitis & other breathing problems
- Strokes
- Road traffic accidents
- Stomach cancer
- Tuberculosis
- Suicide & other non-medical causes

A The main causes of early death (that is, not due to old age) in LEDCs and MEDCs

The number of people living with HIV continues to rise, in spite of advances in medical knowledge. Sub-Saharan Africa is the most affected region, but Botswana, Lesotho and Swaziland have the highest rates, with 22–29% of their total populations being infected (table **C**). Many African countries now use the 'ABC' slogan to advise people on how to avoid HIV/AIDS:

- **A** stands for *abstinence* (from sexual activity)
- **B** means *be monogamous* (have only one sexual partner)
- **C** stands for *contraception*.

This advice has helped African countries like Kenya and Uganda to reduce their HIV infection rates (photo **D**). Scatter graph **E** presents a possible link between population infection percentages and GDP.

1 Infected mosquito bites the skin

2 Mosquito parasite reaches the liver where it starts to reproduce

3 Many parasites enter the bloodstream and infect red blood cells

4 Infected blood cells burst, infecting other cells

5 Blood cells no longer able to supply enough oxygen to the body

6 Victim suffers fever and lacks energy

7 Uninfected mosquito bites skin and becomes infected – it will infect the next person it bites

B How malaria spreads

Skills link

You can learn more about scatter graphs in Section 4.3 page 253.

Population and settlement

	Botswana	World
Life expectancy (years)	54.5	69.0
Adults as % of total population	67.6	74.6
Average age	23.2	30.1
People living with AIDS	348 900	36.7 million
% of total population infected with AIDS	23.9	0.8
Children orphaned as a result of HIV/AIDS	Approx. 130 000	Approx. 17 million

Note: all figures are estimates

C Botswana: some of the effects of HIV/AIDS

D A new AIDS hospital in Lusaka, Zambia

Now Investigate

1 **a)** What is the most noticeable difference in the causes of early death shown for LEDCs and MEDCs in the two graphs in Figure **A**?

   b) Suggest some reasons for these differences.

2 Using diagram B, the text and the internet, suggest how people can help to reduce the spread of malaria.

3 Study graph **E**.

   a) Place a ruler or the edge of a piece of paper along the position of the best-fit line.

   b) According to this line, what appears to be the general link between the fertility rate and HIV/AIDS infection rates?

   c) How might the fertility rates be linked with the number of 15–49 year olds who are infected by HIV/AIDS?

E Relationship between HIV/AIDS and fertility rates in eight East African countries

Section 1.1: Population dynamics   15

Anti-natalist population policies

The governments of several countries have imposed direct laws, or policies, to control their population growth rates. This includes China, which has the largest population in the world.

CASE STUDY

China – a country with a low rate of natural population growth

A country like China needs to keep its population growth under control. The policies it has put in place in order to do this are described as **anti-natalist policies**:

- *anti* means to be against (or in disagreement with)
- *natalist* is anything to do with childbirth.

This term describes any policy that aims to control or limit a country's birth rate rather than stimulate it. China's strategy was the 'one-child policy', introduced in 1979.

Before 1979

After 1949, China experienced a population explosion, or 'baby boom'. The government decided to restrict family size and recommend that people married later in life. But between 1958 and 1961, droughts and floods caused the deaths of 2 million Chinese. Then the harvests returned to normal and the Chinese leader encouraged people to have as many children as possible, creating a second 'baby boom'. China's birth rate soared to 5.8 children per couple – well above the 2.1 needed to keep the population stable. This is known as the **'replacement level'**. In the 1970s, the Chinese government again wanted families to have fewer children. In 1979, it introduced its 'one-child policy'.

Did the policy work?

Family planning advice and contraceptives were made freely available, and a 'One-child Certificate' was awarded to families who had followed the policy. They were also entitled to extra benefits (diagram **A**), while those who had additional children were penalised (diagram **B**). Baby girls and second children were often abandoned, or secretly adopted by childless families.

The policy was generally more successful in the cities than in rural areas. In country areas, farming families needed a son to help work the land, so these families were usually allowed a second child if the first was a girl.

> **Fantastic fact**
>
> Two in every eleven people in the world today lives in China!

> **Topic link**
>
> Look back at Topic 1.1 pages 2–5 for more on the population explosion.

> **Topic link**
>
> For more details of China's current and predicted population structure look at Topic 4.3 on page 262.

A Benefits of being a one-child family

State benefits awarded:
- Better housing
- Better childcare
- Better chances of promotion for government employees
- Cash bonuses
- Longer maternity leave

Population and settlement

1.1

Since 1979

In 1992, China relaxed the rules and adoption was legalised. In 2004, the city of Shanghai introduced a local law allowing divorcees who re-marry to have a second child without incurring the usual penalties. In 2008, the National Population and Family Commission stated that the one-child policy would continue for at least another 10 years. However, in 2015, the Chinese government announced a new two-child policy to help address its major demographic crisis, in which more and more elderly people are being supported by fewer and fewer workers.

10-year period between population census years	% population change in China	% population change in Asia	% population change in the world
1970–1980	20.0	23.7	20.5
1980–1990	14.8	22.0	19.6
1990–2000	10.8	15.7	15.2
2000–2010	5.8	12.1	12.9
2010–2015	2.5	5.4	6.5

D Population trends in China, Asia and the World, 1970–2015

China
2010: 164 (60+), 262 (0–15), 921 (16–59)
2050: 454 (60+), 247 (0–15), 750 (16–59)

World
2010: 500 (60+), 1750 (0–15), 4400 (16–59)
2050: 1636 (60+), 1615 (0–15), 4500 (16–59)

Figures in millions
■ 0–15 years ■ 16–59 years ■ 60+ years

E Age dependency in China and the world

Problems of age dependency

China now has a very 'unbalanced' **population structure**, with more men than women – 117 men to every 100 women. Another concern is **age dependency** (graphs **E**), which means that the elderly population becomes dependent on the younger generations. It is described as China's '4-2-1 problem', because many single children (1) will become responsible for caring for their parents (2) *and* their four grandparents (4).

China's fertility rate is now about 1.6, which is still above its official target. However, the one-child policy does seem to have avoided the financial burden of 400 million extra births, which has facilitated China's development as a global economic superpower.

State Penalties Imposed:
- Government employees sacked
- Basic rice allowance withdrawn for all extra children
- Government employees' retirement pensions cancelled
- Extra children denied the same quality of education and healthcare as the first child
- Fines imposed (could be up to four times a family's income)
- Farmers who couldn't pay fines in cash had cattle taken from them

B Penalties for not following the one-child policy

- China had already achieved success in reducing its fertility rate in the 1970s – that is even before the introduction of its one-child policy! It had dropped from 5.8 children per woman in 1970, to only 2.7 in 1978.

- China's adult workforce is predicted to decrease by almost 10 million a year after 2025.

- Parents of only children who've died young have been demonstrating outside public buildings. They want compensation for financial hardship in their old age because no-one can look after them.

- More than 24 million Chinese men could find themselves without a wife by 2020. A major reason for this is the high number of sex-specific abortions, due to China's traditional bias towards male children. Ultrasound scans, first introduced in the late 1980s, have increased this practice. In some provinces (especially rural areas), 130 boys are actually born for every 100 girls.

C Recent media statements about challenges and changes in China.

Section 1.1: Population dynamics   17

> **Now Investigate**

1. Draw a timeline for population events in China since 1945. Add labels for the following years, giving details of what happened in each:

   1949, 1958–61, 1970, 1979, 1992, 2004, 2008, 2015.

2. a) Search the internet to find more media statements about China, similar to those in Figure C.

   b) Using pages 16 and 17, together with your own search results, evaluate the long-term effects of China's population control policies.

Pro-natalist population policies

Other governments have created policies to encourage people to have more children in order to boost their population growth rate. These are known as pro-natalist policies (*pro* means 'for'). In Western Europe, for example, between 1980 and 2016, no country had a fertility rate above the critical 2.1 population replacement level (table A). In fact, 47% of all the world's countries now have a fertility rate below 2.1. One reason for this is that, as countries become richer, women marry later in life and delay starting a family.

Skills link

See page 16 for an explanation of 'replacement level'.

Country	Fertility rate, 1980	Change in fertility rate, 1980–2016	Fertility rate, 2016
Austria	1.62	– 0.15	1.47
Belgium	1.68	+ 0.10	1.78
Denmark	1.55	+ 0.18	1.73
France	1.95	+ 0.12	2.07
Germany	1.56	– 0.12	1.44
Ireland	3.25	– 1.27	1.98
Italy	1.64	– 0.21	1.43
Luxembourg	1.49	+ 0.12	1.61
Netherlands	1.60	+ 0.18	1.78
Norway	2.10	–0.24	1.86
Portugal	2.18	– 0.65	1.53
Spain	2.20	– 0.73	1.47
Sweden	1.68	+ 0.20	1.88
Switzerland	1.80	–0.25	1.55
UK	1.90	–0.01	1.89
Western Europe	1.88	–0.18	1.67

■ = fertility rate 2.1 and above
■ = fertility rate below 2.1

A *Most fertility rates in Western Europe have stayed below 2.1 since 1980*

Fantastic fact

The world's average fertility rate is 2.42. In Western Europe it used to be 2.7, but is now only 1.67.

Topic link

Look back at Topic 1.1 page 5 for more about how fertility rates affect population growth.

Population and settlement

Germany has the largest population in Europe, but it is still concerned about its declining fertility rate. New measures to increase the birth rate include subsidising childcare and contributing to parents' income while they are caring for infants.

France: population strategies

France has some of the most extensive state-funded childcare facilities in Europe. Diagram **B** shows some of the ways France is encouraging people to have more children in order to maintain its fertility rate. Immigration from southern Europe and former French colonies in North Africa has contributed one quarter of all population growth in recent years, but the growth is due mainly to immigration, and not to a rise in the fertility rate.

France's pro-natalist policy has clearly been successful in restoring its fertility rate almost to the population replacement level (table **A**). One of the country's most popular strategies has been the *Carte Familles Nombreuses* ('Large Family Card'). This gives families with three or more children reductions on the national train network and half-price fares on the Paris Metro underground system. Families living in Paris, the French capital, also have a *Carte Paris-Famille* ('Paris Family Card'), which gives children free entrance to all swimming pools and subsidised entry to other sports facilities provided by the city.

> **Skills link**
>
> See Section 4.3 pages 251–252 to learn more about drawing bar graphs.

PRO-NATALIST MEASURES
- Up to 20 weeks' paid leave for first child, rising to 40 weeks' for the the third child
- All childcare facilities subsidised by the government
- System of crèches for toddlers
- Up to 3 years' entitlement to time off work, to be shared by both parents
- Tax deductions towards home-help costs for working mothers
- Subsidised state nursery schools for children aged 3 or over
- Free pre-school facilities for children aged 2 and 3
- Loss of earnings payments for parents of a third child
- Graded income tax system – the bigger the family, the less tax to be paid

B *Pro-natalist measures taken by the French government, mainly to encourage more working women to have babies.*

Section 1.1: Population dynamics

Now Investigate

1 **a)** What do you think of the French 'Family Card' schemes?

   b) Would your family, or any family that you know, qualify for this card if it was available in your country?

2 **a)** Use the data in table **A** to create a bar graph showing the fertility rates for each country, for 1980 and 2016. Shade the two bars for each country in different colours. Add an appropriate key to your graph.

   b) Draw a horizontal line across your graph at Fertility Rate 2.1; annotate this line to explain its significance.

   c) Comment on the success (or failure) of these countries in maintaining their fertility rate since 1980.

3 **a)** Make a copy of the following table. Complete your table with reference to diagram **B** and the text, putting ticks where appropriate in the last three columns.

   b) From the results shown in your table, what kinds of benefit are most likely to persuade French parents to have a larger family?

Type of benefit	Economic	Educational	Recreational
Childcare facilities			
Crèches for toddlers			
Entitlement to time off work			
Graded income tax system			
Large Family Card			
Loss of earnings payments			
Maternity leave			
Nursery schools			
Paris Family Card			
Pre-school facilities			
State nursery schools			
Working mothers' tax deductions			
Total (ticks)			

Section 1. Topic 2

Migration

Learning objectives:
- explain and give reasons for population migration
- demonstrate an understanding of the impacts of migration

Why, where and how do people move around?

People on the move

All over the world people are moving around. This is called **migration**. As geographers, we are concerned with how these movements take place both within a country, for example from rural areas to the city, and from one country to another. There are many different reasons why people need to move. Some of these are voluntary movements but there are also forced migrations when people have no choice but to flee their home.

The bright lights of the big city

In many parts of the world, life in rural areas can be very hard. For example, rural areas in less economically developed countries have very few services for local people. People in rural areas hear of the big cities where there are jobs and opportunities. Friends and family write letters telling them about freely available health services, housing and education (although this may not always be true). The factors that encourage people to move to towns and cities, in a process known as rural–urban migration, are shown in figure **A**. Things that make people want to leave are called *push* factors and those that attract them to a different area are known as *pull* factors.

Push factors	Pull factors
• Lack of running water	• Good education facilities
• Lack of services	• Better food supply
• No local schools and hospitals	• Available services
• Lack of farm machinery	• Entertainment
• Unemployment	• Variety of jobs
• Population increases resulting in lack of food	• Medical care
• Natural disasters	• Better quality of life

A *Migration push–pull factors*

The problem is that life in the city rarely turns out as well as people from rural areas expect it to be. Read about the experiences of Bagwis Manaloto, who moved from rural Luzon to Manila in the Philippines.

B The migration of Bagwis Manaloto (pictured right)

When my father died, our farm was divided between me and my brothers.

It was impossible to grow enough rice to feed my family.

I sold my land to one of my brothers and took my family to what I thought would be a better life in Manila.

But things are much worse here in the city. Thousands of people are arriving every month and the jobs have gone. We couldn't afford the high prices for a house so had to build one ourselves in the slums.

The water is dirty and makes us sick but we can't afford a doctor. It's hard enough finding money for food. I wish we'd stayed in the country.

The peace and tranquillity of the country

While cities in less economically developed countries are finding it hard to cope with all the extra people moving in, the opposite is happening in richer parts of the world. In many more economically developed countries, **counter-urbanisation** is taking place. People are getting fed up with crowded, polluted and congested towns and cities and are moving out into rural areas. There are a number of reasons why this type of migration is taking place:

- Many jobs are now found on the outskirts of cities. Commuting (daily travel) to these out-of-town areas is getting easier.
- As people get richer they want bigger houses with gardens – there is much more housing of this kind available in rural areas.
- Rural areas are often seen as a much safer place in which to raise a family, and they often have better schools.
- City centres may have higher crime rates, vandalism and social problems.

Counter-urbanisation in the capital of Scotland

Edinburgh, the capital of Scotland, has seen a lot of movement of wealthier families to surrounding rural areas. These families use local services and may save them from being closed down.

Population and settlement

However, migration can also cause problems for the small rural towns, such as North Berwick, that they have moved to (photo **C**).

In recent years many people have been moving into Edinburgh – it is one of the UK's most popular cities. Many young people are taking advantage of the city's increasing job opportunities and entertainment facilities.

- Higher property prices mean local people can no longer afford houses in the area.
- Pressure on services such as schools and hospitals.
- Many new families commute to Edinburgh, shop in the city and bring little money into local businesses.
- Increased numbers of cars make roads dangerous for local children.
- Building new houses destroys the countryside and habitats for wildlife.
- Some recent arrivals do not mix well with the local people.

C *Problems of counter-urbanisation in North Berwick*

Now Investigate

1. Have you moved around different places during your lifetime? Where did you move from? Where did you move to? What were the reasons for your migration?

2. What is the difference between:
   a) temporary and permanent migration
   b) voluntary and forced migration?

3. Using examples, explain in detail why people would want to move from:
   a) rural to urban areas
   b) urban to rural areas.

4. Think about the rural–urban migration taking place in your own country.
   a) Write down all the push and pull factors that might make somebody move to your country's main city.
   b) Would you prefer to live in the city or in a rural area? Explain your answer.

Fantastic fact

The greatest rural–urban migration is currently in China. Many cities are expanding their population by 10 per cent a year.

Moving from one country to another

Both migration within countries and migration between countries are extremely important on a global scale. **Emigrants** are those leaving a particular country and **immigrants** are those coming in. As with

Section 1.2: Migration

A *Major global migration routes*

internal migrations, this can be either voluntary or **forced migration**. Some of the world's major migration routes are shown on map **A**.

Many people move to find a better life for themselves and their families. These people are known as **economic migrants** and they often want to return home when they have earned enough money. In the meantime many will send some of what they earn back to their families. Some may enter a country unofficially without making themselves known to the authorities – these are called **illegal immigrants**.

Forced migration on an international scale is much more serious and happens for a variety of reasons:

- when people are persecuted or threatened because of their religious beliefs
- as a result of war when people are forced to leave their homes
- when people are forced into slavery, again often as a result of war
- because of racial discrimination
- when famine strikes a country and the people have to move to find food
- because of natural disasters such as earthquakes, volcanic eruptions, floods or hurricanes.

People who are forced to move are called **refugees**. The United Nations estimates that there are over 65 million refugees in the world today. Many of these refugees are forced to live in poverty in camps with little food, water or access to healthcare and education (photo **B**).

> **Skills link**
>
> One clear way to illustrate information about migration on a map is to use arrows like those shown on map **A**. Some maps also use flow lines where the arrows are wider or thinner depending on the information they display. For more details, see Topic 4.3 page 257.

B *A refugee camp in Dabaab, Somalia*

24 Population and settlement

Now Investigate

1. Using an atlas and map **A**, describe some of the major global migration routes. You should refer to specific countries in your answer.

2. Why might you want to migrate to another country? What might be the advantages of leaving? What things would you miss about your home?

3. Do people migrate to your country? What are the reasons for this immigration?

4. What are the main reasons for forced migrations? Can you think of any examples in the countries near where you live?

5. List all the advantages and disadvantages of migration for Senegal. Do you think it has a positive or negative effect for the country overall? Explain your answer.

6. What would be the possible impacts in France and other European countries of many people from Senegal migrating to them?

CASE STUDY

International migration: Senegal to Europe

Senegal is a fairly small country (about one-third the size of France) in West Africa. It has a population of around 16 million, which is growing at a rate of just over 3 per cent each year. For many years after independence from France in 1960 it was the destination for immigrants from the rest of Africa. They were attracted by Senegal's stable government and opportunities there for jobs and setting up businesses. This has changed completely over the last decade for a number of reasons:

- An economic crisis from the 1990s onwards saw a huge drop in living standards.
- There was a big increase in unemployment and a lack of jobs even for educated people.
- Rapid population growth has meant competition for the few jobs available. It has also put pressure on resources such as food supplies.

Many young Senegalese males have decided to emigrate to find work to support their families. Originally, many of them went to France because of Senegal's links with that country – the old colonial power – and because they were attracted by images of life in Europe seen on the television and in magazines. More recently, increasingly large numbers have settled in Spain and Italy (diagram **C**).

- Spain 18.8%
- Italy 14.1%
- France 9.8%
- Other European countries 3.3%
- USA/Canada 7.5%
- Cote d'Ivoire 6.6%
- Guinea-Bissau 3.2%
- Mali 2.4%
- Other African countries 31.7%
- Other (no data) 2.6%

C *The destinations of Senegalese migrants*

Section 1.2: Migration

Disadvantages of Senegalese migration

For migrants — DISADVANTAGES:
- Emigrants are often healthy young males who would be capable of doing useful work at home
- Highly qualified emigrants lose self-esteem in poor jobs
- Financial problems
- Pressure from family back home to send money
- Racial discrimination
- Isolation and lack of friends leading to depression
- Lack of jobs available in new country
- Exploitation in low-paid jobs
- Possible death in sea crossings to Europe (often via the Canary Islands)

For Senegal — DISADVANTAGES:
- Many emigrants are educated – the population left behind are less able to build a better country
- An elderly population is left behind, putting pressure on Senegal's healthcare system
- Jealousy and resentment arises against migrants when they return home, causing social problems
- A gender imbalance is created, with many more women than men being left behind

D *Disadvantages of Senegalese migration*

This migration has had a number of benefits for Senegal. Migrants send a total of US$2 billion to their families every year, contributing around 14 per cent of Senegal's total gross domestic product. They often return having learned new skills that can be put to use in developing their own country. The reduction in population also means a decrease in the demand for scarce resources. However, as diagram **D** shows, there are many disadvantages both for Senegal and for its emigrating population.

Despite the possible advantages of living abroad, many migrants are not happy. A large percentage of Senegalese migrants interviewed in Germany said they wished they had stayed at home.

Section 1. Topic 3

Population structure

Learning objectives:
- identify and give reasons for and implications of different types of population structure

Why are there more older or younger people where you live?

Walk along a busy street in your local area, and guess the ages of the people you see. How many are elderly people? How many are young adults and children? If you recorded what you saw, the information wouldn't be very reliable, because many people could be indoors or in other places. A lot would also depend on the day and the time.

In order to find out about a country's population accurately, a **census** is taken. This is an official count of all the people living in a place (usually a country) at one specific time. People are asked questions about their age and gender. The data collected from the answers helps to monitor changes in the country's population structure and in its total population. A census can also investigate issues such as ethnic background and certain measures of the quality of life. Many countries carry out a census regularly, at 10-year intervals. Some countries are unable to conduct regular censuses, because they are expensive and difficult to organise, and people need to be able to read and write in order to answer the questions.

Census data is used to plan how many facilities will be needed in the future, such as schools and hospitals. It also provides a guide as to how many people of working age will have to support the very young and the elderly in the future. Age/gender census data is usually displayed as an **age/sex pyramid** (diagrams **A** and **B**).

Topic link
- Look back at Topic 1.1 page 17 to check on age dependency.
- See Topic 4.1 page 262 to learn more about how an age/sex pyramid is constructed.

Fantastic fact
On average, women live 4 years and 1 month longer than men.

Further research
You will find population figures and pyramids for most countries on the internet. Type in the name of the country, 'age/sex pyramid', and the year you are investigating.

*Note the significant proportion of people under the age of 15.

A *Age/sex pyramid for Haiti, a typical less economically developed country*

*This pyramid has a much higher proportion of people over the age of 65 than pyramid **A**.

B *Age/sex pyramid for Germany, a typical more economically developed country*

Section 1.3: Population structure

Now Investigate

1 Carry out a class census, or one of your school year, to discover its gender structure. Then use your results to answer these questions:

  a) How many boys are there in your census group?
  b) How many girls are there in the group?
  c) What is the total number of students in the group?
  d) What is the percentage of boys in the group? Use this simple formula and a calculator to find the answer:

  $$\frac{\text{Number of boys}}{\text{Total number of students}} \times 100 = \text{.....\% of boys in the group}$$

2 a) If you can, use the same formula for *all* the boys and girls in your school. Then write a statement comparing percentages in your class/year and the whole school.

  b) Find out the gender structure for your own country, and then compare it with that of your whole school.

  c) Suggest some reasons why the structures for your school and your country might be different.

3 List at least five ways in which census information might be useful to a country.

4 Use the data in the table below to create an age/sex pyramid. Refer to graphs **A** and **B** to see how the pyramid should be presented.

5 With reference to your age/sex pyramid, which of the following statements are true?

  a) There are fewer females than males over the age of 60.
  b) There are fewer elderly people aged 60 or over than young people in the 0–15 age range.
  c) The numbers of males and females are about the same in most 5-year age groups below 60 years.
  d) This graph shows the population structure of a typical less economically developed country.

6 Using arrows pointing to the appropriate places, add the *true* statements as labels to your pyramid. Then re-write any false statements about your pyramid to make them true, and add those as labels.

Male % of total population	Age range (years)	Female % of total population
1.5	Over 80	3.3
1.4	75–79	2.0
1.9	70–74	2.3
2.5	65–69	2.8
3.7	60–64	3.8
3.5	55–59	3.6
3.6	50–54	3.5
3.6	45–49	3.5
3.3	40–44	3.2
3.0	35–39	2.8
3.2	30–34	3.1
3.3	25–29	3.1
3.1	20–24	3.0
3.1	15–19	3.0
2.8	10–14	2.7
2.8	5–9	2.6
2.7	0–4	2.7

Changing stages of economic development

You learned (on pages 27–28) that the age/sex pyramids for more and less economically developed countries generally have different shapes – especially in the 'childhood' and 'elderly' age groups. The model is a way of showing how birth and death rates change as a country develops economically and progresses through several stages.

On these two pages are several age/sex pyramids typical of countries at each stage of economic development. These show how population structures are affected by changing birth and death rates.

The age/sex pyramids in diagrams **A** and **B** are examples of population structures for each of the five stages of economic development. There are now only a few remote communities at Stage 1 of economic development such as some tribes living in the tropical rainforest of the Amazon Basin in South America (map **C**).

> **Fantastic fact**
>
> There are no longer any countries at Stage 1 of economic development.

A *Age / sex pyramids for the first four stages of economic development*

Section 1.3: Population structure

CASE STUDY

Japan – a country with a large, ageing population

Japan is a prosperous, highly industrialised country, and success in their business lives leads many of its people to postpone both marriage and child-rearing. As a result, it now has a negative population growth rate of –0.2, compared to the world average of 2.42, and the critical replacement population level of 2.1. Also, its current life expectancy has risen to 85 years (world average 69). The result is an elderly dependency ratio 3.5 times higher than the global mean.

The consequences of these demographic trends include:

- a much greater national need for healthcare provision

- the financial challenge for caring for so many more older people; some pensioners are so desperate for basic support that they deliberately commit crimes that carry prison sentences

- the pressure on employees to work excessive overtime means that more of them are committing suicide or, quite literally, working themselves to death (a fate called *karoshi* by the Japanese).

Japan is one of the few countries that has progressed through all five stage of economic development. The shape of its age/sex pyramid today (diagram **B**) is typical of those at Stage 5 of the Demographic Transition Model.

B Age/sex pyramid for Japan, a typical Stage 5 country

C Location of countries/places at different stages of economic development

Further research

Use the internet to find and print out an age/sex pyramid for your own (or a neighbouring) country. Describe the main features of the population structure of your chosen country.

Topic link

What you have learned about population structure will help you when you study Topic 1.1 pages 2–20.

Population and settlement

Now Investigate

1. How do governments in countries such as Japan respond to the issues which arise from the increasing percentage of older people?

Section 1 . Topic 4

Population density and distribution

Learning objectives:
- describe the factors influencing the density and distribution of population

Why do some people have more neighbours than others?

Many people are living very close together in the place shown in photo **A**. But the place in photo **B** is very different! Here there are very few people. Take a very good look at both of these places – perhaps one of them is like the place where you live.

Five key terms are used frequently in this topic. Some you may already know, but it is important that you understand what each one means:

- **Population distribution** – the way people are spread out over the Earth's land surfaces.
- **Population density** – how many people live in an area (usually one square kilometre or 1 km^2).
- **Densely populated** – describes places where many people live.
- **Sparsely populated** – describes places where very few people live.
- **Uninhabited** – describes places where nobody lives.

There are many reasons why people live where they do. Some people don't have a choice – a few countries never allow anyone to enter or leave. Fortunately, most countries do not impose such restrictions and their people are free to move elsewhere in search of a higher standard of living.

Map **C** shows that the world's population distribution is very uneven. One reason is that there is twice as much land in the northern hemisphere as there is south of the Equator. In this topic we look closely at the distribution of both sparsely and densely populated areas.

A *In cities, many people live very close together*

B *In other parts of the world, people are more scattered across the landscape*

Topic link
See Topics 2.1 and 2.5 to find out more about extreme environments.

Topic link
See Topic 1.2 pages 21–26 to learn more about why people migrate from one place to another.

Fantastic fact
Antarctica is the only continent where *everyone* is a visitor!

C *World population: distribution and density*

Population per sq. km
- over 250
- 101 – 250
- 51 – 100
- 11 – 50
- 0 – 10

Population and settlement

1.4

Challenges of extreme environments

Photos **D–G** show four particularly extreme environments which are either very sparsely populated or totally **uninhabited**.

D A hot desert   **E** A dense forest   **F** A mountainous region   **G** A polar region

Now Investigate

1. Which of the two places shown in photos **A** and **B** would you prefer to live in? Why?

2. Study photos **D–G**.
   a) Explain why each of these regions is a challenging place for people to live.
   b) Where would *you* prefer to live? What environments would be most and least attractive to you as places to live?

3. a) The following table lists the population and physical size of each continent. Calculate the population density of each continent. (To do this you need to divide the population for each continent by its area.)
   b) Which are the most and least densely populated continents?

Continent	Total population	Total area (km²)	Average population density (people per km²)
Africa	1 216 000 000	30 065 000	40.45
Asia	4 436 000 000	44 579 000	
Oceania	40 000 000	7 687 000	
Europe	739 000 000	9 938 000	
North America	579 000 000	24 256 000	
South America	423 000 000	17 819 000	

4. With the help of an atlas, add the following information to an outline world map.
   a) Shade in all the most sparsely populated areas shown on map **C** (<10 people per sq. km).
   b) Locate and name at least five hot deserts and five mountain ranges.
   c) Locate five large forested areas, adding names to them where possible.
   d) Locate and name: (i) Antarctic wilderness (ii) north polar wilderness.
   e) Give your completed map a suitable title and a key.

Section 1.4: Population density and distribution   33

Areas of high population density

In some parts of the world, there are very good reasons why people live in certain places (photos **A**, **B** and **C**). For example:

- Flat or gently sloping land makes it possible to farm and build towns, roads and railways (**A**, **C**).
- Fertile soil is ideal for growing crops and rearing animals (**B**).
- When floods occur, most rivers deposit alluvium (silt), which is rich in the minerals needed by plants for growth (**B**).
- Climate – adequate, reliable rainfall and suitable temperatures are needed for crops to grow and ripen (**A**, **B**).
- Fossil fuels – resources such as coal, oil and gas can be used to generate electricity and meet transport needs (**C**).
- Mineral deposits provide essential raw materials, for example iron ore for industries such as steel-making and car manufacture (**C**).
- Fishing – coasts, rivers and lakes provide plentiful, nutritious food (**A**, **B**).
- Fresh water – rivers and lakes are a major source of fresh water, and some can be used to generate power (**B**).
- Coasts and other waterside locations can be developed into ports with trading links to other countries (**C**). Such places are also often popular with tourists and retired people (**A**).

Towns and cities grow rapidly at suitable settlement sites (photo **C**). They also provide employment opportunities for people. Migration of people from other, less favourable places also increases the size and density of the population.

> **Topic link**
>
> - See Topic 1.2 pages 21–26 to learn more about migration.
> - See Topics 1.5 and 1.6 pages 39–51 to learn more about the site and situation of settlements.

A Many coasts are densely populated because they offer a wide range of opportunities for work and leisure

B A densely populated agricultural area along the Nile Valley, Egypt

> **Fantastic fact**
>
> The most densely populated areas of all are urban settlements such as towns and cities. At present, over 54% of the world's people live in urban areas.

At present, 40% of all people on Earth live within 100 km of a coast. Photo **A** is a typical scene in many highly developed and densely populated coastal areas. The bullet points above suggest some of the reasons why this particular stretch of coastline has attracted so many people.

34 Population and settlement

1.4

> **CASE STUDY**
>
> ## Singapore – a densely populated country
>
> Singapore is one of only 10 countries in the world that has all its people living in urban areas. It is a small island, but this in itself does not explain why it is so heavily urbanised. Its location at the most southerly tip of the Asian mainland means it is at a major shipping 'crossroads'. Ships sailing between Indian Ocean ports and the industrialised countries of China, Japan and Australia refuel and discharge or load their cargoes here, creating thousands of jobs for local people. Large, modern industrial estates employ many more, and are one of the main reasons why Singapore is so successful (photo **C**).
>
> Only 2% of all adults of working age are unemployed in Singapore. Natural population increase and immigration bring a rise in the total population of almost 5% every year. Providing homes for so many people in such a small area has led to the building of 28 new towns – four of these have over 200 000 inhabitants each. Two-thirds of all Singaporeans now live in new towns.
>
> **C** *Singapore is a busy international port*

Now Investigate

1. a) Would you describe the place where you live as an area of high or low population density?

   b) Which of the reasons for settlement listed above applies to the place where you live?

2. The list of bullet points on page 34 explains why people live in particular areas. Use this information to suggest which annotations could be added to photo **C**. You should enhance your annotations in order to develop each idea.

   Note: Annotating is *not* the same as labelling! Labels only identify what is there; annotations explain *why* places are important. See Topic 4.4 pages 263–268 to learn more about annotation.

3. a) Find several photographs of densely populated countries (they should look different from photo **C**).

   b) Annotate copies of these photographs to explain why the places are densely populated.

4. With the help of an atlas, add the following information to an outline world map.

   a) Shade in all the most densely populated countries shown on map **C** on page 32.

   b) Name all of the countries you have shaded (those with a population per sq. km >101).

   c) Make sure your map includes the Equator and the two Tropics. These should be named, and labelled with their latitude (in degrees).

   d) Give your completed map a suitable title and a key.

Section 1.4: Population density and distribution

Areas of low population density

North Africa is one of the most sparsely populated regions on Earth. It is also over-populated in many ways, because there are too many people for the few resources available to them. The main reason is that the Sahara, the world's largest hot desert, occupies most of the region. The area to the south of it is experiencing increasingly severe famines.

> **Topic link**
>
> See Topic 1.1 pages 8–12 to learn more about over-population.

CASE STUDY

The Sahel – a sparsely populated area

The area to the south of the Sahara is called the Sahel (map **A**). Diagram **B** highlights reasons why the Sahel today is known as Africa's 'famine belt'.

Farming is the main economic activity in the Sahel. Dry-land crops such as millet, sorghum and cowpea are the main food crops. The main cash crops are groundnuts (peanuts) and

A *Climate in the Sahel region*

36   Population and settlement

cotton. Most farmers are nomadic herders, who migrate northwards during the wet season, then return when that area becomes too dry. Many farmers now use cell phones to get weather forecasts and move their animals to places where rain is predicted to fall. Some water is available where there are rivers and lakes but, in many areas deep wells are the only reliable source of water. During the worst famines, many cattle die as much from starvation as from thirst, because there is not enough water to irrigate fodder crops to feed them.

Now Investigate

1. Describe how the natural environment of North Africa changes from north to south. You should include changes in both climate and natural vegetation in your answer. Hint: use an atlas and the internet to help you.

2. Imagine you are a farmer in the Sahel. You have received a letter from a friend who lives far away and has no idea what farming in your area is like. Your friend blames you and other farmers for all the recent problems of the Sahel region. Write a reply explaining why many of the problems in the Sahel are beyond the farmers' control.

PROBLEMS FACED BY THE SAHEL

- Sahel's population doubles every 20 years – faster than its increase in food production
- Aid agencies now subsidise 30% of food in the region – many people now dependent on food aid
- Region includes three of the four poorest countries on Earth
- Many farmers grow cash crops on their best land instead of food
- Anopheles mosquito on the increase, so more people suffering from malaria
- Many farming methods unsustainable – annual crop yields continue to fall
- Few natural resources to stimulate local industry and provide exports to increase wealth

B *Why the Sahel is sparsely populated*

Fantastic fact

The largest desert in the world took its name from the Arabic word for desert: *sahara*. *Sahel* is another Arabic word, meaning 'on the edge' of the desert.

Soil degradation

A major problem faced by farmers in many parts of the world is **soil degradation**. This is the process of the soil becoming less fertile. It can happen in three different ways:

- **Erosion** Soil can be eroded and carried elsewhere by strong winds. Over-grazing by cattle is a common cause of soil erosion.

- **Salinisation** In a hot, dry climate, where evaporation rates are high, the salts (minerals) in water can build up in the soil, causing it to become toxic (poisonous) to plants.

NATURAL FACTORS
- Lower total annual rainfall
- Less protective natural vegetation
- Fewer plant roots to bind the soil
- Heavy rain causes rapid erosion of exposed soil
- Greater evaporation of water from unprotected land surface

Climate change: change in the environment due to human activity

HUMAN FACTORS
- Trees cut down for fuelwood and building materials
- Over-cultivation due to economic pressure to grow more cash crops – leads to soil degradation and erosion
- More animals (cattle, sheep, goats, camels) leads to overgrazing
- Trampling by animals increases soil erosion

C *Factors in the process of desertification*

Section 1.4: Population density and distribution

- **Leaching** Soil is leached when heavy rain dissolves valuable plant nutrients (food) in the topsoil, then washes them downwards below the depth that plant roots can reach.

Desertification

Desertification is the process by which semi-arid environments become desert-like. It is *not* the spread of true deserts, but rather what happens to the areas next to them. In the Sahel, for example, 80 000 km² become too dry and infertile every year for farming as a result of desertification. Desertification is clearly a global problem:

- One-third of the world's total land area is already desertified or is under serious threat of becoming so. Climate change is a major natural cause of desertification because it raises global temperatures and changes seasonal rainfall patterns (diagram **C**).

- Twenty per cent of the world's population lives with the constant threat of desertification.

- An estimated 850 million people are directly affected by desertification, mostly in Africa.

> **Topic link**
>
> - See Topic 3.7 pages 213–226 to learn more about human activity and the environment.

Section 1. Topic 5

Settlements and service provision

Learning objectives:
- explain the patterns of settlement
- describe and explain the factors which may influence the sites, growth and functions of settlements
- give reasons for the hierarchy of settlements and services

Why do people live in the countryside?

Do you live in the countryside (a rural area)? Or in a town or city (an urban area)? Do you know *why* you live where you do? Perhaps it is because the family members who support you have lived there for a long time, or maybe you moved there because of personal circumstances. Geographers like to ask questions, and to find out the reason for the locations of towns and villages. There are many reasons why people first create a settlement in a particular place.

Every **settlement** is different. Your own village, town or city will have its own unique arrangement of roads and buildings. How it looks today depends on how old it is, the shape of the land it is built on, and what has happened there in the past. In fact, history is a good place to start when investigating places, because most settlements, however large they are now, started off very small in what were then completely rural areas (photo **B**). Just a few places don't develop in this way, because they are planned and built as complete '**new towns**'.

Deciding where to build a new settlement is very important, because it may only become successful if it is built in an appropriate location. Diagram **C** lists the main village site **factors**, and explains why each one is so important to the success of a new settlement. **Site** is the land on which the first part of a settlement is built. The more beneficial site factors a settlement has, the more likely it is to flourish, to have more **functions** (activities) and to grow in size and importance.

Accessibility, or the ability to reach places, is one of the most important of these factors, because people need to trade with other people and places. Other key factors in the early growth of settlements include the availability of water, food and basic raw materials such as wood and stone.

A *Most towns and cities began as small villages*

B *A small village in a rural environment*

> **Topic link**
>
> What you learn in this topic about rural settlement will help you when you study Topic 1.6 pages 50–63, on urban settlement.

Section 1.5: Settlements and service provision 39

On a river meander
Bend in river provides a natural defence

River confluence
(joining of two rivers) Doubles the chance to use natural transport routes, e.g. for trade

'Dry point'
Higher, dry land above wet ground

In a valley
Natural routeway, fertile land for farming

River bridging point
Where river is narrow enough to build a bridge

In a gap between hills
Convenient routeway

Higher ground
Easier to defend, and drier land

Sheltered coast
Protected harbour can be built – trade, fishing

Road junction
Direct routes to other settlements

Near to woods
Source of timber for cooking, heating, building, tools, furniture

Near to a spring
Provides reliable water supply

By a river
Water for drinking, washing etc. and for power, transport, fishing

Flat land
Building easier, and space for settlement to expand

C *Settlement site factors and their advantages*

Now Investigate

1 Investigate the location of a settlement you know well, then list all the factors in diagram **C** that help to describe its site.

2 a) Re-arrange the site factors in diagram **C** into three groups according to how important you think they are:
   i) must-have
   ii) good to have
   iii) could do without
   b) Explain your selection of the 'must-have' site factors.

3 a) Suggest some site factors that are likely to *hinder* the growth of settlements. Try to think of up to five factors.
   b) Explain why each of these factors is a disadvantage for a settlement.

> **Topic link**
>
> You can learn more about meanders in Topic 2.2 page 86.

Population and settlement

Rural settlements on Ordnance Survey maps

Over time, villages often develop quite distinctive shapes and patterns. The three most common types are: **dispersed**, **linear** and **nucleated** (table **A**). Many villages have combinations of two or more of these basic patterns.

> **Topic link**
>
> See Topic 4.1 pages 235–237 to help you answer the questions on this page.

Dispersed settlement	Linear settlement	Nucleated settlement
Individual farms and houses are widely scattered over a rural area (countryside) and are linked by a network of tracks and minor roads.	Linear settlements are long and narrow, with most of their buildings along a road, river bank or shoreline.	Buildings are tightly clustered around a road junction, church or bridge. Nucleated settlements are about the same distance across in different directions.

A *Different settlement types*

Now Investigate

1. a) Find the following places on map **C** on page 42. A four-figure or six-figure grid reference is given for each settlement. Note that not all settlements are named.

    i) Almondale 1249
    ii) Cabiche 140480
    iii) east side of 1451
    iv) Grande Rivière 1351
    v) La Feuillet 1453 and 1454
    vi) north-east part of 1352
    vii) west side of 1149

   b) Which type of settlement pattern – dispersed, linear or nucleated – does each of these places have?

2. Look for the following settlements on map **C**, and list the advantages of the *site* of each settlement:

    a) Bois d'Orange 1153
    b) Grande Rivière 1351
    c) Gros Islet 1356.

B *St Lucia airport, Castries*

Rural settlements in St Lucia

Only 19 per cent of the population of the island of St Lucia lives in an urban area. The Ordnance Survey (OS) map extract **C** shows clearly the many small settlements in this part of the island and two larger places. Port Castries is the largest settlement on the island, and the capital of St Lucia.

Section 1.5: Settlements and service provision 41

C Ordnance Survey map extract of part of St Lucia, 1:50 000 scale

42 Population and settlement

1.5

Life in rural areas

Worldwide, 37 per cent of all people live in villages and work on farms. In India, though, the figure is much higher – 52 per cent. So even in this rapidly industrialising country, rural areas are still very important.

Chembakolli – a village in southern India

Chembakolli is one of 200 villages in southern India inhabited by the Adivasi tribe (map **A**). *Adivasi* is a local word meaning 'the people of the forest' – a good name for them because the forest used to provide all the food they needed as well as materials for building huts. The forest still provides fuelwood for cooking and for heating water for washing, although many of the trees have already been cleared to create extra farmland. The forest also provides a habitat for deer, rabbits and wild boar which are hunted by the Adivasi.

Most of Chembakolli's 50 families are farmers. Their main crops are rice, onions, tomatoes and peppers. These are all **subsistence crops** (grown to feed the local people), but some farmers have started growing tea as a **cash crop**, which they can sell to earn money for themselves. Every member of a Chembakolli family helps to grow these crops, and the women and older children are usually also responsible for looking after the goats and chickens. Only the better-off villagers can afford to buy a cow. Most people work very hard just to survive, and rely on the summer monsoon rains for the success of their crops (graph **C**).

All the farmwork is done by hand (photo **B**), although elephants are used to help with heavy tasks such as moving logs from the forest. Some of the men add to their family's income by working on the tea and ginger estates owned by more wealthy farmers. This helps to buy materials the children need for school.

Map **D** shows that the village now has a range of basic facilities, and a school for the younger children. It does not yet have an

> **Fantastic fact**
>
> India has the world's second largest population, but it is sometimes called the country of 800 000 villages.

A Location of Chembakolli in southern India

B Farming by hand is hard work

C The monsoon climate has a dry season as well as a very wet season

Section 1.5: Settlements and service provision   43

electricity supply. The village well is used for washing cooking pans and for drinking water. Typhoid is a common, life-threatening illness because the well is also used by animals. Diarrhoea is another common symptom, which can be fatal, especially for children and old people. The village now has a small clinic, and a doctor makes regular visits.

Key:
- Villagers' huts
- Rice fields
- Village market
- Tea plantations
- Wood
- Coffee plantations
- Road
- Track
- CH Community hall
- HC Health centre
- PO Post Office
- PS Police station
- BT Bathing tank
- W Well

D *Chembakolli is a nucleated settlement, clustered around the temple*

Chembakolli is linked by bus to other villages and the nearest large town, Gudalur, which has a population of 49 500.

Gudalur is a different world: it has supermarkets, cinemas and a hospital. Some people in Chembakolli have never travelled along the road to the town, even though it is less than 20 km away!

E *A typical street scene in a rural town in the Tamil Nadu region of southern India*

Topic link

To learn more about climate graphs, see Topic 4.3 page 251.

Now Investigate

1 How is life in Chembakolli village different from your own? Use the following headings to structure your answer:
- Food and water
- The work that people do
- Health problems and medical support

2 a) Describe the monthly temperature and rainfall patterns shown in graph **C**.

b) How do these patterns compare with those for your own region?

c) What problems is Chembakolli's climate likely to cause for:
  i) farmers
  ii) other village people?

Further research

Study maps of your local region and try to identify examples of the different types of settlement: dispersed, linear and nucleated. You might take photographs or obtain pictures of your chosen examples. You could then produce a display of all the resources you have collected, annotating them to highlight their main features.

Population and settlement

1.5

The settlement hierarchy

All settlements can be arranged according to their functions and size of population. This is called a hierarchy. Diagram **A** shows a **settlement hierarchy** based only on population size. Its levels range from isolated buildings such as farmhouses, to the world's 31 **megacities**, each having over 10 million inhabitants. It is impossible to give precise ranges for some of the settlement 'layers' because definitions of towns and cities vary widely from country to country. For example, Swedish cities must have at least 50 000 people, but Romanian cities need only 5000.

Settlement hierarchies can also be based on functions (table **B**). These are the services a settlement provides for its inhabitants and for people living within easy travelling distance. Clusters of houses called 'hamlets' are too small to support any permanent facilities such as shops and schools; their only service provision is likely to be a bus stop.

A *A settlement hierarchy based on population size*

Pyramid levels:
- Megacity — Over 10 million
- Conurbation — Over 1 million
- City — Over 100 000
- Town — 2500–100 000
- Village — 100–2500
- Hamlet — 10–100

Settlements at the top and bottom of the settlement hierarchy	Educational facilities	Shopping facilities	Transport facilities
Megacity	University	Out-of-town regional shopping centre	International airport
	College	Specialist shops	Regional airport
		Department stores	Major rail and road 'hub'
	Secondary school	Supermarket	Railway station
		Local row of shops	Bus station
	Infant/ primary school		Taxi rank
Isolated farm or house		Local general store	Bus stop

B *Function hierarchies based on service provision*

Fantastic fact

The smallest 'city' in the world is believed to be Hum, in Croatia (in Eastern Europe) – a 900-year-old hill-top community with only 23 inhabitants.

Settlements at the top of a hierarchy fulfil a wide range of functions. Castries, the capital of St Lucia, is a good example of this. Although its population is only 20 000, it is the largest settlement and has many of the functions of megacities. Two of the main functions of Castries are as a port and a centre for sports. Photo **C** shows the main harbour at Castries, with its quays at full capacity with large visiting cruise ships.

C *Harbour at Castries with a large cruise ship at every quayside*

Section 1.5: Settlements and service provision

Many countries, especially less economically developed countries, are dominated by one very large, densely populated city. Graph **D** shows one way of plotting the populations of the 10 largest cities of a country to show their relative sizes.

D City size rank order

Now Investigate

1 a) What is the population of the settlement where you live?

b) What level of population settlement do you live in, according to the hierarchy shown in diagram **A**?

2 Create at least one hierarchy like those in table **B** for a place you know well, from this list of other settlement functions: entertainment facilities, medical facilities, sports facilities. Start with the smallest and the largest, for example a village football pitch (smallest) to an international stadium in a major city (largest).

3 Using the map extract on page 42, copy and complete the following table by adding:

a) the four- or six-figure grid references for its named features

b) the missing 'first' and 'second' features at the grid reference positions shown.

Function	First feature grid reference	First feature	Second feature grid reference	Second feature
Administration	082482		–	–
Culture	085475	Caribbean Museum	–	–
Education		St Mary's College	083472	
Health	077490		099496	Health Centre
Hotels		La Toc Hotel	085483	
Industry		Industrial area	106494	
Leisure	084494		106511	Halcyon Beach Club
Places of worship	091485			St Joseph's Convent
Public buildings		Police HQ	089487	
Public utilities	092485			Reservoir
Residential	082500		098486	Rose Hill residential area
Sport		Golf course	096480	Stadium
Transport	092498			Anchorage for ships

c) Study photo **C** to locate the main quays in Castries Harbour on the map extract, then write their six-figure grid reference positions on the last line of your table.

4 **a)** Using graph **D** as your guide, plot these urban populations onto two separate graphs.

City rank order	Urban area populations in France, a more economically developed country		Urban area populations in Peru, a less economically developed country	
First	Paris	12 341 000	Lima	7 737 000
Second	Lyon	2 214 000	Arequipa	841 000
Third	Marseilles	1 727 000	Callao	813 000
Fourth	Toulouse	1 271 000	Trujillo	747 000
Fifth	Lille	1 166 000	Chiclayo	577 000
Sixth	Bordeaux	1 158 000	Iquitos	438 000
Seventh	Nice	1 005 000	Huancayo	377 000
Eighth	Nantes	898 000	Piura	325 000
Ninth	Strasbourg	769 000	Chimbote	317 000
Tenth	Rennes	690 000	Cusco	312 000

Note: These are the populations of urban conurbations, not just the cities at their centres.

b) Compare your two graphs, and highlight any similarities and differences between them.

Service provision in an area

All settlements perform at least one function for the people who live there, or are within easy travelling distance. For example, an isolated house fulfills a function as a home for those who live there. Functions will only be provided if there is sufficient demand for them. For example, a cake shop can only survive if there are enough people who:

- like eating cakes
- can afford to buy that shop's cakes
- are within easy travelling distance of the cake shop.

Online shopping is increasingly important to many businesses – but probably less so for cake shops and other businesses selling perishable food.

The number of people needed to support a business or service is called its **threshold population**. The size of a threshold population is closely linked to the needs of that particular activity. For example, a secondary school needs a cluster of primary schools to provide enough students to make it viable (table **A** on page 48). Graph **B** presents suggestions for population threshold requirements for some non-educational services.

Fantastic fact

The catchment area for the highest-quality jewellery sold in central London is the whole of the British Isles!

Section 1.5: Settlements and service provision

Facility	Threshold population
Small village primary school	500
Pre-school nursery	1000
Town primary school	3000
Secondary school	10 000
College	50 000
University	100 000

A *Population thresholds in the educational hierarchy*

Care needs to be taken when using population threshold data. For example:

- Some communities are wealthier than others, and better-off people can afford to buy more goods or services, so fewer people are needed to make the same service viable.

- Not all people share the same interests or needs. For example, in a community where many retired people live, a shop selling football kit would be less likely to succeed than one specialising in aids for the elderly!

- Communities often have very different preferences and traditions. In France there is a long tradition of eating hand-crafted bread, so a baker's shop in that country can thrive in a community of only 600 people. However, in Britain, where more mass-produced bread is eaten, the population threshold of a similar shop would have to be three times greater.

B *Population thresholds vary widely between different services*

CASE STUDY

Isle of Wight – service provision on a small island in southern England

A good way of comparing the population thresholds of different services is to carry out a land use survey. Figure **D** and graph **E** show results of a survey of service provision for the Isle of Wight, which has a population of 139 000. Its largest town, the coastal holiday resort of Ryde, has 24 000 inhabitants. Photo **C** shows the town of Ryde.

Because each type and level of service has its own population threshold, it also requires a minimum area from which enough people can be drawn. This is called its **catchment area**. Low order goods such as bread and newspapers, which are cheap and bought frequently, have much smaller catchment areas than high order (expensive) items like beds and cars. Another term for 'catchment area' is **sphere of influence**.

Population and settlement

1.5

C *An aerial view of Ryde*

D *Distribution of services on the Isle of Wight*

E *The number of businesses in some of the Isle of Wight's different kinds of services*

The Isle of Wight also has one of each of: Citizens' Advice Bureau, college, hospice, large department store and law courts.

Now Investigate

1. List 10 items owned by your family. For each one, find out how far away from your home it was bought.

2. Imagine that you have been given the job of planning a new leisure centre to meet the recreational needs of your local community. What criteria (for example transport and threshold population) will you need to consider to make sure that the new centre will be a success?

3. Suggest why the threshold population of a doctor's surgery might be different from that of a dentist's surgery.

4. Look at map **D** and explain why Newport has more services than Ryde.

Section 1.5: Settlements and service provision   49

Section 1 . Topic 6

Urban settlements

Learning objectives:
- describe and give reasons for the characteristics of, and changes in, land use in urban areas
- explain the problems of urban areas, their causes and possible solutions

What kind of settlement do you live in?

Pedro lives in a large city, while Maria's home is in a small town. (figures **A** and **B**).

> I live in a big city. It's got everything – including crime! All the big department stores are here, and the latest fashions. My Dad's mad about cars and there are showrooms here selling every make you can think of. There's a great social scene, with plenty of discos, nightclubs and cinemas. There are theatres and museums, too, as well as colleges, universities and hospitals …

A Pedro

B Maria

> My town is quite small. Its shops sell the basics like food, of course, but not much else. You can get second-hand cars and vans here, but anyone who can afford to buy a new car has to go to the city. There isn't much for young people to do in the evenings, so we find our own amusement – and that sometimes gets us into trouble! I can't wait to move to the city when I leave school.

The previous topic introduced the idea of a settlement's site – the small area where its first buildings were built. Here we look at **situation** – the position of a settlement within a much larger region. Site and situation are both about places – the difference between them is scale and distance. To grow, and move up higher in the settlement hierarchy, a hamlet or village needs both a site and a situation with many advantages.

Paris: location and growth of a capital city

Both the site and the situation of Paris have many advantages. It has an ideal island site (map **C** and photo **D**), and a situation in the centre of the most fertile region in France, an area known as the Paris Basin (map **E**). Having an abundant supply of food, and being at the centre of road and later railway networks, helped Paris to grow faster than any other French city. Today it is a huge

Fantastic fact

One in every five French people lives in the Paris conurbation.

50   Population and settlement

built-up area, known as a **conurbation**, which includes many settlements that were once separate towns.

The population of Paris is now almost six times greater than France's second biggest settlement, Lyon (graph **F**). Much of the population increase in Paris has been due to the migration of people from the poorer regions of France.

> **Skills link**
>
> See Topic 4.4 pages 265–267 to learn more about how to draw and annotate a sketch map.

C The site: the oldest part of Paris is built on two islands – the Romans used the Ile de la Cité as a river crossing-point along a military road

D Ile de la Cité is now dominated by important buildings such as Notre Dame cathedral

E The situation of Paris, which is an important focus of European road and rail links

F French cities with populations greater than half a million

Now Investigate

1. Do you live in a large city, a town, or a smaller settlement? Compare your own settlement with those of Pedro and Maria. Does it have more or fewer advantages than theirs?

Section 1.6: Urban settlements

2 Using information on these two pages, and the internet, state whether each of the following statements is *true* or *false*. Re-write any false statements to make them true.

　　i)　Early settlers had a plentiful supply of water and fish from the river Seine.
　　ii)　One of the islands provided an easy crossing point of the river.
　　iii)　The land on the banks of the river Seine is steep and difficult to build on.
　　iv)　The river made transportation by boat very difficult.
　　v)　The original site of Paris consisted of two islands in the river Seine.
　　vi)　Islands in the river Seine provided a safe, easily defended site for early settlers.
　　vii)　Paris is about 175 km upstream from the mouth of the river Seine – which is located on the Channel coast; it is also approximately 300 km by land from the port of Le Havre.
　　viii)　The general relief of the Paris Basin (i.e. the height and relief of its land area) is low; it is undulating land surrounded by escarpment-shaped ridges.

3 Describe the location (situation) and main functions of Paris. Use information from map **E** – together with any you obtain from an internet search and any other resources that are available to you.

　　i)　The size of the Paris conurbation, from north to south and east to west
　　ii)　Rail and road links (national and regional)
　　iii)　Location of international airports
　　iv)　Any nearby industrial areas
　　v)　Land use in the Paris Basin

4 Using both the Ordnance Survey map on page 42 and map **E** on page 51 as a guide, draw a sketch map to show the location of Castries, the largest settlement on the island of St Lucia. Base your map on the area within the grid lines 47–52 and 7–13; annotate your map to show the advantages of both the site and the situation of the town.

How does urban land use change, and why?

The *proportion* of the world's population living in urban areas has been growing for the last 200 years. This process is called **urbanisation**.

Keetan lives in Kolkata, one of the largest cities in India. Read what Keetan has to say about the place he calls home (figure **A**).

A Keetan, a resident of Kolkata in India

Hi! I'm Keetan. My dad is a taxi driver. Sometimes he takes me with him so I can get to know my city.

Yesterday we started off in Howrah, in the northern part of the city. There are lots of squatter settlements here – we Indians call them bustees! Dad usually has to drive around these areas, because there aren't many proper streets between the houses – just narrow dirt tracks, which become flooded in the heavy monsoon rains. We then drove south, through the textile area, where thousands of small businesses make all kinds of clothing. Then 1 km further on is the city centre, with its huge, modern office blocks and hotels and some fine old stone buildings from when India was a British colony. Nearby are the docks, on the east bank of the Hooghly river, with lots of factories nearby.

We came back home through the area where the better-off people live. This is quite close to the city centre where there are big stores which have everything you could ever dream of!

1.6

Two models can help us understand how towns and cities develop. These are based on the location of **land use zones**, areas which have one or more important urban functions – commercial, industrial, residential, recreational – as well as facilities such as roads and schools which form the **infrastructure**. These make it possible for a place to function effectively.

The land use model in diagram **B** shows a series of concentric circles, all of them sharing the same centre point. This theoretical model applies to a town that has grown at exactly the same rate in every direction.

The model in diagram **C** is more realistic, because it allows for growth at different rates in all directions. It also shows that functions can extend to the edge of the built-up area. For example, industrial developments often follow canal, road and railway routes linking the city centre and the countryside. Also wealthier people try to build their houses where they won't be affected by industrial pollution.

It can be difficult to match these models to the towns and cities of today because:

- many old inner city areas have been redeveloped and their original functions changed; for example, retail parks have replaced areas of poor-quality housing
- new by-pass roads around towns have attracted industrial and residential developments away from busy inner city areas
- both models assume that the oldest part of a town will always be in the middle, but many town and city centres are closer to one side of the urban area.

Fantastic fact

The annual rate of global urbanisation exceeds 2%.

Topic link

See Topic 1.2 pages 21–22 to learn why some cities are growing so fast.

B *The Burgess urban land use model*

C *The Hoyt urban land use model*

Key:
- Central Business District (CBD)
- Industry
- Low quality housing
- Middle quality housing
- **a** Rural–urban fringe
- **b** High quality housing

Central Business District (CBD) — Inner zone — Suburbs — Rural–urban fringe

D *Transect across a typical city in a more economically developed country*

Section 1.6: Urban settlements 53

These models are based on urban areas in more economically developed countries, but most cities in developing countries share similar characteristics. Diagram **D** is a transect through a typical city in a more economically developed country, from its modern commercial centre to the outer edges. Cities in less economically developed countries have similar land use patterns, including a **Central Business District** or **CBD**, at their heart, although in some cities the suburbs have developed as squatter settlements.

> **Topic link**
>
> See Topic 1.7 pages 66–68 to learn more about squatter settlements.

Now Investigate

1 Imagine that, like Keetan, you have the chance to travel around a city or large town in your own region. Write about what you might see on the way, for example where there are different kinds of buildings and what they look like. How is your town or city similar to and different from Kolkata?

2 These questions are based on diagrams **B**, **C** and **D**.
  a) Which urban zone is in the same central location in all of the diagrams?
  b) Which model is more likely to show how a town's growth has been influenced by natural land and water features?
  c) Which model recognises that people may have some choice in where they live?
  d) Which model recognises the role of transport in urban development?
  e) Explain how the zones in a more economically developed city might be different from those in a less economically developed city.

Urban zones

There are four main types of urban zone:
- the Central Business District or CBD
- the inner zone
- the outer zone (suburbs)
- the rural–urban fringe.

You will need to know the main characteristics of each zone, and be able to recognise each zone on photographs, maps and street plans.

Central Business District

The Central Business District (CBD) is the commercial 'heart' of a settlement and is easily recognised on photographs by its impressive buildings. The first large buildings were made of stone and designed to show the wealth and importance of a city. More recent big buildings are just as impressive, but are generally made of steel and glass (photo **A**).

> **Fantastic fact**
>
> Half of all people in the UK now live in the outer zone (suburbs) of a city.

A *Part of the CBD in Shanghai, China*

54 Population and settlement

Although the CBD is smaller than the other zones, it is an economic centre of any major settlement. It is also the central meeting point for road and railway routes and has plenty of space for car parking. This good access makes the CBD an ideal place to locate banks, offices and large department stores and specialist shops selling **comparison goods** such as expensive furniture, watches and antiques. Major public buildings like cathedrals, theatres, hotels and museums often cluster around parks and gardens – the few open spaces that are not built on.

Only the rich can afford to buy spacious accommodation in the CBD, and many people rent small 'studio' apartments instead. They want to live in the centre because they like the excitement of city life and prefer to spend more money on rent instead of on high commuting costs. The street patterns in most European city centres developed in a random, irregular fashion – unlike the grid patterns of newer cities like Chicago and Detroit in the USA, and island capitals such as Castries in St Lucia and Port Louis in Mauritius.

The inner zone

In many more economically developed countries this zone dates from the 19th century, during the Industrial Revolution, when factories and houses were built next to each other and people worked long hours and walked to work. Much **redevelopment** has taken place in this zone to replace low-quality housing and remove old industries. They are replaced by inner ring roads, retail parks, recreational facilities such as multi-screen cinemas and extra car parking areas.

B The old and the new in an inner zone

In less economically developed countries, the inner zone often includes some high-quality housing close to the cultural and social attractions of the city centre.

The outer zone (suburbs)

In less economically developed countries, squatter settlements are very common (photo **C**). There are many challenges for the people living there, but they are very resilient and try hard to improve their quality of life. The location of such settlements means that the inhabitants can take advantage of employment opportunities in both the inner zone and on the rural–urban fringe.

In more economically developed countries, many families in the outer zone live on estates of large houses with gardens and garages, and many people commute daily to work. Retired people often live in single-storey bungalows. In other more economically developed countries, apartments, villas and condominiums are the more usual type of housing (photo **D**). The standard of living

C Scene in the outer zone of a less economically developed country

tends to be high, but there are generally few local facilities such as schools, health centres and shops, because most people have cars and are able to travel further.

Rural–urban fringe

This zone is where town and country meet. Photo **E** shows that it can be a very 'busy' area, in spite of its semi-rural location and appearance.

D *Suburban scene in a more economically developed country*

Now Investigate

1. a) Find at least one photograph of the CBD of a major city in your own country and annotate it to show its main land use functions.

   b) Do the same for a city in another, contrasting country.

   c) Compare *and* contrast the two scenes, referring to your annotations for each group of land use functions.

2. For this activity use the Ordnance Survey map on page 42. For Castries:

   a) write down the grid references for the squares in which the CBD is located

   b) list all the key buildings which indicate that it is a CBD.

3. Make a larger copy of the following table. Complete your table by writing in its correct column each rural–urban fringe activity you can see in photo **E**.

Agricultural	Commercial and industrial	Recreational	Transport	Other

E *A typical rural–urban fringe landscape*

56 Population and settlement

1.6 The environmental impact of pollution

Our actions and behaviour can damage our local environment. The ways in which we harm our environment are known as pollution (diagram **A**).

Pollution causes some measure of harm to the environment. Wherever people live, work or travel there is some form of pollution. Spend a few minutes thinking about your area – what people do there, and how their activities might pollute it. Consider all types of pollution – some are less obvious than others (take a careful look at items **A–D** on these pages).

> **Fantastic fact**
>
> When the Eiffel Tower was built in 1889, many French people thought it was the ugliest thing they had ever seen. Now the French love it, and 'their tower' has become one of France's best-known global images.

Air pollution

Air pollution is one of the most serious reasons for damage in the urban environment. It has many causes, including traffic exhaust fumes from air, road and rail traffic when gases such as sulphur dioxide are emitted. Air pollution is also caused by smoke from houses, factories and power stations. This type of pollution is often worst on very foggy or hot days (photo **B**), because that is when **smog** – a combination of *sm*oke and f*og* – is most likely to form. Smog is very dangerous to health, and can cause serious breathing problems in people, especially the young and elderly.

THE FOUR TYPES OF POLLUTION

- **Water pollution**, e.g. untreated sewage flowing into a river, oil tanker spilling oil into the sea
- **Air pollution**, e.g. exhaust fumes from cars, smoke from factory chimneys, dust from quarries
- **Visual pollution**, e.g. litter blown about, a natural landscape spoiled by quarrying
- **Noise pollution**, e.g. aircraft flying low overhead, heavy traffic on main roads

A Types of pollution

Other kinds of pollution

Other environmental problems in urban areas include:

- noise pollution – for example from passing traffic and aircraft taking off and landing (diagram **C** on page 58)
- water pollution – due to industrial and domestic waste and causing diseases such as bilharzia, cholera and typhoid
- visual pollution – people have different reactions to new buildings or other constructions, and may consider some of them to be offensive to the eye (photo **D**).

B Smog over Tel Aviv, Israel

What makes a city 'green'?

Copenhagen, the Danish capital, is one of the world's 'greenest cities' and has received several major awards for its ecological achievements. It became the world's first 'Bike City' (2008–11),

Section 1.6: Urban settlements

was European Green capital in 2014 and was ranked first on the Global Green Economy Index in 2016 by Dual Citizen Inc. These facts explain why:

- Biomass and processed waste provide over 50% of the city's heating, with oil contributing only 5%.
- A new district cooling system takes cold water from the harbour, saving 70% of the energy used by traditional air conditioning.
- 45% of all domestic waste is recycled.
- It has reduced its water consumption by 26%.
- Its CO_2 emissions were reduced by 20% within 6 years; it is on-track to become completely carbon-neutral by 2025.
- It has 454 km of dedicated cycle lanes.
- 56% of Copenhageners commute to work or school by bicycle every day.
- The water in the Inner Harbour is so clean that people can swim in it safely.
- It hosted the 2009 United Nations' Climate Change Conference.

C Levels of noise measured in decibels (dBA)

D Would you like to have a working wind turbine near you?

Now Investigate

1. Write down at least five activities in your local community that might cause pollution. Suggest the kinds of pollution they are most likely to cause. You could display your ideas in several ways:
   - as a table, with activities listed in the left column, and their effects described in four other columns – one for each type of pollution
   - as a sketch map, annotated to show the location of each type of pollution
   - as a series of annotated photographs, with each annotation describing a different cause or effect of pollution

   or as a combination of these.

2. a) In your opinion, would a wind turbine in your own community be a beautiful (and useful) landmark – or an example of visual pollution?
   b) Give reasons for your answer.

Population and settlement

The effects of rapid urban growth on the rural–urban fringe

Rapid urban growth doesn't just change the centres of towns and cities; it can also have major effects on nearby countryside. Urban areas expand to accommodate their increasing population – a process called **urban sprawl**. They can also 'urbanise' the rural areas near to them because people:

- have greater mobility, due to improved transport networks
- have more 'spare' money to spend on non-essentials such as holidays and recreational activities like camping and golf
- have longer holidays and more leisure time at weekends
- lead a hectic life working in the city and so prefer to live in a quiet, country village 'retreat'.

It is not easy to limit the impact of rapid urban growth on rural–urban fringe areas, because these areas provide ideal locations for a wide range of land uses such as golf courses, power stations, modern industrial estates, retail parks and supermarkets (photo **A**). Fringe areas are also the kind of place where people seeking a better quality of life wish to live – even if that means having to spend more time and money commuting daily to work. This outward movement of people is called **counter-urbanisation**. It often results in small, traditional villages becoming more suburbanised in character.

In some places **green belts** around cities have helped to control urban sprawl, by limiting new residential and other developments in rural–urban fringe areas. Another strategy is to build new towns well away from a city's boundaries, which helps both to meet the need for more housing and reduce the rate of urban sprawl (photo **B**).

> **Topic link**
>
> You can learn more about counter-urbanisation in Topic 1.2 page 22.

A Why modern retail parks are located in rural–urban fringe areas

- Residential area (workforce for retail park)
- Land available for future expansion of businesses
- Main road leading to/from motorway nearby
- Retail units selling large items, e.g. furniture
- Large parking area

B A new town

Conflict in the rural–urban fringe

Each land use places a different demand on rural–urban fringe areas, often causing conflict between different groups of people. For example:

- a coal-burning power station creates air pollution, and this could increase the health problems of patients in a nearby hospital

Section 1.6: Urban settlements

- farmers are often involved in conflict because careless visitors can damage their crops or allow valuable animals to stray onto busy roads
- quarries are often sited in otherwise attractive areas of countryside, but the product (stone) has to be transported to where it is needed for building (houses and other buildings, roads), causing conflict among people living nearby (photo **C**).

> **Topic link**
>
> You can learn more about environmental issues in Topic 3.7 pages 220–226.

- Noise pollution: machinery in quarry, lorries transporting stone from quarry
- Air pollution: dust
- Visual pollution: dust, machinery, exposed rock faces
- Roads: congestion and vibration caused by lorries transporting stone
- Local settlements: affected by noise, air and visual pollution

C *Quarrying has many damaging effects on the local environment*

Now Investigate

1 a) Refer to the map extract of Port Louis in Mauritius, on page 312. Copy the table shown below. Complete your table by identifying the various land uses on the rural–urban fringe of Port Louis or by giving a grid reference for the land use stated in column 2. You may use four-figure grid references to complete each cell in the first column.

Grid references	Type of land use
971057 and 987066	
978067 and 978069	
972032 and 984053	
	Industrial estate
985069 and 997065	
	Power substation
	Race course
990038 and 984032	
990039 and 990047	
	Sports ground
964028 and 998022	

Population and settlement

b) Use four colours to highlight the following land uses in the table:

   Economic (including power generation)   Recreation   Transport   Others

   Include a key to show the meanings of your four chosen colours.

2 What activities take place in the rural–urban fringe of a large urban area in your own region?

3 **a)** Suggest reasons why the rural–urban fringe is the ideal location for at least five of these land uses:

   fishing   golf   hospitals   modern industrial estates   power station
   reservoirs   supermarkets

   b) Pair-up at least eight land uses on the rural–urban fringe that are likely to be in conflict, and suggest why. You can use each type of land use more than once.

4 What kinds of pollution and other environmental problems are quarries likely to cause for people living in rural–urban fringe areas? Consider all sources and types of pollution.

Urban change

To understand what a modern city is like, you need to know how, when and where it started, and how it has since developed and changed.

CASE STUDY

London – an example of changing land use

The Romans first built Londinium beside the river Thames almost 2000 years ago (map **A**). This site was chosen because it was easily defended and the Romans knew that it could become an important route centre. The actual site is now occupied by London's financial district, between the areas now known as Westminster and the 'East End'.

From the earliest times, the western and eastern sides of London have developed in very different ways (photos **B** and **C**). The East End has always been heavily industrialised and housed many of London's poorly paid workers. By contrast, Westminster is well known for its royal palaces, government buildings, large houses and expensive shops.

The East End developed first. Roman ships could not sail under London Bridge, the lowest bridging point across the Thames, so a port was established downstream of this.

Fantastic fact

In 1900, London was the world's largest city, with 6.5 million people.

Industries developed behind the quays, as well as low-quality housing for the dock and factory workers, many of them refugees who migrated here from mainland Europe.

Westminster developed later, around the 11th-century abbey and became the preferred location for royalty, the very wealthy, and the most influential people in government. One reason for them choosing Westminster to live was that the prevailing winds blow from the south-west, so any air pollution from the East End's industries blows towards the North Sea, well away from Westminster. The large parks in this part of the city were originally hunting forests for the nobility, and they have been

A *Original site of London*

B *London's East End*

C *Westminster*

D *London Docklands today*

E *Modern development of East London*

DOCKLANDS	OLYMPIC VILLAGE
22 000 new homes, many in renovated warehouses	High-speed rail link to central London
10 000 upgraded local authority houses	Park and ride car parks
New shopping centres	Wetland habitats restored
New college/university campuses	New bridges across main roads
Indoor sports centre and yacht marina	Olympic Stadium – accommodates 80 000 people
Docklands Light Railway – 10 minutes to central London	Aquatics Centre – future training and competitive events
London City Airport – over 4 500 000 passengers a year	Velodrome – links to cycle circuit and cycle routes across London
New road link to M11 motorway	Olympic Village – 3300 new homes, 30% affordable housing
43 000 new jobs	370 000 m² for future business developments
1500 new businesses	Media centre – office facilities for 8000 people

62   Population and settlement

used as recreational areas ever since. It is quite unusual to find so much open space in the heart of a city, where the competition for land is intense.

By the 1980s, sea-going ships had become too big for the East End docks, so most of the industries that depended on them for imported raw materials had re-located elsewhere. The East End's economy had seriously declined and local unemployment had reached record levels. In 1981 The London Docklands Development Corporation was established to redevelop the whole area and give it a new lease of economic life. Photo **D** shows what this area looks now.

The 2012 London Olympic Games were held in the valley of the River Lea, a northern tributary of the River Thames, just east of London Docklands. A major aim of the project has been to transform this area of dereliction and deprivation into one where people will want to live and work long after the games have finished. Map **E** shows what has been done to transform the whole of this area.

Now Investigate

1 Explain why Westminster developed in a very different way to that of London's East End.

2 a) Outline the reasons why it became necessary to regenerate both the London Docklands and the Lea Valley area.

b) In what ways are the regeneration plans for both areas similar? Your answer could take the form of a comparison table.

Further research

Investigate the impact of a previous Olympic Games on its host city. For example, the 2004 Games was in Athens – you could find out how it stimulated economic growth and improved recreational facilities in that city.

Topic link

More detail about the environmental impact of rapid urban growth and its effects on the rural–urban fringe can be found on pages 57–60.

Section 1.6: Urban settlements

Section 1 . Topic 7

Urbanisation

Learning objectives:
- identify and suggest reasons for rapid urban growth
- describe the impacts of urban growth on both rural and urban areas, along with possible solutions to reduce the negative impacts

What problems are caused when cities grow?

People travel for a number of reasons, as shown in diagram **A**.

Commuting and going to school or college are the most common reasons for travel. These are also the main causes of traffic congestion because they peak at certain times on work days (graph **B**). The morning and late afternoon/early evening peak travelling times are often called 'rush hours', because of the usually frantic nature of travel at those times. Congestion is worst in the CBD, where many main roads meet, and some of the oldest roads are too narrow for modern traffic.

Rush hours are a very inefficient use of the resources both of a city and of individual families. Car ownership continues to grow in most countries (see graph **C**), and most commuters prefer to travel alone rather than car sharing. Young children are often driven the short distance to school, instead of walking to school.

Traffic congestion wastes fuel and causes air pollution along busy routeways. It is now a common feature of most large settlements, but there are several ways in which it can be reduced, for example by:

> **Topic link**
>
> See Topic 1.6 page 57 and Topic 1.7 pages 70–72 to learn more about the effects of pollution in cities.

A Why people travel

B The changing volume of road traffic on a typical work day

C Rising car ownership in India since 2000

64   Population and settlement

- making public transport services more frequent, affordable and reliable
- encouraging the use of public transport by imposing 'working-space levies' on companies offering free employee parking within inner city areas
- building **rapid transit systems** such as underground railways and surface city links (guided buses and trams) – photo **D**
- integrating transport systems so that train and bus timetables are linked, allowing passengers to transfer easily between different modes of transport and use inter-changeable tickets
- installing roundabouts and imposing speed restrictions to reduce road accidents which cause traffic hold-ups
- encouraging car-sharing, to reduce the volume of commuter traffic
- introducing traffic light systems which monitor flow and adjust signal timings to maximise traffic flow at peak times
- operating bus-only lanes on wide roads during rush hour periods
- making narrow roads one-way and restricting parking along busy (or narrow) roads
- pedestrianising busy shopping streets and building by-passes and ring roads to divert through-traffic away from city centres
- providing low cost park-and-ride facilities on city approach roads
- raising inner-city parking charges to discourage the use of private vehicles in city centres
- introducing **congestion charges** for vehicles entering the busiest city zones
- creating protected bike lanes to encourage cycle use
- incorporating bike hire into a city's integrated transport network.

D *A section of the Metro Monorail in Sydney, Australia*

Fantastic fact

Passenger vehicle ownership in India has nearly tripled in the last 10 years. It is predicted to increase by 775% by 2040!

Now Investigate

1. Is there a rush hour in your neighbourhood? What times of the day are the busiest?
2. a) If your family or a friend has a car, keep a week-long tally of how often it is used for each type of journey shown in the spider diagram.
   b) Display your tally-totals in the form of a bar graph, then comment on what your completed graph shows.

Section 1.7: Urbanisation

3 For each rush-hour period shown in graph **B**, write down its approximate:
- start time
- finish time
- peak traffic volume.

4 Quoting data from graph **C** as necessary, describe how car ownership in India has changed since 2000.

5 Using a street plan or Ordnance Survey map of an urban district you know well, annotate it to show examples of congestion reduction strategies. (Hint: Two of the more common strategies are traffic lights and roundabouts.)

Squatter settlements

As a visitor to any city centre in a less economically developed country, you might think that traffic and pollution were the only serious problems caused by urbanisation. Travelling beyond the centre would quickly change that first impression! This is because you would see huge areas of deprivation (see map **A**) – the **squatter settlements**, also known as **shanty towns** – where many people are unemployed and can't afford to live anywhere else. City authorities are aware of the conditions in these areas, but they can't afford to improve them all.

Two of the greatest challenges facing newcomers to less economically developed cities are getting a job and finding a place to live. The two problems are connected, because those lucky enough to be in full-time employment may only earn enough to provide food and shelter for their families. Wages are low, even for the employees of **transnational companies** such as clothes manufacturers. They are far below those earned in the **formal sector** of employment, by professional people like lawyers. Textile workers receive little money even though they spend many hours each day in difficult working conditions.

Education in rural areas is very basic, so many migrants are illiterate and lack the practical skills that employers look for. Many immigrant families are so desperate that children as young as 6 years old are sent out to earn money doing jobs like shoe-shining and peddling cheap goods on the streets.

Life in squatter settlements

In the world's fastest growing less economically developed cities like Dhaka, Kolkata and Mexico City, over half of the population are squatters. Some countries have so many squatter settlements that they have their own names for them: *barriadas* in Peru, *favelas* in Brazil, *bustees* in India and *bidonvilles* in north Africa.

Topic link

You can find out more about how people make a living from informal employment, in Topic 3.1 page 143 and Topic 3.3 pages 172–173.

Topic link

To learn more about rural to urban migration see Topic 1.2 pages 21–22.

Fantastic fact

At least one in seven people on Earth now lives in slum conditions such as squatter settlements.

Topic link

See Topic 1.6 pages 52–56 to learn more about land use zones in cities.

1.7

CASE STUDY

Mumbai – a rapidly growing urban area

Key:
- Squatter settlements
- City centre
- High-class residential area
- Built up area
- National park
- Cultivated areas
- Jungle areas
- Salt pans/mud flats

A Many districts in Mumbai have over half of their people living in slum conditions

250 families migrate to Mumbai, which is partly why 62 per cent of its total population live in such settlements.

B Dharavi in Mumbai, India – a typical squatter settlement

Most of the dwellings in Dharavi have no water or electricity and families have to rely on other people to provide what they need – at a high price. In some streets, every household has its own tap, and these families take great pride in hosing down the street to keep it clean. Most workers have employment in the **informal sector**, such as recycling plastic bottles, oil drums and cardboard boxes. Textile workers cluster together in districts called *kaarkhanas*. People in both types of employment usually work from home, not in factories, so there is serious air pollution and constant noise in many residential areas.

Dharavi is often called 'the largest slum' in Asia' (photo **B**). It is huge – an area of over 2 km² on what used to be a mangrove swamp – right in the centre of Mumbai. It is one of many squatter settlements in this rapidly expanding city, whose population increased from 2.9 million in 1950 to 22 million in 2015. Every day, an average of

Photo **C** on page 68 shows a typical squatter settlement in India. There are significant problems for people who live in areas like this:

- **Disease** As there are no effective sewage or household waste disposal systems and community taps may be shared by up to 50 families, disease is rife and life expectancy remains low.

Section 1.7: Urbanisation 67

- **Poor building construction** These settlements are illegal, so the city's minimum building and safety standards are not enforced (photo **B** on page 67).
- **Risk of fire** Fires can spread very quickly between the wooden shacks built so close together.
- **Unsuitable location** Shortage of land means that newcomers often settle in dangerous and unsuitable places, such as steep hillsides prone to landslides.
- **Crime and anti-social behaviour** Domestic stress levels are high, so family breakdown is common and many children are abandoned.
- **Lack of education** The city authorities do not recognise illegal settlements, so do not provide schools and health centres. This leaves migrant families at a great disadvantage, because almost 40% of all residents of Mumbai are recent immigrants, and 23% of them are children.

C *Shacks in squatter settlements are made of any available materials*

Further research

Use online resources to investigate ways in which people in squatter settlements are positive and do much to improve their quality of life.

Now Investigate

1 a) List the difficulties faced by shanty town squatters, under these three headings:

Environmental problems   Social problems   Economic problems

b) Now consider some of the possible good things about living in a shanty town, again listing your ideas under suitable headings.

2 Describe and suggest reasons for the distribution of Mumbai's bustees as shown in map **A**.

3 Major events such as football's World Cup have often led to squatter settlements being cleared, to provide extra land for the construction of sports and accommodation facilities. Imagine that you are a local newspaper or TV reporter and you have been asked to produce a report which contrasts the short-term needs of event organisers with the much longer-term effects on displaced squatter communities.

You will need to include suggestions about how the displaced people are likely to feel about the disruption to their lives, what kinds of places they could be relocated to, and ways in which their lives might improve after leaving the squatter settlements.

How will people in the favela feel? Where will they go? Are the authorities right to do this? Will the clearance improve people's lives?

Ways of upgrading residential areas

Pages 66–68 described the challenges faced by many families living in squatter settlements in less economically developed cities, and some of the ways in which they try to improve their quality of life. The following case studies provide information about two different strategies used by poorer countries to reduce the amount of low-quality housing in their cities. They are called **self-help** and **site and service schemes**.

68 Population and settlement

A self-help scheme in Brazil

In this type of scheme, town and city authorities support families wishing to improve their homes. Grants, building materials and small cash loans are provided to help them to start work. Water and sanitation are vital to people's health, so self-help schemes often include standpipes which groups of households can share. People are often encouraged to buy their land, which makes them feel it is worth the effort of making improvements. Whole communities may also be assisted in building schools and health centres.

Roçinha in Rio de Janeiro is one of Brazil's largest *favelas*. It first developed on a steep hillside in the 1950s and now has 70 000 inhabitants, although some estimates put this figure as high as 300 000. Its early dwellings were small wood and canvas cabins, but most have since been enlarged and improved with bricks and tiles, and with vital help from the local authority (photo **A**). With its many shops and small businesses, most parts of Roçinha now look more like a well-ordered residential area than a poverty-stricken squatter settlement!

A *A self-help scheme in Roçinha, Rio de Janeiro*

A site and service scheme in Egypt

Site and service schemes are much more ambitious than self-help schemes because they need enough land to create whole new developments. Water, sanitation and electricity services are provided for each plot before any building starts. In small schemes, the people use the materials they can afford at that time; any improvements can made later, after the families have saved enough money to pay for them.

The 6th of October City near Cairo is a good example of such a scheme. This new town was founded in 1979 to relieve pressure on over-crowded Cairo. Many of its 500 000 inhabitants live in high-rise blocks of flats (photo **B**) and work on its large industrial estates. New whole-community facilities such as schools, shops, mosques and parks are included in all of Egypt's new towns, which were viewed as the best way of housing Egypt's rapidly expanding population.

B *High-rise flats in 6th of October City*

Housing problems are not confined to less economically developed countries. In the 19th century, during the Industrial Revolution in Europe and North America, millions of migrants from rural areas were accommodated in cheap, rapidly-built terraced houses. These now form the inner residential zone of some industrial cities in Europe and North America (photo **C**). By the mid-20th century, many of these needed to be renovated (upgraded) by re-wiring them and fitting new windows,

C *Low-quality terraced housing in Harlem, New York*

Section 1.7: Urbanisation

indoor bathrooms and toilets. Those that had deteriorated to become slums were demolished and replaced with completely new buildings – a more expensive process called **redevelopment**.

Many people displaced by redevelopment were re-housed in high-rise flats. These were welcomed at the time, because they offered a higher standard of accommodation – but in the process of moving many communities disappeared. These high-rise flats have since become much less popular due to the inconvenience of living in such tall buildings.

Another solution has been to build **new towns**. These provide all the facilities that people need – including recreational and employment opportunities. In the 1940s–60s, the UK built more than 30 new towns, most of them within 50 km of large, overcrowded cities. Singapore, which was a British territory until 1963, built 22 new towns during the same period (photo **D**).

D *A 'new town' area in Singapore*

Now Investigate

1. Define clearly the terms 'renovation' and 'redevelopment', to show that you understand the difference between them.

2. List up to eight possible disadvantages of living in a high-rise block of flats.

3. Write a brief 'revision summary' for each of the two urban renewal case studies.

4. Imagine that you are in charge of your local area's urban planning department. You have been given a grant of $250 million to improve the quality of life for people in your area. You must invest all of that grant in one of two ways:

   either redevelop just one part of your area, by building a complete new town on that site

   or

   renovate every dwelling in the whole of your local area, using both self-help and site and service schemes.

   a) Decide which option *you* would take.
   b) Give detailed reasons to justify your decision.

Fantastic fact

Each of Cairo's new towns houses more than 500 000 people – so they are really 'new cities'!

Further research

Identify a squatter settlement or other area of low-quality housing in an area of your choice. Produce a case study about that settlement, including a location map and some annotated photographs to describe it. Add as much detailed information as you can about its dwellings.

More sustainable cities

Rapid urbanisation creates many problems for the world's cities and the people living in them, but much can be done to make them more sustainable, or 'green'. Some strategies that aim to do this include:

Population and settlement

- reducing all forms of pollution – especially air pollution due to emissions from vehicles and factories
- using fewer natural resources such as fossil fuels, for example by making vehicle engines more efficient and encouraging people to use public instead of private transport
- disposing of waste materials in environmentally less damaging ways – mainly by recycling
- improving the natural environment within urban areas by creating more recreational open spaces and planting more trees and other plants.

Curitiba – Brazilian city leads the way!

Curitiba provides a good example of what can be done to control some of the worst effects of urbanisation. It was a typical Brazilian city that originally developed due to its position on the main beef-cattle route to São Paulo. In the days before motor transport, herds of cattle were driven along this route.

When agriculture was mechanised during the 1950s, 60s and 70s, fewer farm workers were needed. People who lost their jobs migrated to cities like Curitiba, whose population grew by 6 per cent every year during those three decades. They created squatter settlements around the city and the population of the conurbation increased from 150 000 to almost 3.5 million. Today, however, the people of Curitiba say they live in the best place in the world! Here are some reasons why:

- **In the 1960s:** Curitiba's new 'Master Plan' is approved. Its aim is to control urban sprawl, reduce city centre traffic congestion, provide affordable public transport and build more direct highways leading out of the city.

- **In the 1970s:**
  - city centre shopping streets are pedestrianised
  - bus-only lanes are introduced
  - many streets are made one-way
  - industrial areas are established on the city's outskirts, where air pollution is less likely to affect the main residential zones (photo **A**).

- **In the 1980s – Curitiba's 'Greenest Decade':**
  - urban 'green zones' are created to protect them from future unsustainable developments
  - the mayor, Jaime Lerner, allocates 1.5 million young trees to deprived neighbourhoods
  - 17 large urban parks are established, some of which deliberately celebrate different ethnic groups within the city's population (photo **B** on page 72).

A *Industrial location on the rural–urban fringe of Curitiba*

Section 1.7: Urbanisation

- **In the 1990s:**
  - botanical gardens are created
  - buses capable of carrying 270 passengers are introduced on the busiest routes; high-speed bus stops called 'tubes' mean that buses have fewer emissions because they are designed to both discharge and embark passengers at the same time
  - the Bus Mass Transit system reduces car journeys by 70 per cent (a huge saving as cars emit twice as much carbon dioxide as buses).

B *A park in the centre of Curitiba*

- **Since 2000 – the success story continues:**
  - the city introduces sight-seeing buses for tourists, so they don't have to use taxis or their own cars
  - a new technology park is built with research facilities to develop non-fossil fuels
  - Curitiba now has the highest recycling rate in the world
  - buses in the city carry 50 times more passengers than they did 20 years ago
  - 150 km of urban pathways have been created, for use by walkers, cyclists and roller-boarders
  - a city-wide waste re-cycling programme is introduced
  - all bus routes are colour-coded and provided with the size of bus best suited to the needs of passengers using that particular route (photo **C**).

C *A three-section bus and 'tube' bus stop*

Fantastic fact

It is cheaper and more 'green' to use sheep instead of machines to cut the grass in Curitiba's parks! Their wool is sold to raise money for local orphanages.

Now Investigate

1. How has the city of Curitiba managed to fulfil each of the four sustainability strategies listed at the top of page 71? Your answer may take the form of a bullet-pointed list.

2. Investigate the environmental problems in a city of your choice (anywhere in the world), and the measures taken to reduce these problems. Three possibilities to consider are Cairo, Mumbai or Rio de Janeiro.

Topic link

You can learn more about sustainable development in Topic 3.7 pages 227–234.

Section 2 . Topic 1

Earthquakes and volcanoes

Learning objectives:
- describe the main types and features of volcanoes and earthquakes
- describe and explain the distribution of earthquakes and volcanoes
- describe the causes of earthquakes and volcanic eruptions and their effects on people and the environment
- demonstrate an understanding that volcanoes present hazards and offer opportunities for people
- explain what can be done to reduce the impacts of earthquakes and volcanoes

Why does where you live make a difference?

Your constantly changing planet

How would you feel if you lived near a volcano? Perhaps you do! Or perhaps you live in an earthquake zone. If so, is it a scary experience or just something you are used to? Whether you live in such an area or not, the ground under your feet is constantly changing. It is always moving, although often no more than a few millimetres a year. This has been going on since the Earth was formed 4600 million years ago. The powerful forces that make this happen are responsible for some of the world's most dramatic scenery – **fold mountains**. These forces also create volcanoes and earthquakes, natural hazards that affect millions of people.

The structure of the Earth

When it was first formed the Earth was liquid rock but, as it cooled down, the outer surface hardened to become a thin **crust**. Underneath the crust is the **mantle** which makes up 82 per cent of the volume of the Earth and is 2900 km thick. This layer is a liquid and flows rather like really hot jam. Underneath are the extremely hot liquid **outer core** and solid **inner core** which, at its centre (6400 km from the Earth's surface), is 5500 degrees Celsius (°C) – diagram **A**.

A The structure of the Earth

Plate tectonics

The Earth's crust is broken up into a number of enormous pieces called **tectonic plates**. There are seven major plates, some of which are bigger than continents. These plates are constantly on the move, rubbing against, crashing into or moving away from each other. The edges where this happens are known as **plate boundaries** or **margins** (map **B**) and it is here that most of the world's volcanoes and earthquakes are found.

> **Fantastic fact**
>
> It took more than a billion years for the molten surface of the Earth to cool down enough to form the crust.

B Tectonic plates, plate boundaries and their direction of movement

C Convection currents in the mantle

Plates are made up of two types of crust. Continental crust is light but very strong. It cannot sink and it cannot be destroyed. Oceanic crust, on the other hand, is heavier and sinks under the continental crust. It is continually being destroyed and replaced. The plates move because they are floating on the extremely hot mantle. The mantle is made of a liquid called **magma** and the intense heat coming from the Earth's core gives rise to convection currents. These currents push under the plates and cause them to move (diagram **C**).

The study of plate movement and the effects it has on the formation of volcanoes and earthquakes is known as **plate tectonics**.

> **Further research**
>
> Search the internet for 'tectonic plates' or 'structure of the Earth' to find out more.

Types of volcano

Volcanoes are often described in terms of how active they are:

- **active** – still erupting quite frequently
- **dormant** – not currently erupting but could do so in the future
- **extinct** – highly unlikely to erupt again.

In addition to their activity, the volcanoes found along the world's plate boundaries are described by their shape and composition. The two main types are shield and strato- (diagrams **D** and **E**).

Shield volcanoes are low with gently sloping sides. They are formed from thin, runny lava and have fairly frequent, gentle eruptions.

D A shield volcano

E A strato-volcano (also known as composite volcanoes)

74 The natural environment

While other volcanoes are mainly made up of lava, **strato-volcanoes** (also known as composite volcanoes) have alternating layers of ash and lava. Eruptions can be very violent and result in pyroclastic flows mixing hot steam, ash, rock and dust. These flow down the mountain sides very fast at temperatures up to 400 degrees Celsius.

Now Investigate

1. Draw an annotated diagram showing the structure of the Earth. Add labels showing the crust, mantle and outer and inner cores.

2. a) Name the plate that you live on.
   b) Name the plates next to your own.
   c) Describe the direction of movement between your plate and that of its neighbouring plates.

3. Construct a table to show the differences between shield and composite volcanoes in terms of structure, characteristics of lava and type of eruption.

Plate boundaries

Recent earthquakes and volcanoes are found on the edges of the plates making up the Earth's crust. You may know of volcanoes in your region that are not on plate boundaries but these are probably very old and will have moved since the time they were **active**. Map **A** shows the areas where volcanoes and earthquake activity are found around the world.

A *Worldwide distribution of earthquakes and volcanoes*

Section 2.1: Earthquakes and volcanoes

These **zones of activity**, where the plates are in almost constant motion, are the **plate boundaries** or **margins**. These margins can be classified as either constructive, destructive or conservative. A fourth type, a collision margin, consists of two plates of continental crust moving towards each other. It is in these areas that fold mountain ranges are formed.

Constructive margins

When two plates move away from each other a constructive margin is formed. Molten rock (magma) rises from the mantle to fill the gap that is created and this forms new oceanic crust. The process is also known as sea-floor spreading because these margins are found under the ocean. The mid-Atlantic trench, for instance, is widening at a rate of around 3 cm a year, taking Europe further away from the Americas. Earthquakes and volcanoes can both occur in these areas.

Destructive margins

Where plates containing oceanic crust move towards those containing continental crust, a destructive margin is formed. The heavier oceanic crust is forced underneath the continental crust in an area called a subduction zone. Friction (and the increase in temperature as the crust moves downwards) causes the crust to melt and some of the newly formed magma may be forced to the surface to form volcanoes. The structure of a typical volcano formed in this way is shown in diagram **D**. The increase in pressure as the plate is forced downwards can also trigger severe earthquakes.

Conservative margins

Where two plates slide past each other (often at different speeds) no new landscape is formed and, therefore, there is no volcanic activity. However, earthquakes can occur at these conservative margins if the plates get stuck. Pressure will build up until it is released, causing the earth to jerk violently. The most famous example of this type of plate boundary is probably the San Andreas Fault in California.

Measuring seismic activity

Seismic activity is the name given to the movement of the Earth in an earthquake. Once an earthquake has taken place, it can be measured using a seismograph (or **seismometer**). This is a machine that records how much the Earth shakes and plots this on a graph. The strength of the earthquake (its magnitude) is measured using the Richter Scale. An increase of 1 on the scale means the shaking is 10 times greater, so the damage is likely to be much more severe.

B A constructive plate margin

C A destructive plate margin

D Structure of a volcano

E A conservative plate margin. As well as moving in opposite directions, plates can also move in the same direction but at different speeds

76   The natural environment

Now Investigate

1. Look at map **A**. What patterns can you see in the distribution of earthquakes and volcanoes? You may want to use an atlas to find the names of some of the areas on the map.

2. Describe the worldwide distribution of volcanoes and earthquakes. You should include some named examples either from the information on these pages or by using an atlas.

3. a) What kind of a plate margin is the plate boundary nearest to you?

   b) Describe and explain how the plates are moving at your nearest plate boundary.

   c) How does this movement relate to tectonic activity in your part of the world?

4. What is seismic activity and how can it be measured?

Further research

Put the words 'collision, conservative, constructive margins' into a search engine to find out more about the different activity at plate boundaries.

Fantastic fact

The strongest earthquake ever recorded was a magnitude 9.5 event in Chile in May 1960.

Earthquake – Japan 2011

Background

Japan is well prepared for earthquakes. It is located on a conservative plate boundary between the Eurasian, Pacific and Philippine plates and the country experiences about 20 per cent of the world's most serious seismic events. Schoolchildren are taught earthquake drills from a very young age, households keep earthquake survival kits in handy locations, and buildings are made 'earthquake-proof' to sway as the earth moves. Messages are sent to mobile phones within seconds of an earthquake happening, to tell people what to do and where to find help.

The country was well prepared, therefore, for the huge earthquake of Friday 11 March 2011. At magnitude 9.1 on the Richter Scale (which measures the **intensity** of an earthquake) it was the most powerful ever to hit Japan and the fourth strongest in world history. The earthquake itself caused few deaths and there was relatively little damage (map **A**). It did, however, produce a deadly tsunami which swept over the Japanese coastline, destroying buildings, roads and farmland. The wave washed people, houses, trucks and cars both inland and out to sea.

The case study below gives more detail of the greatest natural disaster in Japan's history.

CASE STUDY

Tsunami! Japan, 11 March 2011

When earthquakes occur at sea they can jolt the seabed upwards. This creates huge waves which move away from the **epicentre** in all directions. In the case of the Japanese earthquake the wave quickly travelled the 80 km to the coast at Sendai, the capital city of Miyagi prefecture. As it approached the shoreline and the seabed became shallower, the wave rose to 10 metres high and swept over the coastal defences (photo **B**).

The tsunami spread across the Pacific but, luckily, caused little damage in other countries (photo **C**).

The point where an earthquake strikes is the **focus**. The **epicentre** is the point directly above this on the Earth's surface.

A The Japanese earthquake of 11 March 2011

B The tsunami hits the coast of Japan

Topic link

Look at Topic 1.1 on pages 6–7 to find out how natural hazards can affect population growth.

C The tsunami spreads across the Pacific

D Fukushima Daiichi Nuclear Power Station

78 The natural environment

Within hours of the earthquake taking place, social networking sites on the internet were helping people donate to disaster relief funds and to find out about the location of loved ones. Facebook set up a donations page, Google launched Person Finder and online gaming sites allowed people to donate money to the emergency relief effort as they played.

As can be seen from figure **E**, the effects on people and infrastructure were huge. The clean-up operations were ongoing many months after the earthquake itself. At Ishinomaki, for instance, on Japan's northeast coast 28 000 houses were lost and, even two months after the event, thousands more were still clogged with mud and debris and waiting to be salvaged.

Japan's nuclear nightmare

One major long-lasting effect of the tsunami was the damage caused to Japan's nuclear programme. The six-reactor Fukushima Daiichi nuclear power plant (figure **D**) was damaged when the huge tidal surges knocked out the reactor cooling systems leading to meltdowns and radioactive leaks. Tens of thousands of people were evacuated from the surrounding area as sea water was dropped from helicopters to try to cool the reactors and prevent further leaks. In the days that followed the public outcry led to all of Japan's nuclear plants being shut down. The clean-up of the contamination caused and the decommissioning of the reactors is expected to take decades to complete.

Fatalities	18 000
Injuries	5363
Missing	8492
Evacuated	206 400
People without access to safe water	500 000 (approx.)
Damaged houses	88 873
Damaged roads	3970
Damaged bridges	71
Damaged ships	20 000 (approx.)
Economic cost	US$232 billion

E *Effects of the Japanese earthquake and tsunami*

Now Investigate

Use the information here, and on previous pages in this topic, to prepare an A4 page report on the Japanese earthquake. Include information on the causes (including the plates involved) and the effects on both people and the landscape.

Extension

If you want to go further, add extra detail to your report explaining how Japan prepares for earthquakes and how technology helped to deal with the disaster.

> **Further research**
>
> The 2011 Japanese earthquake is already the most studied in human history – search for extra information on the internet.

Why live next to a volcano?

When volcanoes erupt they can cause huge destruction and many deaths. Despite this, millions of people around the world live near to active volcanoes. This is because of both historical factors and the economic opportunities that volcanoes can bring.

- The land around a volcano is often very fertile – the ash from eruptions forms an excellent soil for growing crops and providing food for animals.

> **Topic link**
>
> There is more information on how people cope with natural hazards in Topic 2.5 pages 128–30.

Section 2.1: Earthquakes and volcanoes

- Farming near volcanoes has been going on for centuries, so small settlements have grown over time into important regional centres.
- More recently, many volcanoes have become tourist attractions and local businesses have sprung up around them, providing much needed employment.
- Despite the economic opportunities, many volcanoes are in poor countries so the people do not have the money to move away when disaster strikes.

Living with an active volcano can bring prosperity to a region but, if it erupts, this can be wiped out in a matter of minutes.

CASE STUDY: Living with a volcano in Montserrat

Before 1995 the small Caribbean island of Montserrat was famous as a peaceful, sunshine-filled tourist destination. Most of the 11 000 people living on the island depended on the tourist industry and on farming the fertile volcanic land.

Montserrat sits on the destructive plate boundary between the small Caribbean plate and the Atlantic plate. These two plates are moving towards each other resulting in seismic activity as the denser oceanic crust is forced downwards under the continental crust.

The Soufriere Hills eruption

In July 1995 increased activity from the Soufriere Hills volcano (which had not erupted for 400 years) caused the authorities to order everyone to move out of the south of the island. As volcanic activity increased many went abroad to other Caribbean islands or to the UK. By April 1996, the south of the island was empty.

A *The Soufriere Hills volcano on the Caribbean island of Montserrat*

The lava within the mountain was made from andesite. So thick that it could not flow, the lava piled up in the summit **crater** as a **lava dome**. This grew rapidly until, eventually, a huge eruption in June 1997 resulted in five million cubic metres of lava flowing from the dome on top of the volcano down its northern side. Scorching hot clouds of fine ash and small rocks – known as pyroclastic flows – spread out to the north and west and lahars, caused by thick deposits of ash mixed with heavy rain, flowed over homes and farmland. These combined effects killed 19 farmers who had entered the southern **exclusion zone** set up by the authorities. It was reported that they were gathering crops to feed the people who had moved to other parts of the island. Many towns and villages, including the former capital of Plymouth (photo **B**), were buried and over 60 per cent of the south and central areas of the island became uninhabitable. Some of the major effects are shown on map **C**.

Further research

Use key words 'Montserrat' and 'Soufriere Hills' to find more information about Montserrat and its volcano.

The aftermath

The population of the island is now around half what it was before the eruptions began and entry to the south is still not allowed. Life has improved for those who remain.

80   The natural environment

The north, which has remained lush and green, has seen a great deal of development as housing, schools and hospitals have been built to serve the remaining population. The people who are left are beginning to make a living from tourism again and visitors are being encouraged to take 'volcano tourism' holidays to see the still smoking Soufriere Hills. They can also view the destruction it caused, by taking a boat trip along the island's south coast.

One of the world's most modern monitoring stations – the Montserrat Volcano Observatory – has been built since the eruption and has ensured that Soufriere Hills is now one of the best monitored volcanoes in the world. Scientists conduct:

B *Plymouth after the eruption of Soufriere Hills*

- seismic monitoring – to detect movements of tectonic plates
- deformation monitoring – to detect movement of the ground on and around the volcano
- environmental monitoring – assessing the gas and ash released and the effects on the environment
- volcanological monitoring – to observe the growing lava dome and the chemistry of the lava.

C *Post-eruption Montserrat*

Legend:
- Pyroclastic flows
- Exclusion zone
- Volcanic dome
- Evacuated settlement
- Destroyed settlement

Now Investigate

1. Using a named example, outline the reasons why people might choose to live near active volcanoes.

2. Study the map of Montserrat after the eruption (**C**). Using map evidence only, describe the effects of the eruption of Soufriere Hills on both people and the landscape.

3. What will life be like for residents if they go back to live in the south of Montserrat? Write a brief essay explaining their thoughts on what they find.

Skills link

As geographers we tend to use maps with a grid system so that we can accurately locate and identify features. However, maps come in many shapes and forms. More details on how to interpret different kinds of map can be found in Sections 4.1 and 4.2.

Section 2.1: Earthquakes and volcanoes

Section 2 . Topic 2

Rivers

Learning objectives:
- explain the main hydrological characteristics and processes which operate in rivers and drainage basins
- demonstrate an understanding of the work of a river in eroding, transporting and depositing
- describe and explain the formation of the landforms associated with these processes
- demonstrate an understanding that rivers present hazards and offer opportunities for people
- explain what can be done to manage the impacts of river flooding

What's the story of your river?

Your constantly changing river

It is likely that you live fairly near to a river. Even if you don't, there will be at least one major river in the country where you live. You will also have heard of the world's major rivers, such as the Mississippi, the Amazon and the Nile. What you may not know is that all these rivers have similar features (although on different scales) and that these features are formed by similar processes.

Drainage basin processes

Rivers are the main feature of a **drainage basin**. This is the area drained by a river and all its tributaries enclosed by the **watershed**, the highest land bordering the basin. All water entering the drainage basin from precipitation and melting ice and snow ends up in the river. There are a number of different processes operating in a drainage basin (figure **A**):

- **interception** – precipitation falling into the drainage basin can be intercepted by the leaves of trees and by ground vegetation
- **infiltration** – some of the precipitation that reaches the ground continues downwards through the soil
- **overland flow** – some of the precipitation reaching the ground flows over the surface until it reaches a river channel
- **evaporation** – water on tree leaves, vegetation or lying on the ground or in river channels can be evaporated back into the atmosphere
- **throughflow** – infiltrating water continues down slopes through the soil towards the river channel

A *Drainage basin processes*

B *A river's long profile*

82   The natural environment

- **groundwater** flow – some infiltrating water continues into pores and cracks in the underlying rock and flows towards the river as groundwater.

River processes

Diagram **B** shows a river's **long profile** from its beginning (the **source**) to its end (the **mouth**). Along the profile it gets flatter and the bottom of the river (the **bed**) gets smoother. The volume of the river also increases as more water is added to it.

Rivers have **energy** which means they do **work** as they flow. This work is either **transportation** or **erosion**. When a river runs out of energy, **deposition** occurs.

> **Fantastic fact**
>
> There is some disagreement as to the world's longest river. Latest research shows it is the Amazon at 6800 km compared with the Nile at 6695 km, but the debate rages on.

Processes of transportation

Rivers carry a lot of particles of different sizes – boulders, pebbles, sand and silt. Collectively this is known as a river's **load**. A river with lots of energy will be able to carry much more load.

Processes of erosion

Transported material is used by a river to erode its banks and bed. As the **velocity** (speed) of a river increases, so does the amount of load it can carry and the amount of erosion it can carry out. There are four ways (processes) in which a river erodes:

- **hydraulic action** – when the force of the water knocks particles off the sides (banks) and the bed of the river
- **corrasion** – when sand and stones carried by the river rub against the bank and bed and knock off other particles; this process is also known as **abrasion**
- **attrition** – when boulders and large stones carried by the river (normally along the bed) collide with each other and break up into smaller pieces
- **corrosion** – when acids in the river dissolve the rocks that make up the bank and bed; this process is also known as **solution**.

Minerals that are dissolved in the water are transported in **solution**

The lightest particles of soil and sand make the river look cloudy as they are carried along in **suspension**

Smaller particles such as stones bounce along the river bed by **saltation**

The heaviest particles – large stones and rocks – roll along the bed in a process called **traction**

River bed

C *Processes of transportation*

Deposition

Along a river's long profile there will be places and conditions that cause it to slow down, for example following a spell of dry weather, when it spreads out over a wide valley or when it flows into a lake or the sea. As it slows it loses energy and can

D *Deposition in a river*

Section 2.2: Rivers 83

no longer carry its load. Deposition takes place with the largest stones dropped first, then pebbles, sand and smaller particles (photo **D**). Dissolved material may remain in solution and eventually be carried out to sea.

> **Now Investigate**
>
> **1** Write down definitions for the following:
>   a) river features: *source   mouth   bed   bank   load*
>   b) river processes: *corrasion   attrition   hydraulic action   corrosion*
>
> **2** Find out about your nearest river. If possible, use a map to draw a rough sketch of its long profile. Include sites of interest such as major towns, cities and other landmarks.
>
> **3** a) Why does deposition take place in a river?
>   b) Explain how this deposition takes place, referring to the different types of material carried by a river.

River features (1)

A river's course

Along its length a river goes through three stages known as the upper, middle and lower courses, shown on diagram **B** on page 82. The length of each of these will depend on the particular conditions where the river flows, such as the type of rock, the landscape and the climate. In the different courses different processes of erosion, transportation and deposition are dominant. The effectiveness of these river processes will vary according to how much water is in the river and how fast it is flowing. It will also depend on the nature of the load which, in turn, is influenced by the bedrock the river is passing over.

A *Cross-section of a river in the upper course*

Features of the upper course

Near the source the river has a steep-sided, V-shaped valley with a steep gradient, and the water in the river channel occupies most, if not all, of the valley floor (diagram **A**). The load is large because it has not had enough time to be eroded. Most of the load is found on the bottom of the river so it is known as **bedload**. There is plenty of friction between the water and the large bedload and this can slow down the river's velocity. Common features of the upper course include waterfalls, rapids and **potholes** (**B**).

B *Potholes forming in a river*

84   The natural environment

The formation of the Upper Ddwli Falls, South Wales

Waterfalls

Waterfalls tend to occur where the river crosses resistant rock and the softer rock downstream is eroded more rapidly. Under the waterfall a plunge pool is formed where erosion by hydraulic action and abrasion is greatest. The harder rock is undercut and collapses, causing the waterfall to retreat upstream.

Potholes

If the river bed is uneven, pebbles can become trapped. Swirling currents cause the pebbles to rotate and erode circular holes in the river bed.

Alternating bands of hard and soft rock crossing the course of a river form an uneven bed and areas of turbulent water called **rapids**.

Features of the middle course

In the middle course the river channel is wider and deeper with gentler valley sides and a wide flood plain (diagram **C**). The river has been joined by others (its **tributaries**) at points of **confluence** and these have added more water to the channel. Lateral erosion (from side to side) becomes more important than vertical erosion and the river begins to bend (or **meander**) across its flood plain. Bedload size decreases and there is more chance of deposition.

The main features of the middle course are meanders and oxbow lakes (**D**) but waterfalls are also common.

Meanders

The velocity of a river can change across a river channel. There will be more erosion on the side where velocity is greatest. On this faster-flowing side the river cuts into the bank and becomes deeper. Increasing deposition on the opposite side of the river forms a slip-off slope and the meander takes on a fairly common shape. Meanders maintain this shape as they erode sideways and move across the flood plain.

Fantastic fact

At almost 1 km from top to bottom, Angel Falls in Venezuela (also known as Kerepakupai Meru) is the highest waterfall in the world.

Rapids form in areas of differing rock type

Upper Ddwli Falls, South Wales

C *Cross-section of a river in the middle course*

Section 2.2: Rivers

Oxbow lake

As the loop of a meander gets bigger, the outsides of the bend get closer together. It becomes known as a 'swan's neck' meander. In times of flood the river may erode a new channel to straighten its course and completely cut off the meander neck. The old channel becomes an **oxbow lake** as its ends are sealed by deposition. Eventually the oxbow lake may dry out completely and become filled by vegetation.

> **Skills link**
>
> Make sure you are able to identify specific river features so that you can sketch them accurately when doing fieldwork. Go to Topic 4.4 pages 263–267 for more information on how to draw field sketches.
>
> *Remember*: You should learn how to draw diagrams and label them to explain the formation of various river features. But don't forget you also need to know the processes behind their formation.

Formation of a meander

D *Formation of an oxbow lake*

1 Swan's neck meander
2 River takes shorter route in times of flood
3 Oxbow lake is cut off as river starts new route
Deposition occurs at the ends of the oxbow lake

Now Investigate

1. Describe the differences in channel cross-section between the upper and middle courses of a river.

2. Draw diagrams with detailed labels to explain how **a** waterfalls and **b** meanders are formed.

3. Explain how changes in rock type in the upper course can lead to different river features.

River features (2)

Features of the lower course

In the lower course near to the mouth the river is broad and deep (diagram **A**). The bedload is transported in either suspension or solution and deposition becomes the most important process. The river is fast-flowing because there is very little friction with the bed, banks and load.

2.2

A *Cross-section of a lower course flood plain*

The river meanders across its **flood plain** – the area either side of the channel which floods if the river bursts its banks. The wide flood plain in the lower course is covered in clay, silt and sand from flooding events (known as **alluvium**). The river channel's edges have natural ridges called **levees**. When the river floods, the largest particles are deposited first, building the levees up higher with each successive flood. Finer material is spread out in layers over the rest of the flood plain.

The mouth of the river

The river channel can take on a number of different forms when it reaches the sea (or a major lake). These forms will depend on the rock type, the strength of the waves and tides and the amount of load being carried by the river. The river may end in a wide, deep **estuary**, which is especially useful for shipping, or it could finish as a narrow mouth. In many cases a **delta** may mark the end of a river's long profile.

CASE STUDY: The Mekong delta, Vietnam

Deltas form when rivers carry lots of sediment. As it reaches the sea, a river's velocity slows down dramatically and massive deposition occurs. As sediment is dropped and blocks the water flow, the river divides up into separate channels called **distributaries**. Deposition continues, the delta forms and it builds upwards and outwards. Photo **B** shows this happening at the end of Vietnam's Mekong river.

The travel guide company Lonely Planet describes the Mekong delta as 'a watery landscape of green fields and sleepy villages, everywhere crisscrossed by the brown canals fed by the mighty Mekong River'. The delta is formed of silt deposits dropped as the river enters the sea. These deposits continue to extend the shoreline by as much as 80 metres a year. The river is so large it has two tides every day.

Fantastic fact

More than 60 million people depend on the Mekong river and delta for their livelihood.

Section 2.2: Rivers

The sediment that forms the Mekong delta is very good for farming and provides the soil that produces enough rice to supply 90 per cent of Vietnam's total with some left over for export – 6 million tonnes worth US$3 billion per year. The delta is also home to the growing of sugar cane, fruit and coconut and many fish farms which make the region the largest seafood breeding and catching hub in the country. Farming has led to the delta becoming one of the most densely populated regions of Vietnam and contributed to an annual economic growth of 11.7 per cent for the first decade of the 21st century.

Key industrial projects in the gas industry with gas-powered fertiliser plants and thermal power stations have also contributed to the improved economy but an even bigger growth area has been in tourism. Marketed as 'Four Countries – One Destination', Vietnam has joined forces with Laos, Myanmar and Cambodia to offer so-called 'unique, stress-free, exotic tourism'. The range of tourism on offer includes eco, community-based, sea and islands and cultural visits. In 2016 a total of more than 10 million tourists visited the country – representing a 26 per cent growth over the previous year.

Although it is currently very productive, there are fears for the future of the Mekong. China has so far built (or planned) eight dams in the upper reaches of the river (photo **D**). The effects of this downstream could include increased salt in the soil and a loss of fertility that could lead to a drop in rice production. There is also evidence that rainfall patterns are changing and there are more drought years which is leading to reduced flow in the river channel.

Most importantly, perhaps, could be the effect of climate change on the delta. As it is so low-lying the delta could easily flood if the sea level rises because of melting ice caps and higher ocean temperatures. There are fears that, if current predictions about flooding are correct, some areas of the delta will become uninhabitable over the coming decades.

B *Satellite image of the Mekong delta*

Topic link

For information on flooding in Bangladesh see Topic 2.5 pages 133–134.

Further research

Using 'Mekong delta' as a search term will help you access plenty of information to develop this case study.

C *Rice farming in the Mekong delta*

D *Hydro-electric power on the Nam Tha river, Laos*

The natural environment

2.2

Now Investigate

1. Is your nearest river in its upper, middle or lower course? Can you identify any of the common river features in your local river? If possible, go and make field sketches to show what they are like.

2. Describe the formation of a flood plain and explain the processes that are involved.

3. Describe the layout and features of the Mekong delta as shown on photo **B**.

4. a) Using a named example, describe how a river delta is formed.

   b) Explain some of the economic opportunities that the delta may present.

   c) Outline some of the threats that may face people living in the delta in the future.

The world's great rivers

The world's greatest rivers often play a very important part in the history and development of the countries where they are found. They have a huge impact on the people, the economy and the landscape, which continues to the present day. Many of these rivers provide excellent case study material, and they still have the standard features of the upper, lower and middle courses.

CASE STUDY — **The mighty Mississippi, USA**

The Mississippi is North America's biggest river. At its source, at a height of 446 metres above sea level at Lake Itasca in Minnesota (map **B**), it is just over a metre wide and half a metre deep. It flows through a series of lakes, and passes over a number of important rapids, before dropping 20 metres at the Falls of St Anthony in Minneapolis. The falls were originally a large waterfall, but they have now been straightened and smoothed by engineers, and a channel with locks has been added to help boats continue up the river (photos **C**).

Many tributaries, such as the Missouri, Illinois, Wisconsin and Rock, add water to the river, vastly increasing the amount of load it can carry. Different types of rock mean that in some sections the river is channelled through 60-metre deep gorges while in others it meanders out over a wide flood plain (photo **D**).

Historically the economic opportunities provided by the river have influenced the development of the USA. The silt deposits

- The total area covered by the river and its tributaries (called the **river basin**) is the fifth largest in the world (map **B**).
- At 3734 km it is the second longest river in the USA (after the Missouri at 3767 km).
- The river releases almost 600 million tonnes of load each year – along its course and into the sea.
- The flood plain is 200 km wide at its widest point.
- The Mississippi flows through 10 states.
- In 2015 the river generated over US$400 billion in revenue and supported 1.3 million jobs.

A *Mississippi river facts*

Section 2.2: Rivers

formed on the huge flood plains have made the areas around the river amongst the most fertile regions of the USA. Sugar cane, rice, tobacco and cotton plantations became widespread in the 19th century with the river providing the main transport routes for export around the world. Today over 500 million tonnes of commodities are transported along the river each year and 92 per cent of the USA's agricultural exports, including feed grains, soya beans and livestock, are produced in the Mississippi river basin.

B The course of the Mississippi river

C The Falls of St Anthony 150 years ago (left) and today (right)

> ### Topic link
>
> Look at Topic 2.5 on page 132 to see how Hurricane Katrina made landfall close to the Mississippi Delta.

> ### Skills link
>
> It is important that you can identify river features on maps as the basis for answering questions on how these features are formed. For more information on how to do this check out Topic 4.1 pages 240–242.

D The meandering Mississippi

90   The natural environment

The Mississippi also provides huge recreational opportunities with more than 11 million tourist visitors each year. In the upper reaches of the river alone, this is worth US$1.2 billion to the economy each year; sport fishing and waterfowl hunting bringing in US$100 million and US$58 million respectively. Other economic benefits in the upper reaches come from the 29 power plants that provide energy to a vast array of factories and homes. The river is used for cooling purposes in 80 per cent of these energy production facilities.

> **Fantastic fact**
>
> In 2002, the Slovenian endurance swimmer Martin Strel swam the whole length of the Mississippi in 68 days.

Flooding on the Mississippi

At various points along its course the Mississippi has built up its bed so that it flows above the level of its flood plain. Huge deposits have created natural levees and these have been artificially strengthened to stop the river overflowing its banks. Other flood prevention measures have also been put into place, such as the building of dams and channels to take water out of the main course. Despite these efforts there have been several major floods over the last fifty years. Following particularly severe floods in 1993, many scientists and engineers argued that floods were a natural part of the river's life and that prevention measures should be abandoned. However, it is difficult to do this when so many people live along the river's flood plain.

One of the worst areas for flooding is the point where the river finally enters its delta at the Gulf of Mexico and spreads out through a number of distributaries. Very careful management is needed here in order to stop the build-up of sediment causing even more floods.

Section 2 . Topic 3

Coasts

Learning objectives:
- demonstrate an understanding of the work of the sea and wind in eroding, transporting and depositing
- describe and explain the formation of the landforms associated with these processes
- describe coral reefs and mangrove swamps and the conditions required for their development
- demonstrate an understanding that coasts present hazards and offer opportunities for people
- explain what can be done to manage the impacts of coastal erosion

How and why is your coastline changing?

Specialised ecosystems develop along coastlines, with plants and animals adapting to extreme – and constantly changing – habitats.

Coastal processes

A *Coasts around the world*

The photos in **A** show a variety of coastal environments around the world. Coasts may be on high or low land, in wet or arid (very dry) locations, and be densely vegetated or with little plant life.

Coasts are constantly changing. Every high tide brings some minor change; every storm brings much greater changes. The main agent of change is the sea itself – the power and effects of its waves. But coasts are also affected by earthquakes and tsunamis, weathering, and changing sea levels.

Waves are created by the wind blowing across the sea's surface. In mid-ocean, waves appear to rise up and down but in fact what we

> **Topic link**
>
> Look back at Topic 2.1 pages 77–79 for more on earthquakes and tsunamis.

92   The natural environment

see is the effect of a circular motion *within* the water. As each wave approaches the shore, the gradient of the sea bed becomes steeper and the sea shallower. Contact with the beach slows down the wave, causing it to rise higher and eventually to 'break'. Breaking waves cause water to rush up the beach (**swash**) then draw the water back down the beach (**backwash**).

High, powerful waves are the result of windy conditions. The distance the wind blows over the sea (**fetch**) and the length of time it blows, also contribute to the height and strength of waves (map **B**).

B The directions of maximum fetch affecting the coastlines of the British Isles

Two very different types of wave affect coastlines: **constructive waves** build up beaches and **destructive waves** remove material from them (diagram **C**).

In a similar way to rivers, waves erode, transport and deposit materials. Coastal erosion involves the same four processes – attrition, abrasion, solution and hydraulic action. Weathering processes also break up exposed rock surfaces above the high-tide line. Much of the sea's load is made up of **sediment** which is transported and then deposited in the sea by rivers. Material is also weathered and eroded at the coast itself. When waves become less powerful, the water cannot transport as much sediment, so deposition occurs (see pages 96–98).

Constructive waves
- Wave crests far apart
- Gently sloping wave front
- Breaking wave spills forward
- Strong swash pushes material up the beach
- Gently sloping beach

Swash is stronger than backwash, so waves run gently up the beach – material is carried onto the beach and deposited there.

Destructive waves
- Waves close together
- Steep wave front
- Breaking wave plunges forward
- Steep beach
- Strong backwash pulls material out to sea

Backwash is stronger than swash, so waves crash onto the beach – material is eroded from the coastline.

C *The features of constructive and destructive waves*

Fantastic fact

The biggest wave ever recorded was caused by an earthquake off the coast of Alaska on 9 July 1958; its height was an incredible 525 metres.

Skills link

Check out Topic 4.4 pages 266–267 to see how to draw, annotate and label a sketch.

Section 2.3: Coasts

> **Now Investigate**

1. If you are familiar with a coastline in your region, try to answer these questions as fully as you can. Otherwise use some of the photos in **A** to help you.
   - What are the main landscape features, such as cliffs, that can be seen on your chosen coastline?
   - How is the coast likely to be affected by high tides and strong winds?
   - How is it used?
   - Is it a safe place to visit / live and work ... or is it sometimes dangerous?

2. Briefly describe *either* the most interesting memories you have of a visit to the coast *or* what you might see and do during a visit to the coast.

3. In what ways are constructive and destructive waves different?

4. Describe and explain the factors that affect the power of a wave. Illustrate your answer with fully annotated diagrams.

5. Choose two of the photographs included on these pages. Practise your field-sketching skills as if you were actually at the coast. When you have completed this topic, add annotations to demonstrate your understanding of the processes at work at each location.

Coastal erosion

The rate of coastal erosion depends on a number of factors, for example the:

- geology of the area – softer rock such as clay is easily eroded, whilst harder rock, for example granite or chalk, is more resistant
- type of wave – destructive or constructive
- shape of the coastline – **bays** are often sheltered from the full force of the sea while **headlands** are exposed (diagram **A**)
- width of the beach – beaches absorb wave energy and protect the coastline from the power of the waves, so a wider beach gives more protection.

Cliffs and wave-cut platforms

Cliffs are steep, sometimes vertical, rock outcrops along a coast (see top-right photo in **A**, on page 92). You might think that all cliffs are made of hard, resistant rock, but they can also be formed of softer rocks such as clay. Wave erosion is most intense at the base of a cliff face – especially where there is no beach to absorb wave energy. Large waves breaking on a

A *Development of headlands and bays*

The natural environment

cliff face combine hydraulic action with strong abrasion to erode a **wave-cut notch** (diagram **B**). As the notch develops, it gradually undercuts the cliff above, eventually leading to cliff collapse and inland retreat and creating a **wave-cut platform**.

Cliffs formed of resistant rock usually retreat at a steady rate. However, where the rock is weaker, the process of undercutting can suddenly accelerate the slipping and **slumping** of cliff materials.

B *Development of a wave-cut platform*

Caves, stacks and stumps

The most resistant rocks contain some weak points which are eroded more easily than the surrounding rock. Even a small crack or **fault** can start the erosion sequence shown in diagram **C**.

C *Erosion from cave to stack to stump*

Fantastic fact

Holderness, in eastern England, is Europe's fastest eroding coastline. Parts of it retreat 2 metres every year!

Coastal erosion on the Australian coast

Port Campbell National Park, in Victoria, south-east Australia, has a range of coastal features including **arches**, **caves**, dunes, islands, beaches, **stacks**, **stumps** and cliffs. The cliffs are made of soft limestone, which are weathered and eroded by storms from the wild Southern Ocean. The exposed rock faces are chemically weathered by high levels of salt spray, and pounding waves undercut the cliffs at sea level.

Section 2.3: Coasts

This 'heritage' coast is so rich in spectacular features that it is now protected by National Park status. Its world-famous landforms include 'The Twelve Apostles' and 'London Bridge' (photo **D(i)**) – which is now known as 'London Arch' (photo **D(ii)**). The 45-metre high stacks on this stretch of coast were called 'The Twelve Apostles' to attract tourists, and they became so popular that helicopter tours of the area have become an additional tourist attraction. Over 2 million people now visit the area every year.

> **Further research**
>
> Investigate the development of other erosional features within the Port Campbell National Park, such as the stack system known as the Twelve Apostles.

(i)   *(ii)*

D Until 5 January 1990, this feature was known as 'London Bridge' (i) – and then the sea broke through and it became 'London Arch' (ii)

Now Investigate

1. Describe the main differences between a bay and a headland.

2. Draw a labelled diagram to illustrate the formation of each of these landscape features:
   a) bay and headland coast
   b) notch
   c) wave-cut platform.

3. Using diagram **C** to help you, describe and explain the sequence of events that occurred to produce the feature in photo **D** (ii). (Hint: Begin with the headland being attacked by wave action.) Include an annotated diagram – or a series of diagrams – to illustrate your answer.

Coastal transportation and deposition

On pages 92–93 you learned how the sea is able to transport material up and down a beach. Here we see how sediment moves along a beach and learn about the features that can form when it is re-deposited. Diagram **A** explains the process known as **longshore drift**, which is so powerful that it can remove all the beach material from a stretch of coast. On many beaches that experience longshore drift, long wooden fences, called **groynes**, are built down the beach to reduce the movement of material (photo **B**).

2.3

A *The process of longshore drift*

Material transported by the sea is later deposited, often in sheltered bays or where the coastline changes direction. Beaches are the result of deposited sand, shingle or pebbles. These materials are often well sorted by size. Usually, the larger the sediment, the steeper the beach is likely to be.

Sand dunes are often found at the top of a wide beach, but they are not really coastal features, because they are formed by wind, not by the sea. Sand that is blown inland from a beach is deposited when the wind speed drops, forming a series of ever-shifting dunes. If they are not held in place by specially adapted vegetation such as **marram grass**, dunes can extend far inland (photo **C**).

Photo **D** on page 98 shows how a typical **spit**, with its long, narrow ridge of sand and shingle, grows outwards from the coast. Spits develop where longshore drift is strong and the coastline suddenly changes direction.

Spits that continue to grow across a river estuary, or a bay, are known as **bars**, and a **lagoon** often forms behind the bar (diagram **E**). Like all coastal landforms, bars are temporary features in the landscape. Eventually, either sea currents change direction and break through, or the lagoon fills with sediment deposited by a river flowing into it.

Where a spit begins to grow across a river mouth, a **salt marsh** often develops on the sheltered (inland) side of the spit. Fine sediment builds up in this shallow water and is eventually colonised by **halophytes** (salt-tolerant plants). Further sedimentation increases the height of the salt marsh so that it is submerged less often. Most salt marshes form a network of tidal creeks – shallow inlets which fill with sea water at high tide. These fragile environments provide an ideal habitat for waders and other migrant birds.

B *Where there are groynes, there must be longshore drift!*

Further research

Find out why marram grass is particularly suited to helping to establish vegetation cover in a dune system.

Fantastic fact

The Arabat Tongue, in the Sea of Azov (coast of Crimea) is 110 km long and is the world's longest spit.

Section 2.3: Coasts

C A sand dune system in Natal, Brazil

D Development of a spit: Farewell Spit, South Island, New Zealand

E Like spits and bars, tombolos are low-lying ridges of deposited material, but they link offshore islands to the mainland. A tombolo forms a causeway which can give access to an island at low tide but is submerged at high tide.

Now Investigate

1. Describe how sediment is transported along a beach. Illustrate your answer with an annotated diagram.

2. Explain what you understand by the terms spit, bar and tombolo. Your answer should include diagrams with labels that highlight both the similarities and the differences between these three depositional features.

3. Lagoons and salt marshes are indirectly the result of coastal deposition. Explain why they are both only short-term landscape features.

4. Use any two of the illustrations on these pages to practise your field sketch drawing and annotating skills.

F Features of a typical salt marsh

98 The natural environment

2.3

A coastline of deposition

Just as in many parts of the world coastlines are constantly being eroded, in many other areas the sea continually creates new features.

Coastal deposition in New Zealand

Omara Spit is located on the north-eastern coast of North Island, New Zealand. It is a stable area of land that has developed as a result of marine deposition. Its gentle, low relief has made it an ideal location for the development of a major golf resort and it provides shelter for the harbour of Whangapoua.

Now Investigate

1. Match each of these grid references to one of the coastal features:

   340326   355322   378321

   beach   island   spit

2. List as many pieces of map evidence as you can which prove that the feature between 350320 and 390313 has existed for many years.

3. Locate grid references 331343 and 358315.
   a) For each of these sites, state whether it is likely to be a zone of erosion or deposition.
   b) Give reasons to support your answers.

4. Suggest reasons why there is a headland at Te Rehutae Point.

5. a) Draw a sketch map of the depositional feature between grid references 350320 and 390314.
   b) Annotate your sketch to show the most likely direction of the prevailing wind and the movement of beach materials due to longshore drift.
   c) Add key information about natural vegetation and human activity in the area.
   d) Use your sketch to help you describe how depositional features such as this are formed.
   e) Give reasons why the sheltered area behind the feature is 'swamp' land.

6. Produce a short case study of a bar or a tombolo. Include an annotated sketch of its location and its main depositional features.

7. Draw a series of annotated sketches to tell the story of how the coastal processes of weathering, erosion and deposition take place.

A *Omara Spit, North Island, New Zealand*

Further research

The Ordnance Survey map shows some ways in which this part of North Island, New Zealand is used. Use Google Street View to discover more about people's activities along this coastline.

Topic link

See section 4.1 on pages 236–237 and section 4.4 on pages 265–266 to help you answer these questions.

Section 2.3: Coasts   99

B Ordnance Survey map extract showing part of North Island, New Zealand, 1:50 000 scale

Legend		
Residential area	Native forest	Coastal rocks
Large buildings	Exotic coniferous forest	Shoal or reef
Isolated building	Exotic non-coniferous forest	Sand and mud
Homestead, stockyard	Scrub	Sand
Glasshouse or greenhouse	Scattered scrub	Shingle
Church, cemetery, grave	Shelter belt	Swamp
Training track	Trees	Boat ramp
Golf course, helipad	Orchard or vineyard	Breakwater, wharf, jetty
	Mangroves	Slipway
		Marine farm, seawall

The natural environment

Coral reefs and mangrove swamps

You may live in a part of the world where you are able to visit a **coral reef**, or you may never have seen one – but there is a chance that they affect your life in some way! They protect coastlines around the world from the effects of erosion, allowing coastal communities to live and work in safety. They are also a major source of income from fishing and tourism, provide must-see tourist destinations – and are home to over a quarter of all marine species.

The term 'coral' has two meanings. It is both the community of tiny marine organisms called polyps that live in and build reefs, and the reef itself (photos **A**). Reefs are made of limestone or calcium carbonate ($CaCO_3$), which is produced by the polyps. It is the **algae** which live alongside the polyps that give a healthy tropical reef its bright colours; coral itself is white.

Most reefs grow in warm seas, ideally with a temperature of 26–27 °C and are found in moving, shallow clear water. The salinity (salt content) and temperature of the water need to remain the same throughout the year, as coral is very sensitive to any change in its environment. Ideal conditions occur in tropical seas between the latitudes of 30 °N and 30 °S, near to land. Map **B** shows the worldwide distribution of coral reefs.

Photos **C** on page 102 illustrate the three basic reef types:

- **Fringing reefs** are found near the shorelines of islands or landmasses. They grow in coastal zones that are already protected by a larger barrier reef.
- **Barrier reefs** develop further from the shoreline, often separated from the land by a lagoon.
- **Atoll reefs** are associated with volcanic islands. They look similar to barrier reefs, but are found only around submerged oceanic islands.

> **Topic link**
>
> See Topic 3.4 pages 181–188 to learn more about tourism in coastal regions.

A A healthy coral reef and the polyps that create it

B World map to show the distribution of coral reefs

Section 2.3: Coasts

(a) Fringing reef

(b) Barrier reef

(c) Atoll

C The three main types of coral reef

Mangrove swamps often occur in the same regions as coral reefs, because they have very similar environmental requirements. They need water temperatures above 24 °C during the warmest month and a total annual rainfall of at least 1250 mm. They prefer sheltered places such as river deltas, which have much less wave and tidal action and where large areas of gently sloping mud flats occur between the high and low tidal points. These are highly specialised trees which, being halophytic (salt-loving), can survive in both salt and fresh water.

Mangroves have stilt roots (photo **D**) which give the plants extra support in stormy weather. The roots' other key role is to absorb extra oxygen from the air, necessary because the mud flats have very densely packed particles which alone cannot hold enough oxygen for the trees to survive.

Mangroves produce flowers, which are pollinated by bees and other insects. After pollination, the seeds germinate and grow roots. These can anchor them before they are swept away by the tidal flow. Some mangrove species release their seeds inside capsules, which can be dispersed by the moving water before growing roots and becoming new trees.

> **Fantastic fact**
>
> The annual global value of coral reefs is approximately $30 billion.

D Red mangrove is easily identified by its distinctive arched roots

The natural environment

2.3

> **Now Investigate**

1. List the ideal environmental conditions for coral reef and mangrove swamp development.
2. Make a display of annotated images to show the three different types of coral reef, and some different varieties of coral.
3. Identify threats to both mangrove swamps and coral reefs from human activity and global climate change.

A world famous coastline

The Great Barrier Reef is the world's most extensive coral reef.

> **CASE STUDY**
>
> ### The Great Barrier Reef, Australia
>
> Australia's Great Barrier Reef (map **A**) is so large it can be seen from outer space! It is 3000 kilometres long and up to 65 kilometres wide. It is not a single structure but is made up of thousands of individual reefs and 900 islands. The Great Barrier Reef is home to a huge diversity of species, many of which are vulnerable or endangered. The reef alone comprises over 400 species of coral.
>
> However, like reef systems around the world, the Great Barrier Reef is now endangered as never before, primarily because of threats from human activities.
>
> Millions of tourists visit the reef every year to see the spectacular sights of over 1500 species of tropical fish, turtles, whales and dolphins. They have created thousands of jobs in the catering, accommodation and transport industries. Managing such a large area also requires teams of highly trained park rangers, whose main task is to minimise physical damage to the coral and carry out biosecurity checks on all visitors to prevent foreign seeds or creatures entering the country and upsetting the delicate balance of Australia's unique wildlife.
>
> **A** *The Great Barrier Reef*
>
> #### Threats to the reef
>
> - **Climate change** – possibly the greatest threat of all, because coral cannot tolerate environmental change. Major **coral bleaching** events occurred in 1998, 2002 and 2015 onwards, and scientists

Section 2.3: Coasts

believe that by 2030 such events will occur every year. Rising sea temperatures also cause some species of fish to migrate to cooler waters, which in turn affects food chains across the reef (diagram **B**).

- **Pollution and declining water quality** – these are also major issues (diagram **D**). Agricultural activities in Queensland are the main source of pollutants in the Coral Sea.
- **Overfishing** disrupts food chains and can have a very dramatic effect on reef systems. One such effect, due to overfishing of the giant triton, is an explosion in the population of the crown-of-thorns starfish (photo **C**). The starfish is a major predator of coral polyps and, if its numbers increase, whole reef systems could be destroyed.
- **Shipping** can also damage coral. In April 2010, a bulk coal-carrier ran aground on a reef, spilling over 4 tonnes of its fuel, causing a 3.7-km-long oil slick.
- **Tourism** – visitors are the greatest human threat to the reef system but they are one of Australia's main sources of income. Tourism is therefore increasingly being 'managed' to promote ecological sustainability.

Much of the reef is protected by the Great Barrier Reef Marine Park Authority (GBRMPA). It is also a World Heritage Site. Sustainability is the key aim of the management strategies. However, the main environmental threat is climate change – which is a global rather than a purely national issue.

B *Effects of a rising sea temperature*

(a) Giant triton
(b) Crown-of-thorns starfish

C *Two species key to the reef's survival – or destruction*

> **Topic link**
>
> See Topic 3.7 pages 229–231 to learn about managing and protecting the Great Barrier Reef, and pages 213–221 for more about the impact of human activity and economic development on the environment.

104 The natural environment

2.3

Flow diagram: Effects of nutrient pollution on coral reefs

- Increased use of fertilisers (especially nitrogen and phosphorus) → Increased nutrient content in runoff and so in sea water
- Increased nutrient content → Intensifies disease in corals → Coral bleaching and eventual death of reef system
- Increased nutrient content → High nitrate levels toxic to corals → Coral bleaching and eventual death of reef system
- Increased nutrient content → Encourages growth of algae and phytoplankton → These plants use up available oxygen → Polyps starved of oxygen → Coral bleaching and eventual death of reef system
- Encourages growth of algae and phytoplankton → These plants obscure sunlight → Coral bleaching and eventual death of reef system
- Increased nutrient content → High phosphate levels → Slows growth of reef structures
- Increased nutrient content → Directly linked to population explosion of crown-of-thorns starfish → Starfish eat polyps → Coral bleaching and eventual death of reef system

D Effects of nutrient pollution on coral reefs

Now Investigate

1. Create a display of images showing healthy and bleached coral. Annotate your work to show the causes and effects of coral bleaching, and highlight the conditions necessary for healthy coral growth.

2. Write a short brochure for tourists visiting a coral reef, explaining what they should and should not do when visiting such areas, and why this is important. This could take the form of a Code of Good Practice which includes five things that visitors should do and five things they should *not* do. Illustrations could show the effects of breaking the Code.

3. How can tropical storms and changing sea levels affect coral reefs? Think about environmental changes caused by these events. You could use online or library resources to help you with this activity.

Further research

Create a case study similar to the one on these pages for a coral reef system of your choosing. If you live in a tropical area, you may like to investigate a reef in your own region.

Fantastic fact

A single crown-of-thorns starfish can consume 6 square metres of living reef in a year!

Section 2 . Topic 4

Weather

Learning objectives:
- describe how weather data is collected
- make calculations using information from weather instruments
- use and interpret graphs and other diagrams showing weather and climate data

What is the weather like where you are today?

The weather affects us all. Take a few moments to look out of the window and observe what the weather is like now. Then, before you answer question 1, think back to what it was like when you came to school this morning – and how it might affect the things you do today.

A *Weather around the world*

Fantastic fact

Earth's extremes of weather include:
- highest annual rainfall is in Mawsynram (north-east India): 11 872 mm/year
- lowest annual rainfall (and longest drought) for an urban area is in Arica (Chile): 0.71 mm/year and a drought lasting 173 months
- driest place is Dry Valleys (Antarctica): 0.00 mm of rain/year
- hottest inhabited place is Dallol (Ethiopia): daily maximum temperature averages 41.1 °C
- sunniest place is Yuma, Arizona: 4050 hours of sunshine each year.

Weather is the state of the atmosphere at a given time. It can change very rapidly – even in quite small areas. Our weather is due to several elements within the atmosphere affecting each other. Photos **A** show you a variety of weather events in locations around the world.

As geographers, we are interested not only in day-to-day weather events but also in finding out what the weather is usually like around the world. This idea of 'typical' weather is known as **climate**. It is defined as average (mean) weather over several decades, or at least 30 years. By 'averaging out' elements of the weather such as temperature, precipitation and sunshine hours,

106   The natural environment

we are able to disregard extreme and/or unusual weather events and identify what the weather is usually like in different places. This helps us to understand how weather actually 'works'. It also shows us that, for most of the time, the processes at work in the air behave in predictable ways. Map **B** is a simplified map of global climate distributions. Each climate type can be represented by a climate graph – just four are included on this map.

Topic link

See Topic 4.3 page 261 to learn how climate graphs are constructed.

B Distribution of the world's main climates

Legend:
- Tundra/ice cap/mountain: cold
- Hot desert/semi-desert: low rainfall
- Tropical: distinct wet season
- Equatorial: rain all year
- Mediterranean: mild wet winters, dry summers
- Sub-Arctic: severe, cold winters
- Continental: warm to hot summers, cold or very cold winters

Now Investigate

1. a) What is the weather like as you look through your window?

   b) Is the weather always like it is today where you live? Hint: Is it usually stable and predictable, or very changeable?

   c) If it is changeable throughout the year, are there recognisable seasons where you live?

2. For each of the photos in **A**, identify the elements of the weather that you can see *and also* those that you have to imagine by observing their effects.

Topic link

Refer to Topic 2.5 pages 115–127 for help with these questions.

Further research

Investigate recent extreme weather events in your own country or region.

Section 2

108

3. Describe how the weather event in each image may affect the lives and economy of the people who live in that place.

4. Using your own knowledge, suggest a country or even a city where each photograph might have been taken – and at what time of the year.

5. Describe the global distribution of climate types shown in map **B**. Make sure you include equatorial areas and hot deserts when you do this. Hint: Start close to the Equator and use compass directions and the named lines of latitude to locate places.

6. Choose two of the four climate types shown on map **B**.

    a) State where in the world each climate type occurs.

    b) Describe each of your chosen climates, using data from the graphs to help you. (Refer to page 261 for help if necessary.)

How can you investigate the weather?

Can you tell how hot – or cold – it is where you are today? By looking around, you should be able to spot clues about the temperature. Is the Sun shining? What sorts of clothes are people wearing? Is any method of heating or cooling turned on? This gives an idea of what the temperature is – but can you measure and record it precisely? Is there a thermometer available in your classroom?

Measuring and recording the weather

Weather is observed, measured and recorded at a weather station. Ideally this should be located on open ground to minimise the effects of local relief and any built-up areas. The basic equipment required for a weather station is shown in figure **A**. Thermometers are always kept inside a **Stevenson screen**, and other equipment is sited close by.

Measuring temperature

Temperature is measured using a special type of thermometer. This is a **maximum-minimum thermometer**, designed to record both the highest and lowest temperatures in a 24-hour period (figure **A**). Diagram **B** shows how to read data from this type of thermometer and how to re-set it after the information has been recorded. Like all other weather data, temperature must be logged daily and at the same time each day. Thermometers used for weather recording have to be kept in the shade. This is why a Stevenson screen is so important, because we measure the *air temperature* – not the temperature in direct sunlight, which can several degrees higher.

> **Fantastic fact**
>
> The Stevenson screen is named after a 19th-century Scottish engineer called Thomas Stevenson. As well as being a pioneering meteorologist, he was also famous for designing lighthouses.

> **Skills link**
>
> See Section 4.3 pages 251–252 to learn more about how a climate graph is constructed.

The natural environment

2.4

Maximum-minimum thermometer

Shields instruments from rain, wind, Sun

Cabinet may house: dry-bulb thermometer, barometer, hygrometer, maximum-minimum thermometer

Rain gauge

Hygrometer

Located in open area, away from buildings and tall vegetation

Door faces away from direct sunlight

Painted white to reflect sunlight

Cabinet at least 1.5 metres above the ground, and slatted, to allow free flow of air

Barometer

Anemometer

Wind vane

A The Stevenson screen and equipment for a weather station

Alcohol used because it has a very low freezing point

Temperature scale increases with height up the tube

Minimum thermometer — Maximum thermometer

°C — Alcohol — °C
−25 — 40
−20 — 35
−15 — 30
−10 — 25
−5 — 20
0 — Metal indices — 15
5 — 10
10 — 5
15 — 0
20 — −5
25 — −10
30 — −15
35 — −20
40 — Mercury — −25

Scale decreases with height up the tube

Maximum temperature 30°C (bottom of index shows temperature)

Minimum temperature 24°C (bottom of index shows temperature)

After taking reading, re-set both markers using a magnet to draw them down the tube until they rest at the top of each column of mercury

B Using a maximum-minimum thermometer

Section 2.4: Weather   109

Measuring rainfall

Rainfall is measured using a **rain gauge**, which must be located well away from trees and buildings so that water dropping from them does not distort the data. Information is usually recorded every day in a simple table and then used to plot a graph. Bar graphs are usually used but, if the data is to be displayed alongside temperature in a climate graph, a histogram is more appropriate.

Measuring sunshine

Sunshine is usually recorded on a **sunshine recorder** using a glass ball, mounted on a frame (diagram **C**). When the Sun is shining, it burns a line along the paper as it moves in the sky. The total length of burnt line shows how long the Sun has been shining that day.

C *Sunshine recorder*

(Labels: Bowl, Glass sphere, Adjustment screw)

Now Investigate

1. Write a step-by-step guide to instruct another student how to measure and record air temperature accurately.

2. a) What is a Stevenson screen used for?
   b) Where would you locate a Stevenson screen within your school's grounds?
   c) Justify your decision to locate it at this site.

3. Draw an annotated sketch to show where, why and how you would set up a rain gauge.

More complex weather measurements

Measuring relative humidity

Relative humidity describes the amount of **water vapour** in the air. Air contains water vapour due to **evaporation** and **transpiration**. How much it holds depends upon its temperature, because warm air can hold more vapour than colder air. Diagram **A** shows you how a wet and dry bulb thermometer (a **hygrometer**) is used to calculate the humidity of the air. The greater the difference between readings on the two thermometers, the drier the air and the lower the relative humidity. Relative humidity is always stated as a percentage: 50% is considered to be 'dry' air, while 100% is as wet as air can be and is described as being saturated. The humidity of the air is important because it tells us whether or not it is likely to rain – the closer the humidity is to 100%, the more likely it is to rain.

The natural environment

Two standard mercury thermometers

Read current air temperature from 'dry' thermometer

Keep bulb of thermometer in saturated sock

Read temperature from 'wet' thermometer (usually lower because of effect of evaporation from sock: this uses heat)

Sock – must be kept saturated with end in bowl of water

A Measuring relative humidity. After taking these measurements you would need to use a table for calculating the difference between the two thermometer readings in percentage terms

Skills link

Refer to Section 4.3 pages 251–262 to learn more about presenting different weather records as maps and graphs.

Measuring air pressure

Air pressure, or **atmospheric pressure**, is the force put on the Earth's surface by the weight of air above it. Pressure varies from place to place around the world because of the Earth's rotation and differences in temperature and altitude (diagram **B**). However, temperature is the most important factor because when air is warmed, it rises. As it rises, areas of low pressure form at the Earth's surface. Rising air cools, becomes denser and eventually sinks back down to Earth. This causes high pressure conditions. A **barometer** is used to measure air pressure, which is then mapped, using isobars.

Observing and measuring wind

Differences in pressure on the Earth's surface cause air to move from areas of high pressure to areas of low pressure. This air movement is known as wind. **Meteorologists** record two different sets of information about the wind: its direction and its speed. As when measuring rainfall, we also note when wind is absent.

- **Wind direction** is recorded using a **wind vane** (see figure **A** on page 109). It is usual to do this at least once every hour, as wind direction can change frequently. The arrow points in the direction from which the wind is blowing.

- **Wind speed** is measured using an **anemometer** (see figure **A** on page 109). This instrument is rotated by the movement of the air. The number of revolutions is recorded on a meter and automatically converted into kilometres per hour (km/hr). Alternatively, wind strength can be estimated using the **Beaufort scale** (diagram **C** on page 112).

B Global pressure belts

Skills link

An example of a wind rose graph is shown in Section 4.3 on page 255.

Section 2.4: Weather

1 1.1–5.5 km/hr   **2** 5.6–11 km/h   **3** 12–19 km/h   **4** 20–28 km/h
5 29–38 km/h   **6** 39–49 km/h   **7** 50–61 km/h   **8** 62–74 km/h
9 75–88 km/h   **10** 89–102 km/h   **11** 103–117 km/h   **12** More than 117 km/h

C *The Beaufort scale*

Fantastic fact

The strongest gust of wind ever recorded was 408 km/hr. It hit Barrow Island, Australia, in 1996.

Digital equipment

Professional meteorologists often use digital measuring and recording equipment (photo **D**). They also use a range of aerial and satellite images to help them track cloud movements and record changes in the upper layers of the atmosphere. Electronic weather stations have one great advantage: they are able to monitor and measure the weather all the time, observing, recording and transmitting information instantly.

D *A digital weather station*

Now Investigate

1. Write a sentence about each of these pieces of equipment, stating what it records, and the unit of measurement used:

   a) anemometer   b) barometer   c) hygrometer

2. Write a step-by-step guide to instruct a younger student how to measure and record relative humidity.

3. Keep a diary of wind strength in your local area for the next seven days, using the Beaufort scale as your guide. Record your data at least three times every day. Then write an account of how you undertook your work and the problems you might have encountered.

4. Draw a wind rose graph to illustrate the data in the table below:

	Monday	Tuesday	Wednesday	Thursday	Friday	Saturday	Sunday
Direction of prevailing wind	SE	E	SE	SE	S	E	Calm

112   The natural environment

2.4

Clouds

A cloud is a visible mass of water droplets or ice crystals suspended in the atmosphere. Clouds form when air is unable to absorb any more water; it becomes saturated. This usually happens when air cools, because cooler air cannot hold as much water vapour as warm air. Therefore **condensation** occurs and clouds form. Clouds are classified into three main types:

- **cirrus clouds** – high-altitude clouds, often described as being 'wispy'
- **stratus clouds** – sheet-like in appearance
- **cumulus clouds** – often described as being 'bubbly', with huge rounded tops, but also described as being rolled or 'rippled' clouds.

As stratus and cumulus clouds can occur at high, middle or low altitudes, these three categories are subdivided to include information about the altitude of the cloud (diagram **A**).

When meteorologists record cloud type, they also assess how much cloud there is in the sky – the more cloud there is, the greater the chance of rain. Unlike all other weather measurements, calculating cloud cover lacks precision. It is done by estimating how many eighths (**oktas**) of the sky are obscured by cloud. This information is recorded by shading-in segments of a small circle (diagram **B** on page 114).

When you have collected all your weather observations, your data should be recorded on a single weather log sheet. If you have access to a computer, you could set up a spreadsheet on which to record your data.

> **Fantastic fact**
>
> The tallest thunder clouds on Earth form in the Tropics, where their tops have been recorded as high as 22 900 metres.

A *Different cloud types and their characteristics*

Section 2.4: Weather

B Cloud cover symbols

- 0 oktas (no cloud)
- 1 okta
- 2 oktas
- 3 oktas
- 4 oktas
- 5 oktas
- 6 oktas
- 7 oktas
- 8 oktas (no blue sky)
- Sky obscured

C Some cloud types

Now Investigate

1. Investigate what types of cloud are most common where you live. For example, do they vary from season to season?

2. Explain how clouds form and why some of them produce rain.

3. Identify the three types of cloud shown in photos **C** and write a description of each type.

4. a) Copy and complete this table by writing the names of these nine cloud types into the correct cells to show the height range of each.

    altocumulus   altostratus   cirrocumulus   cirrostratus
    cirrus   cumulus   nimbostratus   stratocumulus   stratus

	Height above the ground	Cloud types in this height range
i	Less than 2000 metres	
ii	2000–6000 metres	
iii	More than 6000 metres	

    b) Which of these cloud types can extend through all three levels of the atmosphere?

Further research

Carry out an online investigation into the activities of the Cloud Appreciation Society.

Topic link

What you have learned about weather and climate will help you when you study Topic 2.5 pages 115–135.

114   The natural environment

Section 2 . Topic 5

Climate and natural vegetation

Learning objectives:
- describe and explain the characteristics of two climates: equatorial and hot desert
- describe and explain the characteristics of tropical rainforest and hot desert ecosystems
- describe the causes and effects of deforestation of tropical rainforest

How does climate affect natural vegetation?

Take a moment to think about the climate where you live.

- What are the mean (average) temperatures during the year?
- Does the temperature vary, or is it relatively constant?
- Is it mild, tropical or cold for most of the year?
- Does rain fall throughout the year, or is it seasonal?
- Is the rainfall reliable?

Wherever you are, these aspects of the climate affect the natural vegetation growing locally. This is because plants need heat, light and water – as well as nutrients from the soil – in order to grow well. Where the climate provides all of these, the vegetation is rich and dense. Where one or more key factors are limited or absent, plants have to **adapt** in order to survive.

The climate in equatorial regions

Map **A** shows an almost continuous climate zone along the Equator, extending about 5 degrees north and south of it. It is interrupted only by two areas of high land. Graph **B** illustrates this climate type, which characteristically has:

- high annual temperatures, averaging 27 °–28 °C
- a very low **annual temperature range** (the difference between the highest and the lowest average monthly temperature) – usually less than 3 °C
- frequent, heavy rainfall – often more than 2000 mm per year
- rain – usually **convectional rainfall** all year (there is no dry season), with over 60 mm falling every month
- a **diurnal temperature range** that is greater than the annual temperature range
- no obvious seasons
- high humidity levels
- light winds.

> **Topic link**
>
> Look back at Topic 2.4 pages 110–111 for more information on humidity.

A Parts of the world with an equatorial climate

B Climate graph for Manaus, in the Amazon rainforest

There are a number of reasons for the climate along the Equator being like this:

- **Latitude** Along the Equator, the Sun is high in the sky all year round. This means that this region receives high-intensity insolation, so temperatures are high throughout the year.

- **Altitude** Generally, air temperature decreases with increased altitude. The main areas of equatorial climate are also lowland areas. In such regions, the air at ground level is under greater pressure (because of the increased weight of air above it) than the air in mountain regions. It is therefore denser and can become much warmer than the less dense air at higher altitudes.

- **Atmospheric pressure** Intense heating of the Earth's surface at the Equator means that air which is in contact with the ground is heated, becomes lighter and rises. This reduces the air pressure at the surface, giving rise to extensive areas of low pressure along the Equator. This low pressure is associated with heavy convectional rainfall (diagram **C**).

- **Diurnal temperature range** This is the difference between the maximum and minimum temperatures within a 24-hour period. During daylight, temperatures rise quickly as a result of intense heating from the Sun. However, after dark the heat absorbed by the Earth's surface during the day is quickly lost, causing temperatures to fall rapidly. At the Equator, after afternoon rain, there is less cloud cover. After dark,

C The formation of convectional rainfall

> **Fantastic fact**
>
> On average, temperatures fall by as much as 10 °C for every extra kilometre above sea level, which is why mountaineers wear so many extra layers of clothing.

116 The natural environment

without heat input from the Sun, the remaining cloud cover breaks up. Because of reduced cloud cover, heat is lost into space through the process of radiation and temperatures fall, to around 23° or 24°C, from an afternoon maximum of 33° or 34°C.

> **Now Investigate**
>
> 1. List five or six ways in which vegetation near to where you live has adapted to the local climate.
>
> 2. Use map **A** to describe the distribution of equatorial climates. (Hint: Look at Section 4.2 pages 245–250 to help you do this.)
>
> 3. Give reasons why temperatures in equatorial regions vary so little throughout the year.
>
> 4. Using the text and diagram **C**, explain why rainfall is so high in equatorial regions.
>
> 5. What do you understand by the terms:
>   a) annual temperature range
>   b) diurnal temperature range?

Tropical rainforest vegetation

The plants and animals that live in an area together are called an ecosystem. However, they do not exist in isolation; they interact with each other and their non-living environment – the climate, geology and soils that make up their habitats. Diagram **A** shows that some interactions are two-way (the two components interact with each other and affect each other) whilst others are one-way (one component affects the other, but is not affected by it).

The natural vegetation that has adapted to equatorial climates is known as tropical rainforest. Plants need warmth, light and moisture in order to thrive, together with nutrients from the soil. Growing conditions within the equatorial lowlands are ideal, with rapid growth possible throughout the year. Rainforests, which cover just 6 per cent of the world's land surface, are known for their biodiversity – the wide range of vegetation and wildlife that they support. Tropical rainforests are home to over 10 million different species of plants, animals and insects – in other words, over 50 per cent of all species on Earth live on just 6 per cent of its land surface.

A Ecosystem components and their interactions

Section 2.5: Climate and natural vegetation

B *Nutrient recycling in the tropical rainforest*

Although the tropical rainforests are majestic, they are in fact very ==fragile ecosystems==, dependent for their survival on the rapid and continuous recycling of nutrients. This is because of the ==poor fertility of the soils which support them.== Hot, wet conditions have ==weathered the surface rocks intensively== and so forest soils tend to be deep. However, their depth does not make them fertile. Heavy rainfall ==leaches== nutrients from the soil. Without a constant ==input of leaf litter== from the forest above, nutrients are easily and ==quickly removed.== This produces infertile soils which are quickly eroded – see diagrams **B** and **D**.

C *View of the tropical rainforest in the Loboc River, Bohol, Philippines*

D *A typical rainforest soil*

118   The natural environment

2.5

Now Investigate

1 Plants need warmth, heat and light to grow. Use the information on pages 116–118 to help you explain how these needs are met in equatorial lowland areas.

2 a) How are nutrients recycled in tropical rainforests?
b) Why is this nutrient recycling so important?
c) Create a diagram similar to diagram **B**, to show the effects of **deforestation** on soil fertility.

> **Fantastic fact**
>
> The Brazil nut tree of South America has a seedcase so hard that only one animal, the agouti, can open it, allowing the tree's seeds to germinate.

A tropical rainforest environment

Regions of equatorial rainforest around the world are decreasing rapidly, for a number of reasons. One place that was originally covered almost entirely by rainforest is the island of Borneo, in Southeast Asia.

CASE STUDY: Borneo's tropical rainforest

Borneo is the world's third largest island, and its position on the Equator means that most of its natural vegetation is tropical rainforest (map **A**). It still has a low population density – even though its valuable natural resources include oil, coal, gold, timber and very fertile soil. It is now the world's biggest producer of palm oil, which is used to manufacture biodiesel fuel, cooking oils, cosmetics and soap.

Borneo's climate (graph **B**) is ideal for tropical rainforest because:

- it has high temperatures throughout the year, with a maximum annual temperature range of only 3 °C
- there is heavy rainfall every month – up to 400 mm in places
- its high temperatures and heavy rainfall make the air very humid.

Borneo's monthly rainfall totals vary throughout the year due to the changing direction of the wind belts (map **A**). Most rain falls during the northeast monsoon (November–January), when moist air blows in from the Pacific Ocean. March, April and May are much drier, because the south-easterly winds have blown over Australia's deserts.

Borneo's rainforests are very special – and not just because its 45 metre trees are the tallest in the world. What is really special is

> **Topic link**
>
> See Topic 3.7 pages 225–226 for more information on deforestation in Borneo.

> **Fantastic fact**
>
> Borneo's rainforest is 130 million years old, making it the oldest rainforest on Earth. It beats Amazonia by 70 million years!

Section 2.5: Climate and natural vegetation

what lives in the forest. Its fauna (animal life), some of which is found only on this island, ranges from the cute to the extraordinary! It includes the world's largest range of 'gliding animals', which can move between trees at great height, for example flying lizards, flying frogs and even flying snakes. Borneo is also home to the world's largest moth, flower and carnivorous plant. By far the most popular animal with tourists is the orangutan. Its population on Borneo has halved in the last 50 years – because their natural forest habitat is now much smaller, because farmers kill these animals to protect their crops, and because they fetch a high price on the international pet market (photo **C**).

Unfortunately, Borneo's forests have been in decline since large-scale logging first began in the 1970s (table **D**), and the future of the specialised dipterocarp (lowland) forests now seems bleak. The reasons for the reduction of the rainforest include:

- demand from Malaysia's plywood and paper pulp industries
- increasing global demand for valuable hardwoods for use as building materials
- the race to discover and exploit new reserves of oil and coal
- the increasing rate of oil palm production
- devastating forest fires which are started by local farmers to clear the forest – extra farmland is needed to feed the growing population.

National Parks now protect pockets of the remaining forest, and the three-nation Heart of Borneo Conservation Plan, organised jointly between Malaysia, Brunei and Indonesia, aims to protect 250 000 km² of prime forest habitat (map **A**).

A The island of Borneo

- Mountain rainforest
- Lowland dipterocarp rainforest
- Coastal mangrove swamp
- Mainly farmland
- Three-nation Heart of Borneo Conservation Plan area
- Wet northeast monsoon winds (Nov–Jan)

B Climate graph for Borneo

C A baby orangutan

120 The natural environment

2.5

Now Investigate

1. a) Use graph **B** and the information on these pages to help you describe the monthly temperature and rainfall patterns of Borneo's climate.
   b) With the help of an atlas, discover why any winds from the south-east are likely to produce drier weather for Borneo.
   c) Suggest the possible effects of temperature, rainfall and winds on Borneo.

2. Suggest some ways in which the world could reduce its demand for Borneo's exports.

3. a) Using the data in table **D**, plot a line graph. Make sure that you use numbers at equal intervals on the *x* axis.
   b) Describe how the rate of deforestation in Borneo has changed since 1985.
   c) How does the predicted rate of future deforestation compare with that of the past?

> **Topic link**
>
> See Topic 3.5 pages 193–194 and Topic 3.7 pages 220–226 for more on environmental issues in different parts of the world.

Year	% of forest cover in Borneo
1985	73.7
2000	57.5
2005	50.4
2010	44.4
2020	24.0 (estimate)

D

> **Further research**
>
> Ecotourism is tourism that stimulates the local economy but doesn't harm the natural environment or undermine the traditional culture of the local people. Use online research to help you design a poster or brochure which advises visitors on how to respect the natural environment and the local people. Try to add some information about the advantages of conserving tropical rainforests.

> **Skills link**
>
> Refer to Section 4.3 pages 251–252 to learn how to draw a line graph.

How do living things survive in hot deserts?

Perhaps you live in or near to a hot desert area, and are used to coping with the climatic conditions. For most of us, though, desert survival can be very hazardous. These deserts are hot – often above 30 °C. They are also arid (extremely dry), so every drop of water is precious. How do you minimise your usage, making every drop count, without dehydrating (losing water)? Meeting such challenges is difficult even with technology to help us. Plants and animals, however, have been adapting successfully to such conditions for thousands of years. How could you adapt your normal clothing and activities to cope with extreme temperatures?

> **Fantastic fact**
>
> The longest hot desert drought lasted 400 years, from 1571 to 1971, in the Atacama Desert in Chile.

Section 2.5: Climate and natural vegetation

A Global distribution of hot deserts

The climate in hot desert areas

Not all deserts are hot. They can also be temperate or cold. It is the lack of rainfall that determines if a region is classified as a desert. Any region with a mean annual rainfall of less than 250 mm is a 'desert'. Hot desert climates are mainly found between 5° and 20° north and south of the Equator (map **A**). Except in North Africa and Arabia, where the desert extends from the Atlantic Ocean to the Arabian Sea, all are in the western regions of continents. This is because they receive dry prevailing winds – that is, winds that have blown over land for most of the year. Hot deserts often experience higher daytime temperatures than equatorial regions, at least during the season when the Sun is directly overhead.

Although temperatures are high all year, there is a seasonal pattern with one cooler, wetter season and a much hotter, arid one. These seasons are due to various factors:

- High atmospheric pressure: where there is high pressure, air sinks and warms, so any moisture is evaporated. The rising and cooling process needed to form clouds is prevented by the column of sinking air.
- There is an absence of cloud cover, so:
  - no rain can fall
  - the Sun's heating is intense throughout daylight hours
  - night-time temperatures fall rapidly (diagram **C**).
- Diurnal temperature ranges in hot deserts are greater than those in equatorial regions – the arid air accelerates temperature loss through radiation and so night-time temperatures below freezing are common.

B The Atacama Desert, Chile

122 The natural environment

2.5

- In desert areas such as the Sahara, the prevailing winds blow outward from the continental interior, they cannot pick up water vapour and so clouds do not form.
- In other desert regions such as the Namib and Kalahari, although the prevailing wind blows from the ocean, it has to cross a mountain barrier. This creates a rainshadow effect (diagram **D**).
- In South America and southern Africa, cold offshore ocean currents chill the prevailing winds and so these are unable to evaporate much water vapour. Any moisture they hold falls as showers (or precipitates out as fog) along the coastal zone before reaching inland desert regions.

However, most hot deserts do receive some rain, often during the 'cooler' season, as a result of the north–south movement of pressure systems and their associated wind belts (see diagram **B** on page 111). Changes in atmospheric pressure draw moist winds into desert areas. These winds are heated by contact with the hot desert surface and, as they rise and cool, clouds form, bringing rain.

C Why daytime temperatures are high and night-time temperatures are low

D The rainshadow effect of mountain ranges

Now Investigate

1. Think about how you would need to adapt your clothes and activities to cope with a hot desert climate. You could make notes under headings, or draw labelled diagrams.

2. With the help of map **A**, describe the global distribution of hot desert climates.

3. Suggest reasons why hot desert temperatures remain high all year.

4. Explain why rainfall totals are usually very low in hot desert regions.

5. a) Use the illustrations on these pages, and an atlas, to name one desert that is influenced by each of the following:
    i) a rainshadow effect in southern Africa
    ii) cold ocean currents
    iii) a subtropical high pressure area.
   b) For each of these, draw an annotated diagram to explain how it has contributed to the development of your chosen desert.

Section 2.5: Climate and natural vegetation

Hot desert vegetation

In some ways, hot desert environments are good for plant growth because they provide:

- high temperatures all year
- long hours of daylight
- unbroken sunshine.

However, not only is the rainfall light, it is often unreliable and unpredictable. Also:

- When rain does fall, little infiltration is possible as soils are baked hard, so surface runoff is high. This means that very little of the water that falls is available to plants.
- Hot, dry air means that evapotranspiration rates are high, increasing the amount of water that plants need to survive.
- Desert soils are thin and so cannot support dense vegetation cover (diagram **A**). The lack of moisture means that soil development is restricted. As vegetation is so sparse, there is little organic material to form humus in the topsoil.
- Soil erosion is a problem because of strong winds.
- Large diurnal temperature ranges, with overnight temperatures as low as –4°C, are difficult for plants to adapt to.

Together, these conditions make hot deserts hazardous to both plant and animal life. Indeed, there is very little life in some deserts, especially in those with bare rock surfaces (for example the Arizona Desert), in stony deserts (the Kalahari) and in dune deserts (the mid-Sahara). In other places, a desert may be able to support plant growth, depending on:

- the total annual rainfall
- the frequency of rainfall
- the depth of the water table (photo **B**)
- the salinity of the soil.

Photos **D** and **E** show two plants that have adapted to survive in harsh desert conditions. The following are particular ways in which plants adapt to local conditions:

- **Dormancy**: during drought periods, perennial plants like grasses, which can survive for more than one year, die back. Others, called annuals – which means they only last for a

A *Cross-section of a desert soil*

B *Oases are found in deserts where the water table is at or near the surface*

124 The natural environment

C *Sand dunes in the Namib Desert*

year – produce drought-resistant seeds which lie dormant until the next rain falls. These plants can complete their entire life cycle within just a few weeks (photo **D**)!

- **Water retention:** some plants can store water in their stems, trunks or leaves during wet weather.
- **Leaf adaptation:** most desert plants have adapted to reduce water loss, store water and increase protection from the Sun.
- **Increasing water collection:** plants have developed various methods of acquiring the moisture they need.
- **Tolerance of saline (salty) soils:** salt is toxic to most plants but some have developed salt-tolerance. Desert soils are salty because heat and aridity cause a high level of evaporation. This draws salts upwards towards the soil surface (diagram **A**).

D *The Rose of Jericho survives long droughts by lying dormant*

Now Investigate

1. Draw a spider diagram to show the main reasons why plant growth is very restricted in hot deserts.
2. How do plants increase their ability to collect and store water?
3. How do plants reduce water loss?
4. Explain how each of the following are linked:
   a) drought *and* the rate of plant growth
   b) oases *and* water tables
   c) soil salinity *and* water evaporation.

E *The creosote bush protects its own water collection area of soil with chemicals that slow the growth of nearby plants*

Fantastic fact

The tumbleweed plant gets its name because it rolls down hillsides to disperse its seeds!

Section 2.5: Climate and natural vegetation

Life in the hot desert

Each desert is different, supporting different plants and animals, depending on where it is in the world. People live in these deserts, too – and they all have different ways of making a living there. Here we look in more detail at just one desert located on the southwest coast of the African continent.

CASE STUDY

The Namib Desert

The Namib Desert occupies the coastal edge of Namibia (map **A** and photo **B**).

Within this desert are several distinctive landscapes. The south is dominated by the tallest dunes in the world, while further north sand gives way to a rocky desert of gravel plains and bare, rugged hills. Here there is no surface water, except after rain, when for a short time streams flow into inland basins, but never reaching the sea.

Fantastic fact

Dune 7, in the Namib Desert, is the highest dune on Earth (383 metres from base to summit).

Namib Desert
Area: 81 000 km²
Length (north to south): 1600 km
Width (west to east): 50–160 km

Climate in Namibia

	Walvis Bay	Windhoek
Total annual rainfall (mm)	23	370
Average rainfall in wettest month (mm)	8	81
No. of days/year rainfall is more than 0.1mm	16	41
Average temperature (°C)	16	19.3
Average relative humidity (%)	29	32.6

A *Namib Desert location and facts*

B *Satellite image of the Namib Desert*

126 The natural environment

The climate is arid with sparse, unpredictable rainfall. Temperatures vary from west to east – cooler along the coast, but hotter inland. The most important climate feature is the coastal fog, which is the only source of reliable moisture in the region! Rainfall is very low because of the combined effect of the rainshadow effect of the Drakensberg Mountains (see diagram **D** on page 123) and the cold, offshore Benguela Current. The coastal fogs and variations in temperature are the result of the interaction between two prevailing winds. Cold air from the Atlantic Ocean reduces the effects of latitude at the coast but, inland, sinking air from the Drakensberg Mountains raises summer temperatures to highs of 50°C.

C Plant adaptations in the Namib Desert: (from left to right) the pencil bush, quiver tree and Welwitschia plant

How plants and animals have adapted to desert conditions

As in all deserts, both plants and animals have adapted to the climate. For example, Gha grass is valuable because it helps to stabilise the southern dunes. Photos **C** show a variety of other plants that are adapted to the Namib's harsh environment.

Human activity in the desert

Human activity in the desert is restricted by the arid conditions (table **D**). However, the area produces many of the world's finest diamonds, together with uranium, tin, tungsten, zinc and salt. Mining is crucial to Namibia's economy, but it is a major threat to local ecosystems as it destroys habitats and requires the development of complex infrastructure. Decades of hunting and poaching have devastated big game populations in the country, but Namibia has become the first country in the world to incorporate environmental protection in its national constitution. Today, almost all of the Namib Desert is protected, except for areas where mining is in progress.

> **Topic link**
>
> What you have learned in this topic will help you when you study Topic 3.7 pages 213–234.

> **Further research**
>
> Investigate the climate, vegetation and human economic activities in one of the following hot desert regions: Great Sandy Desert (Australia), Sonoran Desert (USA/Mexico), Thar Desert.

Section 2.5: Climate and natural vegetation

Economic activity	What is involved	Effects on the ecosystem
Diamond mining	Alluvial diamonds are found in gravel beds (alluvial means they have been transported there by water). Enormous quantities of sand have to be removed to expose the diamonds. The excavated sand is dumped elsewhere.	Recovering diamonds destroys fragile habitats by removing vegetation and soil. Sand-dumping buries other habitats.
Nomadic herding	Pastoral farmers graze herds of donkeys and goats in the eastern regions where there is more rainfall and therefore more vegetation.	Animals overgraze the area, exposing it to wind and water erosion. Fragile soils are removed and the barren desert spreads further eastwards.
'Activity' tourism	Off-road driving, poaching, sand-boarding, go-carting.	'Big game' are eradicated. Desert surfaces and vegetation are destroyed.

D *How human activities affect the Namib Desert*

Now Investigate

1. With the help of information in this topic, explain the development of the desert climate in southwest Africa.

2. Select a plant that is adapted to life in the Namib Desert. Describe and give reasons for the plant's adaptations. You could present your answer as an annotated sketch.

3. Suggest how hot deserts be used for economic benefit without causing environmental damage.

When does a natural hazard become a disaster?

I've lost everything and everyone. It was 17 March – just an ordinary day. Father had gone to work as usual. Mother was nursing my baby brother. OK – it had rained hard since December. But nothing told us this day was different. I was outside talking with friends and could only watch helplessly as our family home was destroyed in a flood. I've never seen water so high. It could have swallowed me – but I caught hold of a metal post and hung on tight. I survived. My family – all of them – haven't been seen since. I cry every day.

A *Fermin, aged 13. Survivor of flooding in Leyte Province in the Philippines in March 2011. Human cost: 75 dead. Economic cost: US$43 million*

128 The natural environment

2.5

We live on an active planet. Heat trapped inside the Earth causes earthquakes and volcanoes. Heat in the atmosphere causes extreme weather events. Secondary effects of such events include **tsunamis**, flooding, storms, and **lahars**. Scientists believe, though, that the last 10 000 years have been the quietest ever known on the planet! Natural hazards are a fact of life. What turns them into disasters is their scale and the impact they have on people's lives.

Natural hazard events affect people through loss of life, damage to homes and belongings, environmental damage and people's ability to earn a living. Generally, the larger the scale of the event, the greater we see the disaster to be. But the effect of a natural hazard event is not only the result of its strength and scale. The strongest of earthquakes occurring in an uninhabited area will not have an effect on people's lives. A significantly weaker earthquake affecting a densely populated region or city, particularly in one of the world's poorest countries, may be a serious disaster.

Geographically, natural hazards can be classified into three groups:

- geological events, e.g. earthquakes, lahars, volcanic eruptions
- hydrological events, e.g. floods, tsunamis
- climatic and weather events, e.g. droughts (which can lead to wildfires), **tropical revolving storms**, **tornadoes**.

Note that earthquakes are rarely the primary cause of a disaster. It is their secondary effects – such as the collapse of buildings, fires and tsunami – that can be catastrophic. Similarly, although volcanic eruptions can be disastrous, **pyroclastic flows** and lahars often cause far greater devastation.

Other points to note about particular events include:

- Unlike most other natural hazards, **avalanches** are neither rare nor random events. They are common in mountainous areas where deep snow accumulates.
- Tsunamis are always the secondary effect of an earthquake. Recent tsunamis affecting the Pacific Basin have been disastrous, for example the Japanese tsunami of March 2011.
- Climatic events appear to be intensified by human activity. Scientists are now concerned that rising levels of heat in the atmosphere increase its energy – which in turn causes more intense weather-related features, for example tropical revolving storms (see pages 131–132).
- **Wildfires** are also increasingly common – again perhaps because of **climate change**.

B *The damage caused by some recent disasters*

Section 2.5: Climate and natural vegetation 129

The impact of natural hazards on a population appears to be directly linked to its level of wealth. In more economically developed countries, more money and expertise is available for 'the three Ps' – prediction, protection and preparation (diagram **C**). For example, wealthier countries such as the USA can afford to construct more effective flood defences than a less economically developed country like Bangladesh, which means that their inhabitants are much better protected. For the same reason, there have been many more earthquake victims in Turkey than in the USA.

> **Topic link**
>
> See Topic 2.1 pages 73–81 for more on earthquakes and volcanic events.

Prediction involves working out where and when a hazard might occur. **Where** is often easy – most hazards happen in identifiable zones. **When** is less easy. Storms can be forecast using satellite data. In China, scientists believe that animals act oddly before earthquakes happen. But for most hazardous events, predicting when they will happen is still a major problem.

Protection is mainly about building to high standards, using designs that can withstand shock waves, high winds or rising water levels. Providing shelters and flood defences are also protective measures. But all are very costly. Hurricane Katrina (pages 132–133) and the 2011 Japanese tsunami (pages 78–79) showed that even the richest nations cannot protect against every event.

HAZARD PREDICTION, PROTECTION AND PREPARATION

Preparation is mostly about educating local people and practising for hazard events. Then people know what to do and where to go to reduce the effects of a hazard. In the case of drought, for example, preparation is about educating people to use local aquifers, to dig wells, to reduce water loss through leakage, and to re-use water for different purposes.

C *Predicting, protecting and preparing for natural disasters*

Now Investigate

1. Explain the difference between:
   a) a natural hazard and a natural disaster event
   b) the primary (immediate) and secondary (longer-term) effects of disaster events.

2. Use annotated images to create a mind map showing the three types of natural disaster.

3. Prepare an information leaflet for residents of a vulnerable city, telling them how best to prepare for and protect against a disaster event. Your pamphlet should cover two sides of an A4 sheet, and include illustrations such as photographs. It should provide advice for families as well as for the community as a whole.

> **Topic link**
>
> See Topic 3.7 pages 213–234 to read more about environmental risks of economic development.

2.5

Tropical storms

A hurricane is a tropical storm – an area of very low atmospheric pressure that can develop on either side of the Equator, between 5° and 20° north and south. Such storms are known locally by different names (map **A**) but all are characterised by very strong winds and torrential rain. Typically, they form:

- over extensive tropical oceans, where water temperature exceeds 27 °C
- where the sea is warmed to a great depth at the time of year when sea temperatures are highest
- as a result of strong upward movements of very moist air – as the air rises, it cools and condenses, releasing huge amounts of heat which powers the storm (diagram **B** on page 132).

Hurricanes frequently cause extensive destruction along their path. The main reasons for this are:

- **Strong winds** (with gusts of more 200 km/hr) cause structural damage. In more economically developed countries, power cables are torn down, and roofing, signs and wooden buildings are often damaged – although advance warnings mean that buildings can be boarded-up for safety. In poorer regions, fragile buildings are destroyed and vegetation and crops are damaged, causing economic hardship.

> **Topic link**
>
> See Topic 2.4 pages 111–112 for more on atmospheric pressure and its effects.

> **Fantastic fact**
>
> At first, hurricanes were always given girls' names but, in 1979, boys' names were added, so now they are both used.

A *Global distribution of tropical storms*

- Hurricanes 13/yr (June–Oct)
- Hurricanes 9/yr (Aug–Oct)
- Cyclones 6/yr (Oct–Nov)
- Cyclones 8/yr (Dec–Mar)
- Typhoons 26/yr (May–Dec)
- Typhoons 10/yr (Jan–Mar)

Legend: 10/yr Average number per year; Warm sea areas (over 27°C); Cooler sea areas

Section 2.5: Climate and natural vegetation

B Weather associated with tropical storms

Labels on diagram:
- Path of hurricane
- Eye of storm
- As hurricane passes, wind speeds and rainfall decrease, sunny intervals
- After eye of storm has passed, hurricane-force winds and more torrential rain
- In eye of storm, winds are light, sky clear, little rain
- Air pressure falls, wind speeds increase to over 100 km/hr, torrential rain (more than 200 mm/day)
- As hurricane approaches, clouds form, wind speed increases, rain showers occur with sunny intervals between

- **Heavy rainfall:** often over 200 mm in a single day – leads to river flooding and **landslides**.
- **Storm surges:** intense low pressure raises sea levels. Strong winds drive high seas inland with waves up to 5 metres high. This causes flooding in low-lying coastal areas, and settlements can be washed away. Crops are destroyed and huge areas flooded by salt water – which leaves the land unsuitable for plant growth for years to come.

C Satellite image of Hurricane Katrina

Hurricane Katrina

In August, 2005 a **tropical depression** formed over the Bahamas. It tracked westward towards Florida, gaining strength, and was then classified as a hurricane (named Katrina) as it neared the coast. As it moved inland, it caused structural damage, death and flooding.

D Track of Hurricane Katrina

Topic link

See Topic 3.2 page 164 to get information about food shortages to help you with the two investigations.

132 The natural environment

2.5

but lost energy – as all hurricanes do after they reach land. When it reached the Gulf of Mexico, the storm passed over unusually warm water which re-energised it so much that it developed into a Level 5 hurricane (photo **C** and map **D**). As it followed the Gulf coastline, Katrina became the most costly disaster ever to hit the USA and one of the strongest storms of recent times.

Now Investigate

1. Study map **A**.
    a) Describe the direction in which all tropical storms move.
    b) Describe the distribution of tropical storms as shown on the map.

2. Draw a series of simple illustrations, with labels, to show the conditions necessary for the development of a tropical cyclone.

3. Research five important effects of Hurricane Katrina when it hit New Orleans.

4. Katrina was a natural disaster in a more economically developed country. Investigate a storm of similar strength in a less economically developed country (such as Cyclone Nargis). Compare and contrast its effects with those of Hurricane Katrina.

Flooding in Bangladesh

Bangladesh is one of the world's most densely populated countries, with 1128 people/km². It is also one of the most likely to be flooded, for a variety of reasons:

- **Flash floods** (particularly in the east and north of the country), resulting from heavy rain or snowmelt in the Himalayan mountains to the north, cause river levels to rise sharply and the speed of river flow to increase. Crops and settlements on the flood plains are often destroyed.

- Monsoon rains cause rivers to rise and flood every year. Large volumes of water exceed the local drainage capacity. The areas most affected are the distributaries in the delta region, especially when all three major rivers flood at the same time.

- Storm surges (linked to cyclones) affect the low-lying coastal delta area.

A Bangladesh

Section 2.5: Climate and natural vegetation

- Flooding in Bangladesh has a big impact, mainly because of the way local people live and because Bangladesh is one of the poorest nations on Earth.

Cyclone Aila

On 25 May 2009, Bangladesh and northeastern India were hit by Cyclone Aila. Damage was extensive and affected between 2.5 and 3 million people. Although more than half a million people from Bangladesh's low-lying coastal areas were evacuated, at least 179 people lost their lives, 800 were injured and more than 400 000 were cut off by flood waters. A storm surge devastated western Bangladesh, submerging or destroying many rural villages. The pressure of flood water broke through river embankments, causing extensive inland flooding, and more than half a million people were left homeless. Drinking water was contaminated with sea water and sewage, as toilets were washed away and many dead animals were washed into watercourses. Within four days, 7000 people were suffering from various water-borne diseases, including cholera. Over 100 relief camps were created to shelter refugees. These were funded by overseas aid organisations and by the Bangladeshi government. The final estimate put the cost of the disaster at over US$40.7 million.

> **Fantastic fact**
>
> Eighty per cent of Bangladesh lies on a huge flood plain and delta, which are only 1 metre above sea level.

> **Topic link**
>
> - See Topic 3.2 page 164 for more about food shortages due to drought conditions.
> - See Topic 3.7 pages 213–219 for more information about how people use opportunities presented by the natural environment.

1 Heavy monsoon rains cause widespread soil erosion and raise river levels.
2 Melting snow on mountains in summer increases soil erosion and raises river levels.
3 Removal of trees on lower slopes of Himalayas adds to soil erosion and rate of surface runoff.
4 Silt from eroded soil builds up in rivers which can then hold less water and so they flood more easily.
5 Most of Bangladesh is less than 1 metre above sea level so it is easily flooded by rivers and the sea.
6 Cyclones, which are common in this region, create storm surges along the coast.
7 Ganges delta has many islands made of soft silt which is easily eroded.
8 Dhaka, the capital city (population 7 million) is only 4 metres above sea level, so is vulnerable to river flooding.

B   *The main causes of flooding in Bangladesh*

C   *The effects of Cyclone Aila*

134   The natural environment

However, living in such a flood-prone area does actually have some benefits. The annual river floods cover the land with fertile silt, or alluvium. This means that poorer farmers do not need to buy costly fertilisers to grow their crops. It also means that some areas do not need to be **irrigated**, despite the high temperatures in this region. People choose to live here because they believe that the benefits can outweigh some of the disadvantages.

Now Investigate

1. Draw a sketch map of Bangladesh to show the areas that are flooded regularly, and annotate your map to show the main causes of the flooding. Some of your annotations should highlight differences in the effects of flooding on the richer and poorer people of Bangladesh.

2. Summarise the effects of Cyclone Aila in a series of bullet points or a spider diagram.

3. Explain the link between:
   a) the removal of trees in the Himalayas and increased river levels in Bangladesh
   b) cyclones and coastal flooding
   c) snowmelt and flash flooding.

4. Suggest how Bangladesh might predict, prepare and protect against natural disasters.

Further research

Investigate a recent case of prolonged drought which has had a major impact on the quality of life of people living in that area. (You may find it helpful to refer to the drought in the Horn of Africa described in Topic 3.2 on page 164.) It will help you to structure your information under headings, for example:

- Location – possibly including a regional map
- Timing and duration – when did it happen, and how long did it last?
- Main causes of the drought – were they all 'natural'?
- Impact of the drought – what were its immediate and long-term effects on both rich and poor?

Section 3 . Topic 1

Development

Learning objectives:
- use a variety of indicators to assess the level of development of a country
- identify and explain inequalities between and within countries
- classify production into different sectors and give illustrations of each
- describe and explain how the proportions employed in each sector vary according to the level of development
- describe and explain the process of globalisation, and consider its impacts

Quality of life

What is 'a good life'?

There is a significant link between over-population, under-population, and the quality of life or standard of living in a country. There are different views on what makes for 'a good life' (photo **A**, diagram **B**). People in over-populated countries generally have a lower standard of living, and some are so poor that they actually live below the **poverty line**. But people living in under-populated countries experience problems, too:

- Valuable natural resources are not fully used. Exports of these resources are limited to what can be extracted, so the opportunity to earn more from international trade is lost.

- There are few people to buy locally made goods. Making small quantities of goods is expensive, and companies are often reluctant to build factories where there are likely to be few customers. More foreign-made goods have to be imported, and possibly transported over large distances.

- There are too few people to fill key jobs in engineering, teaching and other important areas of employment.

- It is necessary to attract extra workers from other countries who may face language difficulties or have experienced a very different educational system in their own countries.

The **optimum population** is the number of people needed to make the best possible use of a country's resources.

The answers to the questions in diagram **B** can provide only a rough guide to the kind of life people are living. More accurate measures of quality of life and standard of living are needed. Two of these are the **Human Development Index (HDI)** and the **Where-to-be-born Index**.

A *A shanty town in Manaus, Brazil*

B *What is 'a good life'?*

Economic development

3.1

Human Development Index

The Human Development Index (HDI) was devised by the United Nations. It is based on three crucial sets of population data:

- adult literacy
- life expectancy
- GDP per capita.

GDP means **gross domestic product** and *per capita* means 'per person'. The GDP per capita is obtained by dividing the total monetary value of all goods and services produced in a country in a year by that country's total population.

Where-to-be-born Index

Another useful indicator is the Where-to-be-born Index. This also takes GDP per capita and life expectancy into account, but includes a number of other factors which, together, indicate how 'happy and secure' people feel within their family, workplace, local community and country. On a scale of 1 to 10, the most 'contented' country in the world is Switzerland, but its score is only 8.22 – which proves that there is no 'perfect' place in which to live (table **C**)!

Country	Where-to-be-born Index
The top ten	
Switzerland	8.22
Australia	8.12
Norway	8.09
Sweden	8.02
Denmark	8.01
Singapore	8.00
New Zealand	7.95
Netherlands	7.94
Canada	7.81
Hong Kong	7.80

C *Where-to-be-born Index: the top ten*

Fantastic fact

The USA is the richest country in the world, but 12% of its 312 million people still live in poverty.

Now Investigate

1. a) Do you believe *you* have a good quality of life?
   b) Do you think the people who live in the area shown in photo **A** consider *they* have 'a good life'?

2. Study photos **A** and **D**.
   a) Explain why the people who live in the area shown in photo **A** may be living below the poverty line.
   b) Why do you think the people who live in the area in photo **D** probably have a better quality of life?

3. a) In your opinion, which are the six most important questions in diagram **B**?
   b) Give reasons for each of your six choices.

4. Look at the three main sets of data used to create the Human Development Index, listed above, and at the questions in diagram **B** on page 136.
   a) Which of the questions in diagram **B** do you think could be answered by the data used to create the HDI?
   b) Which of the questions, if any, are unlikely to be useful when calculating a country's HDI?

D *A residential area in an MEDC*

Section 3.1: Development   137

Development

How is development measured?

Development is linked to the wealth of a country. One measurement of a country's wealth is GNP per capita which is a measure of national income per person or how much money is earned per person on average. GNP per capita is used to compare countries and gives an indication of how rich countries are.

GNP per capita does not take into account quality of life which includes important aspects such as level of education, healthcare and access to clean water. These are also important **indicators of development**. The indicators change over time as a country develops economically. Changes in two indicators are shown in graph **A**.

The **Human Development Index** (HDI) describes both economic and social well-being within a country. Each year the United Nations publishes the Human Development Report which uses the HDI to rank the level of development in all countries.

A *Indicators of development in different countries*

HDI rank	Country	Group	HDI score (2015)
1	Norway	Very high human development	0.949
10	Canada		0.920
26	Italy		0.887
36	Poland		0.855
54	Uruguay	High human development	0.795
70	Georgia		0.769
77	Mexico		0.762
79	Brazil		0.754
92	Mongolia	Medium human development	0.735
99	Dominican Republic		0.722
113	Indonesia		0.689
125	Guatemala		0.640
144	Nepal	Low human development	0.558
146	Kenya		0.555
170	Malawi		0.476
175	Mali		0.442

B *UN HDI ranking*

138   Economic development

3.1

In the UN Human Development Report countries are divided into four groups. These groups along with some examples are shown in table **B**.

There are other measurements of development as well as the three used to calculate the HDI. These include infant mortality rate, number of people per doctor, average calorie intake per person per day, percentage of population without access to clean water and proportion of children who attend secondary school.

Countries develop over time and reach different stages of development. In the 1980s the Brandt report divided the world into the rich 'North' and the poor 'South'. The 'North' included the **More Economically Developed Countries** (MEDCs) and in the 'South' were the **Less Economically Developed Countries** (LEDCs). Since then other development categories have been identified. The poorest countries are known as **Least Developed Countries** (LDCs) and **Newly Industrialised Countries** (NICs) are wealthier than other LEDCs. BRIC refer to Brazil, India, Russia and China which are all at a similar level of development. Diagram **C** shows one way of dividing countries according to their level of development.

Least Developed Countries (LDCs) → Less Economically Developed Countries (LEDCs) → Newly Industrialised Countries (NICs) → More Economically Developed Countries (MEDCs)

time

C *Country development model*

Factors affecting development:
- **Natural resources** — Minerals, ores, gas, oil, timber and fertile soils are used to produce goods to sell
- **Workforce** — Skilled, healthy and well-educated workers can produce high-value goods to sell
- **Population** — A high proportion of dependents need money and resources to look after them
- **Trade** — LEDCs sell primary products which have lower value than goods made in MEDCs
- **History** — Many LEDCs were former colonies controlled by MEDCs who used them as a source of raw materials and a market for products but did not help them to develop
- **Geography** — Natural hazards such as drought, floods, and earthquakes will make development difficult. Trade is more difficult from a landlocked country

D *Factors affecting development*

Why are there inequalities between countries which make them more or less developed?

There are a number of factors which affect the level of development of a country. These are shown in diagram **D**.

Why are there inequalities within countries?

Development indicators refer to entire countries. They are average figures for the whole population. They do not show differences between rich and poor people in a country or regional differences within a country. Map **E** shows two examples of regional inequality in the UK. There may be large differences between rich and poor people in a country as shown in box **F** on page 140.

Average life expectancy in years:
- <79
- 79 – 80
- 80.1 – 81
- 81.1 – 82

Average income per week in GB pounds:
- <530
- 530 – 600
- 601 – 670
- >670

E *Regional inequality in UK*

Section 3.1: Development   139

Rich and Poor in Saudi Arabia

Although Saudi Arabia has one of the highest rates of GNP per capita in the world, not everyone who lives there is rich. Those with large disposable incomes can afford to buy expensive cars from the UK and USA, but poor people line up for hours to get water from the local pump. A rise in oil prices might benefit the rich oil sheiks but it also increases the price of fuel, food and houses.

Many families in Saudi Arabia are rich and many employ a driver and at least one maid. However, at the poorer end of society are people like Lulwah. She is 36 years old, a mother of five who sells snacks from a stall in a park in Riyadh. She came to Saudi Arabia from Sri Lanka with her husband who is a waiter. Lulwah says that she took out a loan from a charity to start her catering business. She also makes clothes to sell, but much of her income is used up in rent for the apartment which the family live in.

Fantastic fact

Average life expectancy in Monaco is 40 years longer than average life expectancy in Chad.

F Inequality in Saudi Arabia

What can be done to reduce the inequality between countries?

Differences between rich and poor countries have increased. In 2000 leaders of the UN member states agreed eight development goals aimed at freeing people from extreme poverty and deprivation by 2015. In 2015, these were replaced by the 2030 Agenda for Sustainable Development which identified 17 goals to transform the world. These goals are shown in diagram **G**.

G United Nations Sustainable Development Goals

Now Investigate

1. Compare the changes in life expectancy and average income per person in different countries shown in diagram **A**. Suggest why these changes have taken place.

2. Plot the 12 countries shown in table **B** on a map of the world. What do you notice about the distribution of the four groups?

3. Describe the variation in average life expectancy and income per week in different regions of the UK shown in the maps in **E**. Do the two maps show the same pattern of variation?

4. Read Lulwah's story in box **F**. What do you think are the main problems of her life in Saudi Arabia?

5. Work as a group to research more about the UN Sustainable Development Goals shown in diagram **G**. Suggest one way that progress towards each goal can be measured.

Economic development

Classifying industry

There are many ways in which people can earn a living and help their country's economy. This **economic activity** involves different types of industry – the ways in which products and services are made. The car industry, for instance, includes all the businesses and people involved in making cars, from the designers to the people putting the parts together in factories and those selling the finished models in large showrooms.

All economic activities can be classified into four different types of industry, known as **sectors**:

- the primary (or extractive) sector
- the secondary (or manufacturing) sector
- the tertiary (or service) sector
- the quaternary (or knowledge and information) sector.

Primary industry

Primary industries are those that work by taking something out of the earth. For this reason they are also known as **extractive** industries. Examples include fishing, farming, mining (photo **A**), quarrying and forestry.

Some primary industries produce goods that are sold to the public exactly as they are when taken out of the ground. Farmers, for instance, harvest their crops and sell them directly at markets. Other industries, such as logging, sell **raw materials** that are used to make different products. Trees are cut down and the wood is sent to companies that make furniture, paper or other timber goods.

Secondary industry

Secondary industries take raw materials and make new products from them. This is called **processing** or **manufacturing** and includes industries making everything from clothes and computers to cars and tinned food.

In many cases the raw materials are the products of a country's primary industries, for example oil is processed to make gasoline or petroleum. Raw materials can also be bought from other countries as **imports**. Some secondary industries use the products from other secondary industries to make the things they sell. For instance, in computer manufacture all the components such as circuit boards (photo **B**), cases and cables have already been made by other secondary industries before being put together in the factory. The finished goods can also be sold abroad as **exports**.

Secondary industries are good for a country because they 'add value' to the raw materials. There is much more money to be gained from selling clothes, for instance, than from selling the cotton that is used to make them.

A *Coal miners take their products directly from the ground*

B *Computers are put together in factories*

Fantastic fact

For (almost) guaranteed employment, become a biomedical engineer, working on the application of technology to healthcare – it's the fastest-growing job category in the USA.

Section 3.1: Development

Tertiary industry

Tertiary industries are those that provide a service so they are also known as **service industries**. This sector includes anything from hospitals with doctors and nurses to schools with teachers and other staff, or fire brigades and the police. Other examples are financial services such as banks, everything involved with tourism, and selling in shops (retailing). Call centres (photo **C**) have recently become a very large employer in this sector.

Quaternary industry

The **quaternary sector** is made up of companies that provide knowledge and information. This includes research and development for high-technology companies such as mobile phone manufacturers and those involved with the internet.

C Call centres are a growing industry

Now Investigate

1. Write definitions of:

    primary industry   secondary industry
    tertiary industry   quaternary industry

2. Look at the list of jobs shown in figure **D**.

    a) In a table, classify each job under the heading of the industry to which it belongs – primary, secondary, tertiary or quaternary.

    b) Which industrial sector has the most varied range of jobs?

3. Think about the area where you live. Give an example of an industry from each type of industrial sector that takes place:

    a) in your local area
    b) in another part of your country.

Teacher
Writer
Lawyer
Oil worker
Hairdresser
Computer maker
Fisherman
Tea picker
Diamond miner
Waiter
Sugar cane worker
Steel worker
Car factory worker
Fashion designer
Doctor
Banker
Mobile phone designer
Shopworker
Magician
Crane operator
Builder
IT expert
Farmer
Food canning factory worker
Carpenter
Baby-sitter
Mechanic
Secretary
Farmhand

D Examples of different job types

Economic development

3.1

Changing countries, changing work

Agricultural employment decreases as technology means fewer workers are needed on the land

↓

Ex-farmworkers get jobs in factories and secondary industry increases

↓

Factories become more efficient and need fewer workers → Remaining workers become more highly skilled and better paid

↓

Exports increase as countries overseas demand products made by the factories

↓

Factories employ bigger management, sales and research teams to help increase exports further

A *A process of industrial development*

LEDCs, especially the poorest ones, tend to have a very high proportion of people working in agriculture as subsistence farmers. As countries develop, this proportion changes. One way in which this process of industrial development takes place is shown in diagram **A**.

B *20th-century employment in the USA, 1900–2000*

Graph **B** shows the effects of such development on the employment structure of the USA during the 20th century. There are many countries where this change is happening now. Table **C** shows that countries such as Nigeria and Afghanistan still have a high number of agricultural workers but the percentages are falling in China, India, Bangladesh and Brazil. South Africa has low numbers while in the United Kingdom and the USA the service sector is by far the biggest employer.

	Agriculture	Manufacturing and mining	Services
Afghanistan	22.0	22.0	56.0
Bangladesh	15.1	28.6	56.3
Brazil	5.3	22.7	72.0
China	8.6	39.8	51.6
India	17.3	29.0	53.7
Nigeria	21.1	19.4	59.5
South Africa	2.2	29.2	68.6
United Kingdom	0.6	19.2	80.2
USA	1.1	19.4	79.5

Source: CIA World Factbook

C *Percentage of people employed in different industries in selected countries*

The informal sector

Unfortunately, many LEDCs are not developing quickly enough. This means that, despite the loss of farming jobs, there is not enough industrial employment for all those who need it. Unemployment rates can be very high. Underemployment (where people have some, but not enough work) is also a problem. This has led to the growth of the informal sector.

People with informal jobs do not get a regular wage but work when they need to, perhaps by selling goods on street corners or beaches, washing cars or shining shoes (photo **D**).

D *Working in the informal sector*

Section 3.1: Development   143

Presenting and interpreting data

The study of employment figures gives you a great opportunity to practise a number of skills for presenting and interpreting data, such as drawing pie charts, divided bar graphs and triangular graphs. This section shows how this can be done using the information in table **C**.

Pie charts are a very good way of quickly comparing this information and visually checking for major differences.

Divided bar graphs can be used to present this information in a different format – some people find them easier to draw.

F *Divided bar graphs showing industrial employment in China, India and South Africa*

Triangular graphs can be used to show the information for several different countries at the same time. Although they are more difficult to draw this is probably the best technique for a good visual comparison. Look at Topic 4.3 on pages 253–255 for advice on how to use a triangular graph.

E *Pie charts showing industrial employment in Afghanistan, Brazil and the United Kingdom*

G *Industrial employment shown on a triangular graph*

Economic development

Now Investigate

1 a) Draw pie charts like those in diagram **E** for two of the other countries listed in table **C**. Describe the differences shown across all five charts.

 b) Now try producing the same pie charts using the appropriate software on a computer.

2 Draw divided bar graphs like those in diagram **F** for two of the other countries listed in table **C**.

3 Make a copy of the triangular graph **G** and add the information for all the other countries in table **C**.

4 Describe the advantages and disadvantages of each of the presentation methods shown.

5 Using the information shown on these pages, rank all the countries in table **C** according to their level of development. Explain your answer.

Changes over time – Newly Industrialised Countries

Some LEDCs have economies that are expanding very quickly. They are becoming wealthier by developing their secondary industries. These LEDCs are called **Newly Industrialised Countries** (NICs).

The original NICs developed in Southeast Asia in the 1970s. Also known as the **tiger economies**, they included South Korea, Singapore, Taiwan and Hong Kong. These countries are now regarded as MEDCs and have very advanced economies. Their place has been taken by the new NICs, such as – China, India, Mexico, Brazil and South Africa – which share the following characteristics:

- strong government
- an economy moving away from primary industries and becoming based on manufacturing – often using raw materials produced by the primary industries
- free trade with other countries
- lots of foreign investment because of low tax rates and other benefits
- big, successful home-grown multinational companies.

The employment structure of these countries has changed so that there are fewer people employed in primary industries and the proportion in secondary industries has increased. Over time, as these industries need more services, tertiary sector employment also starts to go up.

NICs may have less strict health and safety laws and workers' organisations (unions) with less influence than those in MEDCs. This makes it easier for companies to operate there but may not be so good for the workers themselves.

> **Fantastic fact**
>
> Some experts think that, by 2050, the world's biggest economies will be China, USA, India, Brazil and Mexico.

As their economies expanded, the number of poor people in the original NICs quickly decreased. The governments encouraged their wealthier workers to invest in businesses to help the economy grow and made huge improvements in education, health and the general quality of life. It is hoped the new NICs will follow the same path.

Brazil – an emerging economy

Brazil is the biggest economy in South America and also the fastest growing. Over the past 20 years its economic growth has been on an almost continual upward climb (graph A). In 2010 it grew by 7.5 per cent while much of the world was suffering from recession.

There are a number of reasons for this success. The country has:

- a very varied (diversified) economy with money earned across many industrial sectors
- government investment in local industry and infrastructure
- encouragement of foreign investment (especially from China) through low taxes, cheap land, grants and loans
- relatively low wages, especially compared with MEDCs
- a large and increasingly wealthy population (who want to buy things) and access to markets throughout South and Central America.

China has a huge presence in Brazil. It is the country's biggest trading partner and spent US$140 billion on everything from oil exploration to building aircraft in 2008 alone. In particular, Brazil provides China with a great deal of food, especially chicken, beef and soybeans. Agricultural land is on the increase in Brazil, not just for food but also for ethanol to power motor vehicles. Around 52 per cent of Brazil's cars run on alcohol made from local sugar cane. There are concerns, however, that the increase in land for farming is leading to deforestation in the Amazonian rainforest (extract C).

A Brazil's economic growth, 1990–2009

B Unequal housing in Parasaipolis, Brazil

146   Economic development

3.1

Cows for Trees in the Amazon

Much has been made of China's demand for soybeans from Brazil but the impact this is having on the rainforest appears to have been overestimated. Soybean farming is mainly taking place outside the Amazon region.

The biggest threat to the trees are cows. Between 65 and 70 per cent of all the deforestation taking place in Brazil is for cattle ranching. The country has the biggest cattle herd in the world, it is the world's biggest beef exporter, and it is planning to double production by 2018.

C

0 = complete equality,
1 = complete inequality

D Brazil's changing inequality, 2002–08

Many Brazilians are becoming much better off and there has been a big increase in the relatively wealthy middle classes. The country's index of inequality (graph **D**) has dropped sharply over the past few years. In spite of this, many Brazilians are still living in poverty in ramshackle houses with no running water or electricity (photo **B**). As the county's economy continues to improve, the challenge will be to make sure all sectors of society get an improved quality of life.

Now Investigate

1. What are the main characteristics of a Newly Industrialised Country?
2. Using the information on these pages, describe economic activity in Brazil. Make sure you refer to primary, secondary and tertiary industries in your answer.
3. What problems could Brazil face as its economy keeps growing?

Globalisation

What is globalisation?

Globalisation describes the increase in connections between places around the world. The connections can be through international movement of people (migration), goods, services and money. Globalisation has resulted in closer economic links between countries and increased international trade. Companies now operate in many countries and many are famous throughout the world. However, globalisation is more than just an increase in trade, it has also encouraged cultural exchange across the world.

Section 3.1: Development

A *Internet users in 2016 as a percentage of a country's population*

Legend: under 20 per cent; 20–40 per cent; 40–60 per cent; 60–80 per cent; Over 80 per cent; no data

Why has globalisation occurred?

The main reasons for globalisation are:

- Improvements in international transport by air and sea in the second half of the twentieth century which helped to move people and goods around the world more quickly and cheaply.
- Development of the internet allowed information and ideas to be spread across the world instantly.
- The growth of **transnational corporations** (TNCs) which moved production into selected LEDCs to reduce costs, especially of labour.
- The growth of TNCs encouraged the development of Newly Industrialised Countries (NICs) with large and growing markets.
- Removal of trade barriers in many countries which allowed the free movement of goods, services and money around the world.

Company	Industry
British Petroleum	Oil & gas
Chevron	Oil & gas
Exxon Mobil	Oil & gas
Gazprom	Oil & gas
General Electric	Technology & electronics
HSBC	Banking & finance
IBM	Software
Royal Dutch Shell	Oil & gas
Total	Oil & gas
Toyota Motors	Vehicles
Volkswagen	Vehicles
Wal-Mart Stores	Retail

B *Some transnational corporations*

Headquarters
Usually in a city in a more economically developed country where the company was established

Research and Development
Usually located in a more economically developed country often in the country where the company began

Branch factories
Often located abroad, usually in less economically developed countries

C *Organisation of a transnational corporation*

What are transnational corporations (TNCs)?

TNCs, which you may know as multinational corporations (MNCs), are companies which have factories and offices in many different countries. A TNC is an MNC that operates worldwide without being identified with a national home base. The US fast-food chain McDonald's is a large MNC - it has nearly 37,000 restaurants in 120 countries. Many of the companies in table **B** will be familiar names. The organisation of a TNC is shown in diagram **C**.

Economic development

Positive effects of TNCs on economic development

- Investment by TNCs in a country, such as building factories, helps to create jobs for local people.
- TNCs usually pay higher wages than local businesses which means employees have a higher income and a better standard of living,
- TNCs bring wealth to the local economy which has a positive **multiplier effect** on other local businesses.
- Local people learn new skills and how to make use of new technologies.
- Most of the products manufactured by TNCs are exported, which benefits the economy of the country.
- TNCs pay tax to the government of the host country. This money can be invested in health, education and infrastructure.

> **Fantastic fact**
>
> Walmart employs 2.3 million people worldwide. This is more than the population of Latvia and Botswana.

Negative effects of TNCs on economic development

- TNCs have a reputation for making employees work long hours in poor working conditions.
- Often profits made by the TNC are sent back to the MEDC where the company has its headquarters rather than benefiting the local community.
- TNCs can close factories and transfer production to other low-cost locations overseas with little warning. Local people are made redundant which brings a negative multiplier effect to the local area.
- There are fewer laws about pollution in many LEDCs so TNCs may pollute the environment without danger of prosecution.
- TNCs become too important in the economy of the host country, which becomes too dependent on the TNC. So the TNC may be able to influence decisions made by the government.
- Manufacturing jobs in MEDCs have reduced and many people are unemployed as TNCs move their factories abroad.

D *Opposition to globalisation*

The future of globalisation

Globalisation is here to stay! International travel and internet access are increasing. TNCs greatly influence people in work and everyday life. Many TNCs have become famous international brands. However, some people are concerned

E *Other features of globalisation*

Other features of globalisation:
- Faster aid response to natural disasters
- Increased awareness of events across the world such as the 2004 tsunami and political events
- Threats to the culture of countries, such as local tradition and language
- Increased awareness of global issues such as deforestation and global warming
- Greater focus on world poverty and inequality
- Awareness of the need for sustainable development

Section 3.1: Development

about this growth and its possible effects. Anti-globalisation protests are a common feature of G20 meetings where the leaders of the most powerful nations discuss world affairs.

Now Investigate

1. Find out what the acronyms BRIC and MINT stand for when referring to groups of countries. Why are the economies of countries such as India, China, Mexico and Indonesia important in the process of globalisation?

2. Draw and complete the table below with six TNCs that are not in table **B**.

Name of TNC	What it makes or provides

3. Explain the multiplier effect. How can it be both positive and negative?

4. Do you think that globalisation is a good thing or a bad thing? Consider its effects on different groups of people.

CASE STUDY
Nike – a transnational corporation

Nike was established in 1972. It is famous for supplying trainers, sports and leisure clothing, and sporting equipment which features the 'swoosh' symbol, which is recognised globally. By linking many parts of the world Nike illustrates the economic features of globalisation. The headquarters of Nike are in Beaverton, Oregon in the USA, where much research and development also take place. It employs 8500 people in Beaverton but this is very small compared to the number of employees who work in factories across the world. Many of these people work in factories which are owned by companies to whom Nike subcontracts work. In 2017 Nike had 620 factories in 42 countries employing over one million workers.

A *Nike factory*

B *Countries where Nike has factories*

150   Economic development

At first Nike made and sold its products in North America and then in Europe. In the 1980s Japan became the first major market in the Far East where Nike also set up a regional headquarters and opened some factories. China is now Nike's fastest growing market where another regional headquarters has been set up.

Most of Nike's factories and employees are in the countries of Southeast Asia (table **C**). The reasons why Nike located factories in these countries are typical of many TNCs:

- labour was cheap
- governments offered incentives to the company to locate there
- raw materials were produced locally and so were relatively cheap to obtain
- countries were close together to reduce transport costs
- free trade took place between countries with no import or export duties
- there was an expanding market as countries developed economically.

Country	Number of factories producing products for Nike	Number of workers	GDP per person ($US) 2015
China	151	191 700	14 500
Vietnam	84	392 450	6000
USA	53	6500	56 100
Indonesia	41	202 200	11 100
Thailand	33	35 400	16 300
Brazil	32	17 400	15 400
Sri Lanka	22	34 300	11 800
Malaysia	18	8500	27 000
Argentina	18	4900	20 300
Mexico	16	11 800	17 300
Taiwan	16	5500	22 500
Japan	15	750	40 800
India	13	30 600	6100

C *Countries containing more than 10 Nike factories*

Nike in China

China is the second largest market for Nike products after the USA. Nike has shops in more than 300 cities. China is also the major manufacturing country for Nike with 151 factories employing 191 700 workers (November 2013). 75% of the workers are female and the average age of a factory worker is 37.

A major reason why Nike was attracted to locate factories in China was the abundant labour supply and cheap labour costs. However this advantage has been eroded by the impact of the one-child policy, which was introduced in China in the late 1970s to control the rapid population growth. As people who were born in the 1950s and 1960s retire this policy is now reducing the labour force. China has an ageing population and is changing from a country with an abundant labour supply to one with a shortage. Factories are reporting difficulties in hiring workers and are having to raise salaries to attract employees from the shrinking supply available. Nike, like other TNCs, has taken the decision to re-locate some factories to Southeast Asian countries where wages are relatively lower. The owner of one large shoe manufacturing company which makes Nike products explains that an employee's monthly salary in eastern China is $500 compared with $300 in Indonesia and $250 in Vietnam.

Nike's problems and solutions

Like other TNCs, factories making Nike products have been accused of paying low wages, expecting workers to work long hours, not providing sufficient training, having poor and unsafe working conditions and allowing supervisors to abuse workers. In 2010 20 000 workers in shoe factories in Vietnam went on strike for higher pay. In 2007 there were demonstrations in Indonesia when Nike decided to stop production at local factories and relocate elsewhere. This had a negative effect on local companies who relied on Nike employees to buy their goods. In China Nike was one of many companies which received bad publicity because factories were causing river pollution through waste discharge from the dying and printing process.

Nike is proud of its work in improving working conditions and protecting the environment. In response to some of the criticisms Nike took more responsibility for inspecting factories in order to improve working conditions and for increasing wage rates. In 1992 the company set up a Code of Conduct for all its factories which included protection of workers' rights and monitoring environmental impacts to make sure companies followed regulations on fire safety, air quality, minimum wage and overtime limits. In 2001 it introduced the Corporate Responsibility Report which set and monitored targets towards improving working conditions and hours, paying fair wages, increasing workers' skills and making them feel more valued to the company. The report also set environmental targets on reducing greenhouse gas emissions and increasing renewable energy use. This was replaced by the Code of Leadership Standards in 2014 to continue the focus on workers and sustainability. From 2012 the company has inspected and monitored the performance of all factories.

Topic link

See Topic 1.1 pages 16–17 for details about China's one-child policy.

Fantastic fact

In Greek mythology Nike was the Goddess of Victory.

D *Nike impacts: where it is aiming to manage its impacts and produce greater benefits*

Now Investigate

1. How does map **B** show that globalisation has taken place?

2. Look at table **C**. What conclusions can you make about where most of Nike's factories are located? Explain why factories in some countries employ more people than those in other countries.

3. Describe the impacts that Nike has had in China and Southeast Asia. Are there more positive or negative impacts?

Section 3 . Topic 2

Food production

Learning objectives:
- describe and explain the main features of an agricultural system: inputs, processes and outputs
- recognise the causes and effects of food shortages and describe possible solutions to this problem

What do farmers grow in your local area?

Your farming industry

Take a look at the farmer in photo **A**. He is one of millions of people around the world trying to grow crops to feed his family or to sell to make a living. In this case he is growing rice – as do many people living in east and Southeast Asia. But why has he chosen this particular crop? Is it because of the landscape or the soil? Perhaps the climate is just right, with lots of sun and lots of rain. Or it may just be because this is what his father and grandfather grew and so it has been a tradition for hundreds of years. There are many different types of farming in the world. The type that takes place in a certain area will depend on a combination of natural and human factors.

A *A rice farmer in China*

Types of farming

The many different types of farming can be classified according to the definitions shown in diagram **B**.

Putting these together can help us describe different types of farming. For example, an extensive commercial pastoral farm will use a large area of land to rear animals in order to make a profit.

B *Classification of farming types*

By what we get out of them
Commercial farming produces food for sale
Subsistence farming produces only enough food for the farmer and his family (with perhaps a little left over to sell)

By what we put into them
Intensive farms use large amounts of money, machines and technology or workers
Extensive farms have smaller inputs but usually use more land

CLASSIFYING FARM TYPES

By what is grown
Arable farms grow crops
Pastoral farms rear animals
Mixed farms grow crops and rear animals

Section 3.2: Food production 153

Farming is not always easy to classify. Subsistence farmers may have a small surplus to sell at a market. Some extensive farms may have periods in the year, such as harvest time, when there is intensive activity involving lots of workers.

Nomads are farmers who move around from one area to another. There used to be many nomads taking herds of animals across Africa in search of grassland to feed them on. Recently, however, many have been forced to settle down into **sedentary** farming with permanent farms and settlements.

The farming system

Another way to describe farming is to use a **systems diagram**. This has three main parts:

- **inputs** – the things that go into the system
- **outputs** – the things that come out of the system
- **processes** – the things that happen to the inputs to turn them into outputs.

A range of inputs, processes and outputs is shown in the systems diagram **C**. The diagram shows there may be some **feedback** in the system so that if the outputs include a profit it may be reinvested as an input of capital.

The decision-making farmer

The rice farmer in photo **A** has chosen this particular crop for a number of reasons. It grows well in the hot, wet climate where he lives. It can be grown in small fields with fertile soil. It does not need expensive machinery or fertiliser. It has been grown in his country for many centuries, so everyone understands how the system works. Most importantly, it gives a high yield (the amount of crop from a given area) so it can feed his large family using only the small plot of land that he owns.

Fantastic fact

Around one-third of the world's population make their living from agriculture but there is considerable variation between countries, from less than 1 per cent in the UK to almost 70 per cent in Cote d'Ivoire in Africa.

INPUTS

Physical:
Climate – temperature, precipitation, length of growing season
Relief and landscape
Soils

Human/economic:
Workforce (labour)
Farm buildings
Machinery
Chemicals (fertilisers/pesticides)
Transport and ease of getting to market
Seeds
Animals and animal feed
Money (capital)
Government influence
Energy (electricity)
Demand for products

PROCESSES

Many and varied depending on farm type but could include:

For growing crops
Ploughing
Planting
Spraying
Harvesting

For rearing animals
Grazing and feeding
Making hay and silage
Milking cows and shearing sheep
Calving and lambing

OUTPUTS

Crops such as rice, wheat, barley and vegetables
Animals and animal products including chicken, pork, beef, wool, milk and eggs
Money (profit)

FEEDBACK

Profit to be used as an input the following year

C *A farming systems diagram*

Economic development

3.2

Now Investigate

1. What type of farming do you have in your local area? List all the types you can think of and then compare your answer with those of others in your class.

2. Write down definitions for each of the following types of farming:

   commercial   **pastoral**   **nomadic**   **intensive**

3. What are the characteristics of:
   a) intensive subsistence farming
   b) extensive arable farming
   c) intensive commercial mixed farming?

4. Choose a type of farming found in your own region. Draw a systems diagram to show its main inputs, processes and outputs.

Inputs to the farming system

Inputs can be classified as either natural (relief, climate and soils) or human (economic and social).

Natural inputs

Climate is one of the main things influencing what type of farming takes place:

- All plants need a minimum temperature in order to grow. When the temperature is above this minimum, the plant will be in its growing season. The length of the growing season must be enough to allow the plant to develop. Low temperatures may cause frosts that kill crops or even freeze the ground so that nothing can grow.

- Mean annual rainfall (or precipitation) determines how much water is available for plants. In very dry areas, such as deserts, few plants can be grown. The type of rainfall is also important as heavy thunderstorms can cause soil erosion and destroy crops. If the rain falls when the temperature is high, the water will evaporate, so little will be available for plants to use.

In some areas of low rainfall, water can be taken to fields by **irrigation** from rivers, lakes and underground water stores. It often requires large amounts of money to set up an irrigation system.

Relief refers to the hills, valleys and mountains found in an area:

- Height influences the type of farming because the temperature drops the higher up you are.

- **Aspect** (the direction the land faces) is important. In the northern hemisphere, south-facing slopes receive more sunlight and are warmer (north-facing slopes in the southern hemisphere).

- Steep slopes often mean that soils are thinner. They also make it harder to use machinery. In parts of Asia, hillsides have been terraced to take account of this (photo **A**). Some of these terraces are hundreds and even thousands of years old.

Soil type and factors such as stoniness and how deep the soil is influence what crops can be grown. **Fertile** soils like those found in river deltas like the Mekong have lots of nutrients that plants need to grow. The quality of a soil can be improved by adding fertilisers, but not all farmers can afford them.

Section 3.2: Food production

A Terraced hillsides in China

B Picking olives from trees in the West Bank village of Al Walaja

Human inputs

Farms need enough workers (**labour**) to do all the jobs necessary to grow crops or look after animals. In some countries this work, such as olive picking (photo **B**), may be seasonal (for part of the year only).

Many of the other human inputs are **economic** and depend on how much money is available to buy, or do, certain things:

- Farm buildings – they are needed for storage of crops and equipment.
- Machinery – it can make farming much easier and means that farmers do not have to pay workers, but it can be very expensive to buy (photo **C**).
- Chemicals – fertilisers can help crops to grow, while pesticides and herbicides will stop them being attacked by insects and diseases. However, chemicals are also expensive and can be damaging to the environment.
- Transport and markets – some crops need to be taken to market quickly before they deteriorate but transport can cost a lot of money and in some countries (for example mountainous regions) transport can be difficult.
- Seeds, animals and animal feed and energy – all cost the farmer money.
- Government influence – in some countries, such as the USA and France, the government gives **subsidies** (payments) to farmers to grow certain types of crops.
- Demand – if there is a shortage of a certain crop, for example because of drought, then demand increases and the price the farmer gets for the crop can rise quickly.

Farmers with lots of money (**capital**), or **agribusinesses** that run big farms, can keep up with the latest technology, are much more efficient and make much bigger profits.

C Machinery can be very expensive for farmers

Topic link

You can find out more about the environmental risks and benefits of agriculture in Topic 3.7 pages 213–234.

Fantastic fact

Strange but true – in some countries, governments pay farmers to do no farming at all on parts of their land in order to help keep the environment looking natural.

156 Economic development

World farming types

The different natural and human inputs combine so that different farming types occur in different parts of the world – some of these are shown in map **D**.

The distribution shown on the map is very general. In some areas specialised crops may be grown. In others, several types of farming may take place. Often, one type of farming gradually merges with another, rather than there being a fixed boundary.

Legend:
- Unclassified
- Nomadic herding
- Extensive subsistence irrigation
- Intensive subsistence agriculture
- Commercial plantation agriculture
- Livestock ranching (commercial pastoral)
- Cereal cultivation (commercial grain)
- Intensive commercial (mixed)
- Mediterranean agriculture
- Crops needing irrigation
- Unsuitable for agriculture

D World farming types

Now Investigate

1. Look at the list of natural and human factors affecting farming. Try to rank a top five in order of importance and write reasons justifying your answer.

2. Describe the global distribution of different farming types shown in map **D**.

3. According to map **D**, what type of farming takes place in the region where you live? How does this compare with the types of farming you identified on pages 153–154?

Commercial farming systems

The main feature of commercial farming is that it is carried out to make a profit. In richer countries this is often done by individual farmers. On the grassland prairies of the USA and Canada, for example, farmers own huge areas of land and grow wheat or have cattle ranches with thousands of animals. The land use is extensive, because it takes place over a large area, and the farm

Section 3.2: Food production

needs big inputs of money, machinery and fertilisers and pesticides. Workers are often employed only for brief periods of the year when harvesting or planting needs to be carried out quickly.

In poorer countries, most farmers do not have enough money to farm on a large scale, so agribusinesses are often in control of the agriculture. Agribusinesses are huge companies that own land in many different countries. Del Monte, for instance, is the world's third largest producer of bananas. It has farms in Costa Rica, Guatemala, Ecuador, Colombia and the Philippines but, like many multinational companies, its headquarters are in the USA.

Much of the commercial agriculture in tropical areas is carried out on plantations. These are vast areas of land that have been deforested and the trees replaced with a single type of crop. This is known as **monoculture** and produces crops that are mainly sold for export to other countries. Examples of these crops, known as cash crops, include rubber, coffee, tea, cocoa, palm oil, sugar cane and tobacco.

> **Topic link**
>
> There is more on the environmental effects of commercial agriculture in Topic 3.7 pages 213–234.

CASE STUDY: Plantation agriculture in Sarawak, Malaysia

Commercial plantation agriculture has long been a feature of the landscape in Malaysia (map **A**). The first British-owned plantations were based on coffee and then later on rubber. The British government provided the money to set up the original plantations and built railway lines and ports to export the crop around the world.

The Malaysian government now runs all the major plantations and has made big changes since the time of the British. The industry now concentrates on growing palm oil (photo **B**). The region of Sarawak, for example, exports around 10 per cent of Malaysia's total. The crop is well suited to this area with its high temperatures and plentiful rainfall (graph **C**).

Much of the land that is being used for palm oil production was previously covered with rare tropical peat swamp forests (maps **D**). There is now

A *Malaysia, Southeast Asia*

158 Economic development

serious concern by environmentalists that all these forests will have been destroyed by 2020.

The palm oil is bringing in lots of money, however, for Malaysia's economy. Most of it is exported to other countries (graph **E**) through the main ports of Kuching, Sibu, Bintulu and Miri.

Inputs to the palm oil production system are shown in diagram **F**.

The production of palm oil now accounts for 6 per cent of the economy of Malaysia.

B A palm oil plantation in Malaysia

C Climate graph for Sarawak

D Destruction of peat swamp forest for palm oil production in Sarawak

E Palm oil production and exports in Malaysia, 1964–2016

Section 3.2: Food production   159

Characteristics of Malaysian plantation agriculture (INPUTS)

- **Increased demand for palm oil**
  - as an edible oil
  - in a wide range of foodstuffs
  - to make soap, cosmetics and paint
  - as a source of energy in **biofuels**

- **Large amounts of reasonably flat land** making it easy for machines to spray pesticides and the fertilisers needed to keep the soil fertile

- **Transport facilities** (roads, railways and ports) to help exports

- **Machinery** including mechanised harvesters

- **A local workforce** (of around 491 000 palm oil workers) who will work long hours for relatively low pay – an average of around US$225 per month

- **A hot, wet climate**

- **Large amounts of money to:**
  - clear the land of forest
  - provide irrigation for crops
  - build houses, schools and hospitals for employees

Fantastic fact

The first Malaysian rubber plants were stolen from Brazil by British spies, then smuggled out to London and taken to Southeast Asia.

F Characteristics of Malaysian plantation agriculture

Now Investigate

1. Find out about any commercial farming that takes place in the region where you live. Describe the characteristics of this local agricultural system.

2. Using graph **E** and the text, describe and explain the growth of palm oil production in Malaysia.

3. What are some of the problems associated with palm oil production in Sarawak?

Subsistence farming systems

Subsistence farming is carried out to feed the farmer and his family. If there is any surplus it will normally be sold in the local community. It is often the dominant form of agriculture in poor countries where people do not have the money, land or technology to increase the amount they produce. The main aim is survival and subsistence farmers are very vulnerable to conditions that cause food shortages.

Shifting cultivation

In the Amazon and Congo rainforests some tribes carry out **shifting cultivation**. They build a small central village and farm crops in gardens nearby. When the soil quality starts to decrease they move their garden to a neighbouring area. Food crops

Economic development

(including plantain, cassava, sweet potato, yam, banana and other fruits) grow easily so very few inputs are needed apart from the natural environment and large areas of land.

The most widespread form of subsistence farming is intensive rice cultivation. Land is all-important (see photo **A** on page 153). Rice is very high-yielding and grows so fast that up to three crops can be harvested each year. Despite this, there is little surplus because of the large number of people the rice has to support (almost 3 billion people in China and India).

> **Further research**
>
> For more facts and figures about rice farming in Bangladesh, put 'Rice Country Profile Bangladesh' into your internet search engine.

CASE STUDY: Rice farming in Bangladesh

Bangladesh has one of the highest population densities in the world. Almost half its 161 million people work in agriculture, with rice being by far the most important crop (map **A**). Some of the features of the rice farming landscape are shown in photo **B**.

The major inputs to the rice farming system are:

- a climate with plenty of rain and high temperatures providing ideal conditions for plants to grow all year round (graph **C**)
- fertile soils from the silt deposited by the flooding river Ganges
- a large population giving a high labour input for building and maintaining fields and irrigation channels, planting, weeding, harvesting and other tasks
- small farms which are becoming smaller as land is handed down to the next generation – the average farm size has been cut by around 50 per cent over the last 50 years and is now around 0.61 hectares.

There is little money available for machinery, so much of the work is done by hand. In addition to the major output (rice), farmers may grow vegetables on small plots of land and pick fruit from trees surrounding their villages. Farmers have also been encouraged to farm fish in the flooded padi fields.

The farmers of Bangladesh have faced tough times recently with world rice prices increasing and natural disasters, including floods, wiping out crops. Despite this, production has continued to rise (graph **D**) because of hard work by rural people. There has also been considerable government investment in new irrigation schemes

> **Fantastic fact**
>
> The average person in Bangladesh eats more than 200 kg of rice every year.

A Land use in Bangladesh

Section 3.2: Food production

Fruit trees to add to diet

Small fields (called padis) which may get smaller when passed on to the next generation

Animals may be used for ploughing instead of expensive machines

Small rice plants may be grown in nursery beds before being moved to bigger fields

Low walls (called bunds) built to keep water in the padi fields

Fish may be added to padi fields to add protein to diet

Rice planted under water from heavy rainfall, flooding or irrigation

B *Features of the rice farming landscape*

to allow year-round rice-growing in drier areas of the country. Over 80 per cent of this irrigation is by pumping from sources found under the ground (known as groundwater stores).

C *Climate graph for Bangladesh*

D *Rice production in Bangladesh, 1998–2014*

Now Investigate

1. Describe the main land use features of Bangladesh using map **A**.

2. What are the main characteristics of subsistence farming?

3. Describe and explain the main features of an intensive rice farming landscape.

4. With reference to a country you have studied:
    a) Explain why it is particularly suited to rice farming.
    b) Describe some of the problems faced by its subsistence farmers.

Skills link

You have to be able to interpret a wide range of maps for the IGCSE Geography exams, including land use maps like the one shown on page 161. Refer to Topic 4.1 pages 235–244 to learn how to do this.

162 Economic development

3.2

Why are there food shortages in some parts of the world?

Your daily food supply

If you are lucky you will have woken up this morning and gone through the day with enough food to eat. This will have provided you with the **calories** your body needs. These calories give you the energy to work properly, to grow and develop into a healthy adult. Unfortunately, this will not have been the case for everyone in your country or in the wider world. As population grows, food is in ever shorter supply. Poor people such as Christian Medina, a miner in Bolivia, are the ones who suffer most (photo **A**).

The right food in the wrong places

It would seem there is a direct connection between an increasing population and there not being enough food to eat. But the story is not that simple. Global grain production – the rice, wheat and maize that is the basic diet for most people – has increased so much over the last 40 years that the amount available per person has stayed fairly constant.

It is estimated that there is enough food in the world for everybody to get 3000 calories a day. The minimum needed to survive is around 2500 calories but, in many countries, there are large numbers of people eating much less than this. Map **B** shows where these people live by displaying the average number of calories eaten per person in each country. It also shows the countries where people eat far more than the amount they need to survive. The problem is not the lack of food in the world but the fact that much of it is not distributed equally.

> Hola. My name is Christian Medina. I've always been poor but I've done my best to provide food and shelter for my family.
>
> We can no longer afford the food we need. My children are hungry and are getting sick. Sometimes I give them all my food but then I'm too weak to work. How are we meant to survive?

A Christian Medina, miner, Bolivia, protesting against food shortages

Skills link

You need to be able to describe world distribution maps like map B. Go to Topic 4.2 pages 245–250 for more information on how to do this.

Kcal/person/day per country in 2010 (world average 2800 kcal/person/day)
- 1600–2000
- 2000–2400
- 2400–2800
- 2800–3200
- 3200–3600
- More than 3600

B World food supply

Section 3.2: Food production

Causes of food shortages

Demand for food from wealthier countries, including India and China, has caused the price of food to increase rapidly. Many poor countries do not grow enough food and can no longer afford to import enough for their people. Recent increases in transport and fuel costs have caused food prices to rise further. Other factors play a part:

- Drought, floods, tropical cyclones and other extreme weather events have caused crops to fail.
- Natural disasters (especially earthquakes) affect food distribution by destroying or damaging roads and other transport links.
- Outbreaks of disease including cholera, malaria and HIV/AIDS mean people are not able to work on their farms and grow food.
- In some years, pests, including locusts, destroy vast amounts of cropland.
- Civil wars, like those in Darfur (Sudan) and in Sierra Leone, disrupt food supplies as farmers are afraid to go out to their fields, transport routes are destroyed and soldiers demand food from local people.
- As population has increased, people have had to farm less suitable land. This has led to erosion of the soil so that it becomes unable to support plant life – this is known as **soil exhaustion**.

Some of these reasons could be due to the world's changing climate. The United Nations has estimated that three-quarters of the world's poorest people live in areas that will be affected by crop failures due to global warming.

Topic link

More on the environmental effects of agriculture can be found in Topic 3.7 pages 213–234.

Fantastic fact

The largest recorded locust swarm covered 1036 km² and was estimated to comprise 40 billion insects.

Drought 2011 – The Horn of Africa

Months of no rain in countries including Ethiopia and Djibouti resulted, by mid 2011, in drought and crop failure affecting more than 10 million people.

Rising crop prices led to widespread malnutrition and starvation. There was a refugee crisis as starving people tried to move to areas where food was available.

The situation was most severe in Somalia. People already weakened by years of war and civil unrest fled to Kenya and Ethiopia at a rate of more than 1300 people each day. This added to the problems of food supply in the receiving countries.

Even when the crisis is over, there are fears it will take many years for the region to recover. Many of the people affected are nomads who rely on their animals to survive. The drought killed their camels and cattle, so they have lost their livelihood and long-term source of food.

C *Drought can cause huge loss of livestock*

Economic development

3.2

Now Investigate

1. Look at map **B** and use it to describe the pattern of global food supply. Remember to name individual countries in your answer and explain what the map shows about them.

2. Try to find out how many calories you eat in a day. You could try searching the internet using 'Calorie Counter' to help.

3. What recent natural disasters can you think of that may have affected food shortages? Name the countries where these disasters have taken place.

4. Describe and explain any factors that could cause food shortages in your own country.

5. Do you think reducing population growth would end food shortages? Explain your answer.

The health effects of a shortage of food

When something is missing from the daily diet, this causes malnutrition. This can be a lack of enough food or of certain minerals or vitamins (panel **A**). Around 900 million people (13 per cent of the world's population) do not have enough food. They are almost all found in LEDCs and many of them are children.

Those who suffer from malnutrition are not able to work because of a lack of energy, mental problems and general poor health. Family incomes fall and people continue to become ill through lack of food.

Problems	Diseases caused
• **Protein-energy malnutrition** is caused by a lack of protein (from meat, eggs and other sources) and food that provides energy (e.g. rice, wheat and potatoes) – it is the major cause of world hunger.	• **Marasmus** causes sufferers to become very thin and stop growing.
	• **Kwashiorkor** is caused by eating too many cereals and not enough protein – the stomach swells, skin peels and the hair turns orange.
• **Micronutrient malnutrition** is when the body lacks certain vitamins and minerals.	• **Anaemia** is caused by a lack of iron.
	• **Vitamin A deficiency** causes blindness and death.
	• **Iodine deficiency** affects the brain and can be fatal.

A *Malnutrition and disease*

Tackling the food supply problem

When poor countries have a problem with food shortages, especially when it is the result of a natural disaster such as a drought, cyclone or earthquake, richer countries often help out with food aid (photo **B**).

Africa is particularly in need of food aid. Problems for specific countries include:

- conflict, drought and piracy in Somalia
- drought, AIDS and high population density causing a shortage of land in Malawi

B *Distribution of food aid*

Section 3.2: Food production 165

- the long-term effects of civil war in Sudan
- locust attack in Niger
- increasing numbers of refugees in Liberia.

There are concerns that handing out food does little to solve long-term problems and many countries become too dependent on hand-outs. Increasingly, governments are trying to help countries improve their agriculture in order to maintain their food security. This means they would have enough food to feed their own people without relying on imports or help from overseas.

The Green Revolution

Since the 1960s scientists across the world have been helping to improve agriculture for subsistence farmers in different regions of the world. They have developed new types of rice, maize and wheat that produce more (give higher yields).

The Green Revolution has brought problems as well as benefits. Overall, however, it has helped crop production to keep up with population growth.

A more recent development has been the **Blue Revolution**. Communities have been encouraged to breed fish – in mangrove swamps, padi fields, lakes and near the coast – to provide more protein.

The Green Revolution

Aims: to scientifically develop new types of rice that give higher yields; to introduce new irrigation schemes; to use new fertilisers to help crops grow and new pesticides to protect them from disease.

Benefits

- Food production has increased, so more people can be fed.
- Higher yields means lower prices, so poor people can afford more food.
- Crops are more resistant to disease, so harvests are more reliable.
- Crops grow faster, so more harvests can be gathered each year.
- The better-off farmers who can afford chemicals and machinery have become richer and employ more local people.
- More jobs are available in businesses supporting farming.

Problems

- Not all farmers have felt the benefits of the Green Revolution.
- The less well-off who could not compete have sold their land and moved to the city.
- Some farmers have borrowed money to pay for crops and are now in debt.
- Machinery has caused rural unemployment.
- Chemicals have polluted local water supplies.
- Irrigation has increased the demand on drinking water stores.
- Some of the new varieties of rice are not as pleasant to eat.

3.2

Genetically modified (GM) crops

The latest technological advances have been in GM crops. The idea is to alter crops scientifically to enable them to withstand pests and diseases and to help them survive droughts or the very salty conditions found in some LEDCs.

These crops have the potential to increase the amount of food that can be grown by enabling farmers to plant in areas that were thought to be unsuitable. However, some countries have banned GM crops until they are proved to be safe for both people and the environment.

Intermediate and appropriate technology

Many of the methods used to increase food production need new technology. Others depend on simpler solutions that are more affordable for poor countries and use existing local skills and technology, for example:

- educating farmers to save water by building dams on seasonal rivers
- saving land from erosion by building small terraces on gently sloping land
- using solar energy (the power of the sun) to pump water for irrigation.

Closely linked to this is the development of *permaculture*. People living in cities are encouraged to grow their own food in urban gardens. The Caribbean island of Cuba is one of many countries where people in cities have set up local markets to sell food on at reasonable prices (photo **C**).

C *Urban gardening in Cuba*

Now Investigate

1. a) List some of the diseases caused by a lack of food.
   b) What effects do these diseases have on the countries where people are suffering?

2. Describe some of the methods used to increase food production and reduce food shortages.

3. Have a look at the food you eat at home. Was it produced locally? What could be done to increase the amount of locally produced food in the area where you live?

Section 3.2: Food production

Food shortages and government action

Governments have an important role to play in both causing and dealing with food shortages. Some of the factors affecting food supply can be dealt with through government investment in the following:

- providing an efficient **infrastructure** for distribution – this includes well-maintained roads and port facilities so that food can be taken quickly to those areas that need it
- building up reserves of food when it is available, to be handed out when drought or natural disaster happens
- avoiding wars and conflicts that can lead to people being deprived of food
- investing money in farming – perhaps by providing loans or equipment to farmers
- making sure that land is available to grow locally eaten food crops – in some countries there has been a concentration on growing food for export.

The most important role of a government should be in caring for its citizens. But not all governments can afford to take action. People feel let down when there is not enough food for them to eat. Recently, as food shortages have increased, people's anger has turned to riots in several LEDCs.

CASE STUDY: Food shortages in Bolivia

Bolivia is a country without a coastline in the interior of South America. It has a very varied landscape including high mountains and lowland rainforests (map A) but much of the land is very limited in its use for agriculture. Only about 2 per cent is considered good arable land (graph B). Producing food is difficult and distributing it across the mountainous landscape to a scattered population is expensive. Drought, frosts, hail (which may all be increased by climate change) and soil erosion add to the food supply problems.

Agriculture is the major employer. Around 40 per cent of the population make a living either from subsistence farming on the high plains or export crops (soybeans, coffee and sugar cane) in the tropical areas. There has been much criticism of foreign-owned agribusinesses in the country. They take up much of the best land, some of it used to produce biofuels for export, which could be used to grow food for local people.

A The landscape of Bolivia naming selected high mountains

168 Economic development

Around 60 per cent of the people are poor and unable to buy enough food. They have been badly affected by recent price rises. In a 12-month period between 2010 and 2011 the price of bread rose between 65 and 100 per cent across the country. Recent fuel price rises also increased transport costs. At the start of 2011, many towns and cities began to run out of sugar and other basic foodstuffs. The people, including miners like Christian Medina (see page 163), became very angry indeed and took to the streets to protest (photo C). Bolivian unions said a family's basic monthly needs had risen to US$1100 a month, far in excess of the minimum monthly wage of $290.

The Bolivian president has blamed the shortages on increased demand from China and India putting up food prices (graph D). Others say the government has encouraged agribusinesses to grow soybeans and other crops for export rather than growing food for people to eat.

B *Bolivian land use*

What can I do but take to the streets? We need action from our government. They can't leave us to starve like this.

When the Bolivians protest, they do so in a very distinctive way by blocking roads and causing general disruption. Many of the country's workers are miners and can easily get hold of explosive dynamite.

In a recent demonstration against rising food prices in the town of Uyuni, marching miners threw dynamite towards the country's president to express their anger. Luckily, as they are experienced users, people rarely get hurt by the flying explosive.

C *Miner protesting in Uyuni, Bolivia*

FAO Food Price Index: 2002–04 = 100

D *The increase in world food prices, 1990–2016*

Further research

Find out more about the case study by searching for 'Bolivia Food Shortages' or 'Bolivia Food Protest' on the internet.

Section 3.2: Food production

The steady rise in the price of food has had a serious impact on the poor of Bolivia. With no extra money to spend when prices rise, the only option for them and their families is to eat less food. Long-term solutions which will help the people of Bolivia to survive are hard to find as there is little extra land available to grow crops on. Decreasing fuel prices would have an effect on transport costs and bring down the price of food but they are dependent on world markets. Biotechnology and genetically modified foods may provide some of the answer as they can increase crop yield but they are expensive because of the extra fertiliser and pesticide they need.

Recently however, there have been signs of improvement in the economy as export prices of natural gas and food commodities have increased. One solution put forward is a 10-year plan by the Bolivian government to invest US$5 billion in providing seeds and expertise to support small-scale farmers and peasants in growing both their own food and a little extra for local consumption. This is seen as a way to counter the influence of the big agribusinesses and foreign investors who currently farm a lot of the land in the country.

Now Investigate

1. How can a government influence a country's food supply?

2. Describe the landscape of Bolivia and explain how it affects the country's ability to feed its population.

3. Imagine you are Christian Medina and your family is suffering from a lack of food. Write a brief essay explaining what you would do to get the government to help.

Section 3 . Topic 3

Industry

Learning objectives:
- demonstrate an understanding of an industrial system: inputs, processes and outputs (products and waste)
- describe and explain the factors influencing the distribution and location of factories and industrial zones

What do you want to be when you start work?

Your future employment

What kind of job would you like to do? There are a huge number of options available. If you like working with your hands, farming or factory work may appeal to you. If you want to use your brain you could be inventing the next generation of Ultra HD televisions. Or you may want to look after others as a nurse or doctor. Some people try several different jobs before settling on a career. It may even be that the job you will do hasn't been invented yet – 20 years ago, for example, there was no such thing as a mobile phone apps designer.

A *A world of jobs*

A *huge range of jobs*

Even at a very young age some people know what work they want to do. This may be because they are born into a family where they are expected to do a certain job. Farmers, for instance, often pass their land on to their children. In other cases, people may be limited by the jobs available in their local area, and some may choose to move away from home to find work.

People living in areas where there is a greater variety of work may have more choice. Those with good standards of education or specialist skills may be able to choose from a number of employment opportunities. Figure **B** gives examples of young people from around the world and their ideas on what they will be doing in the future.

B *Young people from around the world*

Peter Malema: Messina, South Africa

> My father is a miner and my grandfather was before him. There's no doubt I will be too when I am old enough. The work is hard but the pay is good, especially compared to working on a farm which is about the only other thing to do around here.
>
> I don't really think about how dangerous it is. I know people die every now and then but I just have to hope I'm not one of the unlucky ones.

Jesus do Silva: São Paolo, Brazil

> The only place to work around here is the drinks factory. Before it was built there was nobody here but the factory came and the people followed. My dad was one of the first to work, putting the liquid into the bottles.
>
> He's gone now and left me to help mum bring up my brothers and sisters. In a year I'll be old enough to go and ask for a job. I'm sure they'll give me one – there are always people moving on and new workers needed.

Evon Dunn: Kingston, Jamaica

> Lots of tourists are coming to our island nowadays and it's been great for jobs. All my parents knew before was how to catch and sell fish but now there are many different ways we can make money. There's work in the hotels as receptionists, waiters, looking after the grounds and all sorts.
>
> If I can get a decent education I could even become a tour guide. This is where the big money is. Good wages and loads of tips. I'd love to tell the visitors all about our history so it would be just great for me.

Economic development

3.3

Zhijia Jingzhou: Shanghai, China

> We live in a high-tech society. Mobile phones, computers, music players are all part of our everyday life and, living here, we're right in the heart of where it all comes from.
>
> At my school we're big on science and technology. Things are moving really fast and we're all trying to be prepared for the jobs of the future. When I start work I want to be involved in making stuff the whole world wants to buy.

Now Investigate

1. Look at the pictures of different jobs in figure **A**. Can you identify what kinds of jobs are shown? Write down a list of the good and bad points of each job.

2. Read through the different jobs described by the people on this page. Pick two you would like to do and write down why you would like to do them.

3. What kind of skills and qualifications might you need to be able to do these jobs?

4. What do you think is meant by 'the job you will do hasn't been invented yet'?

5. What would be your ideal job? Where would that kind of job be available? What kind of skills will you need to be able to do it?

What things are made in my local area?

Your local manufacturing industry

Somewhere near you somebody will be making things. This may be done in a huge factory with hundreds of workers assembling anything from saucepans to motor vehicles. Or it could be a person in their front room making jewellery from beads and bits of coloured glass. These people are all involved in some kind of manufacturing industry although, obviously, at very different scales (photos **A**). As we have seen, as a country develops, its secondary industry becomes more important than its primary industry because it brings in more money. This is a very important part of economic development for many countries around the world.

A *Manufacturing takes place at a variety of different scales*

Section 3.3: Industry   173

The secondary industrial system

As we have seen, systems diagrams are a useful way of showing how inputs, outputs and processes all fit together to explain how something works. Diagram **B** shows a systems diagram for secondary industry.

As with an agricultural system there are feedbacks. Profit can be reinvested as an input of capital. With an increasing demand for sustainability, waste is often recycled. In food processing, for instance, waste products from plants can sometimes be used as a source of energy to power factories (photo **C**).

> **Topic link**
>
> See page 154 which shows how systems diagrams can also be used to explain how agriculture works.

Industrial location

The following inputs to the industrial system influence **industrial location**, or where an industry is located:

- **Raw materials** – these can be bulky and cost a lot to transport. Some industries, for example shipbuilding, may need to locate close to their raw materials because of this.

- **Energy supply** – in countries with a national electricity supply this will not be a problem. In others, factories may need to locate close to a power station.

- **Natural transport routes** – mountains will make transport difficult, while valleys are much easier.

- **Site and land** – many factories need large areas of relatively cheap, flat land to build on.

- **Capital (money)** – start-up costs can be very high for big factories. Rich investors may be needed.

- **Labour supply** – factories need skilled or unskilled workers or a mixture of both.

- **Transport** – ports, railways and good roads will make transport of raw materials and finished goods faster and easier.

INPUTS
Physical:
Raw materials
Energy supply
Natural transport routes
Site and land
Human/economic:
Capital (money)
Labour supply
Transport
Markets
Government policies
Technology
Environment
Entrepreneurship
Research and development

PROCESSES
Many different types depending on what is being produced but could include:
Processing (of raw materials)
Printing
Weaving, stitching and sewing
Painting
Assembling of goods

OUTPUTS
Products such as cars, clothes, books, toys
Money (profit)
Waste (to be disposed of, sometimes costing lots of money)

FEEDBACK Profit to be used as an input in the following year

WASTE Possibly recycled as raw materials or as an energy supply

B *A systems diagram for manufacturing industry*

174 Economic development

- **Markets** – large numbers of people living close enough to buy products will help businesses thrive.
- **Government policies** – government can encourage industry by offering grants and tax breaks.
- **Technology** – email and other forms of global communication mean that factories can now be built a long way away from company headquarters.
- **Environment** – in some cases, a pleasant landscape and good local facilities attract the best workers.
- **Entrepreneurship** – businessmen may want to set up new companies near where they live or where they were born.
- **Research and development (R&D)** – industries that rely on advanced technology need to locate in countries where there are top scientists conducting research.

Before deciding where to build a factory, businesses will consider these location factors. It is unlikely that any one site will meet all of these requirements, so a decision may be made based on the most important ones. Political factors may also play a part. For instance, an Indian company may make a decision to locate in India rather than in Japan because that is better for its public image.

Fantastic fact

Manufacturing industry generated around US$30 trillion worldwide in 2010.

C *Biomass (waste plant products) being used to power a factory*

Now Investigate

1. Think about your local area. Name as many types of manufacturing industry as you can, including both small-scale producers and large-scale factories.

2. Look at all the factors involved in industrial location. Rank them from the most important to the least important and write down reasons explaining your choice.

3. Draw a manufacturing industry systems diagram for any local industry you can think of.

4. a) Which of the factors affecting industrial location are particularly good in (i) your local area and (ii) your country?

   b) Are there any factors you can think of that will have a negative effect on industrial development where you live?

Manufacturing industries

Traditionally, the most important inputs to the manufacturing industry system were raw materials and a power supply. Transport was difficult, so factories would have to locate near to bulky raw materials. In steel making, for instance, this included heavy iron ore and limestone. Meanwhile power would be made locally using water, wood or, later on, coal. As factories were set up, workers would move to be near them, rather than the other way around.

As time went on, and especially from the beginning of the 20th century, transport of raw materials became much easier, with ships sailing quickly all around the world. Availability of raw materials was no longer an important location factor. Neither was power, as this was now provided by power stations connected to a network able to provide electricity where it was needed. One of the main inputs in modern industry is the cost of employing workers. This is why the world's steel making industry has moved from places with expensive labour like the UK to cheaper countries including China and India (photo **A**).

A similar situation has been the case for many other manufacturing industries.

A *Making steel in India*

CASE STUDY
The textile and clothing industry in Bangladesh

Originally starting in the UK as part of the industrial revolution of the 18th and 19th centuries, the **textile industry** soon spread to the rest of Europe and the USA. In the second half of the 20th century, however, a big change in the location of the industry took place. LEDCs became the world leaders in textile production. There were several reasons for this:

- Many LEDCs with a warm climate changed their agriculture and began to grow cotton – one of the most important raw materials in making clothes.
- The growth of cheaper global shipping routes meant that other raw materials could be transported easily and finished products could be taken to markets in MEDCs.
- Many LEDCs saw making clothes as an excellent 'start-up' industry – one that would let them set up a manufacturing industry and get money from exports very quickly.
- The equipment required little technology – cheap sewing machines were available almost anywhere.
- The industry needed lots of labour, especially women, many of whom may have already had experience of making clothes for their family.
- There was an increasing demand for clothes (which could be sold at much higher prices than it cost to make them) from MEDCs.

The main input has been the availability of a large, cheap workforce in many LEDCs. Caribbean and Central American countries, including the Dominican Republic, Mexico, Honduras and Haiti – all close to cotton-growing areas – were

Fantastic fact

In the UK, only one quarter of all clothes are recycled – the rest are thrown away, when they could be used again.

Year	US$billion
2011–12	19.09
2012–13	21.50
2013–14	24.49
2014–15	25.40
2015–16	28

B *Textile exports from Bangladesh (US$billion)*

176 Economic development

some of the first countries to use their workforce well and set up large factories. Recently, however, there has been a huge growth in production in many countries in eastern Asia including Bangladesh (figure **B**).

The textile industry in Bangladesh shows a real mix between small-scale production in towns and villages and big factories located in the cities. Over 50 per cent of all businesses operate in rural areas but, increasingly, the entrepreneurs who originally set up there have made enough money to move into cities including the capital Dhaka. They have taken over rented buildings and have taken advantage of what one businessman called the 'uneducated, untrained and needy rural unemployed' and brought them to work in the city factories.

In many cases the businesses have taken advantage of lax health and safety laws and pay less than the minimum wage of around US$58 a month to increase profits. The industry has now grown to provide 4 million people with jobs in 5000 factories making clothes worth US$19 million a year for export, mainly to the European Union and the USA.

C *Textile industries in Dhaka, Bangladesh*

The lack of enforced health and safety regulations has, however, caused international concern following the Rana Plaza disaster in April 2013 (photo **D**). On this day an eight-storey commercial building holding a textile factory employing 5000 workers collapsed, killing 1129 people and injuring a further 2515. It was the deadliest garment factory accident in history and led to huge scrutiny of the demand for cheap clothes in Europe. After years of inaction it has caused a rethink by many clothing retailers who have insisted on new safety deals and agreements on fire and factory regulations. It remains to be seen what effect these will have on the future of Bangladesh's most successful industry.

D *The Rana Plaza disaster*

Now Investigate

1. Look at the labels in some of the clothes you are wearing and/or in your cupboard at home. Where do the clothes come from? Does this fit with the information on these pages?

2. What are the main inputs to the textile industry system?

3. Using specific country examples, explain why the global textile industry has moved from MEDCs to LEDCs.

Topic link

Some of the environmental impacts, problems and benefits of manufacturing industry are outlined in Topic 3.7 on pages 220–226.

Section 3.3: Industry   177

High-technology industries

High-tech industries are mainly concerned with the application of technology in many different forms. This includes computers, telecommunications (including mobile phones), robotics and computer gaming systems (photos **A**). Raw materials are usually very small and light so they are no longer a major factor in location. The products made are high value, small and easy to transport so the factories can be built almost anywhere in the world. Industries like this are known as 'footloose' industries.

Inputs other than raw materials have become much more important factors in determining where these industries are located (diagram **B**).

Global distribution of high-tech industries

The research and development involved in high-tech industries means they need to attract new graduates from technical universities and colleges. They often locate in attractive environments where these graduates will want to work – Silicon Valley in the USA, for instance, or the skibelt near the French Alps where employees have plenty of leisure opportunities.

However, outside of the USA and the European Union, most of the countries with major high-tech industries are in eastern Asia (graph **C**). These countries have many of the location factors listed in diagram **B**. Special centres called science and research parks have grown up around the world to house these new industries.

A High-tech products are small and easy to transport

> **Topic link**
>
> More information on the way all kinds of manufacturing industries have environmental risks and benefits can be found in Topic 3.7 pages 220–226.

B Influences on the location of high-tech industries

C Global distribution of high-tech industries

178 Economic development

Science parks

Centres where many high-tech companies are found together are often called science parks. Location factors for science parks include:

- close links with universities because of the need to employ technical graduates and scientists
- large amounts of capital to buy land and build specialist laboratories and offices – often this comes from multinational companies and governments
- excellent global connections through international airports
- super-fast internet connections and reliable infrastructure
- low-density building with tree-lined streets and landscaped gardens to create a pleasant working environment.

Businesses found on these sites include those specialising in biotechnology, medical research and telecommunications.

Science parks were originally created in the USA, and most are still located in MEDCs and NICs. The UK, Canada and Singapore all have large numbers, and they are increasing in China, Brazil and India. More wealthy LEDCs are also starting to build science parks. They cost a lot of money to start up but are bringing in huge amounts of money as the quaternary industries located in them start to take off.

D Biopolis in Singapore

Fantastic fact

Sub-Saharan Africa's first science park – The Innovation Hub – has been built in Pretoria, South Africa.

Biopolis, Singapore

Biopolis is an international research and development centre in Singapore (photo **D**). It is close to the National University of Singapore, Singapore Polytechnic, the Institute of Technical Education, the National University Hospital, and to other major scientific organisations.

There are continuing developments to bring new industries to Biopolis. To attract qualified professionals, facilities include tree-lined streets and parks, shops, cafés, restaurants and a childcare centre. Nearby is luxurious accommodation with serviced apartments, hotels and private houses.

E Hsinchu Science and Industrial Park, Taiwan

Hsinchu Science Park, Taiwan

More than 400 high-tech companies have found a home at Hsinchu in Taiwan, including the world's top two manufacturers of semiconductors (a vital part of any computer). National Chiao Tung University and National Tsing Hua University are found next door and there is even a science-themed amusement park to bring in the visitors.

The park has strictly monitored air quality, following earlier complaints from the public and the workers, and it now prides itself on being very environmentally friendly.

Now Investigate

1. Why are some industries known as 'footloose'? Give some examples of footloose industries.

2. Using graph **C**, describe the global distribution of science parks.

3. Answer *either* (a) *or* (b):

    a) If you live near to a science park or have one in your country, what do you think were the location factors behind it being built?

    b) If you live in a country without a science park, what could the government do to enable one to be built?

Section 3 . Topic 4

Tourism

Learning objectives:
- describe and explain the growth of tourism in relation to the main attractions of the physical and human landscape
- evaluate the benefits and disadvantages of tourism to receiving areas
- demonstrate an understanding that careful management of tourism is required in order for it to be sustainable

Where do tourists go on holiday?

Your local leisure industry

A growing number of people around the world, like Jean-Claude (photos **A**), are lucky enough to have the time and money to go on holiday. Where would you like to go? Are there lots of wonderful places waiting to be explored in your own country? Or would you prefer to travel greater distances and visit other nations? Many countries, especially those where there is no important manufacturing industry, are keen to develop tourism as a way of bringing in money. There are both advantages and disadvantages to this – for local people and for their environment.

> *Bonjour mes amis. My name is Jean-Claude Benoix. I'm very lucky to live in France. My parents both have good jobs and they are given lots of time off to spend with me and my sister.*
>
> *We love to go on holiday – usually at least twice a year. We like to spend one of the holidays taking a camper van and exploring France. It's such a great country to visit and my parents think it's important we learn a bit about its history and culture.*
>
> *For our other holiday we get on a plane and head somewhere more exotic. My sister always wants to find a beach she can lie around on and I'm keen on finding out about local wildlife. Sometimes we go to French-speaking countries but we're all working to improve our English so that we have more choice.*

A Jean-Claude Benoix

Section 3.4: Tourism   181

The growth of global tourism

During the last 50 years foreign travel has become available to a lot more people. In that time the numbers of tourists travelling around the world has increased rapidly. Different parts of the world have seen this growth take place at different rates (graph **B**).

This relatively recent growth in tourism has taken place for a number of reasons:

- Rapid air travel has taken over from slow sea journeys.
- The development of more efficient planes means that air travel is cheaper.
- Transport facilities have improved – cars work better and run on much better roads, motorways and express routes, so journey times have been cut dramatically.
- In many countries wealth has increased so people have more money to spend on luxuries (this is known as disposable income).
- As people have become richer and enjoy a better quality of life, they have demanded more paid holiday-time.
- The internet, advertising, and television holiday programmes have brought wider knowledge of (and a desire to visit) other countries.
- People cope with the stresses of modern life by going on holiday.

The global tourism industry has grown to take advantage of these opportunities. It is now possible to take a holiday for any kind of interest, from sports vacations to health tourism (figure **C**).

The changing tourist

For many years, almost all the world's tourists came from Europe and the USA. This situation is now changing. As NICs and LEDCs get richer, more people from these countries can afford to go on holiday. China may eventually take over from Finland as the world's most well-travelled nation. This is a huge potential market to be developed.

> **Fantastic fact**
>
> The world's most visited tourist attraction is the Las Vegas Strip – 40 million people come to see it every year.

B The growth of global tourism, 1950–2020

> **Examples of speciality tours include:**
>
> - culture tourism to historic Inca sites in the Andes
> - ecotourism, experiencing the natural environment in Belize and Costa Rica
> - volcano-watching tours in Montserrat
> - sports tourism for the FIFA World Cup, the summer and winter Olympic Games and other major sporting events
> - wilderness tours to Antarctica
> - mountain climbing tours in the Himalayas
> - active adventure tourism, including bungee jumping and rafting, in New Zealand
> - bird-watching tours to the Amazon rainforest in Brazil.

C Speciality tourism

Economic development

While many Chinese tourists visit nearby countries such as Thailand and South Korea, some are travelling much further afield to major world cities including Paris, Rome and London.

Now Investigate

1. Jean-Claude and his family would like to take a holiday in your country. Plan a week's visit for them, taking in the major sites they may want to visit. Don't just include the well-travelled routes and most popular attractions – find them something different to do as well. Explain why you have chosen these different places.

2. Study graph **B**.
   a) Describe the general growth of global tourism shown in the graph.
   b) Which regions have shown the most and the least growth over the last 50 years?
   c) Which regions are predicted to have the most growth in the future?

3. What are the main reasons for the growth in global tourism over the last 50 years?

4. Using an atlas, find a country you would like to visit. Prepare a factfile giving details such as how to get there, the currency you will need, and what you plan to do when you arrive. You may need to use the internet to help find the information.

The importance of global tourism

Most countries want to develop their tourist industry. Visitors can bring huge amounts of money into the economy. Worldwide, tourism as an industry was worth US$7.6 trillion in 2016 and supported 292 million jobs. In LEDCs, there is the added benefit that the money coming in may be American dollars. This **currency** keeps its value better than those used in only one or two countries.

Tourism also brings local employment opportunities. Some jobs may be seasonal, for example available only in the summer, but many are all year round. The workers earn money and spend it in their local community, so there are knock-on benefits for shopkeepers and other local business people. This is known as the **multiplier effect**.

For a tourist industry, and the country where it is operating, to be a success, it also needs good **infrastructure**. Governments improve roads, for instance, to allow tourists to travel around easily. Facilities such as swimming pools or ski centres may be built and these can be used by local people as well as visitors. There are other cultural and environmental benefits to come from tourism:

- Many tourists visit cultural attractions such as castles and palaces – without these visitors there may not be the money available to keep them in good condition.

Section 3.4: Tourism 183

- Some visitors want to enjoy beautiful scenery. This means the environment has to be protected from development.
- Tourists from different countries brings increased contact between different cultures. This helps global understanding between people.

The world's top tourist destinations are almost all MEDCs. Table **A** shows that France leads the way with over 80 million visitors a year. The table also shows that, despite this, the USA earns more than four times as much as France in tourist revenue.

Country	International tourist arrivals (millions)		International tourism receipts (US$ billion)
France	84.5	16.6	45.9
USA	77.5	15.2	204.5
Spain	68.2	13.4	56.5
China	56.9	11.2	114.1
Italy	50.7	9.9	39.4
Turkey	39.5	7.7	26.6
Germany	35.0	6.9	36.9
UK	34.4	6.7	45.5
Mexico	32.1	6.2	17.7
Russia	31.3	6.1	8.4

Source: United Nations World Tourism Organisation

A *The world's top tourist destinations*

CASE STUDY: Tourism in an MEDC: France

People visit France to enjoy the many famous historic attractions and the natural landscape:

- Beach holidays in Normandy and on the French Riviera,
- Famous castles such as those at Mont St Michel and Vincennes,
- Almost 40 000 historic monuments including the Arc de Triomphe,
- Dramatic scenery of the Loire and Ardeche Valleys,
- The 3900 museums, such as the Louvre and Cité de l'Automobile, that attract tens of millions of visitors each year,
- Skiing in the Alps in winter, mountain biking and walking in the summer,
- World-famous French vineyards in regions like Champagne and Bordeaux,
- Food with a great worldwide reputation.

Economic development

3.4

France has a very positive image worldwide. Almost 7 million people visit the Eiffel Tower in Paris alone every year (photo **B**). There are 1.2 million people directly employed in tourism in France with a contribution of 9.1 per cent of the national economy. However, not everyone is happy with the development of the tourist industry in France, as shown in figure **C**.

There is increasing competition from other countries – especially from other European nations like Croatia, Slovenia and Estonia. The challenge for the French tourism industry now is to come up with new ideas to make sure the visitors keep coming.

'Once a year, sometimes more, we like to take the caravan and explore our own country. There is so much to see. It's easy to see why we are the world's top spot for visitors.'

Jean-Claude Benoix

B *The Eiffel Tower*

> It's great in the summer when the tourists are here but everything shuts down in the winter – there's nothing for young people to do.

> The people around Paris get lots of money from tourism but here in the countryside we get no visitors at all. We're poor and there's no development unless it's in the areas people want to visit.

> All these people coming by air – it's ridiculous. What on earth is it doing to climate change?

> These tourists really annoy me. They drive along so slowly I'm always late getting to and from work.

> The visitors are so rude. They don't speak French and then get angry with us when we don't understand them – how can that be right?

C *French views on tourism*

Fantastic fact

France has 365 different types of cheese!

Section 3.4: Tourism

> **Now Investigate**

1 There will probably be some kind of tourist industry in your local area.

   a) Make a list of all the jobs you can think of that may be associated with tourism where you live.

   b) Draw a bar graph showing the information in table **A**. Describe the relationship between visitor numbers and tourist revenues.

2 Use the resources on these pages to briefly explain the benefits the tourist industry brings to France.

3 What are the main disadvantages of tourism outlined by the people in figure **C**? Can you think of any other problems the industry may cause?

4 Imagine you represent the French Tourist Board. What can you do to keep visitors coming to France? Think of a memorable slogan to launch a new campaign to advertise the country to overseas visitors.

Tourism in LEDCs

While many MEDCs gain a lot of money from tourism, they are not dependent on the industry. The same may not be the case for a number of LEDCs. Table **A** shows that the national economies of some countries rely strongly on tourism.

LEDCs are often seen as exotic tourist destinations. Peru and Bolivia have mystical Inca ruins which many people are very keen to see. Southern and eastern Africa have rare and dangerous animals. The Pacific islands have miles of beautiful sunny beaches. All these places can use their attractions to bring in money from visitors – but there is a lot of competition. A country can spend a huge amount of money developing tourist facilities, only to find that somewhere else has become more popular. Popular destinations, such as Kenya, can go out of (and come back into) fashion very quickly indeed.

Diagram **B** shows some of the benefits and disadvantages that LEDCs get from tourism. Many of these also apply to MEDCs.

> **Topic link**
>
> There are also environmental risks and benefits associated with tourism. These are discussed later on in Topic 3.7 pages 227–234.

Country	Percentage
Maldives	40.9
British Virgin Islands	34.4
Aruba	28.6
Macau	27.3
Former Netherlands Antilles	23.3
Seychelles	22.0
Bahamas	19.8
Anguilla	19.2
Vanuatu	17.2
Cape Verde	17.2

A *Income from tourism as a percentage of the national economy 2016*

3.4

Tourism in LEDCs

Benefits:
- Better quality of life for local people
- A positive international image may lead to investment from foreign companies
- Encourages people to get an education and set up their own businesses
- Local people may take more care in protecting the environment that tourists come to see
- Improvements in local services and infrastructure paid for by tourism
- More tax money for governments to spend on developing health and education
- The multiplier effects means benefits for the local economy
- Lots of different types of employment

Disadvantages:
- Pollution and waste may increase from tourist developments (en)
- Incomes are low, jobs may be seasonal and working conditions poor (ec)
- Tourist developments may be owned by foreign companies so profits are taken overseas (ec)
- Tourist developments use land that could be used for building homes or producing food (en)
- The culture of a country may become increasingly 'westernised' (c)
- Increased crime rates (theft and even murder) as people become jealous of richer tourists (c)
- Roads, ports and other facilities may be damaged by increased tourist use (env)
- Tourist developments (hotels etc.) may use scarce resources, e.g. electricity, water (env)
- Tourists may not respect local customs, dress inappropriately and take insensitive photographs

B *The benefits and disadvantages of tourism for LEDCs*

CASE STUDY — Kenya

Kenya was one of the first African countries to develop its tourist industry. From the 1930s onwards people came for big game hunting and on safari holidays, attracted by the warm and comfortable climate (figure **F**). After independence from the United Kingdom in 1963, tourism was seen as one of the main ways to improve Kenya's economy. The coast was developed around resorts like Mombasa, and National Parks established to protect animals for tourists (figure **C**). Kenya became Africa's number one tourist destination.

Terrorist attacks in the capital Nairobi in 1998 changed that. Western tourists now felt that Tanzania, Namibia and South Africa were safer places to visit. Riots followed elections in Kenya in 2007. This led to a 36 per cent drop in tourist numbers and £500 million of lost revenue.

> 'For our big holiday last year we went on safari to Kenya. It was amazing seeing all the animals you normally only see on the television. At the end we spent a few days relaxing and snorkelling on the beach. It was one of the best holidays ever.'
>
> Jean-Claude Benoix

Section 3.4: Tourism

With more stability in the past few years, visitors have started to return to Kenya. There has been a 20 per cent increase in numbers year-on-year leading to 2.1 million visitors adding US$5.4 billion to the economy in 2015 (and making it the country's biggest foreign exchange earner). This recovery is good news for the quarter of a million people directly employed in tourism and for all the associated industries, including farming and transport companies, that provide services to the tourist industry.

The management of tourism in Kenya has proved highly problematic for successive governments. Tourists have a huge number of countries they can visit, all offering similar experiences and it is up to entrepreneurs and businessmen to offer something different (see photos **D** and **E**). The government can help by providing decent infrastructure, including roads and airports, to help tourists get around and by implementing laws which will protect the environment that tourists come to visit. When riots or terrorist activities occur, all the hard work can be undone overnight and, as with Kenya, it can take many years to restore public trust.

C *National Parks of Kenya (dark green)*

D *Safari holidays are very popular in Kenya*

E *The coastal resort of Mombasa*

F *Climate graph for Mombasa*

Now Investigate

1. Describe the climate of Mombasa, referring to graph **F**.

2. Outline the advantages and disadvantages to a LEDC of developing a tourist industry. Explain why it still makes a lot of sense for such development to take place.

3. Explain why Kenya has become so popular with tourists, especially those from MEDCs like Jean-Claude and his family from France.

188 Economic development

Section 3 . Topic 5

Energy

Learning objectives:
- describe the importance of non-renewable fossil fuels, renewable energy supplies, nuclear power and fuelwood; globally and in different countries at different levels of development
- evaluate the benefits and disadvantages of nuclear power and renewable energy sources

Where does our energy come from?

Your local energy sources

Energy sources are what give you the power for most of the things you use on a daily basis. Without these sources of energy you would not have television, cell phones, computers, hot water, electricity or gas to cook with. Most energy sources originally come from the sun. Coal, oil and natural gas (which give us 87 per cent of the total energy used worldwide) come from solar energy which has been captured and stored over a very long time. They are being used up very quickly. The amount of energy people use around the world is not the same (figure **A**). In your country the **levels of consumption** (how much energy you use) may be pretty low. In other places power is being used up at an incredibly high rate – for many different purposes.

Energy use around the world

We use a lot of energy but then oil is very cheap here. Today we went to the indoor ski centre – it's a strange sight to see in the desert but we're very proud of it.

It's hot so the air conditioning is on and the sprinklers are working to keep the flowers growing in the garden. I can get cold drinks from the chiller in the fridge or turn on the fans if it gets too uncomfortable.

Ali, Dubai

We live in a fairly poor part of a rich country. We don't have a lot of money and our energy supply is really expensive. We have a gas stove for cooking and everything else runs on electricity. My father has a small moped to get around on and, apart from that, the television is the only other major user of energy that we have.

Birgit, Germany

We've been very lucky that my father's business has done well. We can afford loads of things he couldn't when he was a boy. Now we have a car, television and computer games and music players and a really nicely equipped kitchen. My mother loves the dishwasher – she says it has made things so much easier.

Mum says we need the big car to get all the sports equipment in for my tennis and my brother's football. At home we've got it all – music players, PCs, tea makers and rice boilers and all sorts. I know it's bad, it uses so much electricity but I don't know what I'd do without it all.

Mei Lin, China

Imran, Pakistan

A

Global energy consumption

Over the last couple of hundred years, the amount of energy used around the world has increased massively (graph **B**). This is partly to do with the increase in global population but it is not the full story. The amount of energy we use per person has also increased greatly as we buy and use more gadgets such as mobile phones and music devices.

Most of this power comes from **fossil fuels** which cannot be replaced (figure **C**). They are said to be **non-renewable**. However, the use of renewable power is on the increase as well. This includes types of energy such as wind, water and tidal power that can be used over and over again without running out.

*1 exajoule = approx. 25 million tonnes of oil

B Global energy consumption, 1800–2013

Energy source	Percentage
Oil	33
Natural gas	24
Coal	30
Nuclear	4
Hydro	7

Note: small amounts of energy are also generated from wind, wave, solar and other sources

C Energy sources as a percentage of the global total

Now Investigate

1. Read through the quotes from the different young people around the world.
   a) Who do you think uses the most energy?
   b) Draw a table with two columns marked NECESSARY and UNNECESSARY. Read through all the items used by the young people quoted and write them down under the column you think is correct.

2. Take a look at your own life.
   a) Complete an energy audit, listing all the things you use on a daily basis that require some kind of energy source.
   b) How many of them would you be able to live without?

3. Refer to graph **B**.
   a) Which fuels have seen the greatest increase in consumption?

Topic link

The reasons for the increase in global population, and some of the effects this is having on our world, are covered in Section 1.

Skills link

Ways of presenting geographical data include line graphs and data tables like the ones shown here. You need to know how to interpret line graphs and use the information in tables to produce your own graphs. Go to Topic 4.3 pages 251–255 to find out more about drawing and interpreting line graphs and pie graphs. You may want to check this information before you answer the questions to the left.

190 Economic development

b) In which decades have the biggest changes taken place?

c) Are there any fuels whose use has remained fairly constant over the last 200 years?

4 Using the information in table **C**, construct a pie graph showing the different energy sources as a percentage of the global total.

Fossil fuels – making the world work

An estimated 88 per cent of energy came from fossil fuels in 2016 – oil, coal and natural gas. These resources take many millions of years to form but are being used up at an incredibly fast rate. Already it seems we may be halfway through the available resources of fossil fuels and we have only been using them in any significant quantities for about the last two hundred years.

New coal and oil fields are being discovered all the time but they are getting harder and more expensive to find. There are barely enough to keep up with the huge and growing demands from MEDCs. More recently, the growing populations and industry in China and India are leading to an even greater demand for power.

China produced 47 per cent of the global total of coal in 2016. It uses almost all of this in its power stations and factories. In other countries, Saudi Arabia mines 10 per cent of the global total of oil but the vast majority is sold for export. In the end, the different ways the fuel is used has benefits for both of the countries involved (see page 192).

A The increase in world crude oil prices, 1998–2016

Despite the big drop in prices with the world recession in 2009 and the further drop in 2015, the cost of oil almost constantly grows upwards, but there is little drop in demand.

As nearly everything in the world is transported using oil, the price of goods rises as well.

With growing demand from Brazil, Russia, India and China as they develop their manufacturing industry, there is little sign of significant drops in the price of oil in the future.

B Global movements and locations of fossil fuels

Skills link

Map **B** is another kind of a world distribution map that you may be asked to interpret. More details can be found in Topic 4.2 pages 245–250.

Section 3.5: Energy

- If a country can produce its own fuel it will improve its energy security. This means it does not have to depend on expensive imports, or face the threat that supplies from other countries could be cut off.
- If a country can export fuel it will bring in a lot of money for the economy. Oil gains the most money, and its price is increasing almost all the time (graph A). Coal and natural gas, while more readily available, still bring in lots of export money. The location and movement of fossil fuels around the globe are shown in map B.

CASE STUDY

Coal in China

China's huge economic growth over the past few years has been built on coal. It provides around 80 per cent of all the electricity in the country – twice the global average. It is often said that China builds one new coal-fired power station each week, but nobody knows the real number.

Coal provides power to the factories producing all the goods China sells overseas. It also powers the energy-hungry electrical goods that people in the country are buying as they become more wealthy. Televisions, PCs, music players, cookers, dishwashers and washing machines are all becoming more popular in Chinese homes.

As the headlines in texts C show, these advances may not be coming without some cost to China.

More Miner Deaths Underground

Rescuers are battling against time to rescue 26 miners trapped by a deadly underground explosion in China's main mining area. Gas exploded causing the release of tonnes of coal dust and the collapse of some of the mine's walls. Relatives are gathering for news as the clock ticks by.

China's mining industry is the deadliest in the world with 2600 deaths in 2009 alone. Thousands of illegal pits have been closed down but, while demand is high, miners will always work to make some money despite the dangers.

PUTTING OUT THE FIRE

China's Inner Mongolia region today announced plans to put out some of the long-burning coal seam fires that are destroying large reserves underground. Some of the fires, which start all of a sudden when gas or coal dust gets too hot, have been burning for almost 50 years.

The economic effect of the coal seam fires is not well understood but it is thought that millions of tonnes of coal are burning needlessly every year. They can cause mines to collapse and destroy infrastructure above ground. Being underground, the fires are very difficult and expensive to put out.

A LOCAL AND GLOBAL PROBLEM

Concerns have been expressed that China's concentration on burning fossil fuels is adding to the global problem of climate change. The carbon dioxide produced could be having a huge effect in changing the global temperature.

There are other concerns for people in China. Acid rain, caused by the pollutants from coal-fired power stations, is falling on agricultural land, killing crops and leaving the ground unsuitable for farming. This is a growing problem in a country that needs to feed an increasing population.

C *The human and environmental cost of coal in China*

3.5

> **Now Investigate**

1 Use map **B** to:
   a) describe where the world's fossil fuels are found
   b) describe how they are transported around the planet.

2 Why is it important for governments to ensure that their countries have an adequate supply of energy? What kinds of problems do you think countries will face if they do not have an adequate supply?

3 a) 'China's economic growth has been built on coal.' Do you agree with this statement? Give reasons for your answer.
   b) What are some of the problems associated with China's coal industry?
   c) Do the benefits of the use of coal outweigh the disadvantages for the country?

4 Think about your own country:
   a) What kind of fossil fuels are used nationwide?
   b) Why do some people have concerns about the environmental effects of using these fuels?

The fuelwood crisis

Photo **A** shows a typical scene in some areas of the world – it is especially common in the parts of Africa south of the Sahara Desert. What do you think is happening here? Why have the trees been cut down?

Part of the answer is shown in photo **B**. In many parts of the world, people who have little money do not use fossil fuels. They are not connected to a national electricity grid and, even if there are supplies available, many cannot afford to use electricity. However, they still need fuel for cooking and have to rely on what they can find to burn to make a fire. This is usually either precious fuelwood or animal dung.

An estimated 2.4 billion people use fuelwood for cooking and heating. Much of this is from scrub land and dead wood lying on the ground. As populations have increased there has been more deforestation as living trees are cut down and burnt. This has a number of serious side-effects:

- Removing trees leaves soils open to erosion by wind and water – the soil may be removed over a large area with knock-on effects as farmers can no longer grow crops.

- As trees are removed, desertification is the result and desert areas start to grow – this is a particular problem on the edges of the Sahara Desert.

- As wood becomes more scarce, people have to travel further to find it. In some areas it is not unusual for people to take a whole day to find fuelwood and carry it home.

A Deforestation for fuelwood use

B Collecting fuelwood in Africa

Section 3.5: Energy   193

C Global consumption of fuelwood

D Percentage of total fuel provided by wood in some African countries

- There are personal safety issues in this activity for women, who are usually the ones who collect the firewood.
- In urban areas people may have to buy fuelwood for cooking. As supplies get harder to find the price rises, taking more out of already small family incomes.

Added to these problems is the fact that cooking with fuelwood on open fires in enclosed spaces causes breathing difficulties and respiratory disease, especially for the millions of women who do the work in LEDCs. Despite all of this, the use of fuelwood remains high, especially in countries with large populations (diagram **C**). Graph **D** shows that, in many African countries, almost all the power a family uses comes from burning wood.

Forest destruction for fuelwood in West Bengal, India

Deforestation in the northern part of West Bengal state has, over the past few years, become a very serious problem. The area has attracted immigrants for a number of different reasons. Many have come to work on the tea plantations of Jalpaiguri. Others have been forced from surrounding countries – Bangladesh, Nepal and Bhutan – because of conflict, forced migration and natural disasters.

Cutting down the forests and selling the wood is an easy way for the migrants to make money. They also need it for their own cooking. Many local people, both men and women, are finding much of their time taken up collecting wood when that time would be better used in making money for their families.

More than 70 per cent of the wood taken is from state-owned forests. Armed security guards have had little effect in cutting down the amount taken – estimated to be 72 000 tonnes a week. The fuelwood business is the main source of income in 10 per cent of households in the region (figure **F** on page 195).

E West Bengal (in dark green), India

194   Economic development

3.5

We came here from Bangladesh after we lost our rice farm in the flood. Picking up and selling the wood was an easy way to make money.

I know it's illegal but I have no choice – we have a lot of mouths to feed. Things are more difficult now. I have to travel further and chop down the trees far away from home. Sometimes there are guards. If they catch me I'll be fined – or worse.

I've also noticed other things. The weather is changing and the soils are bare. There's less farming as the soil is not so fertile. Surely this can't be because of what we're doing to the forests?

F *Rashid – a fuelwood collector*

Now Investigate

1 Using diagrams **C** and **D**, and referring to specific countries, describe:
  a) the pattern of global consumption of fuelwood
  b) the distribution of the use of fuelwood in Africa.

2 a) Do you, or people you know, use fuelwood for cooking?
  b) If so, try to find out where it comes from and plot the information on a map of your local area.
  If not, plot the forested areas closest to you which could most easily be used as a source of fuelwood.

3 a) What are the main reasons for deforestation in state forests in northwest Bengal?
  b) Describe some of the effects that may result from the trees being cut down.

4 Read through Rashid's story (figure **F**).
  a) Explain why he feels forced into selling fuelwood when he knows it is wrong.
  b) What do you think will happen if he stops?
  c) What would you do in his situation?

Renewable energies

Time is running out for fossil fuels. Despite our dependence on them they will not last for ever (although some of them may last hundreds more years). A more important concern may be whether we can continue to use them knowing the damage they may be doing to the planet by causing climate change.

To solve these problems, many countries are turning to **renewable energies**. These are **sustainable** and can be used continuously without running out. 22 per cent of global power is currently provided by renewable energy but this is increasing all the time. Some countries want to develop their use of renewable energy because it will:

- help reduce their reliance on expensive fossil fuels
- provide energy security

Hydro-electric 54% Solar 15% Wind 24% Geothermal 1% Power from plants (including biogas) 6%

A *Different renewable energies as a percentage of the global total*

Section 3.5: Energy **195**

- ease the world's energy crisis brought on by increasing demand for resources that are running out.

Many countries are already improving their technology so that they can develop alternative energy sources.

The main types of renewable energy currently available are shown in graph **A**. Benefits and disadvantages are shown in table **B**.

Geothermal

Countries with active volcanoes can use energy from the heated rocks and molten magma under the earth's surface. Hot springs and naturally hot sources of water below ground can also be used to provide power. In Iceland **geothermal** power stations produce around a quarter of the country's electricity and almost 90 per cent of heating and hot water in buildings.

C How geothermal power works

Benefits	Disadvantages
Use almost limitless natural resources, e.g. wind, water, sun.	Often require large-scale power stations that are expensive to build, e.g. wind farms, geothermal plants, solar power stations.
Can use waste products, e.g. biogas.	May need to be set up in difficult environments, e.g. solar in the desert.
Cheap to run after initial set-up costs.	Need major infrastructural development, e.g. dams for hydro-electric power.
Can sometimes be set up on a small scale, e.g. solar panels or small wind turbines on individual houses.	Natural resources (e.g. solar power or wind) may not always be available depending on weather conditions.
Mainly produce little or no pollution after initial set-up.	Can have negative environmental consequences, e.g. silting of rivers dammed for HEP.
Help to fight global climate change by reducing dependence on fossil fuels.	Can have negative effects on people, e.g. flooding of villages to create reservoirs for HEP.

B Advantages and disadvantages of renewable energy sources

Wind

Lines of wind turbines (photo **D**), known as 'wind farms', are becoming increasingly popular as an alternative source of power. These can be on land or offshore (in the sea, where turbines can be 50 metres high) but need a good supply of wind and flat areas to build on. Wind farms are expensive to build but cheap and safe to operate and almost completely pollution-free.

Running water

Water, either as waves, tides or in rivers, is a very successful form of renewable energy. The UK is one country currently

D An offshore wind farm

196 Economic development

experimenting with different forms of wave power. France has tidal barrages (dams) across the mouths of some of its big rivers (including the world's second biggest across the Rance estuary). The most widely used form of water power, however, is in hydro-electric plants across large or fast-flowing rivers (photo **E**).

Solar

As much of the power we use has the sun as its original source it makes sense to harness the energy directly. **Solar** panels convert the heat into electricity. In many countries this is done on a small scale on individual houses. In some, such as Spain, huge lines of solar panels (photo **F**) have been set up and, given perfect conditions of cloudless skies, provide good quantities of electricity.

Biogas

Rotting fruit, vegetables, food and animal waste give off methane which can be burnt as **biogas**. There have been many successful initiatives to introduce this kind of power on a small scale in homes in LEDCs (photo **G**). However, many European countries are also investigating ways of using the technology on a larger scale by connecting biogas plants into natural gas pipelines.

E A hydro-electric power plant

Topic link

More details on the global use of hydro-electric power can be found on pages 202–203.

F A solar farm in Spain

Fantastic fact

One UK farmer said about biogas: 'The dung from four cows can produce enough energy to heat and light a house for a year'.

G A home-based biogas plant in India

Now Investigate

1. Describe the worldwide use of renewable energy as shown in graph **A**.

2. What are the advantages of using renewable energy?

3. Which of the forms of renewable energy described here do you think seems to be most environmentally friendly? Explain your answer.

4. Which forms of renewable energy would be suitable in your local area and in your country as a whole? Explain why they would be suitable.

Section 3.5: Energy

How do we generate electricity?

Your power from a plug

Many of the energy sources described in Topic 3.5 are used to make electricity. Much of the energy you use every day will have been produced in this way. Every time you plug something into a socket or turn on the light, they work because there is a power station somewhere turning energy sources into electricity. A lot of this will be from coal, oil or gas – the fossil fuels – but, increasingly, other energy sources are being used. Nuclear and hydro-electric power are two of the biggest generators of electricity in the world (diagram **A**).

Who uses the most electricity?

Map **B** shows the biggest global consumers of electricity. The USA, with large amounts of industry and a population that likes to buy the most up-to-date electrical equipment, uses more than anybody else. The biggest consumers are almost all MEDCs but an increasing number of the richer and more industrial LEDCs are now using a lot of electricity.

A Worldwide generation of electricity by type of fuel, 2010

- Other 7%
- Oil 5%
- Nuclear 11%
- Hydro 17%
- Coal 38%
- Gas 22%

B Worldwide electricity consumption

Million Kilowatt hours per year
- Under 10 000
- 10 000–50 000
- 50 000–200 000
- 200 000–1 million
- Over 1 million
- no data

Skills link

Map **B** is an example of another type of distribution map that you may need to analyse. You should know where some of the key countries are located so that you can refer to them if you are asked to do so. Turn to Topic 4.2 pages 247–250 to find out what you need to know when describing this type of map, and then answer the questions on page 199.

How is electricity produced?

Most power stations convert energy sources into electricity using turbines. These turbines usually have blades which are forced to turn very fast and this produces the electricity. Making the blades turn can be done in a number of ways:

- Nuclear reactions, burning fossil fuels and geothermal power all produce steam which is used to turn the turbines.

Economic development

3.5

- Hydro-electric and tidal power use running water to turn the blades.
- Large wind-powered turbines are also used in many windy parts of the world.

Since the late 19th century, most energy has come from fossil fuel power stations. These are also known as thermal power stations because they use the heat from burning the oil, gas or coal to produce steam. The three different types of power stations are found in quite different areas.

Coal-fired power stations

Coal is a heavy, bulky raw material, so it is expensive to transport. Power stations (photo **C**) are often found close to the mines and coalfields where the coal comes from. They are also often near the major towns, cities and industrial areas that use the power. When the coalfields start to run out, railways may be built to transport coal from coastal ports to keep the power stations running.

C A coal-fired power station

Oil-fired power stations

Oil-fired power stations (photo **D**) are often built on the coast where oil pipelines bring the liquid ashore or where tankers can bring it from other countries. The coastal estuaries where they are built need to be deep enough to allow the huge oil tankers to come in to port. Regulations in some countries mean that oil-fired power stations have to be built away from population centres, because of the pollution risk and other safety issues.

D A coastal oil-fired power station

Gas-fired power stations

Natural gas is often found under the sea in the same place as oil and is piped ashore in a similar way. Some countries, such as Russia, also have large amounts of onshore gas. This still has to be transported in huge networks of pipes (photo **E**) to the power stations where it is turned into electricity.

Now Investigate

1. Describe the worldwide consumption of electricity as shown on map **B**.
2. Can you find your own country on the map? How does its consumption of electricity compare with that in the rest of the world?
3. Describe, in basic terms, how electricity is produced.
4. Are there any thermal power stations in your country? Find out where they are and write down the important factors influencing their location.

E A natural gas pipeline

Fantastic fact

Iceland uses more electricity per person than any other country in the world – but most of it comes from renewable energy produced by geothermal and water sources.

Section 3.5: Energy

Where to put a nuclear power station?

Most power stations (or plants) producing electricity are very big. One of their requirements is a large area of flat land to build on. As we have seen in the previous section, other factors such as nearness to towns and cities and access to transport links are also important. The location factors for the production of electricity using nuclear power are even more important.

Power from the atom

Nuclear power uses uranium as its raw material. Although this is not a renewable source, much less fuel is needed compared to fossil fuels such as coal or oil. Countries including the USA, France, Japan, Russia and Germany use uranium to produce a lot of their power. However, the waste material from this process is very dangerous and has to be disposed of as safely as possible. This often means burying it deep inside the earth or under the ocean, or re-processing it from fuel that has already been used. Despite this problem, some countries rely heavily on uranium to meet their demand for electricity (table **A**).

France	74.8
Belgium	53.0
Ukraine	46.2
Switzerland	35.9
Czechia	35.3
Finland	32.6
South Korea	30.4
Canada	21.0
Spain	20.5
USA	19.0

A Nuclear power as a percentage of a country's total energy production

Choosing a location for a nuclear power station

What are the factors that influence the location of a nuclear power station? Most are found in MEDCs because the technology needed to develop them is expensive. The main users have been countries that do not have their own supply of fossil fuels (like Japan) or those where energy needs are far greater than other resources can meet (such as the UK and France). Nuclear power plants also need:

- a nearby water supply for cooling the nuclear **reactor** – most are located either next to the coast or beside large lakes
- flat, cheap land – nuclear power stations are quite large and need the space for building. In the UK, for example, most are found on land reclaimed from the sea.

Nuclear power stations are almost always found well away from large towns and cities. Since the 1950s there have been major concerns over the safety of nuclear power and the damage that potential leaks could cause. There have, however, been relatively few incidents of this kind around the world. The meltdown of the reactor at Chernobyl in Ukraine in 1986 caused widespread panic in many affected countries (figure **B**). More recently, in March 2011, there were concerns about the effects the earthquake and tsunami would have on the Fukushima power plant in Japan.

> **Skills link**
>
> Data tables like the one in table **A** can be easily converted into a more visual presentation, such as a graph or chart. To find out more about how to do this go to Topic 4.3 pages 251–255.

> **Topic link**
>
> Find out more about the nuclear power plant meltdown at Daiichi near Fukushima in the Earthquakes section, Topic 2.1 pages 78–79.

Economic development

3.5

Early morning on 26 April 1986: one of the world's worst nuclear disasters took place when a reactor exploded at the Chernobyl nuclear power plant.

Details were slow to emerge from communist Russia but increased radiation levels were found in nearly every other country in the northern hemisphere. Europe was particularly badly affected (see map).

Around 350 000 people were evacuated from the surrounding area.

Contamination is still a problem. Scientists are also unsure about the final number of people who will have died as a result of the accident – the figure is probably around 9000.

Increased radiation across Europe, 3 May 1986

Dose - multiples of normal rate
- No detecable rise
- 10^{-2} - 1
- 1 - 5
- 5 - 10
- 10 - 20
- 20 - 40
- 40 - 100
- 100+

B *Disaster at Chernobyl, 1986*

Despite the concerns over nuclear power, it has been put forward as a relatively clean, safe technology and much better for the environment than polluting fossil fuels. The benefits and disadvantages of nuclear power are shown in table **D**.

C *A nuclear power station*

Benefits	Disadvantages
• The amount of raw material needed is very small compared with other fuels such as coal or oil.	• Many people still have serious concerns over the safety of nuclear technology.
• It contributes relatively little to acid rain, global warming and climate change.	• There is the potential for disastrous accidents to take place. Sometimes, as with the case of the Japanese tsunami, these accidents can be the result of natural disasters.
• There is a lot of research being carried out to address fears over safety.	• People living near to nuclear power plants may suffer from poor health.
• It receives support from many governments around the world.	• Nuclear waste is difficult and expensive to dispose of and can be dangerous for many years.
• Many measures are taken to make sure it is as safe as possible.	• Nuclear power plants are very expensive to build.
• It allows countries to reduce their dependence on fossil fuels and to cut imports of these resources.	• Nuclear power plants are very expensive to close down when they are no longer used.

D *Some benefits and disadvantages of nuclear power*

Section 3.5: Energy

> **Now Investigate**

1. Construct a bar chart using the information in table **A**.
2. Using an atlas, describe the distribution of the countries that rely most on nuclear power.
3. What are the main location factors for a nuclear power station?
4. Where are (or where would be) the best places to locate nuclear power plants in your country? Use maps (if possible) to find at least three suitable locations and give reasons why they are suitable.
5. After reading the information on these pages, do you think nuclear power is a safe and reasonable option for producing electricity? Explain your answer.

Power from water

Hydro-electric power (HEP) is by far the most important way in which electricity is produced from renewable sources. Electricity from HEP is relatively cheap but as for other forms of power, there are benefits and disadvantages (table **B**).

A An HEP station

Benefits	Disadvantages
• Power is cheap to produce and generally reliable.	• Finding suitable sites can be difficult.
• HEP creates very little pollution or waste.	• Dams and HEP stations are expensive to build.
• Dams reduce the risk of flooding.	• Valuable areas of land may be flooded when dams are built.
• Dams are often built in highland areas away from major population centres.	• Dam collapse can cause widespread damage.
• Reservoirs behind dams can be important sources of water.	• There may be visual pollution and environmental damage to wildlife habitats.
• Reservoirs are often used for leisure and tourism.	• Water quality and quantity may be reduced downstream, causing water shortages.
• HEP stations can very quickly increase the amount of power they produce when required.	• Large rivers can deposit a lot of very fine material which clogs up the turbines.

B Some benefits and disadvantages of HEP stations

Flowing water is needed to turn the turbines that produce electricity. HEP stations therefore tend to be found at waterfalls, across large valleys or where water flows down a steep hillside. Other favourable landscape features include:

202 Economic development

- areas with heavy rainfall such as high mountains
- rivers with a large drainage basin which allows more water to be trapped in reservoirs
- steep-sided valleys so reservoirs can be deep and hold lots of water
- narrow valleys to help keep down construction costs
- valley sides and bottom made from **impervious** rock that will not let water drain through and will provide a stable base for a dam.

Major users of HEP include Iceland, Norway, Paraguay, China, Brazil and the Democratic Republic of the Congo.

HEP and the Colorado river, USA

The USA's Colorado river has long been used as a source of HEP. Its source is in the wet Rocky Mountains (graph **C**). The flow of the river is increased by water from melting snow in April and May. It has helped the USA to become wealthy, by providing the power to develop industry and create jobs.

C Climate graph for the Rocky Mountains

The first dams built on the Colorado are now almost 100 years old. Some were originally built for flood control but many, including the Hoover Dam (photo **D**), have always been used to produce electricity. There are 10 other major dams in the Colorado river basin and many smaller ones. Deep canyons and gorges make ideal sites for storing water. Some, like Lake Mead, have become important tourist sites.

A huge amount of energy is produced from the Colorado river – a renewable source. However, people do have concerns:

- Environmentalists are worried about the negative effects on wildlife downstream – reduced flow means there are now few animals in the Colorado delta, where there were once jaguars, porpoises and notable bird species.
- Farmers complain about the effect that irrigation water, which is now full of dissolved salts, is having on their land.
- Native Americans are concerned that flooding has destroyed their sacred sites.

Fantastic fact

The heat produced when making the concrete for the Hoover Dam could have baked 500 000 loaves of bread every day for three years.

D The Hoover Dam

Skills link

Geographers use graphs like graph **C** to describe the climate of a particular place. Climate graphs show temperature and precipitation (rainfall) for each month of the year. Go to Section 4 to find out how to draw and interpret climate graphs.

Section 3.5: Energy

Pico Hydro plants in Vietnam

HEP schemes are often very big – but many people are starting to use the same kind of technology on a much smaller scale.

E Ho Phi Giang

> The Pico Hydro system is really easy to use – far easier than the electricity provided by the government on the national grid system. It is also much cheaper and we have more control over the supply.
>
> Our home now has working lights. My children can do their homework and are getting on well at school, and my wife finds it much easier doing her work around the house.

Pico Hydro units need a constant supply of water and a slope with a 1 metre drop. They can be used in almost any small stream in a mountainous area. For US$20 a family can buy a small Pico unit and produce enough electricity for their own home. Ho Phi Giang (photo **E**), a farmer who lives in Da Bac in Vietnam says the technology has revolutionised his family's life.

Pico Hydro power is becoming more and more common in Asia and Africa. Vietnam currently leads the way with more than 120 000 units in use.

Now Investigate

1. Are there any HEP stations in your country? If so, what are the reasons for their location? If not, are there any areas that would be suitable? You should use an atlas to help you answer.

2. Using graph **C**, describe the climate of the USA's Rocky Mountains. Why does the climate make the area suitable for HEP?

3. Describe the benefits of HEP. You should refer to both large-scale and small-scale schemes in your answer.

Economic development

Section 3 . Topic 6

Water

Learning objectives:
- describe methods of water supply and the proportions of water used for agriculture, domestic and industrial purposes in countries at different levels of economic development
- explain why there are water shortages in some areas and demonstrate that careful management is required to ensure future supplies

How can water supplies be managed?

> Hi! I'm Mary-Lou. I live in the Midwest of the USA and I've just finished washing my parents' car. Do you know that, on average, every American uses almost 600 litres of water every day, and that most of that is for industry and farming? At home, 75 litres is used by each member of the family – for showering, bathing, washing clothes, cleaning teeth and flushing the toilet. Some is also 'lost', due to dripping taps and leaking pipes. Many of my friends have swimming pools in their gardens. These take thousands of litres of water to fill. Dad uses a sprinkler on the lawn, though Mom thinks that watering the grass every summer evening is a *dreadful waste*.

A *Mary-Lou*

> Sannu! My name is Yawo and I live in a small village in northern Ghana. Every drop of water is precious to us here because people can die of thirst if they don't get water. My family always struggled to get enough, until the WaterAid charity helped us to dig a new well. Two-thirds of all our village's water is used for irrigating the crops. Some of this is called *grey water*, because it has been used before, in the house. On average, Ghanaians use about 4 litres of water daily in factories and workshops, but people in my village don't use any for this because we don't manufacture goods, and electricity supplies never reach this far out in the countryside! The rest of our water is used at home. I'm told this is only 12 per cent of what most Americans use every day at home, but at least we don't waste water through burst pipes and leaking taps!

B *Yawo*

The families of Mary-Lou and Yawo use very different amounts of water. They also use their water in different ways. This is because the communities they live in are not at the same level of economic development. Like most Americans, Mary-Lou's house is fitted with a washing machine and a dishwasher. The family also own two large cars and have a big garden. Few families in the Ghanaian countryside can afford such luxuries, and Ghana certainly does not have the wealth to provide a large amount of drinking water for all of its villages.

Using water sustainably

Unfortunately, not all families have enough water to meet all of their needs. Where there is a shortage of water, or **water deficit**, it is essential to use all available sources as carefully as possible. Photos **C** show some ways that people can use water sparingly, in more sustainable ways. Countries too can use their available water in different ways (table **D**). Agriculture and industry both use huge amounts of water. For example, it has taken 10 litres of water just to produce the paper for this page! Some other surprising facts about water use are:

- A slice of bread takes 40 litres to make.
- A pair of jeans takes almost 11 000 litres.
- It takes 1300 litres to grow 1 kg of wheat, but *twelve times as much* to produce 1 kg of beef.

Taking a shower

Car-washing by hand

Drip-feed irrigation

Washing dishes by hand

C How can we use water more sustainably?

Country	GDP per capita (US$)	National water use (av. litres per person per day)	National % water for agriculture	National % water for domestic activities	National % water for industrial activities and electricity generation
Canada	46 200	323	12	68	20
China	15 400	86	67	7	26
Egypt	12 100	200	86	8	6
France	42 400	287	9	17	74
Ghana	4400	36	66	24	10
India	6700	135	86	8	6
Mexico	18 900	365	78	17	5
Russia	26 100	248	18	19	63
UK	42 500	149	3	22	75
USA	57 300	575	41	13	46

D Water use in ten countries

Now Investigate

1. Keep your own personal water-use diary for a whole week, then use it to estimate the total amount of water you have used. If your home has a water meter, use its readings to add some accurate water-use figures for your household.

2. Suggest some ways in which water can be used more sustainably – in addition to those shown in photos **C**.

3.6

3 Study table **D**.

  a) Use data in the table to identify how fresh water use can vary between countries at different levels of economic development.

  b) Suggest reasons for the patterns of use you have identified in (a). (Hint: Some crops, for example rice and cotton, use much more water than others.)

4 a) Draw two spider diagrams, to show the most likely water uses of a family in an LEDC and in an MEDC.

  b) List ways in which the information in your diagrams is similar and different.

  c) Suggest some reasons for any differences you have identified in (b).

Meeting the demand for water

Many people have unlimited access to clean drinking water. However, 1 billion people (that is one in every seven people on Earth) struggle to get enough water to meet their basic needs (map **A**). The number of people who are permanently short of clean drinking water seems likely to rise to at least 4 billion by 2050. The main problem facing these people is not the lack of water, but actually accessing the water. This is because rain doesn't always fall where it is most needed (map **B**), and 99 per cent of all fresh water on Earth is stored in rocks deep underground.

Over the years, people have developed ways of storing water for future use, and moving it to water-deficit areas. **Water transfer** using pipes and aqueducts has been practised for centuries – cities like Los Angeles now transfer water over 300 km in order to meet their needs. Many places that already experience a deficit are likely to face even greater water supply problems in the future. This is due mainly to population increase (see graph **D** in Topic 1.1 on page 3), but also because people use more water as their standards of living rise.

Percentage
- 100
- 90 – 99 average
- 80 – 89
- 60 – 79
- 40 – 59
- no data

Access to safe water
The percentage of the population with reasonable access to an adequate amount of water from an improved source. World average 89%. Statistics are for 2012.

A Access to safe water around the world

Section 3.6: Water   207

Precipitation in July (mm)
☐ Over 25   ☐ 25–50   ■ 50–150   ■ More than 150

B Rainfall around the world

Accessing water sources

Clean water is available from several sources:

- **Lakes and rivers** are the main sources of easily accessible water. However, many of these have been heavily polluted by waste from homes, farms and industries, or are over-used (photo **C**).

- **Aquifers** are underground sources of water. They don't lose water through evaporation, and deep aquifers aren't polluted by towns, farms and factories on the surface. **Bore holes** are used to extract water; however, care must be taken not to extract more from these sources than can be replaced naturally by rainwater and water seeping downwards from lakes and reservoirs.

- **Desalination plants** distil sea water and make it safe to use by removing the salt. This is a very expensive process, and can only be afforded by wealthy countries such as the oil-rich desert states in the Middle East.

- **Large-scale rainwater harvesting** is the collection and storing of rainwater in reservoirs. 'Mega-dams' are now seen as the best way of storing huge quantities of water for the future, even though reservoirs in warmer regions can lose much of their water due to evaporation. The dams are often fitted with turbines for generating electricity, which is sold at a profit. This income helps to pay the building costs and reimburse people whose lives have been disrupted by the new reservoirs.

> **Fantastic fact**
>
> By 2050, the global demand for water for agricultural use is estimated to increase by 19%

C This is what happened when too much water was taken from the Aral Sea's feeder rivers to irrigate farmland chiefly for growing cotton

> **Topic link**
>
> For more about the Aral Sea go to pages 215–217.

Economic development

- **Small-scale rainwater harvesting** can also be very effective. Some cities in Germany and India have laws that require all new properties to have their own rainwater collection and storage systems.

Reducing the demand for water

Many countries are now trying hard to reduce their total use of water and yet still meet their people's increasing needs. The benefits of such measures as those shown in photos **C** on page 206 can be significant. For example, reducing the world's use of irrigation water by only 10 per cent could double the amount available for the domestic supply of everyone on the planet.

Now Investigate

1. a) Make a drawing of your own home.
   b) Annotate your drawing to show how your home could be adapted to harvest and store rainwater.
   c) Add further information about how water reaches your home, and about any treatment the water receives to make it safe to use.

2. Make a large copy of the table below. Your task is to complete your table by adding the possible advantages (benefits) and disadvantages of each source of clean water. It is a good idea to discuss your ideas with other students in your class before you start to do this.

3. For this activity you will need to refer to map **C** in Topic 1.4 page 32 and maps **A** and **B** on pages 207–208.
   a) Briefly describe the main distribution patterns shown in each of these three maps.
   b) Using your answer to (a), suggest reasons for the global distribution of areas where access to water is difficult.

Water source	Benefits of this type of water source	Disadvantages of this type of water source
Aquifers		
Desalination plants		
Lakes and rivers		
Large-scale rainwater harvesting		
Small-scale rainwater harvesting		

Water supply issues

Sawadogo's (page 210) story shows how some people in LEDCs are being given access to clean water. Another way is by water-harvesting. This is a way of saving small amounts of water for future use. Local people build small earth or stone dams across a river or stream to hold back any rainwater. This stored water allows farmers to irrigate their crops and so increase crop yields. If the water is treated to make it safe to drink, it also means women and children do not have to spend so much time collecting water from further away.

> Bonjour! I'm Sawadogo and I live in Burkina Faso, in the Sahel region. It doesn't rain here often and when I was younger we were always short of water. I was often ill because the water we drank wasn't clean. Then they dug a well in the village, with a pump and tap. Now we have a good supply of clean water which is safe to drink. We use some of the water to grow food. We can sell some of the food and earn money.

A *Sawadogo*

Topic link

- Look back at Topic 1.4 pages 36–37 for more information on the Sahel region.
- Look back at Topic 1.1 pages 2–20 for more information on population growth.

Further research

Look for information about some agencies that help to give people a supply of clean water (for example WaterAid or Oxfam). Find out how they do this.

CASE STUDY

Water supply in northern India

An aquifer becomes depleted (gets smaller) when more water is extracted from it than can be replaced naturally. The aquifer beneath the Indian states of Rajasthan, Punjab and Haryana (map **B**) is becoming seriously depleted, at a rate of 1 metre every three years, because so many people are using the water in the aquifer. These states have a combined population of about 135 million, and include the cities of Jaipur and Delhi. The water is also needed for irrigating the crops that are vital to Rajasthan's economy – this region supplies much of India's wheat, barley and cotton. Rajasthan's industries are also expanding rapidly, and many of these use large quantities of water.

India is building more **wells**, dams, canals and water treatment plants, but improving the country's water supply infrastructure is expensive and the rapidly growing cities cannot process all their sewage. Untreated water near to major urban areas is therefore often used to irrigate crops, which endangers the health of the farmers, their animals and their consumers. This means that skin disease, intestinal worms and diarrhoea are increasingly common ailments. Where there are prolonged water shortages, cows produce far less milk and villagers in rural areas have to walk much longer distances to access safe drinking water.

B *Location of the aquifer in northern India*

210   Economic development

3.6

Competition for water in the Nile basin

Egyptian farmers have used irrigation water from the river Nile for thousands of years. Together the White Nile and the Blue Nile and their tributaries pass through ten countries. The Blue Nile brings floodwater and fertile sediment from the Ethiopian Highlands after snowmelt and heavy rainfall there in summer (graph **D**). Graph **E** shows that, without this river water, much more of Egypt and Sudan would be an infertile, hot desert. Egypt was the first country to build dams across the river, such as the Aswan High Dam (photo **C**). Storing the Nile's floodwater is the key to growing more than one crop of rice and cotton each year.

In 1999 the Nile basin countries signed an agreement to promote the sustainable use of the river water in ways that would benefit them all. However, the basin's population of 280 million people is expected to double in the next 25 years, and every country is demanding more water to grow more food and generate more power. The resulting tension has split the countries into two opposing groups: Egypt, Sudan and South Sudan in one group, and countries further upstream in the other. Serious conflict could develop if the demand for more water grows.

C Aswan High Dam and Lake Nasser, the reservoir created by the dam. In 2017, the Grand Ethiopian Renaissance Dam was completed on the Blue Nile. It could take 15 years for its new reservoir to fill up. During this time it will greatly reduce river flow to countries downstream of it.

D Climate graph for Addis Ababa, Ethiopia

E Climate graph for Cairo, Egypt

Fantastic fact

Lake Nasser is the world's largest artificial lake. It extends 100 km south of Egypt into another country, Sudan.

Section 3.6: Water   211

Now Investigate

1. Do you have access to a regular supply of clean water? Keep a record of how many times in one day you use water. State what you use it for, and approximately how much you use (in litres) each time. How much have you used by the end of the day?

2. a) Describe in detail the contrasts between the climates of Addis Ababa (graph **D**) and Cairo (graph **E**).

   b) What is the significance of these contrasts in terms of a supply of water in Ethiopia and Egypt?

3. Imagine that you are a farmer living beside the Blue Nile in Ethiopia.

   a) What are your priorities for using water from the river?

   b) How are those priorities different from those of an Egyptian farmer? Explain your answer to this question.

Section 3 . Topic 7

Environmental risks of economic development

Learning objectives:
- describe how economic activities may pose threats to the natural environment and people, locally and globally
- demonstrate the need for sustainable development and management
- understand the importance of resource conservation

A balancing act?

The human race against the natural world

Many of us live in environments where it is fairly easy to survive. If you live in New Zealand, for example, the climate is mild and there is good farmland (photo **A**), so people can grow plenty of food to eat. Not everyone is so lucky. In Topic 2.5, for example, you learned that life in the hot deserts is far more difficult, with a constant struggle to find water and food.

But humans are very adaptable. Even in places that would seem to provide little opportunity, people have settled, found food and been able to make a living for themselves. Tropical rainforests, polar areas and the high mountains are just a few of the places where people have settled despite the problems posed by the natural environment.

A *A farming landscape in New Zealand*

Finding a good place to live

Most of the densely populated areas of the world have natural environments that provide the basic needs of life – fresh water, food, fuel and shelter. If people have easy access to these then they carry out other activities to make a living and help a country develop. These needs can usually be met in natural environments that provide:

- low, flat land with deep, fertile soils
- a reliable source of fresh water such as a spring or river
- no extremes of climate and a long growing season
- natural vegetation of *temperate* forest or grassland
- natural resources, especially energy supplies but also mineral resources
- natural beauty that is attractive to tourists.

Those parts of the world where commercial agriculture has developed and where people have plenty to eat have most, if not

> **Topic link**
>
> You can learn more about the problems and opportunities presented by tropical rainforests in Topic 2.5 pages 115–120, and by hot deserts on pages 121–127.

> **Topic link**
>
> You can learn more about floods in Bangladesh in Topic 2.5 pages 133–135.

all, of the above features. In places where there are mineral resources, these may have provided the raw materials for industry to develop. Tourists will want to visit some places as those areas become wealthier and more developed and can offer facilities such as top-quality hotels and restaurants.

Problems posed by harsh environments

There are other areas of the world where life is more difficult because of challenges presented by the natural environment. Some of these challenges are shown in diagram **B**.

B *Characteristics of harsh environments*

- High, steep land
- Rocky, bare landscape
- Lack of natural resources, especially fresh water
- Thin, dry and easily eroded soils
- Unattractive or desolate scenery
- Natural vegetation which is desert, poor grassland or dense forest
- Extreme climate

Even in these areas there are often economic opportunities. Tropical rainforests are increasingly attractive to tourists who travel to see the amazing plants and animals there. Ski industries occupy high, steep land in winter and become popular with mountain bikers in summer (photo **C**). Desert areas are attracting more and more visitors who are looking for a different kind of holiday.

Tourism can be the main way of making money in many difficult natural environments, but there are other opportunities too. Areas of high rainfall can provide electricity through hydro-electric power, for example, and tropical rainforest can be a source of valuable timber.

C *Mountain biking in the French Alps*

A balancing act

In many parts of the world the natural environment provides both problems and opportunities. In Bangladesh, for instance, the advantages of the annual river flood are balanced by the devastation that such floods can cause.

In some areas, people have also tried to change the environment in order to exploit it. This has both positive and negative consequences, as can be seen in the case studies on pages 215–219.

Fantastic fact

One of the most popular countries for desert tourism is Dubai. There you can stay in the world's only seven-star hotel and go skiing at the country's own winter wonderland resort.

Topic link

The theme of natural environments has links to a number of topics in Sections 1 and 2, including population distribution, tropical rainforest, deserts and storms. Bear this in mind when you work through those sections.

Now Investigate

1. Think about the area where you live. What are the problems and opportunities presented by the natural environment? For instance, is it really hot? If so, does this attract tourists or provide the ideal location for a solar power plant? Make a list of the problems and opportunities presented by the natural environment in your area, and compare it with a partner's list.

2 Which areas of your country have few people living in them because of the natural environment? Make a list of the possible opportunities that could exist in these areas.

3 Look at the list of basic necessities to be found in the natural environment (water, fuel, food and shelter). Which of these do you think is most important and why? Which is least important?

4 Choose an economic activity – either (a) agriculture or (b) tourism. What features of the natural environment are most useful for your choice of economic activity?

Exploiting the natural environment: disaster!

Some natural environments are harsh and present many challenges to the people living there, but people still try to make a living there, through agriculture and other activities. Sometimes these attempts can have disastrous effects for the environment and the people involved.

CASE STUDY: The Aral Sea disaster

Before 1965, the Aral Sea occupied a huge area of 67 300 km² (a little larger than the island of Sri Lanka), in Kazakhstan and Uzbekistan (map **A**). It was the world's fourth largest lake and was fed by two major rivers. Into the southern end flowed Central Asia's largest river – the Amu Darya – bringing water 1500 km from its source in the Hindu Kush mountains between Afghanistan and Pakistan. The smaller Syr Darya brought water into the northern end of the lake.

The climate of the region around the Aral Sea is arid with high summer temperatures sometimes reaching 50 °C. Winters can be very cold and there is low rainfall throughout the year (graph **B**). Because of this, agriculture is difficult and people traditionally made a living by fishing in the sea. In the 1960s thousands of fishermen landed 40 000 tonnes of fish a year from the Aral Sea. Many more people were employed in industries that supported the fishing. They lived in the towns and two cities on the lake shore.

A The Aral Sea

Section 3.7: Environmental risks of economic development

The sea dries up

In the 1960s Kazakhstan and Uzbekistan were part of the Soviet Union. The government made a decision to use the water in the Amu Darya to grow wheat and cotton. Huge canals were built to divert water through **irrigation** channels to the 3 million hectares of land dedicated to the two crops. This proved disastrous for the Aral Sea. With less water reaching the lake, it began to dry up and shrink dramatically. By 1989 it was already half its original size, and it continued to shrink for many years after that (photos **C**).

B Climate graph for the Aral Sea

C The declining area of the Aral Sea: satellite images from (left to right) 1989, 2003 and 2009

The effects on people and the environment

As the Aral Sea dried up, fishing became more and more difficult. The water was further and further away from the towns where people lived. At first, canals were built to allow ships to get to the lake but, eventually, the ships had to be abandoned. As the water level dropped, the amount of salt it contained (known as its **salinity**) increased until it became almost as salty as the ocean (graph **D**). Most of the remaining fish died and the fishermen had to move away to find jobs elsewhere. Further environmental damage was caused by agricultural fertilisers and pesticides needed for the intensive farming of wheat and cotton. These polluted both drinking water and the water used to irrigate crop land.

Worse was to follow. Summers got hotter and winters colder as the decrease in water affected the climate. Violent dust storms blew salt, sand and chemicals into the air and people developed throat cancers and breathing diseases, including tuberculosis. With no protein from fish, people suffered from **malnutrition** and the number of children dying increased rapidly to become the highest rate in the Soviet Union.

Skills link

Interpreting satellite images is a very useful skill. Used in combination with maps, comparisons can show clear patterns of change in the environment. See Topic 4.4 pages 263–267 and Topic 4.6 on pages 281–282 for more information.

D Relationship between salinity and water level in the Aral Sea over time

Economic development

Signs of recovery

This situation was described by UN Secretary-General Ban Ki-moon as one of the planet's most shocking environmental disasters, but there are now some signs of recovery. The World Bank and the Kazakh government paid for a 13 km long dam to be built to raise the level of the lake. The northern part has grown by 20 per cent and salinity levels have dropped to what they were in the 1960s. Freshwater fish have returned and local fishermen have begun catching them in large numbers again. There are also plans to develop the tourist industry in the area.

Despite these encouraging signs, large parts of the Aral Sea have been subjected to desertification and have vanished for ever. It remains a lesson that there are often unexpected consequences when people try to **exploit** their natural environment.

> **Skills link**
>
> Relationships between different factors can be seen quickly and easily using multiple line graphs like graph D. For more details on how to interpret them, see Topic 4.3 pages 260–262.

Now Investigate

1. Describe the environment of the Aral Sea area using the information in this case study.
2. Referring to photos **C**, draw a sketch map to show how the area has changed over the last 60 years.
3. Describe the relationship between salinity and water level as shown in graph **D**.
4. Write a few paragraphs to explain why the Aral Sea is 'one of the planet's most shocking environmental disasters'.

Exploiting the natural environment: success?

It is clear that extreme damage can occur when the use of the natural environment is not well managed. However, in some parts of the world careful management is allowing people to exploit the natural environment in a sustainable manner.

Polar regions

The polar regions of the planet lie inside the Arctic and Antarctic Circles, north of 66°N and south of 66°S. These areas are extremely cold, mainly covered in ice and have low levels of precipitation. Technically they are referred to as 'cold deserts' because deserts are defined by a lack of rainfall. Life for the people who live in these regions can be extremely hard, with long winters when darkness lasts for 24 hours and temperatures are very low, and with almost

Section 3.7: Environmental risks of economic development

no opportunity for agriculture. Remarkably, there are people who make these areas their home and who manage to survive and do well economically.

> **CASE STUDY**
>
> ## Greenland – the biggest island in the world
>
> Greenland, in the North Atlantic, lies mainly within the Arctic Circle (map **A**) and is the world's largest island (not including those that are classified as continents). It is 95 per cent covered in ice, with one-twentieth of the world's total. Its 55 000 inhabitants live in coastal areas.
>
> Traditionally the main way for the islanders to make money has been through fishing, fish processing, seal hunting and fur trapping. Only 1 per cent of the land is suitable for agriculture but, here, farmers raise cattle, sheep and goats and grow a few vegetables.
>
> The last ten years or so has seen some big changes to this traditional pattern. Greenland has been advertising itself as a major **ecotourist** destination, giving adventurous visitors the chance to see one of the world's last true wildernesses (photo **B**).
>
> Many people come to cruise around the dramatic coastline, to go fishing or hiking, or to view some of the wildlife. There are also many opportunities for specialist tourist holidays. Adventure tourists can go dog-sledding, kayaking or heli-skiing, while other holidays cater for people who want to eat the local food or see unique sights such as the Northern Lights (photo **C**).
>
> ### Digging for wealth
>
> Perhaps the most important recent development for the wealth of Greenland has come partly because of environmental problems elsewhere. A steady rise in local temperatures, perhaps brought about as part of global climate change, means that the vast ice sheet is beginning to melt, making it easier to access the huge mineral deposits on the island (map **D**). Increases in the global price of various metals have also made it attractive for companies to open up mines here.
>
> Angel Mining is currently re-opening the Black Angel Mine to extract lead and zinc. It is also looking at taking gold from another site, and wants to look for other metals and coal.
>
> **A** *Greenland*
>
> **B** *The Kujalleq area on the southern coast of Greenland*

218 Economic development

Other companies in Greenland are searching for diamonds, copper, silver and many other valuable minerals.

These developments bring employment to the people of Greenland and money for the government of the country. Exploitation of resources is being strictly controlled and mining companies have to prepare detailed social and environmental impact assessments to show what effects their operations will have and what they will do to ensure minimal damage to the beauty of the natural landscape.

Despite this, campaigning organisations such as Greenpeace are very concerned about what may happen to this pristine wilderness, especially in light of recent disputes over what Greenland believes are its territorial waters but which, in some areas, are also claimed by Denmark, Russia, Canada and others.

C *The Northern Lights*

Topic link

There is more about the general rise in tourism around the world in Topic 3.4 pages 181–188, while industrial location is covered in Topic 3.3 pages 173–175.

Topic link

Map D is one way of showing information on a map, using symbols. For more information on interpreting different kinds of maps see Topics 4.1 and 4.2.

▲ Gold   ▲ Coal   ▲ Iron ore   ▲ Graphite   ■ Rare earths
▲ Platinum metals   ● Andalusite and antimony
● Molybdenum   ◎ Columbium   ◎ Chromite   ◎ Cryolite

D *Mineral deposits around the Greenland coast*

Now Investigate

1. Where are the world's polar regions? What are the main features that make it difficult for humans to live in these areas?

2. a) Describe how people living in Greenland are able to make a living from their natural environment.

   b) What kinds of problems could be caused by what they are doing?

3. This case study of Greenland suggests many opportunities for tourism in the Arctic. What about on the other side of the world? Using the internet, investigate tourist activities in Antarctica and write a few paragraphs explaining what they are.

Section 3.7: Environmental risks of economic development

How much are we damaging our environment?

Your damaged environment

The economic activities described so far in Section 3 – agriculture, industry, tourism and electricity generation – all have huge benefits for the countries where they take place. But they can cause a number of problems for people, including food shortages, health issues and loss of culture. Most economic activities can also cause great harm to the natural environment. Think, for instance, about agriculture in your local area. What kind of damage does it do to rivers and lakes, soils, the atmosphere and the natural vegetation? Some ideas are shown in diagram **A**.

Damage to watercourses

Lakes, rivers and the sea can all be damaged by industrial activities. Many factories are located by rivers and use the water for cooling and other purposes. This water may be returned to the river containing **toxic** (poisonous) chemicals. This is called **contamination** and means people downstream cannot use the water for drinking supplies or irrigation as it may cause diseases or ruin crops. It may also affect the fish supplies that provide protein for their diet. Smaller-scale industrial activities can also have very damaging effects on the environment. Figure **C** gives an example of how this happens in the Amazonian rainforest in Brazil.

Pollutants and toxic chemicals can also enter underground water systems (known as **groundwater** supplies). They can come from leaks from mines or factories and power stations. These supplies are often pumped to the surface through wells for drinking water. Areas of Vietnam and Korea have been particularly badly affected by groundwater contamination.

Damage to the air

It is often quite easy to see the damage that pollution causes to land and watercourses. Damage to the air can be much more difficult to spot. Smoke pouring out of large factories (photo **B**) is quite obvious and can cause breathing difficulties for those who live nearby. Coal dust produced by mining has a similar effect. In many countries, factories are now forced by law to keep their pollutants to a minimum. This is easier to keep under control in MEDCs. In LEDCs, where laws are less strictly enforced, the environmental damage can go unchallenged.

A The environmental impacts of agriculture

Diagram showing DAMAGE CAUSED BY AGRICULTURE with surrounding boxes:
- Rivers, seas and lakes – chemicals in fertilisers and pesticides can be washed into watercourses
- Wildlife – chased away or forced to leave as natural habitats are destroyed
- Natural vegetation – chopped down to make way for fields to grow crops
- Physical landscape – hills are terraced and the landscape destroyed to increase land available for growing crops
- Atmosphere – farm machinery pumps pollutants into the air while rotting vegetation adds dangerous methane to the atmosphere
- Soils – growing the same crops year after year reduces soil fertility and chemical fertilisers need to be added in larger amounts

B Factories can cause severe air pollution

3.7

C The garimpeiros at work in Brazil

> We are the garimpeiros, looking for gold in the Amazon rainforest.
>
> We have to strip the land to get at the gold. We know we're causing damage. We cut down the trees to get at the earth and then we wash it into the river. Sometimes the river silts up and can't flow any more.
>
> The worst thing we do is washing the gold with mercury. It's a dangerous chemical and kills the fish. Sometimes the local people eat the fish or drink the contaminated water. It damages their bodies and sends them mad.
>
> What can we do, though? There are no jobs anywhere else and here, we may get rich!

Other effects are much harder to detect. Some chemicals react with the water in the atmosphere and fall to the ground as **acid rain**. This can kill crops and, again, contaminate watercourses. In China, there are fears that an estimated 30 per cent of the country's agricultural land is affected by acid rain. This is a serious problem in a country with an expanding population that already has problems producing enough food for its people.

Perhaps the biggest impact of pollutants in the atmosphere is the change in the world's climate brought about by global warming.

How transport affects the environment

Industry can cause less direct effects on the environment. Most factories, mines and tourist developments rely on some kind of transport. This may be to bring in raw materials, move finished products or to carry people around. The transport used will add further pollutants to the atmosphere. Aircraft are particularly damaging because they release pollutants high up in the atmosphere where there are even greater effects on the environment causing global warming.

The effects of chemicals produced by motor vehicles have been shown to be very dangerous. Leaded gasoline (fuel oil) has now been banned in many countries because of health risks. Studies have shown it can be linked to brain damage and other mental health problems. Fuel with a low sulphur content is also becoming more widely available. Kenya and Tanzania, for instance, have introduced it to help reduce the diseases, such as lung cancer, that high sulphur gasoline can cause.

Topic link

- There's more information on groundwater contamination in Topic 3.6 on pages 205–211.
- Global warming is discussed in more detail later in this topic and in Topic 3.5 pages 189–199.

Now Investigate

1. Look at diagram **A**. Choose an example of either tourism or manufacturing industry from your own local area. Draw a similar diagram showing the environmental damage these activities could cause.

2. Using the images on these pages, describe some types of pollution that can result from industrial activity.

Section 3.7: Environmental risks of economic development

3 Think of examples of economic activities where you live. What types of transport do these industries use? Make a list of the possible sources of pollution from industry in your local area.

4 There are many types of pollution affecting people and countries on a global scale. Which do you think are the most dangerous? Give reasons for your answer.

The world gets warmer

Over the last 150 years there has been a gradual increase in the average global temperature. Although this increase has only been around 1 °C, it has had some very big effects – especially when compared with changes over a much longer period of time. Most scientists now agree that this global warming has been caused by human activities (graph **A**). They also predict that average temperatures will continue to increase – perhaps by more than 5 °C by 2100. These changes could have the potential to completely change our world.

The enhanced greenhouse effect

Greenhouse gases are produced by human activities. They are concentrated in the atmosphere and act like a blanket, keeping heat in (diagram **B**). The concentration of these gases is increasing all the time and they come from a number of different sources:

- Burning fossil fuels – coal, oil and gas – in factories, power stations and motor vehicles releases carbon dioxide, sulphur dioxide and other gases.
- Cutting down and burning trees also adds carbon dioxide to the atmosphere.
- Very damaging methane comes from decaying vegetation in padi fields, from cattle and from rubbish tips.
- Nitrous oxides are given off by agricultural fertilisers.

A The effects of human activity on global temperatures

> **Topic link**
>
> There is more about the effects of deforestation, including the greenhouse effect, in Topic 3.5 pages 189–195 and other topics in Section 3.

B The greenhouse effect

222 Economic development

- Halocarbons and chlorofluorocarbons (also known as CFCs) come from fridges and aerosols – although banned worldwide they can remain in the atmosphere for 400 years.

Growing populations mean that the amount of these gases being released into the atmosphere is constantly increasing. This leads to more heat being trapped and higher global temperatures. There are fears that it may already be too late to stop concentrations growing beyond levels that would have disastrous effects for some parts of the world.

The effects of climate change

It is very difficult to predict what could happen as the world gets warmer. Computer models have been used to give us some idea of what might happen in the future, and these predict some of the events set out in diagram **C**.

Although many of these changes are only predictions at the moment, some countries are already coming to terms with the effects of climate change.

> **Topic link**
>
> Topic 1.2 pages 21–26 shows a variety of other reasons why people may migrate from country to country.

THE EFFECTS OF CLIMATE CHANGE

- Melting polar ice caps, ice sheets (in countries like Greenland) and glaciers could cause a sea-level rise of up to 5 metres – a severe problem for the 40 per cent of the world's population who live close to the coast.
- Rising sea temperatures will mean the oceans expand, leading to an average worldwide sea-level rise of 40 cm by 2100 – this would mean widespread flooding of low-lying areas.
- There could be changes in extreme weather events – e.g. temperatures over 40°C causing wildfires in Australia, more hurricanes in the Caribbean, deadly heatwaves in Europe and floods in Egypt.
- Wars may be fought as the global population grows and precious resources such as food and water become scarce in some countries.
- Changes to farming as equatorial areas become too hot and tropical crops are grown further north.
- The coral reefs that provide many countries (including Belize, Australia and the Maldives) with a big tourist attraction could die.
- Extinction of wildlife that is unable to adapt to the changing climate – some scientists estimate up to one third of all species could become extinct over the next 100 years.
- Tropical diseases become more widespread – malaria, for instance, could become common in Europe.

C *Future events as a result of climate change?*

CASE STUDY: Abandoning the Carteret Islands

In 2009 the world's first large-scale evacuation due to climate change took place from the Carteret Islands in the South Pacific. The coral islands, around 80 football pitches in size and home to 2600 people, are gradually being submerged by rising sea levels.

The islands have a maximum height above the sea of 170 centimetres so any sea level rise will have a serious effect (photo **D**). Violent storms across the islands have been increasing, perhaps as a result of climate change, and have brought widespread flooding.

Salt water from storm surges has poisoned the land where islanders used to grow crops, including bread fruit trees, and food has become very scarce. Water from many of the wells has become undrinkable and, at the coastline, the beaches have disappeared and the coconut trees which the islanders used to supplement their diet have been uprooted. The inhabitants have made the decision to relocate to a nearby island called Bougainville, off the coast of Papua New Guinea.

The evacuation was the first time that large numbers of people have been forced to leave their homes, apparently as a result of climate change. It is unlikely to be the last.

D Sea-level rise has destroyed the coastline

'Their numbers might be small, but this is the event that could show the likely mass migration of people from coastal cities and low-lying regions as a result of rising sea levels. The disaster has begun, but so far hardly anyone has noticed.'

George Monbiot, environmental author and campaigner

Now Investigate

1. a) Draw a labelled diagram to show how the greenhouse effect occurs.

   b) Explain how human activities have led to an increase in the greenhouse effect.

2. Using specific examples, describe some of the global impacts of climate change.

3. Think about your local area. Find out what impacts climate change might have on the place where you live.

Destruction of the forests

A Changing global forest cover, 1990–2010

Skills link

Graph **A** shows a lot of information – different time periods and positive and negative scales. Look at Topic 4.3, pages 251–252 on graph interpretation before trying to work out exactly what it shows.

224 Economic development

3.7

As we saw in the previous section, cutting down and burning trees can have an influence on global warming. This process is called **deforestation**. Trees take carbon dioxide from the air and turn it into oxygen by **photosynthesis**. Not only does burning the trees add carbon dioxide to the atmosphere, it also means less gas can be removed in this way.

With the increased use of natural resources there are concerns about the effects on the world's natural ecosystems, including the tropical rainforests. Graph **A** shows global changes in forest cover over a period of 20 years. Some countries, including China, have started planting more trees to increase the size of their forests and help combat the negative effects that deforestation is having on the environment. Many others, however, have come to rely on the money that can be made by cutting down trees. The Brazilian government has opened up the Amazonian rainforest to mining, huge cattle ranches and other forms of agriculture. Deforestation in other countries has also had severe environmental effects.

Fantastic fact

More than 50 countries around the world have already lost over 90 per cent of their natural forests.

CASE STUDY: Deforestation in Borneo

Maps **B** shows that, until 1950, Borneo was covered in dense tropical forest. In the 1980s and 1990s, however, the island suffered a higher rate of deforestation than any other part of the world. Much of the wood was sent to the USA and Japan for chopsticks, furniture and paper. More recently oil palm plantations have been responsible for the destruction of the rainforest.

Deforestation in Borneo has had a number of environmental effects:

- The habitats of many animals have been destroyed or reduced – including endangered species such as the clouded leopard, pygmy elephant and orangutan.
- Forest fires have increased – these cause 'haze' pollution across Borneo and in neighbouring islands (in Indonesia, Malaysia and Singapore).
- Smoke from fires causes environmental health problems, especially breathing difficulties for local people.
- The removal of the forest cover is increasing the amount of soil erosion.

Topic link

See Topic 2.5 pages 115–120 for much more information on tropical rainforests.

B The decline of Borneo's forests

Section 3.7: Environmental risks of economic development

Deforestation has other effects on the economy and on people. It can, for instance, mean fewer tourists coming to visit a country. Soil erosion resulting from deforestation also reduces the amount of land available for agriculture and is an increasing problem around the world.

Environmental effects of soil erosion

In regions such as Borneo, once forest cover is removed from the land, there is nothing left to protect the fertile soil. It is left exposed to heavy tropical rains which wash it away. This can cause huge **gullies** to form (photo **C**). The soil becomes impossible to farm and local people are forced to migrate to other areas which may be even less suitable for farming.

In drier areas, such as the countries that border the southern Sahara Desert and in the Midwest states of the USA, soil erosion by the wind is more common. Once the vegetation cover is removed, the soil quickly dries out and can be easily blown away. The soil again becomes infertile. Farming may still be possible with the use of fertilisers but these can contaminate water supplies.

Soil removed by wind and water can be transported over huge distances. When washed into rivers, the soil can kill animal life, alter the river's flow, lower the water quality and may even increase the risk of flooding. Soil in the air can travel even further. It is not unknown for soil carried on the wind to be blown from the Sahara to southern England where it collects on cars (image **D**).

C *Gully formation due to soil erosion*

D *Satellite image showing sand being blown from the Sahara towards Europe*

Now Investigate

1. Describe the trends shown on graph **A**. Refer to specific regions in your answer.

2. Think about your own country. Where are the woodlands nearest to where you live? Find out if they have any sort of protection.

3. a) Using maps **B**, describe the extent of the deforestation that has taken place in Borneo.
   b) Explain some of the causes and effects of the destruction of Borneo's rainforests.

4. a) What are the two main processes by which soil erosion takes place?
   b) Which do you think has the worst environmental effects? Explain your answer.

5. Are there any areas of your country where severe soil erosion could take place? Use a map or atlas to identify them and outline the reasons that could be behind the erosion.

Topic link

The effects of forest destruction for fuelwood are described in Topic 3.5 pages 193–195.

How can we conserve the environment?

Your chance to save the planet

Topic 3.7 shows that our use of natural resources can be very damaging to the environment. But it does not have to be this way. Governments and organisations across the world are starting to realise there could be alternative ways to live our lives. Many are now looking to become more **sustainable** – using resources in a way that won't leave permanent damage for future generations. Some countries have been forced into action by their own people. Across the world, ordinary citizens are demanding that the natural environment has better protection. Many people are making an effort to use less of the planet's resources (figure **A**).

> Ben Formby has set himself a challenge to use as few resources as possible. Giving up his house, he has moved into a tent pitched in his office car park (so he can walk to work). The PC and radio in his tent are powered by hand-winding.
>
> He cycles to local markets to buy food (without packaging) that has been transported over very short distances. For a complete lifestyle change he has also given up meat and become a vegetarian because of the damage to the environment brought about by the intensive farming of animals.

A *How to be low carbon*

'Think global, act local'

This commonly used phrase helps us remember that we can help look after the Earth by taking action in our own community. We are all consumers, daily using up the planet's resources. When we drive anywhere we use petroleum; when we turn on the television we mainly use electricity generated in a power station; and the food we eat may have been produced using chemicals and then transported over long distances. There are ways, though, in which we can cut down on the damage that our consumption causes.

- How can you cut down the resources you use? Perhaps you could walk or cycle instead of asking for a lift in the car (figure **B**)? Maybe you could buy pizza from a local street seller instead of food from a global hamburger chain? Think about how these actions would save resources.

B *Can you cut down on the resources you use?*

Section 3.7: Environmental risks of economic development

There are three helpful principles you can use:

- **Reduce** – stop using so much stuff. Take your own bag to the shops instead of using a new one. Or either turn off the heating and put on a sweater, or turn off the air-conditioning and allow a free flow of fresh air.

- **Re-use** – use the stuff you have more often, for example wash plastic cups and plates and then use them again, or fill up plastic water bottles at home instead of buying new ones.

- **Recycle** – over 80 per cent of household waste can be used again. This doesn't just mean paper, glass and tin cans but also computers, batteries and video games.

More and more countries are investing in recycling facilities, especially across Europe (graph **C**). This cuts down the amount of waste that has to be buried or burnt or dumped in the sea. It also saves on the energy and resources needed to make new things and used in transporting waste material around the world to be processed. Many developing countries are also heavily involved in recycling (photo **D**).

C *Europe's biggest recyclers*

Fantastic fact

Recycling one tin can saves enough energy to power a television for three hours.

For many of the people of Senegal, small-scale recycling is a daily activity.

Local people recycle everything, including many items thrown away by richer countries. School books, glass bottles and plastic bags are all used again and again. Even fruit peel is collected and used in cheap perfume.

In villages across the country people drink water from cleaned tomato tins. Official papers thrown out by government departments are used to wrap the bread, fruit and vegetables bought from traders on the street.

Craftspeople are also involved in this widespread recycling. Chairs, kitchen utensils and toys are made from metals. Even plastic bags have taken the place of worn tyres in making shoes.

Interest in recycling is spreading and people are becoming ever more resourceful. Some are now collecting waste metal in ever larger quantities and sending it back to the factories in Europe where it originally came from.

D *Recycling in Senegal*

Now Investigate

1 How much of the Earth's resources do *you* consume (use up) every day? *Either* keep a diary for the next 24 hours *or* review what you have done in the last 24 hours. Write down all the activities you can think of that use resources. Try to think of what resources you have used in each activity.

3.7

2 Have a look again at the list you made of your activities over 24 hours that used resources. Decide how many and how much of these resources could be reduced, re-used or recycled. Make a table like the one below to illustrate this and compare it with those of other members of your class.

Activity	Reduce	Re-use	Recycle

3 Graph **C** shows recycling rates in Europe.

   a) How do you think your country compares? Carry out some research on the internet to try and find out what percentage of waste your country recycles.

   b) Do you have any local recycling centres? What can they recycle? Find them and mark them on a map of your local area.

4 Read the text in figure **D**. Do you know of any similar recycling measures carried out by people in your local area? Write them down, and try to add some ideas of your own.

Looking after our natural environments

We can all do something to cut down on the resources we use, but there is a limit to how much individuals can achieve. Governments and organisations also need to play a part in looking after the environment. Take the Great Barrier Reef in Australia, for example.

CASE STUDY: The Great Barrier Reef Marine Park

The Great Barrier Reef, located off Australia's eastern coast, is the largest coral reef system on the planet – it measures over 2500 km in length (map **A**). More than 2 million people visit the reef every year. The majority (up to 90 per cent) are domestic tourists from within Australia. Large numbers of people also come from New Zealand, Japan, the UK, Germany and other European countries. These tourists stay at hotels on individual islands, go diving, arrive by cruise ship or fly in for the day by helicopter. Many come to see the great range of wildlife (figure **B**) – some species are not found anywhere else in the world.

Tourists spend around US$4 billion a year, contributing money to the local economy and creating jobs. However, the large number of people can cause considerable damage to the environment. This can be by using polluting vehicles or damaging the coral when snorkelling and diving.

Section 3.7: Environmental risks of economic development

There are other pressures on the environment. Large towns along the coast have factories and power stations. There is large-scale coastal agriculture using fertilisers and other chemicals. These industries can pollute the sea and destroy the fragile coral. People from the towns located near the reef use the surrounding waters for commercial fishing, and the local Torres Strait islanders have depended on the sea for food for centuries. Overfishing is a potential risk. Meeting the needs of all these users makes **conservation** of the reef very difficult.

The Great Barrier Reef Marine Park Authority (GBRMPA)

The Australian government has made the Great Barrier Reef into a protected area by declaring it a 'marine park'. The GBRMPA is the organisation responsible for looking after the reef (figure **C**).

One of the most important developments by the Marine Park Authority has been to divide the whole reef into zones, creating areas where people are allowed to use the reef in different ways. There are areas for local people to fish, other areas for tourists to dive, and so on.

The GBRMPA has been praised for the way it has communicated with all the people who want to use the park – from tourist companies to local fishermen. It has won many international awards for helping to protect the environment while allowing sustainable development to take place.

The problem of climate change

One of the biggest threats to the Great Barrier Reef comes from climate change. Rising sea temperatures can kill the coral and have a damaging effect on fish and other marine life. Extreme weather events can also affect the area. In 2017, huge floods caused by severe tropical cyclone Debbie washed damaging sediments and pollutants over large parts of the reef (photo **D**).

There is little the GBRMPA can do to stop climate change but it is helping local people prepare for the possible negative effects on the environment and their lifestyles and jobs.

A Australia's Great Barrier Reef

- 30 species of whales, dolphins, and porpoises recorded
- 6 species of sea turtles come to the reef to breed
- 215 species of birds (including 22 species of seabirds and 32 species of shorebirds) visit the reef or nest or roost on the islands
- 17 species of sea snake
- More than 1500 fish species
- At least 330 species of ascidians (sea squirts)

B Natural attractions of the reef

Topic link

For more general information about coral reefs see Topic 2.3 pages 101–105.

Economic development

3.7

Organisations wanting to use the reef have to complete a report explaining how their activities will affect the environment

Permits are given out for fishing, diving, camping and other activities – no permit, no use

Tourist boats are not allowed to stop in certain sensitive areas

MANAGEMENT STRATEGIES

Rangers educate visitors on how their trips affect the reef

Boats patrol the area checking up on illegal activity

Fines of up to US$1 million can be forced on companies polluting the environment

Scientific research is used to monitor the effects of activities on the environment

C Strategies used by the GBRMPA

D Damage to the Great Barrier Reef

Further research

Search for 'Great Barrier Reef Marine Park Authority' to find much more official information on the work of the GBRMPA. Create a factfile displaying the information you find.

Now Investigate

1 Assuming there are 200 000 overseas visitors to the Great Barrier Reef every year, complete a copy of the following table to show the number of visitors from selected countries.

Country	Percentage of total visitors	Number of visitors (total 200 000)
United Kingdom	30	60 000
Germany	10	
Other European countries	21	
Japan	15	
USA	11	
Other countries	13	

2 Display the information shown in your table as (a) a correctly labelled pie chart and (b) a bar graph. Think of the effects all these visitors could have on the sustainable development and conservation of the reef.

3 a) Explain why Australia's Great Barrier Reef needs to be protected.

b) Explain how this protection is being carried out.

Section 3.7: Environmental risks of economic development

Conservation management and National Parks

Australia's Great Barrier Reef Marine Park is just one example of the worldwide network of National Parks. These are areas protected from development, usually because they contain some special environmental feature, fragile environment or wildlife that may be in danger of extinction. There are many different categories of National Park including marine reserves, forest reserves and forest parks, biological reserves and wildlife refuges (figure **A**).

> **Topic link**
>
> There is more on tourism, including national parks, in Topic 3.4 pages 181–188.

National Park	Country	Special feature
Jaldapara Wildlife Sanctuary	West Bengal, India	Indian elephants
Kruger National Park	South Africa	Wildlife
Bwindi Impenetrable National Park	Uganda	Mountain gorillas
Poas Volcano National Park	Costa Rica	Active volcano
Quttinirpaaq National Park	Canada	Tidewater glaciers
Triglav National Park	Slovenia	Limestone scenery and caves
Whanganui National Park	New Zealand	Lowland forest and birdlife
Madidi National Park	Bolivia	Tropical rainforest

A *Examples of National Parks from around the world*

National Parks in the UK

The UK's National Parks were originally set up by the government in 1949. They have three main aims:

- to maintain and improve natural beauty, wildlife and culture
- to help the public understand and enjoy their special qualities
- to make sure local communities can survive economically and socially.

> **Fantastic fact**
>
> The world's first ever National Park was Yellowstone in the USA.

In most parts of the world, National Parks are **wilderness** areas but this is not the case in the UK. The country's high population density means National Parks are areas of the countryside where people live and work. These areas have different kinds of industry and farming that would not be allowed in National Parks in many other countries. For this reason their conservation is affected by many different pressures.

Economic development

3.7

CASE STUDY

The Yorkshire Dales National Park, England

The Yorkshire Dales National Park is an area of beautiful rural landscapes in the north of England (map **B**). It is famous for its limestone scenery and wildlife. Unlike many National Parks, it is renowned as a farming landscape with unique features such as 'drystone walls'. For centuries it has also been an industrial area with quarries mining limestone and lead (photos **C**). It is close to major population centres including the cities of Leeds, Manchester and Liverpool and receives almost 9 million visitors each year. The military also use part of the National Park for war games practice. The variety of uses puts a lot of pressure on those trying to conserve the environment of the Park.

Problems and solutions

Some of the problems caused by the different land uses in the National Park are listed below:

- **Tourism** – causing traffic congestion; leaving farm gates open; parking on narrow roads.
- **Quarrying** – causes noise and visual pollution; lorries cause congestion and pollution; disused quarries are dangerous.
- **Military** – loud noises disturb wildlife and scare tourists.
- **Local residents** – lack of affordable housing for local people; residents treat tourists as a nuisance.

A number of different organisations are trying to find solutions to these problems. Some, like the Yorkshire Dales National Park Authority, are official government bodies. Others, like the Friends of the Yorkshire Dales, are voluntary and rely on donations from the public. Solutions to the problems in the Dales include:

- stopping new quarries being set up
- 'screening' the quarries with trees to reduce pollution
- using self-closing gates in farmers' fields
- allowing 'live' firing by the army only on certain days
- increasing public transport and providing car parks on the edges of popular towns and villages
- forcing quarry companies to return the landscape to its natural state when digging is finished
- helping build rail links to quarries and limiting blasting to certain days of the week

B *The location of the Yorkshire Dales National Park*

C *Landscapes of the Yorkshire Dales National Park*

Section 3.7: Environmental risks of economic development 233

- providing houses at lower prices for local residents
- making tourists feel more welcome.

The organisations involved work to manage the National Park carefully, and there is a lot of communication between all the parties involved. It is only by doing this that the environment will be conserved, and development within the Park will be sustainable.

Remember that some of the details you need to know are covered in previous sections of Section 3.

C *Landscapes of the Yorkshire Dales National Park*

Now Investigate

1. Find out about National Parks in your own country. They are often marked on maps. Investigate why they were set up and what they are protecting.

2. What are the aims of the UK's National Parks? Which do you think is most important? Give at least one reason for your answer.

3. Using photos **C**, describe the varied human and natural landscapes and environments of the Yorkshire Dales National Park. Explain why these landscapes are important.

4. Construct a mind map, using different colours, to show the problems caused by the different land uses in the Yorkshire Dales National Park and some of the proposed solutions.

Section 4 . Topic 1

Map skills

Learning objectives:
- use a co-ordinate reference system and be able to give and read four-figure and six-figure grid references to locate places
- be able to give directions, both in terms of a 16-point compass (such as north, north-north-east, north-east, etc.) and as a bearing from grid north of one place from another
- calculate differences in height by means of contour reading
- interpret, construct or complete a cross-section
- translate the scale of a feature by describing its size and shape in real terms
- be proficient in using the key to identify features on the map
- draw inferences about the physical and human landscape by interpreting map evidence such as patterns of relief, drainage, settlement, communication and land use
- identify basic landscape features such as river valleys and uplands
- give brief descriptions of basic landscape features using suitable geographical terms (such as ridge, plateau, scarp, flood plain) and simple adjectives showing an appreciation of their nature (such as broad, flat, steep-sided, deeply cut, gently sloping)
- recognise essential differences in density of drainage, stream patterns, gradients or sizes of streams in relation to the relief
- describe the physical features of coastlines and the shape and form of river channels as they are shown on large-scale maps
- describe variations in land use
- recognise and analyse patterns of settlement (dispersed, nucleated, linear) and draw sketch maps illustrating these patterns
- interpret and describe features of urban morphology as represented on large-scale maps
- describe the functions of and services provided by settlements
- give reasons for the site and growth of individual settlements
- recognise communication networks in terms of their type and density in relation to physical and human features

About maps

A number of standard mapping conventions are used worldwide, for example blue is used to show water features and brown for the height of the land. However, there are also many variations in map symbols, so all maps include a key displaying any symbols on the map, with their meanings. When 'reading' a map you must always take time to refer to its key.

Giving directions

Diagram **A** shows a sixteen-point compass. Using a compass is the most common way to give directions. A more accurate

A *Sixteen-point compass*

Stage 1 Place the centre point of the protractor over the 'direction from' place on the map (A).

Stage 2 Adjust the protractor so that its 0° line from the centre dot points due North. Do this by making sure that this line is parallel to the nearest vertical grid line on the map.

Stage 3 Use a pencil and ruler to join point A to the 'direction to' place on the map (B).

Stage 4 Read the number of degrees from 0° (i.e. North) to the point where the line AB crosses the edge of the protractor. This is the bearing of B from A – in this example 60°.

B *How to find bearings using a map and protractor*

Section 4.1: Map skills 235

way to give directions is to use bearings. These provide the exact angle between two places, measured from due north. In order to calculate bearings, you need a protractor (diagram **B**). However, you do need to learn the compass points! On most – but not all – maps, north is at the top. Any map that you draw must include a north point. When using a map in an examination, be very careful to check where north is before you write any answers that include directions. Most questions can be answered by making simple statements such as 'The mountains are in the north', 'Most rain occurs in eastern areas' or 'The river flows in a south-westerly direction'. In examinations many candidates confuse west and east. They also often write directions the wrong way round, for example 'east-south' instead of 'south-east'. So do learn the names and directions well.

Scale and distance

Topographical maps are drawn to a **scale** of 1:25 000 or 1:50 000. On the 1:25 000 map this means that 4 cm on the map represents 1 km on the ground. Similarly, on 1:50 000 maps, 2 cm on the map represents 1 km on the ground.

The easiest way to work out distances on topographical maps is to use the scale line. You may be asked to calculate a distance in a straight line – the direct distance from one point on the map to another – or you may have to measure a curved distance, for example along a river or winding road. To do this, place the straight edge of a clean piece of paper between the two points you are measuring. Mark these points on your paper, then move the paper to the scale line. The first point on your paper should be aligned with zero on the scale line. Then check where the second point is on the scale-line and note the distance. If the distance you are measuring on the map is not straight, you will need to do this several times to find the total distance. Always give your answer in metres or kilometres.

C *Grid system on a topographical map*

Locating places using grid references

The grid lines that run from north to south are called **eastings**. They are numbered along the top and the bottom of the map, and the numbers always increase in value from west to east (map **C**). The **grid lines** that run from west to east are called **northings**. They are numbered up the sides of the map, and their values increase from south to north.

4.1

Some map extracts are part of a much larger map – so the grid numbers are very unlikely to start at 00 in the south-west corner!

The grid and grid lines on a map are used to give **grid references**. These are unique locations on that map where a feature or a place is located. Four-figure grid references identify the **grid square** in which a large feature such as a village, a lake or a forest can be found. For example, in map **C** the square marked X is shaded in orange:

- The line along the left of the square is numbered 81
- The line along the bottom of the square is numbered 09.

So the four-figure grid reference for that square is 8109. Notice that the easting comes first, followed by the northing.

However, to pinpoint an exact location, we use a more precise six-figure grid reference. In map **C**, the six-figure grid reference for the school building (Sch) is 805087.

- The grid line to the left is 80, and the school is *five*-tenths (5/10) of the square to the *right* of that line.
- The grid line to the bottom is 08, and the school is *seven*-tenths (7/10) of the square *above* that line.

Now Investigate

1 Look at the map on page 42. Sketch four symbols shown on the map and explain what each one represents.

2 Find an open space outside. Establish which direction is north, and then describe what you can see as you turn to the south, east and west.

Refer to map **C**.

3 Give the four-figure grid references for:

   a) The square entirely filled with woodland
   b) The square that is mostly filled with water.

4 Give the six-figure grid references for:

   a) The post office P
   b) The crossroads.

The shape of the land

Contour lines

Topographical maps show the relief of a landscape. They do this by using **contour lines** – a type of isoline that joins points with the same **altitude** (height) above sea level. Many maps also include **spot heights**, which show the exact height of the land,

> **Topic link**
>
> See Topic 4.2 page 256 to learn more about isolines.

Section 4.1: Map skills   237

marked as a dot and a number stating the height (diagram **A**).

In many countries, relief is shown by colour-shading of the area between the contour lines. See for example the maps on pages 42 and 312.

Contour lines tell us much more than just the height of the land. The patterns they make show us the shape of the land surface and how steeply it slopes. They also give us the information we need to calculate the **gradient** (steepness) of the land.

Cross-sections

A **cross-section** shows changes in relief between two points on a map. It is a kind of line graph, with horizontal distance plotted along the *x*-axis, and the height of the land on the *y*-axis. You may not need to learn how to draw a cross-section for your examination questions, but drawing can help you to understand how cross-sections are constructed and so be able to link them to a map and annotate their features.

A Contours representing relief

Annotating a cross-section

The main aim of any cross-section is to show the shape of the land – so any labels or annotations generally refer to its relief features. However, such profiles can also be used to show other physical features, for example those in river valleys. Aspects of the human landscape may also be shown, for example:

- the sites of settlements
- the locations of routeways
- land uses at different altitudes.

Cross-sections are an ideal way of highlighting relationships between relief features and human activities, for example where routeways follow valley bottoms.

Interpreting cross-sections

Although you may not have to draw a cross-section, you are expected to be able to interpret them in the examination. This involves describing and possibly explaining the relief features shown. Where land is steep, contours are close together, and the cross-section profiles will reflect this (diagram **A**). More gently sloping land is shown by contours that are further apart. Land that rises and falls gently is said to be 'rolling' or 'undulating'. Cross-sections can also indicate where land slopes

> **Topic link**
>
> See Topic 4.3 pages 251–262 to learn more about line graphs.

i An even slope
ii A concave slope
iii A convex slope

B *Cross-sections of three different types of slope*

very evenly (diagram **Bi**), is concave (diagram **Bii**) or is convex (diagram **Biii**).

If you are asked to describe or explain features using a cross-section, you could also comment on:

- the highest and lowest points (and their grid references)
- the difference in height between these points
- how the land slopes in each direction from the highest point, for example steeply or gently, and referring to compass directions as necessary
- the relationship between physical features and any human activities.

Gradient

Gradient is the mathematical term used to describe the steepness of a slope. It is the change in vertical height between two points compared with the horizontal distance between them. It can be given either as a ratio (e.g. 1:10) or a percentage (10%). Diagram **C** explains how a gradient between two points on a map is calculated.

Calculating gradient is an extra and not required by the Cambridge syllabus

To find the gradient between the spot heights at 49 m and 11 m

Stage 1 Calculate the difference in height between the two places: 49 m – 11 m = 38 m

Stage 2 Calculate the distance between the two places. Using the line scale on the map shows that this is 550 m.

Stage 3 To find the gradient, divide the distance by the height difference: $\frac{550m}{38m}$ = 14.5

Gradient is 1:14 5

C *How to calculate gradient*

Now Investigate

1. Draw the contours that would represent a long, isolated hill that has a steep slope on one side, a flat top, and a more gentle slope on the other side.

Section 4.1: Map skills

Landforms and drainage

You are now aware that knowing about contours, slopes and gradients helps us to understand what the relief of an area is like. They can also be used to identify landscape features such as river valleys (figure **A**).

Figure **A** shows typical contour patterns for some of the most common types of relief feature, as you will see on a large-scale map, with photographs of some of these features. Table **B** describes each of these features. You need to be able to recognise all of them on both 1:25 000 and 1:50 000 scale maps, and be able to name and describe each one.

When you describe the relief of an area, remember to:

- Make a few general statements such as:

    'This is mainly a highland/lowland area.'
    'Most of its slopes are steep/gentle.'
    'The land is undulating.'

- Quote actual heights from the map (including the highest and lowest).

Type of landscape feature	Description
Cliff	very steep (vertical) slope
Escarpment	a ridge with one side that is much steeper (scarp slope) than the other (dip slope)
Knoll	small, isolated hill
Pass (gap)	long valley providing a natural routeway through an upland area
Plateau	flat-topped area of high land
Ridge	long, narrow area of higher land
Spur	finger of high land that juts out into an area of lower land
Valley	narrow area of lowland that has higher land on both sides; valleys widen as they approach the sea

A Some landscape features and their contour patterns

B Descriptions of landscape features

240 Geographical skills

- Calculate the height range between these two points.
- Identify and name key features such as mountain peaks and river valleys.
- Give grid references to locate features.
- Use compass directions, for example 'The area of highest land is in the south-east'.
- Mention any coastal features such as cliffs.

Look at figure **A** again, and note how similar the contour patterns for ridges and river valleys can seem on a map – you need to look carefully at the contour heights to see whether the land is rising or falling. It is important to identify these features correctly in an exam – table **C** will help you to do this.

Typical contour patterns	Identifying features
Valley	• Often has a river or stream flowing through it. • Lowest contour values are in the 'middle' of the feature (inside the V). • Contour V-shape points uphill, to higher ground.
Ridge	• Never has a river or stream flowing through it. • Highest contour values are in the 'middle' of the feature (inside the V). • Contour V-shape points downhill, to lower ground.

C *Differences between ridges and valleys*

Describing rivers and river valleys

When you are asked to describe the **drainage** of an area, you should be aware that the question is asking you about both rivers *and* their valleys. You should, therefore, try to comment on all of the following:

- The presence or absence of any surface drainage such as rivers and lakes.
- The names of the main river, any important tributaries and large lakes.
- The density of drainage – estimate the number of rivers and streams and how close they are to each other. Make statements such as: 'There are many rivers and streams in the north and west of the map area, but far fewer in the south.'
- Any major confluence points, giving their grid reference locations.
- Any general drainage patterns that the rivers and streams make (diagram **D**).
- The long profile of the main river. Do this by observing how close the contour lines are where the river crosses them – the closer the contours, the steeper the profile will be.
- The features of the main river, by quoting:
  - its width at the widest and narrowest places – give a grid reference for each place
  - its general direction of flow

D *Two types of drainage pattern*

Section 4.1: Map skills

- evidence of any river features such as meanders, oxbow lakes and waterfalls – give their grid references
- any evidence of flooding, for example levees or marshy land, and locate these, e.g. 'The river appears to flood in the north-west area of the map [quote the grid reference]; the evidence for this is the levees along its banks in grid square ... '.

- The shape of the main river valley (e.g. is it V-shaped?) and its width – is there evidence of any interlocking spurs?
- Evidence of a flood plain – where is it and how wide is it?
- Evidence of any human activity, such as:
  - dams/reservoirs
  - flood control measures, e.g. river straightening or embankments.
- Again, locate these activities using grid squares/references.

> **Topic link**
>
> Look back at Topics 1.5 and 1.6 to remind yourself about your work on settlement.

Now Investigate

1. Look at the map on page 312. Describe the drainage pattern shown.

The human landscape

There are several human landscape features you could be asked about in an examination. Probably the most common of these is settlement. Settlements may be rural or urban – and you may be asked about either of these, so you need to revise this subject thoroughly for both Cambridge Papers 1 and 2.

Describing settlement patterns

To provide a good description of a settlement pattern, follow this system:

- **Stage 1** – write some general statements about where settlements are, for example: 'Most settlements are in the north and north-west.' If there is a large settlement, name it and state how much of the map area it covers.
- **Stage 2** – provide some detailed information, for example: 'Some settlements follow the course of the river *x*' or 'Most villages avoid steep slopes' (photo **A**).

A *A village site at the base of a hill slope is easy to build on, and provides shelter*

- **Stage 3** – make one or two specific points by naming features, giving grid references and referring to the height of the land, for example: 'Settlements appear to be on land below 150 metres' or 'Many are on south-facing slopes'.

Questions may also ask you about the site, situation and shape of settlements.

Site is the area of land on which a settlement is built. You should provide information about its physical and human features. The letters of the word **SHAWL** may help you here:

- **S**helter – from winds and storms (photo **A**).
- **H**eight – above sea level.
- **A**spect – the direction towards which sloping land faces.
- **W**ater supply – from springs, rivers etc.
- **L**and – is it flat or gently sloping, on or above a river flood plain (photo **B**)?

Situation refers to a settlement's location within the larger area around it. Here, the letters **PARC** can be used:

- **P**laces – for example, other settlements and National Parks.
- **A**ccessibility – how easy it is for people to get to a settlement.
- **R**elief – the height and shape of the land.
- **C**ommunications – for example road and rail links.

> **Topic link**
>
> See pages 237–242 for more on the shape of the land and how it is represented on maps.

B *Although water is important, some villages avoid the river's flood plain*

Section 4.1: Map skills

Shape can take one of three basic forms: nucleated, linear and dispersed. You may be able to provide additional information, for example:

- Nucleated settlements are clustered around key points such as road junctions.
- Linear settlements follow routeways, valleys or coastlines (name these where possible).

Maps show many different kinds of human activity. If an exam question asks you to identify and/or to describe these, you must start by studying the key to discover what the symbols on the map represent – and then include a range of the activities set out in diagram **C**. Try to identify any patterns that the activities make across the map's area – and don't forget to include grid references (and place names) in your answer!

C *Human activities represented on maps*

Now Investigate

1. List the three main stages of writing a good description of a settlement pattern.

2. Refer to these stages and write a brief description of the settlement pattern on the map on page 312.

Section 4 . Topic 2

Using maps

Learning objectives:
- be able to identify and describe significant features of the human and physical landscape on maps, for example, population distribution, population movements, transport networks, settlement layout, relief and drainage

••

Examination questions frequently give you a map (often an atlas-type) and ask questions that test your ability to recognise and describe distributions or patterns. Such maps may show the physical or human features of a landscape. More searching questions may then test how well you can analyse information presented in map form – perhaps by asking you to link the information on two or more maps.

A (i) *The relief of Britain*

(ii) *Population density in Britain*

Describing maps

Your main focus when describing maps like those in figure **A** is to keep your answer relevant to the question! Avoid including additional information that you happen to know about the area,

Section 4.2: Using maps   245

try to write a 'word picture' and give a detailed answer worthy of high marks.

1 Read the title of the map and study the key.

2 Start with one or two general statements about key features located on the map.

3 Then add more detail, by mentioning named areas or particular features.

4 Add some specific detail and/or named features

5 Finally, for top marks, note any anomalies (distributions which don't fit the general pattern)

Map skills

1 Study figure **B**.

   Describe the distribution of the world's main forested areas.

   Do this by answering the following questions:

   a) Where is each type of forest located in relation to the named lines of latitude?

   b) Which continents have the largest areas of forest? Which types of forest grow there?

   c) Are there any continents without any forests? If so, which one(s)?

   d) Name one continent in which each type of forest can be found.

B *Global distribution of forests*

Geographical skills

2. Devise a similar set of questions to help you describe the distribution of population within Britain.

3. Use these questions (i.e. your answer to question 2) to write a paragraph describing Britain's population distribution.

Many maps use different shadings and colours to show the physical or human features of an area (maps **A** and **B**). Some types of map you may come across include:

- **Energy and mineral production maps**, locating economic assets such as coalfields.
- **Environmental hazard maps**, highlighting areas where water and air pollution levels are especially high.
- **Natural hazard maps**, locating major tropical revolving storms and other natural hazard events – these may include plate boundaries and names, because the position of plates is a significant factor in the location of earthquakes and volcanic activity.
- **Political maps**, showing country boundaries and names – these often include capital cities and other major urban settlements.
- **Urbanisation maps**, showing the percentage of people living in urban (as opposed to rural) areas.
- **Wealth distribution maps**, showing each country's average GDP per person per year.

> **Topic link**
>
> Map **B** is a 'Eurocentric' global map, because Europe is on its central line of longitude. Turn to page 75 to see an example of an America-centric map.

Now Investigate

1. Look through this book and find three distribution maps. Explain what type of distribution each map shows. Hint: Look carefully at the map title and key.

2. Use map **B** to describe any similarities and differences between the land areas in the northern and southern hemispheres.

Analysing and comparing maps

Some examination questions are based on **thematic maps** which include additional information in the form of bar graphs and pie charts. Other questions invite you to compare two maps of the same area, which might present different types of information, or show similar information taken at different times.

Analysing maps

A Global fossil fuel reserves in 2016

percentage of world total ■ Coal ■ Oil ■ Natural gas

Map **A** is a thematic map with the extra information displayed as bar graphs. In response to the question 'Compare the fossil fuel reserves in the six regions' you would be expected to write statements like these, based on the six bar graphs:

- Every region has some reserves of all three types of fossil fuel.
- Reserves are significant in all regions except for coal in the Middle East, which is only 1 per cent of the world's total, and coal reserves in South America and Africa, which are much smaller than those in other regions.
- North America and Europe-Eurasia still have very large reserves of coal, even though much has already been used here since the industrial revolution, which made these the world's first major industrial regions.
- Europe-Eurasia still has one-third of the world's natural gas reserves, which are available for use as coal stocks begin to run out.
- Asia-Pacific's reserves of coal are much greater than the reserves of oil or natural gas.
- The Middle East is very rich in oil and natural gas – it is the region with the largest reserves of both of these fossil fuels.

Comparing maps

Often, you will be presented with two maps showing data which is linked in some way, then be invited to identify the main linkages and suggest reasons for them. Figures **B(i)** and **(ii)** show a typical pair of maps giving information about Africa. To write successfully about maps in this way:

- Read the question very carefully and be very clear about what it asks you to do.
- 'Read' both maps – their titles and their keys.
- Write a very brief description of the 'independent' map (i.e. the one which shows information which might 'cause' the second map's distribution). E.g.:
  - Dry climate affects about 50% of Africa and droughts are closely associated with drier areas.
  - Both are particularly common across northern Africa although southern Africa is also affected.
  - Central Africa is not a dry region but in the early 1970s (for example) even the east of this region experienced some droughts.
- Write a similar brief description of the second map, making comparisons where possible.

  For example:
  - In many ways, the map of famine-affected regions is very similar to the drought map.

Geographical skills

B (i) *Drought events in Africa*

B (ii) *The extent of famine in Africa*

- In much the same way, famine affects a belt across tropical North Africa.
- However, famines seem rather less common in southern Africa.
- The countries of Ethiopia, South Sudan and Chad (with over 6 million, 5 million and 3 million people affected respectively) are amongst the worst affected famine areas.
- Famine is not common in Central Africa, although it can occur along its eastern seaboard.
- Countries along the northern coastline seem to be unaffected by famine, even though they are dry and droughts do occur.

• Make a final, summative statement such as:
- Overall, it appears that there is a close link between dry climates, drought and famine events in Africa, with areas of least rainfall usually experiencing the most famines.

Now Investigate

1. Using figure **C,** answer this question:
Describe the pattern of nuclear power production across western Europe.

2. Use figures **D(i)** and **(ii)** to answer these questions:
   a) Describe the global distribution of active volcanoes.
   b) Referring to figure **D(ii)**, suggest reasons for this distribution.

3. Using what you have learned in this section, return to figures **A(i)** and **A(ii)** on page 245 and write a detailed account of the link between relief and population density in Britain.

4. Use figures **B(i)** and **B(ii)** to see if there is a link between drought and famine in Africa. Use the guidelines on page 248 to structure your answer.

Section 4.2: Using maps

C *Percentage of nuclear power generated in Europe*

D (i) *The distribution of active volcanoes*

D (ii) *Earth's plate boundaries*

250 Geographical skills

Section 4 . Topic 3

Graphing and mapping numerical data

Learning objectives:
- construct a range of graphs to illustrate numerical data
- present numerical data and locational data on a map
- describe and explain the patterns that such graphs and maps show
- suggest and use appropriate methods of representing numerical data
- describe variations and identify trends in information

One of the easiest and most common ways of presenting data is to draw graphs. There are several different types of graph and it is important for you to know which is the correct one to use.

Simple graphs

Line graphs show data that changes continuously as time passes. Time is always plotted along the horizontal (**x**) axis, and the variable data (such as temperature or number of vehicles) is plotted using the vertical (**y**) axis. Line graphs can also be used to predict how the variable may change in the future. Diagram **A** shows you how to draw a line graph.

Bar graphs are also simple to draw, but are often used wrongly, or not drawn correctly. Many students confuse them with histograms (see below). Bar graphs are only used to show data that fits into categories, for example types of vegetation or road vehicles, but **not** data that changes over time (diagram **B**). Bar graphs are always drawn with a space between each category (bar) on the **x** axis. More complex graphs can be used to display several data sets, and can also be used to compare data year by year.

Histograms look like bar graphs drawn without spaces between the bars – and there is a more important difference too. They are used to show data that is continuous in some way. This may

The y axis is used for the variable data set

Label each axis, stating what it shows

Divisions along the axis are always evenly spaced

Average monthly temperatures for Auckland, New Zealand
Altitude 26 metres

Plot data using small dots or crosses

The x axis is used for the dependent data set

The title should state clearly what the graph shows

Join the dots/crosses carefully with a smooth curve

Note: If you are drawing a temperature line graph it is usual to present the line in red

Plot the data as accurately as possible

A *How to draw a line graph*

Section 4.3: Graphing and mapping numerical data 251

be data that changes as time passes (like monthly rainfall totals for a year) or values that vary across the data set (for example particle size in a soil sample). Remembering this crucial difference between bar graphs and histograms is the key to knowing which type of graph to draw. Diagram **C** shows two types of histogram which you may see in examinations – and which you need to be able to draw and interpret for Cambridge Papers 3 and 4.

Vehicles travelling into city centre along main road 10 August 2010, 10.00–10.15

- The y axis label should include units of measurement if included (here absolute numbers are shown)
- The title should include information about date/time if relevant
- Height of each bar shows data plotted
- Width of all bars should be the same
- Shade each bar a different colour
- Leave a clear gap between each bar
- The x axis label links to graph title

B How to draw a bar graph

Average monthly precipitation for Auckland, New Zealand

- Specific details in title
- Title states the type of graph and what it shows
- Precipitation/rainfall is usually shaded in blue
- Histograms show a change over a continuous period of time

Histogram showing beach pebble length

- The x axis showing continuous change (length of pebbles)
- Pebble length (cm). The axis label includes unit of measurement and the variable
- Mutually exclusive data sets

C Two types of histogram

252 Geographical skills

4.3

Now Investigate

1 Using the information from pages 251–255, which type of graph would you draw to display each of the following sets of data?

   a) The average (mean) height of six different types of vegetation recorded in your sample area.

   b) Population growth over a number of years.

   c) Pedestrian flow along a CBD street (at survey points every 10 m) recorded at 5-minute intervals over one hour.

   d) The tally of different types of land use (expressed as percentages) along a main road.

More complex graphs

Scatter graphs are plotted in a similar way to line graphs, but show two sets of changing data instead of one. This type of graph is used if it seems likely that one set of data is likely to be the cause of changes to a second set. For example, in diagram **A**, a country's GDP is thought to be the significant factor affecting the number of people in that country who own a cell phone. The data set that 'causes' the change is called the independent variable, while the set that is affected by it is the dependent variable. Diagram **B** shows you how to use a scatter graph to identify and then analyse links between data sets.

- Decide which is your independent variable (in this example, GDP) and which is likely to be the dependent variable (cell phone ownership).
- Plot your axes and decide on a suitable scale for each one. Note that the spaces between values must be the same along each axis.
- Plot the data as you would for a line graph, but do not join the dots:

A *How to construct a scatter graph*

	GDP/ person (US$)	Cell phones per 100 people
USA	57 300	119
UK	42 500	125
France	42 400	100
etc. ↓		

Section 4.3: Graphing and mapping numerical data

- Identify the mid-point on your graph.
- Place a ruler through this point. (Hint: A clear plastic ruler makes this task easier.)
- Now rotate the ruler around this mid-point until it divides the dots on the graph so that half of them are above it and half below it.
- Draw a pencil line along the ruler's edge; this is your best-fit line.
- There are two key points to remember:
    - The line does not have to pass through the origin of the graph.
    - While your aim is to split the dots 50:50, it isn't critical if you can't quite do this.

B *How to add a best-fit line to a scatter graph*

Age/sex pyramids show population structure according to age and gender (diagram **C**). They are drawn using two back-to-back, horizontal histograms. Age is plotted on a central **y** axis, and the number of people in each age group is plotted along the **x** axis (number of people is sometimes presented as a percentage of the whole population).

C *A typical age/sex pyramid*

A **triangular graph** is a way of showing three variables on one diagram. The triangular shape allows three axes to be shown. Diagram **D** explains how to read a triangular graph.

D *Reading a triangular graph*

254   Geographical skills

4.3

Pie graphs are sometimes called pie charts or circle graphs (diagram **E**). They are divided into sectors to illustrate proportions. When describing these graphs, you should comment on the size of each sector in relation to the whole graph, and compare the size of each sector with other sectors.

Energy used in Brazil	
Oil	47%
HEP	28%
Natural gas	12%
Coal	6%
Renewables	6%
Nuclear	1%

Types of energy used in Brazil

- Oil
- HEP
- Natural gas
- Coal
- Renewables
- Nuclear

E *Constructing a pie graph*

Wind rose graphs are often simply called rose diagrams. These are the most frequently used type of **radial graph**. They show the orientation of the data being recorded and are most often used to plot wind direction – hence their name (diagram **F**). The graph is made up of eight separate bar graphs, drawn outwards from a central octagon (to show the main compass directions); the length of each bar represents the number of days the wind blows from each direction.

Scale: 5 days

F *A wind rose graph for one month*

Section 4.3: Graphing and mapping numerical data

Mapping data

Not all the data we collect is presented as graphs. Some information is better shown as a map, because we need to include details of the area it covers.

Isolines are lines on maps that join points of equal value. You already know about contour lines, which are a type of isoline showing information about the altitude (height) of the land. Other examples of isolines are isotherms, which show temperature (map **A**), isohyets (rainfall, map **B**), isobars (atmospheric pressure), isotachs (wind speed) and isogons (wind direction).

A **choropleth** map is a type of thematic map. It provides information about a place, such as population distribution or energy consumption (see map **B** on page 198). The map is coloured or shaded to show changing distribution patterns within an area. Such maps can be drawn by plotting isolines, then shading the spaces between them (map **C**).

A *Isotherm map: average January temperatures across Africa (degrees Celsius)*

*Rainfall figures in centimetres

B *Isohyet (rainfall) map for Africa, November–April*

C *Choropleth map of rainfall across Africa, November–April*

256   Geographical skills

4.3

Flow diagrams are usually used to show movement – of people, goods or even ideas – and so need to include a base map of the area where the movements are taking place. The simplest form of flow diagram is called a **desire line map**. Such maps or diagrams are a very effective way of showing the directions of movements (diagram **D**). This type of map is sometimes called a rose or ray diagram.

Desire line maps become **flow line maps** when they are drawn to show information about the commodity being moved, such as the volume of traffic or goods in each direction. This is done by varying the width of each line to show the volume of flow along it (diagram **E**).

Now Investigate

1 Suggest an appropriate graphic presentation for each of the following sets of data:

   a) Number of students moving along corridors in a school over a specified period of time.

   b) Atmospheric pressure readings taken at many points over the continent of Europe.

   c) Frequency of wind experienced in one place from various directions over a 24-hour period.

Direction and distance travelled to Main High School by pupils in Class 9

D *Desire line map*

Pedestrian traffic in Summertown, 10.00–10.15 on 11 November 2011

E *Flow line map*

Section 4.3: Graphing and mapping numerical data

Mapping land use

When geographers talk about **land use**, what we really mean is 'the human uses of land', for example fields, factories and housing. However, we manage and modify the natural environment too, even in wilderness areas, so these areas can also be mapped on land use maps. Such maps can be used to identify almost every natural resource, settlement type and economic activity on Earth.

Today, commercially produced land use maps are based on satellite imagery and aerial photography (photo **A** and map **B**). However, even with modern technology, map-makers often have to visit an area to check details and record the data, in just the same way that you can record land use in your work for your Cambridge Papers 3 and 4.

A Satellite image of New York City

B Land use map of New York City

As you can see in map **B**, finished land use maps are usually presented as colour patches with a key. However, data collection is often done simply by writing onto a base map what each field, building or plot of land is used for, or using a coding system like those shown in tables **C**. Both of these methods are designed for urban or suburban surveying, but a similar coding system can easily be devised for farm surveys or other rural land uses.

S	Shop
O	Office
E	Entertainment
D	Residence/dwelling
H	Hotel/guest house/motel
P	Public building
OS	Open space
R	Resort function
DEM	Building has been demolished
DER	Building is out-of-use and decaying

C *A simple land use coding system*

S1	Hypermarket/supermarket
S2	Grocery store
S3	Fresh meat shop
S4	Fresh fish shop
S5	Fruit and vegetable shop
etc.	
O1	Solicitor
O2	Estate agent/realtor
O3	Accountant
O4	Surveyor
etc.	

A detailed land use coding system

Geographical skills

D Fieldwork recording sheet showing land use along Lancaster Road, Torrisholme, Morecambe

Urban land use can be recorded across an entire built-up area. However, unless you are surveying a relatively small village, it is more likely that you will investigate land use in an urban zone (such as the CBD) or along a transect through a settlement. A **transect** is simply a route along which we walk, recording and counting occurrences of the topic of study, for example plants or building use. In towns and cities this is usually along a street or a road. Figure **D** shows a typical student's data recording sheet for a land use survey along a main road. Figure **E** shows the same information translated into a land use map.

E Land use map, showing land use along Lancaster Road, Torrisholme, Morecambe

F Relief profile linking land use change to physical features

Section 4.3: Graphing and mapping numerical data   259

Rural land use can also be recorded on a base map showing buildings and fields – especially if you are undertaking a farm study. However, if the relief of the land varies, a different type of transect based on a relief cross-section may be more useful. This will allow you to link land use to relief, geology and soil (diagram **F**). A transect such as this might also be useful in a built-up area if you wish to investigate how land use is affected by relief – perhaps to see if land on a flood plain is used differently to that on higher land on either side.

Interpreting graphs

Some questions in your examinations not only ask you to plot graphs and map data, they also require you to interpret (explain) such information.

Line graphs, bar graphs and histograms

- Identify what is plotted along each axis, and the units of measurement used.
- Describe any trends (changes) in the data – do they show an increase or decrease?
- Is any change steady or fluctuating (variable)? Is it rapid or gradual?
- Note any variations from the overall trend(s).
- Quote data from the graph to support every observation.
- If asked to, justify each observation, using your geographical knowledge and understanding.

Compound graphs

Such graphs display changing information over time for more than one variable. Examples can be found on page 159 graph E (a compound bar graph) and page 182 graph B (a compound line graph).

A *A line graph*

Start by following the guidelines above for each data set. Then:

- State the relative importance of each component (variable).
- Identify any patterns or links between the different components.
- Justify any statements you make by quoting data from the graph.
- If asked to, use your geographical knowledge to suggest reasons for the patterns, trends and links that you have identified.

Climate graphs

- Describe the temperature pattern.
- Describe the rainfall/precipitation regime.
- Comment on humidity levels (dry/arid/damp/humid).
- Refer to the weather station's altitude (if provided). If appropriate to the question, comment on how altitude has influenced rainfall and temperature patterns.
- If the question asks you to give reasons for the climate data, do so using your geographical knowledge of climatic factors, for example latitude, movement of the overhead Sun, prevailing wind, continentality and relief.

Temperatures are plotted in centre of the column

Title is 'Climate' (not 'Temperature and precipitation')

Altitude is included because of its effect on both temperature and precipitation

Climate graph for Auckland, New Zealand (26m)

Remember to read temperatures from the left-hand y axis and precipitation from the right-hand axis

B *A climate graph*

Pie graphs

- Note and then use the correct units of measurement – not all pie graphs show percentages!
- Describe the relative size of each sector and identify the largest and smallest ones. Instead of writing brief statements such as 'Oil is the largest sector', provide detailed ones, for example 'Oil was the largest supplier of energy in Brazil in 2006'.
- If there are a number of pie graphs, compare and contrast the data within them. Always quote which graph you are referring to, and provide data from it to support your observations.

Age/sex pyramids

- Identify the units used – they may be percentages or actual numbers of people.
- Comment on the width of the pyramid's base, then its height.

C Age/sex pyramids for China

- Describe the overall shape of the pyramid.
- Identify and comment on the dependent and independent populations. What is the dependency ratio?
- Link every point you make to the country's population structure/policies/issues and quality of life.
- Are there any anomalies, for example bars that are much longer or shorter than the overall trend? Do these indicate the effects of migration/war/famine/'baby booms'?
- Note the likely level of development of the country (less economically developed country/more economically developed country), giving reasons for your decision.

Now Investigate

1. Look through this book and find examples of each of the graph types described above.

2. Choose one of the graphs you identified in (1), and write a clear interpretation of that graph.

3. Study the material in Topic 1.1 on pages 16–17 about population growth in China.

    a) Explain what effect the 1958 and 1961 droughts and floods and the two population explosions had on the shape of the 2013 pyramid shown in figure **C**.

    b) Explain what effect the 'one-child policy' has had on the shape of the 2050 pyramid shown in figure **C**.

Geographical skills

Section 4 . Topic 4

Using illustrations

Learning objectives:
- be able to give simple descriptions of human and physical landscapes (landforms, natural vegetation, land use and settlement) and geographical phenomena from photographs, and aerial photographs
- be able to add specified detail on maps or other material provided to show that they can apply geographical knowledge and understanding
- be able to use supporting material in conjunction with large-scale maps to identify, describe and analyse features and show that they can recognise patterns and deduce trends

Your examination papers are likely to include a photograph or some other type of illustration. For Cambridge Paper 3 (fieldwork) you will be expected to use photographs and/or sketches as a record of the landscape you visited.

Photographs

The photographs you take and use may have been taken at ground level, but in examination papers they are more likely to be aerial photographs or satellite images (photo **A**).

All photographs include information that does not appear on maps, for example land use in rural areas (see photo **A**) and traffic in urban zones. Examination questions may invite you to use a variety of skills, for example:

- Simple descriptive writing about features in a picture.
- More in-depth writing asking you to give reasons based on evidence in a photograph.
- Photograph interpretation – describing and explaining what you can see.
- Completion of a labelled or annotated sketch based on a photograph (see pages 266–267).

Photo **B** shows part of the centre of Shanghai. Possible questions on this image might include:

- 'Describe what photo **B** shows you.'

    Your answer might include observations such as:
    - There are tall/high-rise buildings made of steel and glass.
    - These look like office buildings.
    - They are built very close together.
    - The roads are [insert info based on photo].

- 'Give evidence which suggests that this zone is part of the CBD.'

A *Satellite image of land use in rural Kansas, USA*

B *Aerial view of central Shanghai, China*

Section 4.4: Using illustrations

Here, answers need to be more specific, for example:

- The high-rise buildings are obviously very modern and this suggests that they are office blocks. They are typical of a CBD.
- There is a dense network of straight, narrow streets.

- 'What evidence is there in photo **B** that this city is in a less economically developed country?'

This question tests your knowledge of urban land use models and your ability to use photographs. Your answer should focus on street patterns and building densities, because in less economically developed countries, city centre streets usually form a grid-iron pattern.

> **Topic link**
>
> - See Topics 1.5 and 1.6 for more information on features of settlement.
> - Look back at Topic 1.6 for information on urban land use models.

Interpreting an aerial photograph

'Interpretation' includes both description and explanation. You need to write clearly and use key terms to support your answer. Include information about both the physical and the human environments. You will find the following guidelines helpful.

Physical features

- Describe the relief and gradient of the land.
- Note the presence (or absence) of streams/rivers. Comment on their width and course. Do they meander or flood? Can you see a flood plain?
- Describe the coastline (if appropriate). Is it a lowland coast or are there cliffs? Is there a river mouth? What shape is the coastline? Are there headlands and bays? Is it a coastline of erosion or deposition? What evidence do you have for this?
- In rural areas, comment on the likely soil depth/fertility, supporting your observations with evidence such as vegetation cover and/or agricultural activity.
- Consider settlement sites/sizes/distribution patterns.

C

Human features

- In urban areas, comment on:
  - Street patterns and building densities.
  - Building materials, height and possible age.
  - Possible building functions.
  - Any open space, and what it is used for.
  - The urban zone shown (how can you tell?).

264 Geographical skills

- Whether this place is in a more economically developed country or a less economically developed country (what evidence suggests this?).
- In rural areas, comment on:
  - Street patterns and building densities.
  - Field size and shape.
  - Types of field boundary and land use (is it arable or pastoral land, are there different crops? Tip: field colours may indicate different crops).
  - Access for farm machinery (can it operate easily? how can you tell?).
  - Evidence of manual labour/irrigation/greenhouses.

Now Investigate

1. a) Describe the landscape in photo **C**.

   b) Give two pieces of evidence in photo **C** which suggest that this area is an important tourist destination.

2. Write a brief interpretation of photo **A**, suggesting reasons why this area is important for agriculture.

Other illustrations

Sketching from maps

Sketching is a very useful geographical technique which you do need to learn! This can involve drawing a sketch from a map or a photograph, or even sketching a landscape as part of fieldwork. Many students fear that their artistic skills are inadequate – but geographical sketches are not detailed, accurate representations of a landscape. They are summaries of important features, so drawing them is a skill that can easily be learned.

By following the guidelines below, you can learn how to draw sketches from 1:25 000 and 1:50 000 scale maps. The same guidelines can easily be adapted to help you sketch other types of map, for example those in an atlas. See map E on page 51, which is a sketch map showing the situation of Paris.

- Using a pencil and ruler, draw a frame for your sketch.
- Lightly add the grid lines, numbering them along the bottom and side edges.
- Draw in the main features required by the question (or your fieldwork task). Sketch lightly at first, adding the detail to each grid square in turn to help you locate features accurately. Firm

up your outline sketching when you are happy with what you have drawn. Add colour as necessary, using pencil crayons.

- Try to avoid adding too much detail. Only include information that is relevant to the question. For example, on a sketch map showing the shape and land use zones of a town, it would be relevant to include some information about the surrounding area's relief and drainage, because these will have influenced the growth and shape of the settlement.

- Add a title, a north point, a scale line, a key, and labels or annotations as appropriate.

Sketching a landscape

Sketching from a photograph or outdoors during a field trip can seem difficult – but again, follow the tips below and you will soon master this important skill.

- Begin with a pencil-drawn frame.
- Divide this into quarters, drawing the lines very lightly as you will erase them later. If you can, add similar lines to the photograph, or make an overlay. The lines act as guides when positioning features on the sketch.
- Draw the major linear features first, for example the coastline, rivers and major contour lines. Add any transport networks.
- Add the outline shapes of 'block' features such as settlements, woodland and open spaces. Then complete your drawing by marking on any key features, such as farms or civic buildings.

A Annotated sketch to show the site of Shrewsbury, in the west of England

Annotations:
- Original site of settlement (now CBD) on higher land to reduce the risk of flooding
- Hard engineering to reduce flood risk
- Farmland on fertile, alluvial soils
- Bridges provide access to town – but were easily defended in the past
- More recent development outside river loop
- River provided a natural routeway to other settlements
- Open park land (and recreation uses) occupies land most liable to flood
- River provided a reliable source of water (and fish) for the original settlement

Geographical skills

B *Aerial view showing the site of Shrewsbury*

Erase your guidelines and add colour if appropriate, using pencil crayons.

- Give your completed sketch a title, a north point (if known) and a key. Label or annotate your sketch as appropriate.

Photo **B** is an oblique aerial photograph of Shrewsbury. Diagram **A** is an annotated sketch of its main features.

C *Global warming is one of the most obvious effects of climate change!*

Using cartoons

One distinctive type of illustration that is occasionally used in examinations is the cartoon. These are usually simple drawings which highlight a set of important ideas in a humorous way. Cartoon **C**, for example, shows some possible effects of global climate change.

If you have to answer a question based on a cartoon, study it carefully to identify its key message. Then:

- Write one or two brief statements suggesting the key point(s) the cartoon is making.
- Support your statements by explaining how the artist gets these ideas across.
- State how these ideas are relevant to the key message.

Section 4.4: Using illustrations

Now Investigate

1. Study the topographical map on page 312. Draw a labelled sketch map to show the main settlement features within the area defined by eastings 96–99 and northings 02–06.

2. Draw an annotated sketch to show the main landscape features visible from your school's recreation area (or a local viewpoint).

3. Which possible effects of climate change are illustrated by cartoon **C**?

Section 4. Topic 5

Fieldwork skills

Learning objectives:
- design and plan fieldwork investigations for both physical and human geography studies
- carry out a wide range of techniques, including questionnaires, surveys and ground measurements
- understand why sampling is important and when to use different types of sampling
- know the limitations of the fieldwork investigations you are carrying out

Questionnaires and interviews

When carrying out investigations for human geography we often want to ask members of the public for their views and opinions. This can be the best way to gather information on people's habits and the reasons why, for instance, they visit certain areas or use certain facilities. Examples of investigations where questionnaires and interviews are used include:

- Studies on shopping habits at a local shopping centre.
- Investigations into the impacts of tourism in the local area.
- When looking at how people feel about levels of immigration where they live.
- Studies on the use of different types of transport.

Planning is very important when carrying out this type of investigation. You need to make sure the questions relate to the topic you are looking into and that they are easily understood by the people answering your questions.

Questionnaires

Questionnaires are usually best asked face to face so that you can be sure you will get some replies. They can also be sent out by post or completed online – but then you run the risk that nobody will answer. The most important thing when asking face-to-face questionnaires is to be safe – always carry out such surveys with a friend (photo **A**). There are other things to take care of to ensure you get good results:

- Always be polite, introduce yourself and say why you want to ask questions.
- Keep the questions simple and easy to answer.
- Keep the questionnaire short with no more than 10 questions so that it can be completed quickly – most people will not want to spend a lot of time talking to you.
- Keep a note of when and where you carried out the questionnaire.
- Ask for some personal information, for example age-range, where the person being questioned lives – but keep it general.
- Say thank you when you've finished.

A Carrying out a questionnaire

An example questionnaire for an investigation into National Parks is shown in diagram **B**.

Creating a decent questionnaire takes time and some practice. It is a good idea to try them out at school or with your friends before asking the public, to make sure the questions make sense. This is called a pilot study. It can also be tried out on a smaller number of people who are the same type as those you eventually want to survey.

National Parks questionnaire

Name: Location:
Date: Time:

1 How often do you visit the National Park?
   First time   Once a month   Once a year   Less than once a year
2 What are the main reasons for your visit?
   Sightseeing   Walking   Wildlife   Bird watching
   Watersports   Cycling   Fishing
   Other (please write below):
   _____
   _____

   .....

6 In what ways could your visit be improved?
   Information boards   More facilities   Guided tours
   Better public transport
   Other (please feel free to give any more information):
   _____
   _____

7 Gender: Male   Female
8 What is your age range?
   Under 16   16–25   26–40   41–65   Over 65
9 What town do you live in?
   _____

   ......
Thank you for taking the time to answer my questions.

B *National Parks questionnaire*

Interviews

Sometimes you may want a little more information than the basic details you can get from a questionnaire. Interviews are a way to ask more in-depth questions. For instance, once you have carried out the survey of visitor views using the questionnaire in **B**, you may want to find out what the National Park manager thinks of any suggestions or comments that have been given.

Although you should prepare some questions in advance, interviews can be more open, with fewer answers being picked from a list. You may change some of the questions or ask new ones depending on how the person you are interviewing responds.

Interviews can be carried out over the phone or in person, or even via email or through an internet conversation. However they are done, it is important to keep a record of what is said. You may want to use some kind of recording device, but always make sure you tell whoever is being interviewed that you plan to do this.

Now Investigate

1. What are the main differences between a questionnaire and an interview?
2. Design a questionnaire that could be used to find out about shopping habits in your local area. You should aim to ask between five and ten questions.
3. What ways could you use to display the information you get from asking your questionnaire?
4. Based on your questionnaire, think of five interview questions you could ask about shopping habits when talking to the managers or owners of local shops.

Sampling

Often, when carrying out fieldwork, we want to study groups with similar characteristics (for instance, couples with children living in a nearby town). However, these groups, called populations, can be very large and we don't usually have the time available to study every single member. Instead of trying to find out about them all we can save time by using sampling to look at a small percentage of the total population. Sampling is seen as being a fair and unbiased way of determining the characteristics of the whole group. There are three main types: random, systematic and stratified.

A *Random sampling*

Random sampling

In this type of sampling each member of a population has an equal chance of being chosen. You will need a list of random numbers, to work out which members are going to be sampled. There are applications on the internet that will generate random numbers but many calculators also have a random number key.

Using either of these methods you could end up with a list such as this:

6, 1, 5, 7, 9, 2, 5, 5, 6, 8, 3, 3, 3, 8, 2

This list can then be used to identify which members of a population you will be sampling. If, for instance, you are interviewing visitors to a National Park, you could stand at the gate and direct questions to the sixth person to walk past, followed by the first, followed by the fifth, and so on (photo **A**).

Systematic sampling

Systematic sampling is easier to work out than random sampling because it uses regular numbers. For instance, when interviewing members of the public, you could decide to talk to every fifth person you meet. This technique is also easy to use in physical geography fieldwork. For example, when looking at aspects of weather in a certain area, you could take measurements of wind speed and wind direction every three days.

The main disadvantage of systematic sampling is that you may miss out certain important groups because not everyone or everything has an equal chance of being chosen.

Stratified sampling

Sometimes we only want to sample certain groups within a population. If we were trying to find out the characteristics of different groups of workers in a town, for instance, we would need to concentrate our questionnaires on those groups. We could choose to look at twenty members of three different groups, for example the unemployed, factory workers and professionals. Breaking the population down into groups like this is known as stratifying.

Within our stratified sample we can then use random or systematic sampling methods to work out the particular people we are going to study.

Now Investigate

1. Briefly describe how to carry out the three different types of sampling: random, systematic and stratified.
2. Give examples of fieldwork studies where you would use each of the three types of sampling.

4.5
Environmental quality surveys

The environment includes everything from natural features (mountains, lakes, rivers) to the factories and houses that people build. The environment can easily be spoilt or destroyed by our actions. We can use environmental quality surveys to try and identify problems or damage in the environment, and then set about trying to make it better.

Environmental quality survey sheets often look like the one in diagram **A**. Ticks are marked in the correct boxes depending on how the surveyor feels about the area they are looking at. Each box is worth a number of points. The higher the total number of points, the better the environment. This lets us compare different areas quickly and easily.

In some cases, not all the categories will be relevant. For example, there may be no housing in a pristine wilderness area. That category should then be left blank. You can still make comparisons between areas by calculating the average number of points for each survey, dividing the total number by the number of categories filled in.

B

Environmental Quality Survey Sheet						
Place:		Date:			Time:	
High quality	5	4	3	2	1	**Low quality**
High-quality housing						Poor-quality housing
Peaceful						Noisy
Little traffic						Large amount of traffic
No litter						Lots of litter
No vandalism or graffiti						Large amounts of vandalism and/or graffiti
Clean						Dirty
Attractive surroundings						Ugly surroundings
Clean air (or water)						Air (or water) pollution
Safe						Unsafe
Interesting						Boring
	Total:					

C

A An environmental quality survey sheet

Measuring the quality of the environment is a difficult fieldwork exercise. This is because it depends on what we feel about a

Section 4.5: Fieldwork skills   273

certain place. The results of an environmental quality survey can be completely different from one surveyor to another. It is important that we try to be as unbiased as possible when we carry out this type of survey.

Now Investigate

1. Study the photos **B** and **C** on page 273. Complete an environmental quality survey sheet for each picture. Compare your results with somebody else in your class.

2. Complete an environmental quality survey sheet for at least five different sites around your school. Try to think of ways in which the information you have gathered could be used to improve your school environment.

River measurements

Getting out and studying rivers is great fun but it can also be quite dangerous. Much of the fieldwork means getting wet, and you must find a safe place to carry it out – somewhere reasonably shallow and easy to access with no rapids or fast-flowing water.

River investigations often involve taking measurements at a number of different sampling points and then comparing the characteristics of the river at each point.

Width, depth and cross-sections

Width and depth are measured in centimetres. Measurements are taken with a tape measure and a metre ruler:

- The channel width is measured from the top of one bank to the top of the other. The tape measure needs to be stretched right across the channel at right-angles to the bank.

- The depth of the river needs to be measured at a number of points across the channel all the way from bank to bank – these should be around 20 to 25 cm apart.

- Finally, a note needs to be made of the height of the bank above the top of the river and of the width of the river within its channel.

A *A river cross-section*

274 Geographical skills

The measurements taken can then be used to draw a cross-section. This is best done on graph paper (diagram **A**) but it can also be completed using a computer spreadsheet program.

First decide on the scale you are going to use and then draw in the channel width. Add the measurements for river height and depth. Join up the dots for river depth to form the cross-section. You should now be able to calculate the channel or river cross-sectional area (the depth × the width) by counting up the grid squares that are covered by the channel or river on the graph paper. You can also calculate the wetted perimeter by measuring the contact that the river has with the bank and bed. Rivers with a large wetted perimeter have greater friction.

Measuring velocity

The velocity (or speed) of a river is measured most easily using a flow meter (photo **B**). This is a device with a propeller which turns in the water and gives a reading for the speed in metres per second.

Flow meters are expensive and there are other ways of measuring velocity that are more fun! All you need is an object (or some dye) that floats – for example an orange or a cork – and a tape measure and a stopwatch. Measure a distance of 10 metres along the river bank, throw the object in at one end and time how long it takes to travel 10 metres. Repeat the exercise at least five times to get an average time (photo **C**). This avoids errors if, for instance, the object gets stuck as it travels down the river.

The velocity can then be worked out in metres per second using the equation:

$$\text{velocity} = \frac{\text{distance}}{\text{time}}$$

If possible, measure velocity at various points across the river so that you can compare velocity with river depth using your cross-sections.

> **Topic link**
>
> Remember: you can refer back to Topic 2.2 pages 82–91 if there are any river terms you do not understand.

B *A flow meter*

C *Measuring the velocity of a river using dye*

Measuring a river's load

It is often useful to measure how big the load of a river is. This can be done in order to look at changes from the source to the mouth, or across different river features such as meanders. Wherever your sample point is you should take several measurements across the river's width.

1 At each point, reach into the river, pointing your index finger directly downwards.

2. Pick up the first pebble or particle that your finger touches.
3. If possible, measure the length of the pebble and note it down (photo **D**).
4. Repeat the process at several points across the river.

If the river bed consists only of fine sediment, this can be collected in plastic bottles and left to settle. A visual comparison will then be needed to determine which is the smallest particle size.

Load carried in suspension can also be analysed using a similar collection in plastic bottles.

D *Measuring the size of a river's load*

Changes in gradient

If you are studying a river's long profile you may also want to measure changes in gradient as it flows downhill. This can be done using a similar technique to measuring beach profiles – see page 277.

Coastal measurements

As with rivers, taking measurements along coasts is potentially dangerous. It is important (and more fun) to attempt such fieldwork in pairs or groups, and to take care when working on steep cliffs or near violent seas.

Destructive and constructive waves

There are many clues on a beach to help you identify whether it is affected more by destructive or constructive waves:

- Destructive waves have a stronger backwash than swash so they remove material, leaving a steep and narrow beach.
- Constructive waves have a stronger swash than backwash, depositing material on a more gently shelving beach.

Measuring wave frequency will help you identify wave type. Use a stopwatch and count the number of waves breaking on the beach in a five-minute interval. Then work out the number of waves per minute. While counting, remember also to make a note of the general wave height.

Destructive waves are more frequent and break between 10 and 15 times per minute. They are also taller than the less frequent constructive waves which break between 6 and 9 times each minute.

> **Topic link**
>
> Remember to refer back to Topic 2.3 pages 92–100 if there are any coastal terms you do not understand.

A *Using a clinometer for beach profiles*

276 Geographical skills

Measuring a beach profile

For a complete profile you will need a number of different sampling points along the width of your chosen beach. At each sampling point set up ranging poles (or standard 1-metre poles) from the top of the beach to the low water mark. Then take measurements using the following steps:

1. Walk between the two poles and make a general note of the main changes in the profile (the less and more steep spots).

2. For the points where the slope changes, take gradient measurements using ranging poles and a clinometer (photo **A**). If a clinometer is not available, a protractor can be used to get a general idea of slope angles.

3. Measure the distance along the ground between each set of measurements you take.

4. Use the information you collect on angles and distances to construct a cross-section profile (using graph paper), as shown in diagram **B**.

B Constructing a beach profile

You can use the beach profiles to compare different transects along a single beach or to compare different beaches.

Beach material analysis

To gain a more complete picture of the differences between beach profile transects, measurements of beach material can be made.

You will need to decide which type of sampling system you are going to use and then select a number of points along each transect. At each point a quadrat can be used (with random number tables) to choose which pebbles or particles to measure. Alternatively, simply choose the ten pebbles that are touching your foot. Pebble or sediment size can then be measured using the methods outlined on pages 275–276.

When analysing the distribution of beach material, you need to take account of recent or longer-term events. For instance, has the beach recently been affected by a storm? Or is it so well used that erosion through human activities is taking place on a daily basis?

Measuring longshore drift

Analysing the swash, backwash and how material is transported along a beach can give us an excellent idea of how longshore drift is operating in a certain area. Measuring this is quite simple:

1. Plot a distance of 10 metres along a section of beach and mark the start and end points.

2. Place a float (such as a cork or an orange) in the water at the point where the waves are breaking.

3. Watch the float and time how long it takes to travel the 10 metres along the beach.

As an alternative, you could measure how far the float travels in a specified period of time, for example five minutes.

Taking measurements at different sample points along a beach will show where longshore drift is at its most and least active.

Other indications of longshore drift

Material carried by longshore drift will pile up against natural rock outcrops and built features such as the artificial groynes that are used to stop beach erosion. Take pictures of the sediment piled up against these features (photo **C**) and make a note of the direction in which the sediment lies – this will tell you which way longshore drift is operating along a beach.

Measuring human impact

One final study we can complete along the coast is to look at the effects of erosion as a consequence of people walking on footpaths. Measuring infiltration rates shows how quickly water soaks into the soil and is a good indication of how people's footsteps are compacting the soil.

The basic technique is to put a bottomless cylinder into the ground, pour a measured amount of water into the cylinder and time how long it takes to soak into the soil (diagram **D**). Measurements from a number of different sampling points can then be compared.

C Beach material accumulating against groynes

D How to measure infiltration rates

Geographical skills

Section 4 . Topic 6

GIS and satellite images

Learning objectives:
- be able to give simple descriptions of human and physical landscapes (landforms, natural vegetation, land use and settlement) and geographical phenomena from satellite images and GIS

What is GIS?

A **Global Positioning System (GPS)** is an information gathering system. Most GPS data is captured by clusters of satellites orbiting almost 19 000 km above the Earth's surface (like the one in diagram **A**). Aircraft-mounted cameras and even office scanners are also used in the collection process. As long as satellite signals can be picked up, a GPS can work 24 hours a day, operate anywhere in the world and is not affected by poor weather conditions. A common use of a GPS is in vehicle navigation aids such as TomTom. It is also the major source of information for a GIS.

Because a **GIS (Geographic Information System)** is more complex than GPS, it can analyse as well as gather and display information. By doing this, it helps people to understand patterns, identify relationships and make decisions or plan for future developments more easily than by reading lengthy written descriptions. It can use any data that includes an exact location on the Earth's surface, and adding new information to a system is called 'data capture'.

One of the most basic functions of GIS is producing maps from separate 'layers' of selected information; these are sometimes called 'themes'. The map being compiled in diagram **B** is designed to show how settlement and transport links are related to relief and drainage. A printed map is of course only a snapshot display of information at a particular time. This is why most maps such as town plans become obsolete so quickly. The great advantage of GIS mapping is that its continuous flow of information can be used to update its memory banks and produce complex images whenever required. Its display techniques include adding symbols at precise points, lines to connect places, and shaded areas for large features such as woods and reservoirs.

A A satellite orbiting above the Earth

How do we use GIS?

More advanced GIS programs aid problem solving for businesses and government departments as well as helping them to prioritise tasks in order of their importance. This, in turn, allows these organisations to make accurate decisions quickly and undertake tasks which help them operate more efficiently. For business companies, this usually means making less waste, but much more profit! Diagram C shows some ways in which GIS can help people with issues in the workplace. Other ways include deciding where a

B Layers of GIS information making up a map

Section 4.6: GIS and satellite images 279

new industrial estate could best be located to take advantage of a city's existing transport network or meteorologists might study the path of hurricanes to predict where they may occur in the future.

GIS has been especially helpful to the Ordnance Survey (OS). This is because adding contours and other key landscape features to new maps is a very expensive and time-consuming operation. Whilst it took the OS 22 years to digitise all of its 250 000 maps of the United Kingdom, the ability to instantly update its maps by computer is of huge long-term benefit to the company.

> **Topic link**
>
> Your map for Now Investigate 3 will be used for an activity on page 282.

- It shows me where best to build my new superstore.
- It alerts Police HQ to housing areas where burglaries are most likely to take place.
- It helps scientists to predict volcanic eruptions.
- It plans my shortest route to deliver all today's parcels.
- It highlights those houses which are at most risk of flooding after a storm.
- It uses past weather conditions to help me predict tomorrow's rainfall.

HOW GIS HELPS PEOPLE LIKE ME AT WORK

C *Some modern uses of GIS*

> **Fantastic fact**
>
> GPS locations transmitted from satellites can be accurate to within 3 m on the Earth's surface!

Now Investigate

1. a) What do the acronyms GPS and GIS stand for?
   b) What are the main differences between a GPS and a GIS?

2. Write three lists of features which a GIS might plot using point symbols, lines and shaded areas.

3. To demonstrate how a GIS uses layers of information to construct a map:
   a) Choose an island or a larger but fairly straightforward map area such as Australia.
   b) Make three identical tracings of the coast of your chosen area.
   c) On one tracing, shade and name your chosen area's main relief features. Do the same on the other two tracings for its rivers and lakes, then its main urban settlements.
   d) Staple all three completed maps together, with their coast tracings exactly above each other.
   e) Finally, make a colour-copy of the information showing through all three layers of tracing paper. This copy is your finished map!

280 Geographical skills

4.6

How can GIS and satellite images be used?

Remote sensing is the technology of using satellites to obtain images of the Earth's surface. This process is called capturing and uses a range of sensors to detect different forms of electromagnetic radiation, including X-rays and ultraviolet light. The captured data can then be processed to display the distribution patterns of surface features such as urban settlements and tropical rainforests. Colour-tinting is often used to make it easier to identify and understand such patterns. Stored data can also be compared with more recently captured information to spot past trends and predict future changes.

> **Topic link**
>
> Pages 279–280 describe what a GIS is and how its data is captured.

A *Images of the Kitakami River before and after the tsunami in 2011*

16 January 2011   14 March 2011

Figure **A** shows a pair of ASTER false-colour images, taken before and after the tsunami that struck north-east Japan in March 2011, showing the devastating effect natural hazards can have in a short space of time. The March image shows how the water from the ocean spilled over the banks both north and south of the river Kitakami. Cropland and settlements close to the ocean appear to have disappeared. Only rugged peaks rising above the flood plains escaped inundation.

The emergence of Dubai as a major metropolis and tourist destination is evident in the image sequence in figure **B**. In the bottom image, captured in 2008, artificial islands shaped like palm trees stretch along the shore. Inland, irrigated vegetation stands out in red against the tan-coloured desert. In the top image, taken in 1973, the number and density of roads and buildings is far less than in 2008.

GIS can have useful applications at any scale from local to global. A digitised map of an urban area, for example, can highlight areas which have enough dental surgeries to meet the needs of the community and, much more importantly, those areas which don't! Also, towns and cities are in a constant process of change. It is therefore important to monitor how this happens so that basic public amenities such as bus routes can respond to changing population distributions. Global applications include

B *The growth of Dubai over 35 years*

1973
2002
2008

Section 4.6: GIS and satellite images   **281**

C *GIS was used to produce these maps showing changes to the Arctic's ice sheets*

monitoring the retreat of the polar ice caps due to climate change (see figure C) and the contraction of tropical rainforests due to deforestation and wildfires.

Now Investigate

1. The distribution patterns of the following data sets are often applied to GIS technology:

   farming systems; height of the land; hours of daily sunshine; mid-day temperatures; population densities; pre-historical sites; river patterns, road networks; soil types; annual rainfall totals; types of ecosystem; wildlife distributions; urban areas.

   a) Write the above data sets in their correct columns in this table.

Data sets about natural landscape patterns	Data sets about human landscape patterns	Data sets about climatic patterns

   b) Now write at least two extra examples of data sets of your own in each column.

2. Explain why these pairs of data sets might be successfully applied to GIS mapping technology because they are so closely linked:

   Height of the land *and* total annual rainfall

   Road networks *and* urban areas

   Soil types *and* natural vegetation

3. Suggest ways in which each of these organisations might use GIS technology in the course of their everyday work: real estate agents, emergency/rescue services, energy generating companies, the National Health Service, the Army and travel agents.

4. Use the map you produced for activity 3 on page 280 to show how the distribution pattern of that area's urban settlements is linked to those of its other features.

5. With the help of the maps in **C**, describe the changing distribution of the Arctic's ice sheets.

Fantastic fact

The acronym GIS was first used in 1968, by a British geographer called Roger Tomlinson whilst working in Canada. This led to him being called 'the father of GIS'!

Topic link

You can find examples of satellite images on pages 126, 132, 216, 226, 258 and 263 showing natural and manmade features.

Topic link

GIS and GPS have helped businesses expand around the world leading to globalisation which is described in Topic 3.1 pages 148–149.

Geographical skills

Section 5 . Topic 1

Preparing for your Geography examinations

Learning objectives:
- confidently prepare for examinations
- understand examination questions
- write a detailed case study answer

What themes will be covered in examinations?

The Cambridge Paper 1 Geographical Themes examination is the same for both IGCSE and O Level candidates. Questions are set on each of the three themes:

- **Population and settlement** (population change, migration, population structure, population distribution, urban and rural settlement, service provision, urban land use, impact of urbanisation).
- **The natural environment** (earthquakes and volcanoes, river and coastal processes and landforms, coral reefs and mangrove swamps, weather, climate and ecosystems of the equatorial region and hot desert).
- **Economic development** (indicators of development, food production, industry, tourism, energy and water resources, environmental risks of economic development).

In studying this course you will:

- Learn about geographical events happening in different areas of the world.
- Gain an understanding of geographical processes.
- Have the opportunity to explore how people and the natural environment affect each other.

The examination tests:

1. Your understanding of geographical concepts (ideas).
2. Your knowledge of case study examples.
3. Your analysis of information and data.

You will not be told which objective each question is testing but you will recognise the objectives by the wording of the question.

How to use your time effectively

During any examination it is important to plan your time effectively and the marks available for each section or question

> **Tip**
> - Where there is a choice of questions to answer, it is important to choose the correct questions.
> - You do not have to answer the questions in the order in which they appear on the question paper. Answer your best topic first and your weakest topic last.

are a good guide. Remember that during your examinations, as well as answering the questions, you need to allow time to:

- Read all the questions carefully.
- Choose the questions you want to answer and in which order.
- Check your answers at the end of the examination to correct any simple mistakes you may have made.

To have the time to do all this it may be better to allow yourself 30 minutes to answer each question and use the extra 15 minutes on the other tasks. Look carefully at the number of marks available for each part of a question (shown in brackets at the end of each question). This is a good guide to how much time to spend on each part. Do not spend too much time on one part if it is only worth 1 or 2 marks, or write only a short answer if a question is worth 4 or 5 marks. The number of lines provided for your answer is another guide as to how much detail you need to include.

Choosing the correct questions to answer

In the Geographical Themes examination you have the opportunity to choose which questions you want to answer. You must choose one question from each section, so read them all carefully before you make your choice. To help you to do this think about the following:

- Read all the separate parts of each question, especially the case study, which is worth most marks.
- Make sure you have studied the question topic! Some questions might look easier than others but you may not have enough knowledge about the topic.
- Think about which topics you have revised most thoroughly.
- Do not choose a question just because it has an interesting photograph, map or diagram.
- If you think you have chosen the wrong question you can change your mind once you have begun your answer. It is better to do this than carry on answering a question badly.

Tip
- Do not try to answer more than three questions. You will not have time to answer them properly.
- If you change your mind and stop answering a question part way through, make sure you cross out what you have written.

Understanding the question

Questions in the examination will test different parts of the syllabus. Many questions have a common structure, as shown in the following example taken from a past Cambridge examination paper.

(a) Study Fig. 8, a map showing pollution of a river in an MEDC.

   (i) Describe how the water quality changes along the river between points A and B. [1]

   (ii) Using information from Fig. 8, give **two** reasons for the change which you have described in **(a)(i)**. [2]

   (iii) Explain why, in many countries, waste is released into rivers. [3]

   (iv) River pollution is a threat to the environment. Explain what could be done to reduce this threat and improve the quality of water in rivers. [4]

Fig. 8

(b) Study Fig. 9 which shows newspaper extracts about three proposed new developments on an island in the Atlantic Ocean.

Extract 1

NEW NORTH-SOUTH MOTORWAY PLANNED

Plans have been submitted to build a motorway across the mountains, through the valley of the White River ....

Extract 2

PLANS ANNOUNCED TO BUILD NEW FISH PROCESSING FACTORY

A multi-national company plans to clear woodland and scrub to build a factory to process and can locally caught sardines ....

Extract 3

LUXURY RESORT AND GOLF COURSE PROPOSED FOR SUMMER BAY

Plans have been submitted to build a resort and golf course on the sand dunes ....

Fig. 9

Section 5.1: Preparing for your Geography examinations

(i) Choose one of the proposed new developments and write down the number of the extract which you have chosen.

Explain **three** different ways in which the development could damage the local natural environment. [3]

(ii) Suggest what should be done to ensure that your chosen development is sustainable. [5]

(c) People can benefit when economic activities take place. Such activities include:
- transport
- tourism
- manufacturing industry.

Name an area which you have studied and describe an economic activity which takes place.

Explain how the activity benefits local people. [7]

[Total: 25 marks]

(Cambridge IGCSE Geography 0460 Paper 13 Q6 June 2010)

Part of question	Mark allocation	Type of question
(a) (i)	1	Interpretation of the first resource which shows river quality
(a) (ii)	2	Explanation of change based on the first resource
(a) (iii)	3	Understanding of an idea, waste in rivers, linked to the first resource
(a) (iv)	4	General understanding about river pollution and management
(b) (i)	3	Detailed interpretation and explanation of the second resource
(b) (ii)	5	Explanation linked to the second resource
(c)	7	Case study

The case study

In Geography examinations questions which include a case study aim to test your knowledge about places. Here are two examples of case study questions:

1. Name an urban area which you have studied where there are not enough houses for people to live in. Explain why there is this problem and what has been done to solve it.

2. For a country or area which you have studied, describe the problems for people and the local environment caused by using wood and charcoal as sources of energy.
(Cambridge IGCSE Geography 0460 Paper 13 Q5c June 2010)

Both questions have a *topic*, a *focus* and a *location*.

In **example 1** the *topic* is housing shortage, the *focus* is reasons for the housing shortage and what has been done to reduce the shortage, and the *location* is an appropriate named urban area.

In **example 2** the *topic* is using wood and charcoal for fuel, the *focus* is problems this causes for the local environment, and the *location* is an appropriate country or area.

What is the topic, focus and location in the following case study question?

3   For an area you have studied, describe the benefits and problems of living near the coast.
    (Cambridge IGCSE Geography 0460 Paper 13 Q3c June 2010)

In **example 3** the *topic* is living near the coast, the *focus* is benefits and problems, and the *location* is any appropriate area.

Answering case study questions

Read the following case study question and the two example answers (written by the authors) below it.

Question

Describe how deforestation has affected people and the natural environment in a named area of tropical rainforest you have studied.

Answer 1

In the Amazon forest deforestation has affected the local people and the natural environment. People cannot live in the forest because their livelihoods have been destroyed. There are many reasons why trees are cut down in the Amazon such as to use the timber for furniture and to make paper, to clear the land for new roads and cities, for mining and hydro-electric schemes.

Deforestation has caused atmospheric pollution and it is the main cause of global warming.

When the trees are cut down the heavy rain washes away all the soil. When the trees are chopped down animals in the forest have nowhere to live and many of them die. The soil becomes infertile and nothing will grow.

Answer 2

In the rainforest of Borneo, deforestation has destroyed the forest ecosystem. Since 1980 about half of the tropical rainforest in Borneo has been chopped down. Deforestation has been done to clear land for farming and to use the logged timber for furniture. Many plants and animals have been affected by deforestation. After trees are cut down soil erosion happens as the soil is no longer protected by the tree canopy. Topsoil is washed into rivers and this causes flooding as the river channel is filled up.

When the trees are cut down there are no more leaves to fall onto the ground to rot and make humus so the soil becomes infertile. Animals such as the orangutan that live in the forest lose their habitat, which may cause them to become extinct. Other animals lose their food source as smaller species migrate or die out.

People living in this rainforest are also affected by deforestation. Traditionally groups of farmers have cleared the forest to grow crops and then moved to a different area when the soil became infertile. This shifting cultivation system gave the soil the chance to regain its fertility. When

> **Tip**
>
> - Learn your case study examples thoroughly so you can confidently draw on them in an examination.
> - When you are revising your work, make a list of all the case studies you are learning. Highlight the topic, focus and location.
> - You can use a case study that is local to your school as an alternative to the case studies in this textbook.

the trees are cut down the farmers must stay longer in one place or return there more quickly, which means that the crop yield is lower and the soil becomes infertile. The traditional way of life of these people is also affected by modern industrial and farming developments.

Here is a list of eight characteristics of case study answers. Decide which four apply to each answer. On a copy of the table tick the correct box and identify where each characteristic is found in the answers.

Characteristic	Answer 1	Answer 2
Uses geographical terminology		
Makes simple statements		
Includes information that is not relevant to the question		
Develops (expands on) points that are made		
Does not explain in detail the impact on people		
Includes relevant facts and figures		
Gives a place-specific answer (writes about the actual places)		
Makes inaccurate, general statements		

How a case study question may be marked

If you understand how case studies may be marked it should help you to work to your best abilities. If you are aiming for a high mark your case study answer must increase in quality to reach a higher level. The example below shows how case study answers may be marked.

Question

> Choose an example of rural to urban migration in an LEDC which you have studied. Name the areas between which people moved and explain why many people migrated. You should refer both to pull and to push factors.
> (Cambridge IGCSE Geography 0460 Paper 13 Q2c June 2010)

Low level answer

A low level answer includes limited ideas (simple statements) which explain why people migrated from rural to urban areas.

An answer at this level includes reasons such as:

- There are more jobs in cities.
- There are better services in urban areas.
- There is not enough food in the rural area.

Intermediate level answer

An intermediate level answer includes more developed statements which explain why people migrated from rural to urban areas.

An answer at this level includes reasons such as:

- There are more jobs in cities where people can work as cleaners or shoe shiners.
- There is better access for the family to schools, hospitals and clinics in the city.
- People can buy food from markets rather than having to grow food for themselves on unproductive farmland.

High level answer

A high level answer includes detailed statements about an appropriate named example.

An answer at this level includes details such as:

- People come from the surrounding countryside to work and make money by offering shoe-shines to tourists in Placa de Republica, a main square in the city centre of São Paulo.
- People move to São Paulo to live in the Cinqua Pora area where basic concrete houses are being built, with piped water and sewage pipes. Even in the favelas which have developed on the steep hillsides the people have better access to healthcare and education than in the countryside.
- People living in the valley of the São Francisco River lost their farmland when dams and reservoirs were built along it for HEP generation, so they were forced to move to the city to look for work.

Before your examination you should practise writing answers for all your case studies. If you are aiming for a high mark your answer must:

- include developed ideas
- use the correct geographical terminology, where appropriate
- include detailed ideas about the place you have chosen.

These are included in the example answer to a case study question below. Read it carefully and pick out where detailed and developed ideas and geographical terminology are included.

Question

Name an area where subsistence farming takes place. Describe the farming system and explain why it is taking place in the area.

Rice farming is important in the Lower Ganges valley in India. (named area) One third of the world's population eat rice but it can only be grown in areas with very wet conditions and hot temperatures and sun. This area of India has a tropical monsoon climate, temperatures are around 27° C and rainfall is over 1,000 mm per year, most of which comes in 4 or 5 months which suits rice farming. (place details)

This area has a high population density which suits labour-intensive farming (geographical terminology) like growing rice. The farms are very small, often about 1 hectare divided into many plots, so machinery cannot be used and most of the work is done by the farmer and his family. (developed idea) Water buffalo are used to pull a plough to prepare the padi fields for planting. (developed idea)

The farmer has to construct bunds (place detail), which are embankments, around the padi field to keep the water in the field. The farmer also has to build irrigation canals to get water to the fields in the drier season, and plant crops and harvest them. (developed idea)

Some farmers in the area grow high yield varieties of rice like IR8 (geographical terminology), but the seeds are expensive to buy and not all farmers can afford them. These farmers can sell some of their rice crop but most farmers only grow enough rice to feed their families. (developed idea)

Command words

Many students lose marks in an examination because they do not read carefully or understand the command words in the question. Command words tell you how to answer the question. You need to know what each command word means and follow its instructions. If you do not know the meaning of the command word you will answer the question incorrectly.

The groups of command words below are commonly used in Geography examinations.

Examples of command words used in Geography examinations

Recall information, example or fact
Identify (name, select or recognise something from information you are given)
State (express in clear terms an answer using your own knowledge)
Give (produce an answer either from a given source or information or from your own knowledge)
Identify three coastal landforms shown in photograph B. (photograph shows an area of coastline)
State two differences between the percentage use of water in Europe and Asia. (you need to use a bar graph from the examination paper)
Give three different reasons why rainforests are being cleared.
Give a definition
Define (give the precise meaning of a word or phrase)
Define 'sphere of influence'.
Define relative humidity.
Description
Describe (give the main points about the characteristics or features of a topic)

> **Tip**
>
> Read the command words carefully. Do not explain when the question says 'describe'.

Describe the sphere of influence of the shopping centre. [2 marks] (you need to use a map from the examination paper)

Describe three likely impacts of flooding in the area shown in the photograph. [3 marks] (photograph shows part of a river and its flood plain)

Describe the likely problems for an MEDC, such as Ireland, of having so many old dependants. [5 marks]

Explanation

Suggest (apply your knowledge and understanding to a situation in order to make proposals or give reasons)

Explain (give reasons or make the relationships between things evident and support it with relevant evidence)

Suggest three reasons why many thousands of people were killed by this earthquake.

Suggest why erosion is more likely at point S than point P. (you need to use a diagram from the examination paper)

Explain how the process of hydraulic action may erode the bed and banks of a river. (a three mark question)

Explain why there are high birth rates in LEDCs such as Nigeria. (a four mark question)

Explain why many people live in areas such as Sichuan, even though they are at risk from earthquakes. (a five mark question)

Explain the factors which attract high technology industries to an area.

Other commands

Estimate (use your judgment to give a value to a figure)

Locate (indicate the position of a place or feature from or on a resource)

Predict (suggest what may happen based on information which is provided or available)

Sketch (make a simple drawing to show the key features)

Estimate the height of the land where the weather station is located. (located on a map which shows the relief of an area)

Locate a city on the map where the population has increased between 1995 and 2015.

Predict how the population structure of the country may change by 2050. (using population pyramids in the exam paper)

In the box below draw a **sketch** of a river meander. Label the areas of erosion and deposition.

> **Tip**
>
> Notice the different mark allocations which mean that the descriptions will need different amounts of detail.

> **Tip**
>
> - Using a named example does not by itself make a high level case study answer. You must include more detail about the place in your answer.
> - Command words are often linked together, as shown in the following question:
>
>   **Name** and **explain** two processes by which a river transports its load.

Resources

Before you answer each question, check that you are looking at and using the correct resources from the examination paper and resource booklet. The resource booklet may include a number of photographs, so it is particularly important that you study the correct one.

Examples of types of resources used in Geography examinations

Map	World map to show distribution of the tropical rainforest or tectonic plate margins Map of a country or continent to show contrasts or information such as the distribution of nuclear power stations Local map of an area such as a river basin
Graph	Line graph to show population change over time Bar graph to show employment figures in different countries Climate graph to show temperature and rainfall in a hot desert Pie chart to show types of employment in a country Scatter graph to show the relationship between the strength of earthquakes and the number of deaths Population pyramid to show population structure
Photograph	These can show many things, for example type of vegetation, industrial sites, types of farm, areas of a city, natural landscapes
Diagram	Geographical idea or theory such as settlement hierarchy Sketch of a feature such as a cliff
Information	Newspaper article Factfile Website image These can show many things, for example a volcanic eruption, government announcement about population policy, growth of tourism in a country

In an examination you may have to read and interpret information from the resource. This is shown in the following examples.

Question

Study the map which shows information about internal migration in the USA. Describe the distribution of states where there are high rates of migration into the state.

Question

Study the three photographs which show different parts of Amman, the capital city of Jordan. Describe the main urban land use in each of the areas in the photographs.
(Adapted from Cambridge IGCSE Geography 0460 Paper 11 Q1b (i) and (ii) June 2009)

Make sure you are prepared for your examinations

When preparing for your examinations it is good practice to:

- Learn your work and revise it thoroughly. There are different ways to learn your notes and your teacher will give you advice about them. Try out a few different ways to find out which suits you best.
- Ask your teacher for questions from previous examinations which you can use for practice. Sometimes it is useful to do this under test conditions.

5.1

- Ask your teacher how they mark your answers. You are given advice on pages 288–290 about how a case study question may be marked. Using this advice may help you to write high level answers.

Examples of two answers

You have now found out more about the Geographical Themes examination and how to improve your skills to be successful in the course. Next you have the opportunity to look in detail at examination questions from a past paper. There are two example answers which have been marked by teachers – one answer would receive a high mark and the other answer would receive a medium level mark. Each example answer is followed by a suggestion of how the answer may be marked and possibly improved.

Read the questions and look at the resources, then study the two example answers. Can you understand how the marks may be awarded and the answer might be improved?

(a) Study Figs 1A, 1B and 1C, information about migration from Poland in 2006. Poland is an MEDC which joined the European Union (EU) in 2004.

Migration from Poland in 2006

Fig. 1A

Scale 1mm = 1% of emigrants

Section 5.1: Preparing for your Geography examinations   293

Top 10 Migrant Jobs in the UK

- Factory worker 37%
- Warehouse 10%
- Packer 9%
- Catering 9%
- Cleaner 9%
- Farm worker 5%
- Waiter/ess 6%
- Hotel maid 6%
- Carer 5%
- Retail 4%

Fig. 1B

Emigration from, and immigration to, Poland 2000 – 2006

immigration (in 000's)
emigration (in 000's)

Fig. 1C

(a) (i) Name the country which was the destination of the largest percentage of migrants from Poland in 2006.

(Cambridge IGCSE Geography 0460 Paper 12 Q1a(i) November 2010)

[1 mark]

Answer 1

UK (✓)

Teacher's comment

The answer correctly identifies the country from the map.

Answer 2

UK (✓)

Teacher's comment

The answer correctly identifies the country from the map.

(a) (ii) For each of the following, suggest one reason why a greater percentage of migrants from Poland to the UK:

   A were employed in factories rather than on farms

   B were employed as cleaners rather than teachers. [2 marks]

(Cambridge IGCSE Geography 0460 Paper 12 Q1a(ii) November 2010)

Answer 1

A: The factory (secondary) sector has a larger number of jobs available compared to the declining farming (primary) sector. (✓)

294 Exam preparation

B: Teaching requires people to be qualified and most immigrants lack the qualifications and experience, but they don't have to be qualified to be cleaners. (✓)

Teacher's comment

Both reasons would be correct. In A the focus is on the different number of jobs, in B the focus is on the different need for qualifications. Notice how a comparison was made in both answers.

Answer 2

A: There were more factory jobs available for the migrants. (✓)

B: There were more jobs available as cleaners.

Teacher's comment

The first reason would be correct. Although reason A is brief it does make a comparison between the number of jobs in factories and on farms. Reason B would not be credited because it repeats the same idea. The significant difference between jobs as cleaner and teacher is the level of qualifications required. Use comparative words like 'more' or 'larger' when the question requires a comparison to be made.

(a) (iii) Using Fig. 1C, briefly compare the amount of emigration from, and immigration to, Poland between 2000 and 2006. [3 marks]

(Cambridge IGCSE Geography 0460 Paper 12 Q1a(iii) November 2010)

Answer 1

Between 2000 and 2006 the number of emigrants was almost double the number of immigrants (✓). In 2004 the number of emigrants was almost the same as the number of immigrants (✓). In 2006 the number of emigrants was nearly three times more than the number of immigrants (✓).

Teacher's comment

The answer correctly identifies three differences from the graph. The answer recognises the general imbalance between emigration and immigration. It then includes comparison in particular years. Credit would be given for using information from the graph. This answer does that by including words such as 'almost double', 'almost the same' and 'nearly three times more'.

Answer 2

In 2000 about 7000 people immigrated to Poland and almost 20 000 emigrated from Poland. Between 2001 and 2005 immigration stayed low, emigration, on the other hand, fluctuated with some years having a high emigration rate and some years not (✓). In 2006 the immigration rate was at its highest at about 11 000 people and the emigration rate was also at its highest at about 36 000 people (✓).

Teacher's comment

The answer includes two comparisons between rates of immigration and emigration. The statement which describes the situation in 2000 would not be credited because no comparison is made. The answer would need to emphasise that emigration was more than immigration. There would be no credit given for just reading data from the graph. A comparison is made between immigration and emigration rates between 2001 and 2005. The final idea would be credited because it makes a comparison in a particular year, 2006.

(a) (iv) What difficulties might be faced by migrants from Poland when living in countries such as the UK? [4 marks]

(Cambridge IGCSE Geography 0460 Paper 12 Q1a(iv) November 2010)

Answer 1

Migrants may face discrimination because they are foreigners (✓). It will be difficult for them to mix with people from a different culture (✓). They will only be able to get low-paid jobs and will be the first to lose their jobs if the company is not doing well (✓). Because of low wages they will only be able to afford low quality housing (✓). Also may have to work very long hours for little pay.

Teacher's comment

There would be many possible answers to this question; the answer correctly identifies four different difficulties. The answer also suggests another difficulty of working long hours which is to receive little pay. Remember that the mark allocation (in this example it is 4 marks) may help you to decide about how many ideas to include. This answer suggests five difficulties. It could be a good idea to give more ideas than the number of marks in case they are not all credited.

Answer 2

The migrants do not have enough money for decent housing so end up living in poor quality housing (✓). They cannot afford to live in nice areas. Many people from Poland might not be able to speak English so it will be difficult for them (✓). The children will not be able to understand lessons at school. Overall it will be very difficult for them.

Teacher's comment

The answer explains two difficulties: having to live in poor houses and being unable to speak English. The answer could gain more credit by suggesting why the migrants have little money. The final sentence does not improve the answer because it just repeats the question. The answer needs to include more ideas.

(b) Study Fig. 2, an article about migration from Poland to the UK.

'Nearly 600,000' new EU migrants

Almost 600,000 people from Poland and the seven other countries which joined the EU in 2004 have applied to work in the UK, where full work rights have been given to all citizens of EU countries. Each morning in Hammersmith, west London, many Poles gather to look in a shop window at adverts for work. Here you will find graduates scribbling down details of work in catering and cleaning, delivering pizza takeaway leaflets and ironing.

"I am not here to claim benefits," says Radek, 25. "I am here to earn money, as much as I can make and then go home. At home in Poland unemployment is 20 to 25% and the wages are very low." He notes down the number of a builder from an advert looking for plasterers, kitchen fitters and electricians. "I can do all of those, I studied at Poznan technical college as an electrician. I have a qualification." Newly arrived Poles, like many immigrants to Britain before them, are often doing the work that Britons seemingly no longer want to do. For example, when Tesco needed 140 new lorry drivers recently, it hired Poles because of the lack of British applicants.

Fig. 2

(b) (i) Use your own words to give **three** reasons why many people from Poland have migrated to the UK since 2004. [3 marks]

(Cambridge IGCSE Geography 0460 Paper 12 Q1b(i) November 2010)

Answer 1

Polish people have migrated to the UK to get better paid jobs (✓) as wages in Poland are low. They hope to earn more money in the UK. They have also migrated to the UK because of the EU policy which protects people's rights to have a job in different countries (✓). Another reason is that there is a high unemployment rate in Poland so it hard for them to get jobs (✓). Another reason is that Britain has a lot of vacancies where manual labour is required.

Teacher's comment

The answer includes three valid ideas about jobs, employment rights and higher pay. The question instruction is to 'use your own words' so credit would not be given for copying from the article. The final idea about job vacancies is the opposite of the previous statement that there is a lack of jobs in Poland. The idea of jobs has already been credited. It would be acceptable in a question that asks for 'three reasons' to number your ideas 1, 2 and 3 and write each answer on a different line.

Answer 2

People have migrated from Poland to the UK because there are more job opportunities (✓). The jobs are better paid than the jobs in Poland (✓). Full working rights have been given to all citizens of EU countries.

Teacher's comment

The answer includes two simple valid ideas: that there are more job opportunities, and wages are higher in the UK. The final reason is copied from the article and would not be credited because the question instruction is 'use your own words'. This is an example of where an answer does not follow the command words.

(b) (ii) Explain the problems which may be caused in Poland by this migration. **[5 marks]**

Cambridge IGCSE Geography 0460 Paper 12 Q1b(ii) November 2010)

Answer 1

> The migrants are usually men which means that families are separated. (✓) There are also less qualified, unskilled and semi-skilled people available to do the jobs in Poland. (✓) This can harm the economy and slow down development. (✓dev) It is usually the young who move away and leave the elderly which increase the dependent population for the government. (✓) If too many men move away this can cause a sex imbalance as there are more women left who will have to go to work (✓) and leave their family which can be against tradition (✓), especially in farming areas of the country.

Teacher's comment

This answer includes well-developed ideas. The answer focuses on the problems of splitting up the family and loss of the economically active workforce. However, more than one point is made about both problems which develop the answer and would gain extra credit. You may have heard these called 'development' marks which are credited when the answer includes more detail. In this answer the loss of qualified workers could slow down economic development, and men migrating means women have to go to work, which is against tradition. In a question worth more marks you may be awarded development marks, so try to make your ideas as detailed as possible.

Answer 2

> Most of the people who migrate from Poland are men so the sex structure of the country will be uneven. (✓) Most of the people who leave are the people who are economically active so there are less people working in Poland (✓) which means that it will affect the economy. The men leave so women have to look after the family as there is no father at home. (✓)

Teacher's comment

The answer identifies three problems, but does not develop them to gain further credit. The answer could explain a possible impact of gender imbalance in the country and could suggest what would be an impact of the migration on the economy of Poland, rather than just saying it will 'affect the economy'. All the ideas could easily be developed to score more marks. You should always try to give more detail to your answer when the question is worth more marks.

(a) Name an example of a city or country to which large numbers of people have migrated from other countries. Describe the effects of international migration on your chosen city or country. **[7 marks]**

(Cambridge IGCSE Geography 0460 Paper 12 Q1c November 2010)

5.1

Answer 1

Many Mexicans have migrated to the USA, particularly to cities like Los Angeles in California which is near the border between Mexico and the USA. They have moved to get better paid jobs and because their living conditions in Mexico were poor.

Most migrants are young adults who get jobs in the USA, working on farms or in services like cleaning or in shops. Often this work is for low wages and they work long hours. They do the jobs which Americans don't want to do. The Mexicans pay taxes to the government which helps to pay for services and supports the country.

Many of the migrants cannot afford good houses so they live in poor conditions in communities with other Mexican people. Many Californians do not like the immigrants because they say that they take some of the jobs which could be done by Americans. Also some of the immigrants have large families which need education and healthcare.

Many Mexicans try to cross the border into the USA illegally. Along some parts of the border fences have been put up with searchlights. Although there are many border police many of the illegal migrants are not caught. They end up living in the poorest slum conditions and cannot get jobs because they don't have work permits. This causes problems for the American government as sometimes there are riots and fights between the Mexicans and some American gangs who feel threatened by them.

Teacher's comment

This is a high level answer.

In paragraph 1 the answer names a city and country to which Mexicans have moved. The answer then gives some brief reasons why the migrants moved but this would not gain any credit because it is not what the question asks.

The focus of paragraph 2 is jobs. The effect is explained that Mexicans do low-paid jobs which Americans will not do. The idea is then developed as the Mexican workers pay taxes.

Paragraph 3 concentrates on a negative effect of immigration, that there is often conflict between Mexicans and Americans because of the competition for jobs and the needs of the large Mexican families.

Paragraph 4 focuses on illegal immigrants who cause social unrest because of their poor living conditions and conflict with American gangs.

All of the ideas are developed with extra detail. The answer contains a number of developed ideas which relate to the named example so it should be awarded a high mark. Go back to the case study ideas on pages 288–290 to check how this answer meets the requirements of a high level answer.

Section 5.1: Preparing for your Geography examinations

Answer 2

Turkish people moving to Germany

In Germany separate communities have formed such as different shopping areas for the Turkish and the Germans. The country has different cultures, food, dress and way of life. Often the Germans feel that the Turks are taking away their jobs. The Turks have poor living conditions.

In Turkey men leave and women and children stay. A great part of the working population migrates and elderly and young are left to be looked after by the government. The population becomes an ageing population.

Teacher's comment

This is a low level answer. The chosen example is appropriate to the question but paragraph 1 contains no developed ideas. Simple effects are included: segregated shopping areas, different cultures, and competition for jobs and the poor living conditions of the migrants. However, none of these ideas is developed and so would not be credited as intermediate level answers. Go back to the case study ideas on page 288 to check how this answer only meets the requirements of a low level answer. The answer could have given examples of different shopping centres or described how the culture is different between the two nationalities or how the Germans react to the competition for jobs. All of these would develop low level ideas into intermediate level answers. You should always try to develop your ideas, because even if you only develop one idea your answer should be credited at intermediate level.

Paragraph 2 is irrelevant to the question. It focuses on the effects of migration in Turkey rather than the country that is receiving the migrants. Try to avoid going away from the question when you are answering. You will not gain credit for an answer that does not fit the question.

Section 5 . Topic 2

Preparing for your Geography examinations

Learning objectives:
- confidently prepare for examinations
- understand different types of examination questions
- apply the map and graph skills you have learned

What skills will be covered in examinations?

The Geographical Skills exam is taken by both IGCSE and OL students. Some examination questions are based on map extracts and test map reading and interpretation skills. You will learn how to 'read' and understand maps in Topic 4.1 on pages 235–244.

The other questions test a variety of different skills but also your understanding of geographical concepts and your decision-making ability about different issues.

In studying for this examination you will have the opportunity to:

- Use the geographical skills which you have learned.
- Interpret a map.
- Make geographical judgements and decisions.

The examination tests:

1. Your use of geographical skills.
2. Your interpretation and analysis of geographical data.
3. Your decision making.

You will not be told which objective each question is testing but you will recognise the objectives by the wording of the question.

How to use your time effectively

During any examination it is important to plan your time effectively and the marks available for each section or question are a good guide. Remember you also need to allow time to:

- Read all the questions carefully.
- Study the map extract and resource booklet.
- Check your answers at the end of the examination to correct any mistakes you may have made.

> **Tip**
> - The Geographical Skills examination tests much more than geographical skills. It also tests understanding and decision-making.
> - The questions will test topics from any part of the syllabus. Unlike the Geographical Themes examination, you do not require knowledge of specific places. The resources will give you the information you need to answer each question.

To have the time to do all of this it may be best to allow yourself 30 minutes to answer the map question and 50 minutes to answer the other questions. You can then use the remaining 10 minutes on the other tasks. You will need more time to answer the map question because it is worth more marks, and to give you enough time to work accurately. Look carefully at the number of marks available for each part of a question (shown in brackets at the end of each question). The higher the mark allocation, the more detail is required. The number of lines provided for your answer is another guide as to how much detail you need to include. Not all questions on the Geographical Skills paper require extended writing. Some questions may only need one word or a short sentence answer. You may be told to complete a table, put a tick in a tick list, or draw or sketch an answer.

> **Tip**
>
> Make sure that you attempt all questions. It is very easy to miss out a question if there are no answer lines.

Understanding the question

It is important to prepare for examination questions which use a map extract, often of an area with a scale of 1:25 000 or 1:50 000. An example of such a map is shown on page 312. Typical tasks in these questions are:

- Use the map symbols in the key to identify features on the map.
- Give four-figure and six-figure grid references.
- Find places on the map using four-figure and six-figure grid references.
- Work out the direction of one place from another, using the 16-point compass.
- Work out the bearing of one place from another.
- Use the scale to measure distance between places on the map.
- Use contour lines and spot heights to work out the height of places.
- Interpret and construct cross sections.
- Describe natural or physical features, such as relief of the land, river and river valley, coastal area.
- Describe human features, such as types of settlement, road network.
- Describe distribution of features, such as types of farming, settlement pattern.
- Suggest or give reasons for features, such as distribution of settlement, location of farming types, direction of river flow.
- Use map evidence to identify features, such as functions in a town, different types of transport or services, comparison between two river valleys.

302 Exam preparation

How to use your geographical skills to the best of your ability

- Be accurate in measuring on the map.
- Give the correct units of measurement.
- Use the edge of a piece of paper to measure distance (see page 236).
- Use the information provided with the map, such as scale, key to map symbols, compass point.
- Practise basic map skills, such as grid reference, compass bearing (see pages 235–237).
- Understand and learn how to draw a cross-section.
- Practise how to identify and describe features shown on the map.
- Follow the command words (see pages 290–291 if you do not know what these are).

Common command words used in a map reading and interpretation question are:

Identify/Name	**Identify** the features shown on the map extract. **Name** five services found at the settlement.
Mark	**Mark** the position on the cross-section of …
Measure	**Measure** the distance along the road. **Measure** the bearing.
State / Give / Circle	**State** the compass direction. **Give** the four-figure grid reference. **Circle** the six-figure grid reference (when a choice of answers is given).
Calculate	**Calculate** the difference in height.
Describe	**Describe** the physical features of the river.
Suggest	**Suggest** why there are few settlements inland.

Other examination questions which test your geographical skills

These questions focus on different topics and may include a variety of resources (see pages 309–310). The following questions are taken from a past Cambridge examination paper and show the different ways you could be tested. Make a copy of the table on page 308 and complete the table for Questions 3, 4 and 5.

Section 5.2: Preparing for your Geography examinations   303

2 Study Fig. 5, which shows the structure of the total New Zealand population, and Fig. 6, which shows the structure of the Maori population in 2006. The Maori people form part of the population of New Zealand.

Total New Zealand population, 2006

Maori population, 2006

Fig. 5

Fig. 6

(a) In 2006, 10% of the male Maori population were aged 15–19 and 5% of the female Maori population were aged 50–54. Complete Fig. 6 by adding this data. [2]

(b) Complete the following sentences by adding the words **greater** or **less**.

(i) The percentage of 0–14 year olds in the Maori population is .... than the percentage of 0–14 year olds in the total New Zealand population. [1]

(ii) The percentage of over 55 year olds in the Maori population is .... than the percentage of over 55 year olds in the total New Zealand population. [1]

(iii) The percentage of over 35–49 year olds in the Maori population is .... than the percentage of over 35–39 year olds in the total New Zealand population. [1]

(c) In 2006, the Maori population formed 14% of the total New Zealand population.

(i) Using evidence from Figs 5 and 6 only, suggest how this may change over the next 50 years. [1]

(ii) Explain your answer to **(c) (i)**. [2] [Total: 8 marks]

(Cambridge IGCSE Geography 0460 Paper 2 Q2 June 2009)

3 Photograph A (below) shows an area of small-scale subsistence agriculture in Asia.

(a) Describe the relief of the area shown in Photograph A. [4]

(b) The natural vegetation of the area is tropical rainforest but the forest has been affected by human activity. Which of the following statements describe the distribution of forest shown in Photograph A? Circle **two** correct statements.
- Covering the whole area
- On the highest land
- On the steepest slopes
- In valleys
- Completely removed [2]

(c) Soil erosion is a problem in the area shown in Photograph A. What features shown in the photograph may encourage soil erosion? [2] [Total: 8 marks]

(Cambridge IGCSE Geography 0460 Paper 2 Q3 June 2009)

4 The United Kingdom plans to increase the percentage of electricity it produces from renewable energy sources. Fig. 7 shows the percentage produced from renewable sources in 2005 and the targets for 2010, 2015 and 2020.

(a) State the target for the percentage of electricity to be produced from renewable sources in 2015. [1]

Fig. 7

(b) The target for electricity from renewable sources in 2020 is 20%. Plot this information as a pie chart on Fig 8. Use the key provided. [3]

Key

☐ non-renewable sources   ■ renewable sources

Fig. 8

(c) Wind power is one renewable energy source. Fig. 9 shows a wind farm and some of the advantages and disadvantages of wind power.

It will not run out	Potential effect on house prices and tourism	Can be generated on land or on sea
Visual impact	WIND FARM	Turbines may kill birds
No carbon dioxide emissions or air pollution		Minimal risk of serious accidents
Amount of wind is variable		May increase electricity costs for consumers
No need to dig underground for it	Older wind farms cause some concern over noise	Quick to build and easy to remove

Fig. 9

A new wind farm is to be built. Using Fig. 9 only, suggest how this may affect:

(i) energy supplies [2]

(ii) the natural environment. [2] [Total: 8 marks]

(Cambridge IGCSE Geography 0460 Paper 2 Q4 June 2009)

5 Fig. 10 is a map showing the islands of Japan and the surrounding region. Plate boundaries, plate movements and selected earthquakes are shown.

The depth of the focus of each earthquake is shown. The focus of an earthquake is the place in the Earth's crust where an earthquake originates.

Key

▬▶ Direction of plate movement

╱ Plate boundary

∗ Earthquake focus shallower than 100 m below the Earth's surface

• Earthquake focus between 100 m and 400 m below the Earth's surface

○ Earthquake focus deeper than 400 m below the Earth's surface

Fig. 10

(a) Which of the following statements describe the plate movements shown on Fig. 10? Tick **two** correct statements. [2]

Statement	Tick
plates sliding past each other	
plates moving towards each other	
plates moving away from each other	
plates moving north-west and south-east	
plates moving north-east and south-west	
plates moving north and south	

(b) Describe **one** feature of the distribution of the following earthquakes shown on Fig. 10:

   (i) Earthquakes with their focus shallower than 100 m below the Earth's surface [1]

   (ii) Earthquakes with their focus between 100 m and 400 m below the Earth's surface [1]

   (iii) Earthquakes with their focus deeper than 400 m below the Earth's surface. [1]

(c) Explain why and how earthquakes occur in the area shown on Fig. 10. [3]

(Cambridge IGCSE Geography 0460 Paper 2 Q5 June 2009)

> **Tip**
> Use all the information provided for you. Only relevant information is included in the maps, diagrams, data tables etc.

Make a copy of the table below and complete it for Questions 3, 4 and 5.

Part of question	What you must do to answer the question
2 (a)	Complete the horizontal bar on the population pyramid.
2 (b) (i) (ii) (iii)	Interpret the data shown in the population pyramids.
2 (c) (i)	Suggest a possible change using evidence from the population pyramids.
2 (c) (ii)	Explain why the change you suggested might happen.
3 (a)	
3 (b)	
3 (c)	
4 (a)	
4 (b)	
4 (c) (i) (ii)	
5 (a)	
5 (b) (i) (ii) (iii)	
5 (c)	

Command words

Command words tell you how to answer the question. You need to know what each command word means and follow its instructions. If you do not know the meaning of the command word you will answer the question incorrectly.

> **Tip**
> Underline or highlight the command word to make sure you read it carefully.

Exam preparation

5.2

Identify the common command words used in examinations in the questions below.

- How many primary schools are there in Chatteris?
  (Cambridge IGCSE Geography 0460 Paper 2 Q2a November 2009)

- Using the information in Table 1 only, suggest the minimum population needed for a settlement to have a doctor's surgery.
  (Cambridge IGCSE Geography 0460 Paper 2 Q2c November 2009)

- Which one of the following statements about Fig. 3 is correct? Tick the correct statement.
  (Cambridge IGCSE Geography 0460 Paper 2 Q2e (ii) November 2009)

- Describe the physical features of the area shown in the photograph.
  (Cambridge IGCSE Geography 0460 Paper 2 Q3a November 2009)

- It is planned to build a dam in the area in order to provide a water supply for an urban area. Using evidence from the photograph, suggest **two** advantages and **two** disadvantages of the area for this purpose.
  (Cambridge IGCSE Geography 0460 Paper 2 Q3b November 2009)

- Name feature **X** shown on Fig. 5.
  (Cambridge IGCSE Geography 0460 Paper 2 Q5b (i) November 2009)

- Explain how feature **X** may have formed. You may add labels to Fig. 5.
  (Cambridge IGCSE Geography 0460 Paper 2 Q5b (ii) November 2009)

- Using the information from Fig. 6 and Table 3 only, give **four** advantages of the Western Cape for outdoor tourism.
  (Cambridge IGCSE Geography 0460 Paper 2 Q6c November 2009)

Resources

An examination paper contains a lot of different resources which you will use to answer the questions. Check that you are looking at the right resource. The resource booklet will include photographs, so it is particularly important that you study the correct one.

Examples of types of resources used in a Geographical Skills examination

Map	World map to show distribution of areas where there are food shortages Map of an island to show tourist developments Local map of an area around a city
Graph	Line graph to show change in birth rate and death rate over time Bar graph to show number of tourists to countries Climate graph to show temperature and rainfall in a hot desert Pie chart to show types of energy source Scatter graph to show the relationship between the population of villages and the number of shops Population pyramid to show population structure

Data table	Change in employment figures over time Climate data for contrasting areas in world
Photograph	These can show many things, for example areas of a city, types of farming, natural landscapes and features
Diagram	Geographical idea or theory such as Demographic Transition Model Sketch of natural features such as a lowland river valley Weather instruments
Information	Newspaper article Factfile Annotated (labelled) map These can show many things, for example a disaster such as famine, types of erosion in different natural areas, climate contrasts in a country

During examinations you may have to plot or draw information on a resource or read and interpret information from the resource. This is shown in the following examples.

Table 2 shows weather information for Pretoria, South Africa, for five days in 2006.

(i) Use the information in Table 2 to complete Fig. 9.

(ii) Which date has the greatest range of temperature? [2 marks]

(Adapted from Cambridge IGCSE Geography 0460 Paper 2 Q5a (i) and (ii) June 2008)

Read Fig. 4, which is an account of volcanic activity at Montserrat. Using information from Fig. 4 only, name **two** volcanic hazards affecting Montserrat. [2 marks]

(Adapted from Cambridge IGCSE Geography 0460 Paper 2 Q2b (i) November 2008)

Make sure you are prepared for your examination

You might think that you cannot revise for a skills exam. There are no case studies to learn, and you do not know which topics the questions will focus on. However, you can revise very effectively for this type of examination by:

- Practising how to answer map reading and interpretation questions from previous examinations.
- Revising the techniques you will use in examination.
- Re-reading your work which you revised for the Geographical Themes examination, except for the case studies. There will be questions in the Geographical Skills paper which test your understanding of different geographical ideas and your ability to make decisions.

> **Tip**
>
> Be accurate in plotting and interpreting maps and graphs.

Examples of two answers

You have now found out more about the Geographical Skills examination and how to improve your skills. Next you have the opportunity to look in detail at examination questions from a

5.2

Cambridge past paper. There are two example answers – one answer should achieve a high mark and the other answer should achieve a medium level mark. Each example answer is followed by a suggestion of how the answer may be marked and possibly improved.

Read the questions and look at the resources, then study the two example answers. In the exam, the map extract will be provided with a full key. The map shown on the next page is not reproduced with a key and is not to scale, but is provided as an example only.

Can you understand how the marks may be awarded and the answer might be improved?

(a) Fig. 1 shows part of the coastal area of the map. Study Fig. 1 and the map extract and answer the questions below.

Fig. 1

Identify the following features shown on Fig. 1.
  (i) the vegetation in area A
  (ii) the named or public building at B
  (iii) two services or functions in grid square C
  (iv) the type of road at D
  (v) the name of river E
  (vi) feature F in the ocean. [6 marks]

(Cambridge IGCSE Geography 0460 Paper 21 Q1a November 2010)

Answer 1
  (i) Tea (✓)
  (ii) Factory (✓)
  (iii) Hospital and power substation (✓)

Section 5.2: Preparing for your Geography examinations   311

Study the map extract, which is for Port Louis, Mauritius. The scale is 1:25 000.

(iv) Motorway (✓)
(v) Lataniers River (✓)
(vi) Coral (✓)

Teacher's comment

All features were correctly identified.

Answer 2

(i) Tea (✓)
(ii) Fcty
(iii) Hospital and power substation (✓)
(iv) Northern Entrance Road
(v) Lataniers River (✓)
(vi) Coral (✓)

Teacher's comment

Four of the six features are correctly identified. Answer (ii) would not be accepted because although the correct label has been copied from the map this is not a building. The key (which will be provided in the exam but is not shown in this example) must be used to answer the question correctly. Answer (iv) would also not be credited. The instruction is to identify the type of road not the name of the road. Do not lose marks carelessly by not reading and obeying the command word.

(b) Fig. 2 is a cross-section drawn from 975038 to 000038 through Priest Peak.

Fig. 2

Using labelled arrows, mark the following features on Fig. 2:

(i) the Citadel
(ii) Priest Peak
(iii) a power line. [3 marks]

(Cambridge IGCSE Geography 0460 Paper 21 Q1b November 2010)

Answer 1

Fig. 2

All three features are located correctly on the cross-section with labelled arrows.

Teacher's comment

All three features are located accurately on the cross-section with correctly labelled arrows.

Answer 2

Fig. 2

Citadel and Priest Peak are located correctly on the cross-section. The power line is located in the wrong position.

Teacher's comment

The answer correctly locates the citadel and Priest Peak. The position of the power line is inaccurate and would not be credited. Remember that when marking features on a cross-section you should use an arrow and label it. Do not just write the name above the cross-section. For example do not write Priest Peak above the hill without identifying the hilltop with an arrow. Another common error in labelling a cross-section is to point the labelled arrows at the base line of the cross-section not the cross-section line itself.

(c) The Port Louis area is an important commercial port in Mauritius.

 (i) State **two** features shown on the map which suggest that the area is a port. [2 marks]

 (Cambridge IGCSE Geography 0460 Paper 21 Q1c(i) November 2010)

5.2

Answer 1

1. Harbour (✓)
2. Dry dock (✓)

Teacher's comment

Both features would be credited. The answer correctly identifies both features from the map as instructed in the command words.

Answer 2

1. Harbour (✓)
2. Deep water quay (✓)

Teacher's comment

Both features are correctly identified from labels on the map. No further description would be needed.

(c) (ii) Using evidence from the map extract, describe **three** natural advantages of the area for the development of a port. [3 marks]

(Cambridge IGCSE Geography 0460 Paper 21 Q1c(i) November 2010)

Answer 1

1. The bay makes a natural harbour for the city (✓).
2. The headlands protect the harbour (✓) and the ships going into and out of the docks.
3. Lataniers River provides transport for goods that are produced further inland so that they can be exported from the river.

Teacher's comment

The answer correctly identifies the bay and surrounding headlands and describes how they will protect the harbour. Although the answer about the river may be true it is not really an advantage for the port and so would not be credited.

Answer 2

1. Flat land in most areas of the map.
2. Close to the sea, it's on the coast of the Indian Ocean.
3. Clear of coral at the port (✓) so that ships will not damage it.

Teacher's comment

The first idea is too vague. The answer would need to state that there is flat land next to the coast in order to be credited. Similarly, the second idea is far too general. Many areas are on the coast of the ocean. The answer does not describe why a port has developed at this particular place. The lack of coral would be an

Section 5.2: Preparing for your Geography examinations 315

acceptable reason. It appears from the map that there is a natural break in the coral reef at this location.

(d) (i) Find the CBD (Central Business District) of Port Louis. State the **four-figure** grid reference of the square containing the CBD. [1 mark]

(Cambridge IGCSE Geography 0460 Paper 21 Q1d(i) November 2010)

Answer 1

9703 (✓).

Teacher's comment

The grid reference is correct.

Answer 2

9702

Teacher's comment

The answer identifies the fishing port rather than the CBD. Look carefully at the map to find evidence of the CBD. There are a number of buildings shown on the map which indicate the CBD of Port Louis including two cathedrals, a mosque, the law office and the Supreme Court.

(d) (ii) State the meaning of the map symbol shown at 986029. [1 mark]

(Cambridge IGCSE Geography 0460 Paper 21 Q1d(ii) November 2010)

Answer 1

Minor trigonometrical station (✓)

Teacher's comment

This is an accurate answer. It has located the point correctly using the grid reference and then used the key to distinguish between the symbols for the major and minor trigonometrical points.

Answer 2

Peak of Moneron Hill

Teacher's comment

The answer uses the six-figure grid reference correctly to identify the area of Moneron Hill. However, the answer also shows that the question has not been read carefully enough because the map key has not been used to identify the map symbol on the top of the hill.

(e) Fig. 3 shows the area around Quoin Bluff. The area shaded is over 100 metres above sea level.

> **Skills link**
>
> You will find out more about how to interpret a six-figure grid reference on pages 236–237 of Section 4 Geographical Skills.

Fig. 3

Describe the relief of the area shaded on Fig. 3. [4 marks]

(Cambridge IGCSE Geography 0460 Paper 21 Q1e November 2010)

Answer 1

The relief is very steep (✓). The area has a pass high in the mountains (✓) between the top of Quoin Bluff and Spear Grass Peak. The area has some cliffs (✓). The western side of the location is more gently sloping than the north or south. The area reaches a height of over 500 metres (✓).

Teacher's comment

This answer should achieve an excellent mark because it shows an understanding of the key word 'relief'. Four simple descriptive ideas would be credited, these are steepness, the pass – a feature of upland areas, cliffs which are indicated in the key, and the highest point.

Answer 2

The contours are very steep sloped (✓). It has the shape of a smooth ridge (✓). The Quoin Bluff gets higher towards the centre. Near the 100 m contour we can see a lot of scrub and scattered trees all around Quoin Bluff. In square 9601 there is a small tea plantation. There is also a district boundary passing exactly through the middle of Quoin Bluff.

Teacher's comment

This answer could be improved. It shows understanding of the term 'relief'. Credit would be gained for recognising that the land is steep and that there is an upland feature called a ridge. However, the answer then fails to maintain a focus on 'relief' and describes irrelevant features of the area. Try to avoid going away from the question focus when you are answering. You will not gain marks for an answer which does not fit the question.

> **Skills link**
>
> You will find out more about how to describe relief of the land on pages 237–239 of Section 4 Geographical Skills.

2. The city of Cambridge in the UK lies close to important transport routes. People commute to work in the CBD from the suburbs and surrounding villages. The city suffers from traffic congestion. Fig. 4 below shows features of the transport routes in and around Cambridge.

Key

- motorway and dual carriageway
- other main road
- P — car park with bus to CBD
- CBD — central business district
- built up area
- railway and station

Fig. 4

(a) What features, shown on Fig. 4, help reduce traffic congestion for long distance travellers who do **not** wish to visit Cambridge? [2 marks]

(Cambridge IGCSE Geography 0460 Paper 21 Q2a November 2010)

Answer 1

The M11 motorway (✓) helps to reduce traffic congestion as well as the railway (✓).

Teacher's comment

Both features would be credited.

318 Exam preparation

Answer 2

The motorway and dual carriageway do not go through Cambridge. This means that they are able to avoid traffic congestion that occurs by going around Cambridge (✓).

Teacher's comment

The motorway and dual carriageway would only be credited as one feature; even though the idea is developed, the answer would not be given any more credit. A better answer is to name the features, such as the M11 motorway and the A11 main road.

(b) (i) Find the village of Melbourn on Fig. 4. A commuter travels from Melbourn to Cambridge CBD.

Estimate the distance, to the nearest kilometre, that the commuter travels ....kilometres.

State the compass direction in which the commuter travels.

[2 marks]

(Cambridge IGCSE Geography 0460 Paper 21 Q2b(i) November 2010)

Answer 1

18 (kilometres) (✓)

North-east (✓)

Teacher's comment

Both answers are correct

Answer 2

14 (kilometres)

North-east (✓)

Teacher's comment

The measurement is incorrect. The correct compass direction is given.

(b) (ii) Describe and give a reason for the location of the car parks shown on Fig. 4. [3 marks]

(Cambridge IGCSE Geography 0460 Paper 21 Q2b(ii) November 2010)

Answer 1

People are able to park their cars outside the city and travel to the CBD (✓) by bus (✓). This reduces the amount of vehicles in the CBD (✓) because more people fit in a bus than in a car.

Teacher's comment

The answer describes the location of the car parks as 'outside the city' and explains the location by stating that people can travel to the CBD by bus which reduces congestion.

Answer 2

The car parks have been strategically located around the CBD, most of them outside the built-up area (✓). They could have located them around Cambridge so it is easier for the people to park near where they live and get a bus to the CBD (✓).

Skills link

You will find out more about how to measure distance on maps on page 236 of Section 4 Geographical Skills.

Teacher's comment

The answer describes the location well as 'outside the built-up area'. The explanation would not be credited for the idea of proximity to where people live, as this may not be true, but the bus link to the CBD is credited.

(c) Suggest **one** way of reducing traffic congestion caused by commuters from the suburbs of Cambridge. [1 mark]

(Cambridge IGCSE Geography 0460 Paper 21 Q2c November 2010)

Answer 1

The commuters could travel there by metro, they would get an underground train into the CBD (✓). They could also cycle there if there were routeways.

Teacher's comment

There are many possible answers to this question. This answer correctly suggests a type of public transport – underground train. The answer includes another correct suggestion which is not needed.

Answer 2

They could take a bus or train to the city centre (✓).

Teacher's comment

The suggestion to use public transport is correct.

3 Study Fig. 5, which shows the Earth's tectonic plates and plate margins and Fig. 6, which shows the world distribution of active volcanoes.

Fig. 5

5.2

Fig. 6

(a) Using arrows, as shown below, label on Fig. 5 a plate margin where:

(i) Plates are moving away from each other (←—— ——→)

(ii) Plates are moving towards each other (——→ ←——)

[2 marks]

(Cambridge IGCSE Geography 0460 Paper 21 Q3a November 2010)

Answer 1

Fig. 5

(i) Arrows positioned on the boundary between the South American and African plates (✓)

(ii) Arrows positioned on the boundary between the South American and Nazca plates (✓)

Teacher's comment

Both sets of arrows are drawn in correct locations.

Section 5.2: Preparing for your Geography examinations 321

Answer 2

Fig. 5

(i) Arrows positioned on the boundary between the South American and Nazca plates

(ii) Arrows positioned on the boundary between the Eurasian and African plates (✓)

Teacher's comment

The arrows to show the plates moving away from each other are on the wrong boundary. The arrows showing plates moving towards each other are in a correct location.

(a) Which **two** of the following statements about active volcanoes are correct? Tick only **two** statements. [2 marks]

(Cambridge IGCSE Geography 0460 Paper 21 Q3b November 2010)

Statement	Tick
They are mostly found in the centres of plates.	
They are mostly found at plate margins.	
They are found at every plate margin.	
They may be found in the centres of plates.	
They are only found at plate margins.	

Answer 1

They are mostly found at plate margins. (✓)

They may be found in the centres of plates. (✓)

Teacher's comment

Both statements are correct.

322 Exam preparation

Answer 2

They are mostly found at plate margins. (✓)

They are found at every plate margin.

Teacher's comment

One correct statement is identified. Although it is correct that active volcanoes are found at plate margins they are not found at every plate margin.

(c) Fig. 7 is a map showing some of the effects of the eruption of Mount St Helens, USA, in May 1980.

(c) (i) Which effect of the eruption:

- covered over 600 km² north of the crater
- occurred in a single, 22 km long band west of Spirit Lake
- covered an area from the crater to 8 km further north? [3 marks]

(Cambridge IGCSE Geography 0460 Paper 21 Q3c(i) November 2010)

Fig. 7

Answer 1

Sideways blast (✓)

Debris avalanche (✓)

Pyroclastic flow (✓)

Teacher's comment

All three effects were correctly identified from the map.

Answer 2

Sideways blast (✓)

Mudflow

Pyroclastic flow (✓)

Teacher's comment

Two effects were correctly identified. The mudflow is not correct, even though it is west of the eruption. It is the debris avalanche that is located west of Spirit Lake.

(c) (ii) Suggest a reason for the distribution of mudflows shown on Fig. 7. [1 mark]

(Cambridge IGCSE Geography 0460 Paper 21 Q3c(ii) November 2010)

Answer 1

The pyroclastic flow and sideways blast did not allow the mudflows to flow north so they flowed east, south and west following the same paths as rivers and creeks. (✓)

Teacher's comment

The answer is over-elaborate but does include the correct idea that the mudflows followed the valleys.

Answer 2

The distribution is mainly caused by the rivers, the South Fork Toutle River and the North Fork Toutle River. (✓)

Teacher's comment

The idea that the mudflows followed the river valleys is credited.

4   Figs 8 and 9 show features seen at a weather station.

Fig. 9

Fig. 8

(a) (i) Why is the box shown on Fig. 8 raised above the ground? [1 mark]

(Cambridge IGCSE Geography 0460 Paper 21 Q4a(i) November 2010)

Answer 1

So that the thermometers do not measure the heat radiated from the ground. (✓)

Teacher's comment

This would be an appropriate answer.

Answer 2

So that insects or the material on the floor that could get into the box cannot be reached and does not ruin it.

> **Topic**
>
> You will find out more about how to interpret and understand weather instruments on pages 108–110.

324   Exam preparation

Teacher's comment

The reason given is irrelevant. The answer is incorrect.

(a) (ii) Why are the sides of the box shown on Fig. 8 louvred (slatted)? [1 mark]

(Cambridge IGCSE Geography 0460 Paper 21 Q4a(ii) November 2010)

Answer 1

To allow ventilation of the air (✓) so that the thermometers give an accurate reading of shaded areas.

Teacher's comment

This answer gives correct reasons: for ventilation and shade.

Answer 2

The sides of the box are slatted so that when it rains water will not get inside and ruin it.

Teacher's comment

This would not be a valid reason. The answer is incorrect.

(b) (i) What feature of the weather does the instrument shown on Fig. 9 measure? [1 mark]

(Cambridge IGCSE Geography 0460 Paper 21 Q4b(i) November 2010)

Answer 1

Wind speed (✓)

Teacher's comment

The answer is correct.

Answer 2

Wind

Teacher's comment

The answer would not be credited because different aspects of the wind can be measured (speed and direction). The instrument in Fig. 9 measures wind speed.

(b) (ii) What units are used to record this weather feature? [1 mark]

(Cambridge IGCSE Geography 0460 Paper 21 Q4b(ii) November 2010)

Answer 1

Metres per second (✓)

Teacher's comment

There are a number of different units which are used to measure wind speed. The answer correctly names one of them.

Answer 2

How much it spins.

Section 5.2: Preparing for your Geography examinations

Teacher's comment

The answer shows an understanding of how the anemometer works but this is not a unit of measurement.

(c) Clouds are recorded without using any equipment. Fig. 10 shows three types of cloud.

Fig. 10

(c) (i) Name the **types** of cloud shown on Fig. 10. [3 marks]
(Cambridge IGCSE Geography 0460 Paper 21 Q4c(i) November 2010)

X
Y
Z

Answer 1

X Stratus

Y Cumulus (✓)

Z Cumulo-nimbus (✓)

Teacher's comment

Two of the cloud types are identified correctly. The answer mixes up stratus cloud with cirrus cloud in answer X.

Answer 2

X Wind-blown cloud

Y Cumulus (✓)

Z Storm cloud

Teacher's comment

The answer correctly identifies one cloud. The description of a cumulo-nimbus cloud as a storm cloud is accurate but it is not the name of the cloud.

(c) (ii) State the units used to estimate the amount of cloud cover. [1 mark]

(Cambridge IGCSE Geography 0460 Paper 21 Q4c(ii) November 2010)

Answer 1

Oktas (✓)

Teacher's comment

This is the correct unit.

Answer 2

Eighths (✓)

Teacher's comment

This alternative answer would also be acceptable.

Section 5 . Topic 3

Preparing for your Geography examinations

Learning objectives:
- confidently collect data through fieldwork to test a hypothesis
- present and analyse the data you have collected
- make some judgments about the hypothesis that you are testing

What are coursework assignments?

Candidates for the Cambridge O Level examination do **not** submit a coursework assignment as part of the assessment but instead sit the Geographical Investigations examination (Paper 3).

Candidates for the Cambridge IGCSE examination can choose between an examination paper (Paper 4) **or** complete one coursework assignment which is set by your teachers and approved by Cambridge Assessment International Education.

The coursework assignment is worth 60 marks but instead of having a time limit like the other examinations, the coursework assignment has a maximum word limit, which is 2000 words. The examination board suggest to your teachers that the coursework assignment should take between four and five weeks to complete in classwork and homework time. Your teacher will decide when you do your assignment and how long you will have to complete it.

Your teacher can also decide on the topic to investigate. It is likely that the topic that is chosen will be:

- interesting to investigate
- relevant to the course and topic which you are studying
- investigated in an area that is local to your school or within easy travelling distance, so you can easily visit the place and possibly return to do further work if necessary
- broken down into different hypotheses or ideas to be tested.

In completing the coursework assignment you will be:

- encouraged to think for yourself and test a hypothesis
- given the opportunity to use your geographical skills away from the classroom
- able to gain understanding of geographical concepts and theories by testing them.

Doing a coursework assignment tests three objectives:

1. Your understanding of the geographical concepts (ideas) which you are testing through fieldwork.
2. Your data collection and presentation techniques and your analysis of the data.

3   Your conclusions about the ideas you are investigating and your suggestions for how to improve the investigation.

Why do fieldwork?

The coursework assignment will probably be based on fieldwork. Fieldwork is an important part of geography. It gives you the opportunity to go out of the classroom and find out geographical ideas for yourself. You do this by testing these ideas in real places and with real people. This may take place in the grounds of the school, in a local village or town, in a river or coastal area near to school, or further away if you go on a field trip for one or more days.

Fieldwork gives you the chance to learn the methods that geographers use to test ideas and concepts. It gives you the opportunity to work with other students in measuring and collecting data. You will probably discuss in class suitable hypotheses (ideas) to test during your fieldwork, but you should also have the chance to think of and test some hypotheses of your own.

Follow the 'route to geographical enquiry'

Whatever fieldwork investigation you undertake you should follow the 'route to geographical enquiry'. It will help you to plan, undertake, and write about your fieldwork investigation.

1 Identify a topic to investigate and think of some hypotheses to test

Although your teacher may decide the topic, you will have the opportunity to discuss it in class and agree some hypotheses to test. You may also think of some extra hypotheses to test yourself. To think of a suitable hypothesis you need to make a sensible guess of a possible outcome of your investigation. A suitable hypothesis is 'The river will flow faster as it goes downstream', or you could write this hypothesis as a question: 'Does the river flow faster as it goes downstream?'

2 Collect relevant data to test your hypothesis

You can either collect data by yourself or in a group. Often you will do this with other students. You will need to think about safety whilst collecting data, what equipment you will need to take, and how you can make sure that the data which you collect is reliable and accurate. As well as collecting 'primary' data – that is, the information you collect yourself – you can also get data from 'secondary' sources such as the internet, books, maps and newspapers.

3 Record and present your results

You might include maps at different scales to show the location of your study area. Put statistics that you have collected during the fieldwork into tables so that they are clear to read. Draw a variety of graphs, not just one type, but make sure they are appropriate for the data you are displaying. If appropriate, plot some data on a map. Also use field sketches and photographs to illustrate your work.

4 Analyse your results

You must explain what your maps, tables, graphs and diagrams show. Identify the general patterns or trends which your results show. Look for any individual results that do not fit the pattern – these are called anomalies.

5 Make a conclusion about your hypothesis and evaluate your investigation

Look back at your hypothesis. Then refer to your results and analysis to make a conclusion about whether the hypothesis is true and supported by evidence, or not true because there is no evidence to support it. Maybe the evidence of your fieldwork does not clearly prove or disprove your hypothesis. This is also an acceptable conclusion. Your conclusion may lead you to suggest how you might improve the investigation if you were to repeat it, or what extra work you could do with more time.

> **Skills link**
>
> You will find out more about how to record and present your results on pages 251–262.

Practical hints to make your fieldwork successful

Safety

Make safety your first priority. Be sensible to stay safe. Rivers, beaches and town centres are just some fieldwork locations that can be dangerous places. What hazards and dangers do you think a student would need to be aware of at each of these locations?

Possible hazards and dangers

- Rivers: deep water, fast-flowing current, wet and slippery rocks, polluted water, animals in the river.
- Beaches: large waves, strong current, wet and slippery rocks and groynes, being cut off by rising tide.
- Town centres: traffic along busy roads.

Precautions

Take the following precautions. They can save a lot of worry.

- Work in pairs or small groups.
- Tell an adult where you are going and what time you will return.

- Take a mobile (cell) phone, making sure it is fully charged.
- Don't do fieldwork in bad weather or when it is dark.
- Wear sensible clothing and footwear.

Equipment

Make sure that you take the correct equipment with you and that you know how to use it. Test the equipment before you set off to make sure that it is working properly.

Planning

Plan your investigation before you set off. If more than one person or group is collecting data, make sure that everyone knows what to do. Each person or group should use the same method of measurement, use the same questionnaire, and do the tally count for the same length of time.

In their evaluation many students say that errors such as inaccurate measuring or different groups not doing the task in the same way have made their results unreliable. Good planning removes this problem.

Practice investigation

It is a good idea to do a practice or 'pilot' investigation before you do the 'real' fieldwork. This gives you the chance to check equipment and your methods, and it might give you an idea of what results you might expect to get in the actual investigation. A practice investigation can be done near school, for example in a local stream or road. You do not need to use your actual investigation site.

Collecting data

Collect as much data and information as you can in the time available. It is better to have more data than you need than not have enough. You can always discard some when you begin to analyse it back at school.

Recording data

Prepare a form for recording your results before you begin your fieldwork. It is much easier to fill in a prepared form than having to write you results out in full. If you are doing fieldwork in wet conditions, keep your recording sheet in a plastic bag or envelope. Many fieldwork investigations are spoiled by having illegible results because the recording sheet has soaked up water!

Politeness

Be polite when speaking to people and asking them questions. Remember that you want them to help you. Explain the purpose of the interview or questionnaire. People will be more willing to give you answers if they know why you want them. Don't ask questions that are intrusive or personal.

The questionnaire on the right was produced by two students. They were investigating the 'catchment area' of their local football club and opinions about whether the club should move its ground to a new location.

Explain why their teacher did not approve the questionnaire.

Reasons why the questionnaire was not approved

The introduction does not give any background information about the fieldwork.

Jo does not explain why she needs to ask the questions.

Question 1 is irrelevant and personal.

Question 2 is too vague and may not get a precise answer and it is too personal.

Question 3 is badly worded and it would be better if possible alternative answers were given.

Question 4 is probably going to get only one answer – to watch the match.

Question 5 is a closed question and needs to be followed up by asking why the person has given their answer.

Question 6 is too vague and will get too many different locations to be useful.

Question 7 is a closed question and needs to be followed by asking the reason for the answer.

The final comment is abrupt and impolite.

How your coursework may be marked

If you understand how your coursework may be marked it will help you to improve your geographical enquiry. Your assignment may be marked in 'levels' from a low level for simple work to a high level for detailed work that links together well. Your work may be assessed under different headings. Your work must improve in quality to reach a higher level. The five headings that are often used to mark your coursework are:

- Knowledge with understanding
- Observation and collection of data
- Organisation and presentation of data
- Analysis and interpretation
- Conclusion and evaluation

Hi, my name is Jo and I need to ask you some questions.

1. What is your name?
2. Where do you live?
3. How did you get to the ground?
4. Why have you come?
5. Do you think the club should move the ground or stay here?
6. Where would you like the new ground?
7. Would you go to the new ground?

OK that's it.

Skills link

You will find out more about how to produce a questionnaire on pages 269–271 of Section 4 Geographical Skills.

5.3

Building the skills needed for success in your coursework assignment

Knowledge with understanding

You need to show good knowledge of the topic that you are investigating in your coursework, for example why land values vary in a city. The best place to do this is probably in the introduction, but you will also be able to show your knowledge in the analysis and conclusion. Do not have too many hypotheses to test (between two and four is best). Make your hypotheses clear to understand and not too complicated. You will then be able to explain what you are trying to find out and why. Including an extra hypothesis to the ones being tested by the class may help you to show more clearly your understanding of the topic.

Observation and collection of data

Describe clearly how you carried out your fieldwork and the methods or techniques you used. There are many different fieldwork techniques that you can use. Some of the more common ones are listed in the table below. These techniques are described in Section 4 Geographical Skills. A high level answer should also explain why you used these methods (not just because your teacher told you to!).

Common fieldwork techniques

Questionnaire
Interview
Sampling
Perception study, e.g. as part of an environmental survey
Land use mapping, e.g. the CBD, farm
Field sketching
Counting, e.g. pedestrians or traffic
Measuring:
River, e.g. depth, width, velocity, cross-section, wetted perimeter, load, gradient
Coast, e.g. longshore drift, beach material, waves, beach profile, cliff profile
Weather, e.g. temperature, rainfall, wind speed and direction, pressure, relative humidity, cloud cover and type

Organisation and presentation of data

You may choose to put your work in a logical order. This order will probably be:

1. Explain what you are investigating and state your hypotheses.
2. Describe your methods of investigation.
3. Display your results.

4 Analyse your results.

5 Make a conclusion to your investigation, evaluate your fieldwork and suggest improvements.

For example, it may not be so effective if you describe your investigation methods before explaining why you are investigating the topic.

It is also important to use a range of methods for presenting the data that you have collected. Some methods are more complex than others and so may gain more credit. Results displayed in bar graphs or pie charts, even if they are computer generated, are not considered as challenging as other techniques, such as a map with proportional symbols or flow lines.

Analysis and interpretation

It is good practice to include a high level method of presentation, such as a scatter graph with a trend line drawn on it, and use this as part of your analysis by including a written commentary next to the graph that identifies the important information shown on it. You may also link the graph to your original hypothesis and make a comment about whether the evidence supports it or not. By linking the data and analysis you can show a high level of understanding. This is a much better approach than drawing lots of graphs and having a separate section for analysis.

Conclusion and evaluation

If aiming for a high level grade you may refer back to your hypotheses and summarise the information that you have found to support each one. You should also refer to the information that was inconclusive or suggested the opposite of what you expected to find. From this you can make your own conclusion about the hypotheses.

A high level evaluation will identify how reliable the information that you collected might be and what factors affected its reliability. Do not focus your evaluation on what went wrong during the fieldwork, such as 'there was not enough time to collect data' or 'people would not answer my questions'. These may have affected your results but they are really weaknesses that should have been avoided.

You may include in your evaluation your thoughts about how useful the results might be and which groups of people might benefit from the conclusions you reached. For example, you might suggest how an area may be improved based on your results of a perception survey. You might also include in your evaluation new hypotheses that could be tested in future fieldwork.

> **Skills link**
>
> You will find out more about how to draw proportional symbols and flow lines on page 257 of Section 4 Geographical Skills.

5.3

Make sure you are prepared for the coursework assignment

When preparing your coursework assignment it is good practice to:

- think of clear hypotheses to test
- prepare your investigation before you go to do the fieldwork
- collect relevant data
- link your analysis to the different maps and graphs that you draw
- think carefully about what your investigation shows about your hypotheses and write about this in your conclusion.

Examples of two coursework investigations

You have now found out more about the coursework assignment and how to produce good coursework. Next you have the opportunity to look in detail at two examples of good coursework. These are followed by comments and advice that you might get from your teacher.

Study the two example assignments. Can you understand whether it is a strong or a weak answer? Read the teacher's comment, which explains the awarding of the level and, where appropriate, suggests how the work could be improved.

Example 1 A river study

Knowledge with understanding

The investigation begins with a general introduction about the river and the area that it flows through, describing the relief of the area and the location of the source and mouth of the river. This is supported by two maps: a small-scale map showing the position of the river in the country, and a large-scale map showing the river drainage basin.

The investigation identifies five survey sites and locates them on the map of the drainage basin. It also describes the landscape at each site and explains why these sites were chosen.

The aim of the investigation is: 'To find out if this river has typical characteristics of a river'. The five hypotheses that will be tested to investigate the river are:

1. River velocity increases with distance from the source.
2. River depth increases with distance from the source.
3. The length of the river cross-section increases with distance from the source.
4. The wetted perimeter of the river increases with distance from the source.
5. Bedload size and roughness decrease with distance from the source.

There is a brief explanation of each hypothesis, for example Hypothesis 5:

> I believe that this would be an appropriate hypothesis because a typical river's bedload size decreases with distance from the source due to the increase in velocity in the water. This increase in velocity increases the river's ability to transport rocks and to erode them, making them smaller and more rounded. I believe that as you get closer to the river's mouth, the bedload would gradually change from larger, more angular boulders to small, round pebbles.

Teacher's comment

This is a high level piece of work. The introduction contains relevant background information about the river. The maps help to put the river 'in context' so that it is clear where the investigation has been carried out. The large-scale map is useful to show the locations of the investigation sites. The aim of the study and the hypotheses are straightforward and stated clearly. The explanation of each hypothesis shows understanding of the processes that are being investigated. Five hypotheses are more than usual but the results will provide a comprehensive conclusion to the study's aim.

Weaker fieldwork studies:

- do not include maps so they do not locate the investigation
- do not explain why the hypotheses are being tested
- contain a lot of theory often copied from a textbook – a little theoretical background is useful but the main focus must be on the practical tasks.

Observation and collection of data

Data collection is done by the individual as part of a group. Having identified five investigation sites, the group go to each of the sites in turn to do their fieldwork. For each hypothesis the investigation includes a list of the equipment that the group used, with photographs and drawings where needed. The method of data collection for each hypothesis is described in detail. This is supported by field sketches of each site and labelled photographs of the group making their measurements. The method used to test hypothesis 1 (River velocity increases with distance from the source) is described as follows:

> To find the average velocity at each point in the river we measured out a length of 10 metres along the river using the tape measure. One member of the group stood at each end of the 10 metre distance. The person upstream had the float and the other person had the stopwatch. The person placed the float in the river when the person downstream started the stopwatch. When the float reached the person downstream she stopped the stopwatch, called out the time taken and it was recorded. This was repeated five times to make sure that the result was reliable, and then an average time was calculated.
>
> To limit air resistance the group used a thin piece of wood (painted red so it could be seen easily). This floats on the surface. However, this technique only measures the surface velocity of the river, which is not the greatest velocity due to friction slowing it down. A more accurate way to measure velocity is to use a flowmeter but we did not have this equipment. In the test, sometimes the float got stuck behind rock or reeds in the river or got washed into the side of the river and did not move. So we had to repeat that test.

Photographs show the group laying out the tape along the bank to measure 10 metres downstream, and the float in the river.

Teacher's comment

The measuring method is described and explained in detail and meets the requirements of a high level investigation. The method is justified and comments are made about where the test is weak and the problems encountered whilst collecting the data.

Weaker fieldwork studies:

- do not describe the method in detail
- do not explain the method used
- focus on problems that are due to 'operator error', such as not timing the test accurately; these are not weaknesses in the methodology of the fieldwork but are examples of poor fieldwork technique.

Organisation and presentation of data

The fieldwork report is organised so that there is a different section for each hypothesis. Each section follows the same order:

1 Description of the method (as shown above).
2 Record of data collected in a data table.
3 Presentation of the data in an appropriate graph.
4 Analysis of the data.

The data collected at one site to test hypothesis 2 (River depth increases with distance from the source) is shown below. This data was also collected and plotted on graphs for the other four sites.

Distance across river (m)	Depth of river (cm)
0	0
0.5	13
1	21
1.5	16
2	17
2.5	21
3	20
3.5	18
4	21
4.5	19
5	15
5.5	14
6	6
6.5	0

A different type of graph or diagram is used to illustrate each hypothesis, including a sketch of the river with flow lines to show velocity in hypothesis 1, and a multiple bar graph to show bedload size and roughness in hypothesis 5.

Teacher's comment

This is acceptable as a high level piece of work. The coursework has a clear structure that makes it easy to follow and understand. The method, results, data presentation and analysis are linked for each hypothesis. The diagrams and graphs can be easily compared to see any changes downstream.

A computer program was used to produce the graphs. Whilst this is acceptable, the graphs must be appropriate and accurate. In the graph above the distances across the river are points 1–14, not the actual distance across the river as shown in the data table. The river should also be shaded to show the channel clearly.

Weaker fieldwork studies:

- do not show organisation in the written work
- put all the results together, all the graphs and diagrams together, all the analyses together – there is no integration of the different parts, which makes it difficult to relate the results, presentation and analysis for each separate hypothesis
- do not contain a variety of appropriate presentation methods – they are often restricted to one type of graph.

Analysis

The investigation includes an analysis of the results for each hypothesis. Each analysis begins by describing what the results showed, including the identification of a pattern that supports the hypothesis and picking out anomalies that do not fit with the hypothesis. The results of hypothesis 4 (The wetted perimeter of the river increases with distance from the source) are shown below, with an analysis of these results.

Investigation site	Length of wetted perimeter
1	2.0
2	6.4
3	11.8
4	7.8
5	8.1

Section 5.3: Preparing for your Geography examinations

> You can see from the graph that site 1 has the shortest wetted perimeter. However, site 3 has the longest measurement, which does not fit the overall pattern that the wetted perimeter gets longer away from the source. The wetted perimeter at site 3 is more than three metres wider than site 5, which should be the largest according to the hypothesis. The graph also shows that sites 1, 2, 4 and 5 fit the pattern as the wetted perimeter gradually increases in length.
>
> Overall these measurements prove the hypothesis is correct. The river is typical in terms of its wetted perimeter, as it increases from 2 metres at site 1 to 8.1 metres at site 5. Site 3 is much wider than would be expected. This might be because the river is joined by a tributary at this site and so the river channel is wider.

Skills link

You will find out more about how to interpret maps and graphs on pages 245–257 of Section 4 Geographical Skills.

Teacher's comment

There is a clear analysis of the results for each hypothesis. It includes a description of how the results change downstream and suggests why the results may vary, including an explanation of any anomaly, as shown above. The explanation may not clearly explain the anomaly but it shows understanding of a possible reason. This is supported by a photograph of site 3, which does not fit the overall pattern. Each separate piece of analysis refers to the original hypothesis.

Weaker fieldwork studies:

- include a simple level of analysis which is usually a description of the graph or results
- do not attempt to explain the results
- do not identify anomalies
- include the analysis at the end of the investigation report but it is not linked back to individual hypotheses.

Conclusion and evaluation

The investigation goes back to the original aim of the study, which was stated in the introduction. An overall conclusion is made that the river has typical characteristics that change downstream. This is followed by a separate conclusion to each individual hypothesis, as shown below for hypothesis 1.

> My first hypothesis 'River velocity increases with distance from the source' was proved to be correct. I discovered that site 1 did have the slowest velocity and that site 5, furthest from the source, did have the fastest velocity. This shows that the river is a typical river in terms of river velocity. However, site 3 was irregular and had a greater velocity than sites 4 and 5, meaning that this point in the river was not typical.

Later in the conclusion the point is made:

> Site 3 did not fit the pattern of any of the hypotheses, so it must be an anomaly. I think that the main reason for this is that the river is joined by a tributary before that site and therefore there is suddenly a lot of extra water in the river. This might explain why the results are different for site 3.

Finally there is an evaluation of the investigation. The evaluation picks out some weaknesses in methodology and suggests how the investigation could be improved in the future, for example as in the following comment about measuring velocity:

> The equipment that was available to us was not very accurate, which meant that our measurements could have been inaccurate. When measuring the velocity of the river the float would only show the surface velocity of the river and would get slowed down by obstacles such as large rocks.

The evaluation also suggests strengths of the investigation that would make the conclusion acceptable. It states:

> As we were in groups of four there were many helping hands when collecting the information. We could have one person recording the results, whilst the other members of the group took the measurements. Also the investigations and measurements were repeated a few times so that we got enough data to calculate an average for all the measurements.

Teacher's comment

The conclusions are well thought out. They are relevant to the data that has been collected and fit the analysis of these results. There is also an overall evaluation of the investigation that draws together the conclusions about the separate hypotheses. The investigation also recognises weaknesses in methodology and suggests how they can be improved. The suggestions are sensible and practical and will increase the reliability of the results.

Weaker fieldwork studies:

- do not link the conclusion back to the original aim or hypotheses
- often just repeat the analysis in the conclusion
- have a negative evaluation that blames the other members of the group for inaccurate results
- suggest improvements such as 'repeat the experiment', 'take more care in measuring', 'check our results carefully' but there is no explanation how these will be done.

Example 2 A study of tourism

Knowledge with understanding

The investigation report begins with a question:

> Why has my local area grown as a centre for tourism and what impact has the growth of tourism had on the area?

In the introduction the investigation briefly describes the physical and human attractions of the area and locates the area on a map of the country. It then states that the aim of the study will be 'To find out what attracts tourists to this area and what impact tourism has had on the area'. The three hypotheses to be tested are:

1. Tourists will be attracted by both physical and human factors.
2. The impact of tourism on local people will be more positive than negative.
3. Areas near the coast will have most visitors compared to areas that are inland.

Each hypothesis is supported by a brief explanation of what outcomes are expected. For hypothesis 3:

> In tourist areas there will be more traffic and pedestrians than areas where locals live. The areas near the coast will be busiest because this is where many tourist attractions, such as the beaches and entertainment parks, are located. Areas that are not near the coast will not be as busy because people in these areas are working and shopping and doing their daily tasks.

Teacher's comment

This would be a high level piece of work. The introduction makes it clear what is the main focus of the investigation and where the investigation is taking place. It is clear that there are two parts to the investigation:

1. Why do tourists visit the local area?
2. What impact does tourism have on the area?

The aim is reflected in the hypotheses. These hypotheses are quite complex and each one contains two elements to consider: physical and human factors in hypothesis 1; positive and negative impacts in hypothesis 2; coastal and inland in hypothesis 3. The explanation of the hypotheses, like the one shown above for hypothesis 3, shows clear understanding of what the investigation predicts that the outcomes will be.

Weaker fieldwork studies:

- do not locate the study area
- use simple hypotheses
- do not suggest what the outcome of the investigation will be.

Observation and collection of data

Collection of data is done by the individual working as part of a group. Each hypothesis requires a different method of investigation. Hypotheses 1 and 2 were researched by different questionnaires, and hypothesis 3 was investigated through a traffic survey and a pedestrian count done in different parts of the area. These different fieldwork techniques provide opportunities for planning and organisation. This is shown in the description of the method used to test hypothesis 1 (Tourists will be attracted by both physical and human factors) as follows:

> We conducted interviews with tourists. Our first task was to devise a questionnaire that we could use with visitors. We produced the questionnaire shown below. First we had to ask if the person we wished to interview was a visitor. If they were not, we thanked them and moved to the next person. We divided the attractions into physical and human groups. We asked for the overall attraction last to see which group people thought was more important. We went to the main tourist area where there are lots of hotels to use our questionnaire.

Teacher's comment

The collection of data is of good quality because a range of investigation techniques are used. These different methods also provide opportunities for working in pairs and in a group. The questionnaire shown on the right, which is used to investigate hypothesis 1, is easy to understand and can be completed quickly. Possible responses to the questionnaire have been considered in advance and the task of recording the answer has been made easier by providing a number of alternatives to choose from. This technique will also make the calculation of results easier. The questionnaire contains a brief introduction to explain why the survey is being carried out. It is also polite and contains simple instructions. However, it does not explain if any sampling technique was used to select people to interview in order to get an unbiased sample.

Weaker fieldwork studies:

- include only one technique such as a questionnaire
- do not organise the methodology to make results easy to calculate
- do not explain why different techniques are being used.

Organisation and presentation of data

The fieldwork report is organised so that for each hypothesis the tasks are put in the same order: description of the method, recording and presentation of data, analysis. The different fieldwork techniques produce varied pieces of data that are recorded in tables under the appropriate hypotheses.

Tourist questionnaire

We are doing a tourism survey as part of our Geography coursework. If you are a visitor please will you answer the following questions?

1. What are the main physical attractions which you are visiting?
   - Waterfalls ☐
   - Mountains ☐
   - Hot springs ☐
   - Botanical gardens ☐
   - Wildlife reserve ☐
   - Butterfly farms ☐
   - Gorge ☐

2. What are the main human attractions which you are visiting?
   - Hill villages ☐
   - National museum ☐
   - Flower market ☐
   - Temples ☐
   - Royal palace ☐
   - Prehistoric sites ☐
   - Royal pagoda ☐

3. Overall which attracted you most to this area?
   - Physical attractions ☐
   - Human attractions ☐

Thank you for your time.

Skills link

You will find out more about how to produce a questionnaire on pages 269–270 of Section 4 Geographical Skills.

You will find out more about sampling techniques on pages 271–272 of Section 4 Geographical Skills.

For hypothesis 1 the results rank the physical and human attractions, which are plotted on two bar graphs. For hypothesis 2 the results show positive and negative impacts, which are plotted on pie charts. For hypothesis 3 the results show traffic data, which is drawn as flow lines on a local map, and pedestrian flows, which are used to plot an isoline map of the area.

Teacher's comment

The structure of the coursework is logical and easy to follow and understand. There is a variety of methods of displaying the data that has been collected. These methods include simple techniques such as a bar graph or pie chart, and more complex techniques such as flow lines and isoline construction. These presentation methods are appropriate for the data that they are being used to display. The presentation of pedestrian and traffic data makes it possible to see the contrasts needed for high level analysis.

Weaker fieldwork studies:

- use simple map or graph techniques, and often only one presentation method is used
- do not use maps to display fieldwork data – everything is shown on graphs whether or not it is appropriate to do so
- only use results for one area.

Analysis

Each set of results is analysed in turn by summarising what the results show and then explaining why these results were found. The analysis for hypothesis 1 (Tourists will be attracted by both physical and human factors) is shown with the results of the questionnaire survey below.

Q1 Physical attractions	Number of visits made
Mountains	42
Waterfalls	35
Wildlife reserve	34
Gorge	20
Hot springs	19
Botanical gardens	13
Butterfly farms	7
Total	170

> **Skills link**
>
> You will find out more about how to draw flow lines and plot an isoline map on pages 256–257 of Section 4 Geographical Skills.

Q2 Human attractions	Number of visits made
Outdoor market	45
Hill villages	33
Temples	27
Prehistoric sites	11
National museum	10
Royal pagodas	8
Royal palace	6
Total	140

Q3 Overall opinion	Number of tourists
Physical attractions	38
Human attractions	32

You can see from the results that the mountains and waterfalls attracted many people. This is because of the beautiful natural scenery and also because there are human attractions in the area such as whitewater rafting, trekking trails and the hill villages. This will also explain why these villages are a main attraction, because they are only found in this area. The wildlife reserve is also a popular attraction as it is world-famous and many visitors want to go to it.

The most popular human attraction was the outdoor market which is in a main tourist area of the city. It is easy to get to and many people will go there to buy the craft products and local foods. The temples are also popular with visitors who are interested in the history of the country.

Overall the physical attractions are more popular than the human attractions, but there is not much difference between them. The overall opinion of visitors is that they are attracted by both types of attractions. Most visitors go to both physical and human attractions that are in the same area, such as the mountains and the villages.

Teacher's comment

There is a clear analysis of the results for each hypothesis, as shown in the analysis of hypothesis 1 above. The analysis describes the main pattern of results and highlights the main attractions. It comments that physical and human attractions may be found together, which will help to explain the pattern of results. It also suggests why these attractions are most popular. The final point of analysis is excellent. It does not simply state that physical attractions are more popular but shows understanding that there is little difference between the results.

For the other hypotheses the analysis describes the patterns shown by the maps and graphs and any results that do not fit the overall pattern. The analysis of a flow-line diagram and an isoline map and the analysis of how the tourist and local areas are different would all be high level responses.

Weaker fieldwork studies:

- describe the results of a survey but do not explain the results
- do not describe spatial variations on a map
- do not explain variations between areas.

Conclusion and evaluation

The investigation includes a conclusion to each hypothesis in turn. Most investigations conclude that the hypothesis is correct. However, a high level conclusion will also refer to results that do not agree with the hypothesis. The conclusion to hypothesis 1 is as follows:

> I conclude that it is both the physical landscape and its culture that attract tourists to the local area. From the results of the questionnaire you can see that they mostly come for the mountains, shopping, waterfalls and the hill villages. More people say that they are attracted by physical than by human attractions but I think many visitors will come to see both. The most popular attraction is shopping at the outdoor market, which attracts many visitors because it is easily accessible.

There is an excellent evaluation of the investigation. It identifies four factors that could have affected the results. These include factors affecting the questionnaire and pedestrian and traffic counts shown below.

> We asked 70 people to complete the questionnaire, which is a good sample size. We would have asked more people but some tourists did not speak English as their first language and so did not understand what we were asking.
> The problem with the traffic survey and pedestrian count is that they were not all taken at the same time of the day. This meant that the results could be affected by factors like people going to and from work. If we repeat these surveys we would have to make sure that different groups do the counts at the same time.

Teacher's comment

The conclusion tends to repeat some of the ideas from the analysis section and neither agrees with nor rejects the hypothesis. The conclusion does include a decision about hypothesis 1 but does not say exactly what this decision is.

The evaluation is well thought out and includes practical difficulties such as trying to use a questionnaire with people for whom English was not their first language. This is a common problem with questionnaires. One way to overcome the difficulty is to have one member of the group who can speak the local language. Carrying out the pedestrian count and traffic survey at different times is a common error and this should be considered when planning an investigation. Overall this section is satisfactory, but could be improved.

Weaker fieldwork studies:

- use the conclusion to describe again the methodology and how the results are presented
- state that the hypothesis is correct or incorrect but give no explanation to support this conclusion
- suggest that a way to improve the investigation is to 'gather more information'
- suggest improvements such as 'repeat the experiment', 'take more care in measuring', 'check our results carefully' but there is no explanation how these will be done.

Section 5 . Topic 4

Preparing for your Geography examinations

Learning objectives:
- confidently prepare for examinations
- understand examination questions
- make the best use of resources in an examination paper

What investigation skills will be covered in examinations?

Candidates for the Cambridge O Level examination do not submit a coursework assignment as part of the assessment but instead sit the Geographical Investigations examination (Paper 3). Candidates for the Cambridge IGCSE examination can choose between an examination paper (Paper 4) or complete one coursework assignment, which is set by your teachers and approved by Cambridge Assessment International Education. In studying this course you will be:

- encouraged to think for yourself and apply your understanding to different geographical questions
- given the opportunity to use geographical investigation skills.

The examination tests:

1. Your understanding of the ideas being investigated.
2. Collection and presentation of data and your analysis of this data.
3. Your conclusions about the ideas being investigated and suggestions to improve the investigation.

You will not be told which objective each question is testing but you will recognise the objectives by the wording of the question.

How to use your time effectively

During any examination it is important to plan your time effectively and the marks available for each section or question are a good guide.

You also need to allow time to:

- read the question all the way through to make sure you understand the investigation topic
- study the insert and check which question each resource is used with
- check your answers at the end of the examination and make sure you complete any answers which you may have missed out.

To have the time to do all this it may be better to allow yourself 40 minutes to answer each question and use the extra 10 minutes on the other tasks. The mark allocation (shown in brackets at the end of each question) is a good guide about the length of answer or amount of detail required. The higher the mark allocation, the more detail is required. The number of lines provided for your answer is another simple guide as to how long your answer needs to be. Remember that in an examination that is an alternative to coursework, answers may also involve doing tasks such as:

- plotting data onto maps and graphs
- doing calculations
- reading information from maps and graphs.

These tasks do not require any extended writing but the mark allocation can still be used as a guide as to how much time you should spend on answering the question.

> **Tip**
> Keep a check on time during your examinations and use all your time.

Understanding the question

Questions in examination will test different themes from the syllabus. One question may test a 'human' theme and the other question may test a 'physical' theme. There are three components of each question: the introduction, the hypotheses, and the individual parts of each question.

> **Tip**
> Follow the mark allocation.

The introduction

The focus of each question is explained in the introduction, which 'sets the scene'.

What is the focus of the following question?

Question 1

A group of students studied how a river changes downstream. They wanted to see if the river was typical of most rivers.
(Adapted from Cambridge IGCSE Geography 0460 Paper 4 Q2a June 2009)

The focus is a river investigation.

The hypothesis

Each question includes two hypotheses. These describe what is being tested in order to reach a conclusion that can be explained. The hypothesis is a statement that you may find evidence to support or to disagree with, or you may not make a definite decision.

> **Tip**
> Make a decision about the hypothesis where needed and state this decision.

Section 5.4: Preparing for your Geography examinations

The following hypotheses follow the introduction above.

The students decided to test the following hypotheses:

Hypothesis 1: Velocity increases downstream.

Hypothesis 2: The size and shape of the bedload changes downstream.

(Adapted from Cambridge IGCSE Geography 0460 Paper 4 Q2a June 2009)

The questions

One question is shown below.

The students selected six sampling sites along the course of the river. Suggest three factors the students should have considered in choosing the sample sites.

(Adapted from Cambridge IGCSE Geography 0460 Paper 4 Q2a June 2009)

Important words

Many students lose marks in an examination because they do not read carefully or understand important words in the question. Before you answer a question you should read it carefully. Use a pen to underline the important words or use a highlighter. The important words are:

- 'Command' words which tell you what to do in the question.
- 'Context' words which tell you what the question is about.

Command words are particularly important as they tell you how to answer the question. You need to know what each command word means and follow its instructions. If you do not know the meaning of the command word you will answer the question incorrectly.

The important words in the following questions are highlighted:

Define (command word) the term **'sampling'** (context words)?

Is the hypothesis: **'The number of visitors to the safari park varies during the year'** (context words) accurate? **Give evidence** (command words) from the Table and Fig. to support your view.

What are the important words in the following questions?

- To measure atmospheric pressure the students used a barometer. Describe how the students would do this investigation.
- Whilst doing the investigation one student suggested that tourism may increase the amount of litter in the area. Suggest a suitable hypothesis to test this idea and describe how the students could investigate your hypothesis.
- Describe two possible problems in measuring river velocity.

> **Tip**
> Read the command words carefully. Do not explain when the question says 'describe'.

> **Tip**
> Support your decision with evidence from resources where required.

5.4

- What is a pilot study and why is it important in an investigation?
  (Adapted from Cambridge IGCSE Geography 0460 Paper 41 Q1c (i) November 2010)

- What decisions would the students have to make on organising and carrying out the survey on the impact of tourism?
  (Adapted from Cambridge IGCSE Geography 0460 Paper 41 Q1c (ii) November 2010)

- Identify one similarity and one difference between the results for the two sites.
  (Adapted from Cambridge IGCSE Geography 0460 Paper 41 Q1d (ii) November 2010)

- State two human activities which could cause air pollution.
  (Adapted from Cambridge IGCSE Geography 0460 Paper 41 Q2a (i) November 2010)

- Use information from Figs 1 and 2 to explain why the level of acidity in rainfall varies with the wind direction.
  (Adapted from Cambridge IGCSE Geography 0460 Paper 41 Q2c (v) November 2010)

Examples of command words used in Geography examinations

Recall information, example or fact

Identify (name, select and recognise something from information you are given)

State (express in clear terms an answer using your own knowledge)

Give (produce an answer either from a given source or information or from your own knowledge)

Identify one similarity and one difference between the results at the two sites.

State two safety precautions that students should take when doing fieldwork in a river.

Give three characteristics which may indicate the position of the centre of the town.

Give a definition

Define (give the precise meaning of a word or phrase)

Define 'sphere of influence'.

Define 'sampling'.

Description

Describe (give the main points about the characteristics or features of a topic)

Describe two differences between the rainfall patterns at the school and the airport. [2 marks] (you need to use a graph from the examination paper)

> **Tip**
>
> Notice the different mark allocations, which mean that the descriptions will need different amounts of detail.

Section 5.4: Preparing for your Geography examinations 351

Describe one appropriate sampling method used to obtain a sample of people to be interviewed. [3 marks] (you must answer by using your own knowledge of what you have revised)

Describe how students could carry out an investigation into one other aspect of life in a squatter settlement. [4 marks] (you must answer by using your understanding of how to do a fieldwork investigation)

Explanation

Suggest (apply your knowledge and understanding to a situation in order to make proposals or give reasons)

Explain (give reasons or make the relationships between things evident and support it with relevant evidence)

Suggest two **reasons** why the students did the pedestrian count at five different times during the day. (only two reasons are required)

Suggest reasons why the velocity of the river varied between the two sections of river. (look at the mark allocation for a guide of the number of reasons required)

Suggest why a pilot study is important

Explain the process of longshore drift.

Explain what the students could learn from the investigation about the impact of longshore drift on the movement of pebbles?

Identify similarities and differences

Compare (identify or comment on similarities and / or differences)

Compare the buildings shown in the two photographs.

Compare the land use in the two areas shown on the map.

Make a judgment or reach a conclusion

What conclusion (decide if the hypothesis is true or false and be prepared to explain your conclusion)

Justify (support a conclusion with evidence or argument)

Using the data that they collected, **what conclusion** could the students make about the hypothesis?

Justify your conclusion with evidence from the rainfall graph and wind rose diagram.

Data

Estimate (use your judgement to give a value)

Calculate (work out from given facts, figures or information)

Support your answer/conclusion (use data or other information)

Estimate the average measurement from the top of the groyne to the beach.

Calculate the average rainfall per day at the airport.

Use data from Fig. 4 to **support your conclusion**.

Tip

Command words are often linked together, such as 'describe and explain'.

Tip

Your answer needs comparison or contrast in a sentence. Do not give two separate descriptions and then assume the comparison or contrast is made.

Tip

If you use a calculator to do a calculation, you may still need to show your working.

Other commands
Devise (create a questionnaire to gain information or opinions)
Plan (create a method to obtain or plan information)
Devise a questionnaire to investigate the benefits and problems of tourism for local residents.
Plan an investigation to measure how the velocity of a river changes downstream.

> **Tip**
> Be careful not to miss out these practical questions. There will not be any answer lines so answer on the resource indicated. This may be a map, graph, table or diagram.

Resources

Before you answer each question, check that you are looking at and using the correct resources from the examination paper and resource booklet. This is particularly important in the Alternative to Coursework paper as you are instructed to look at and use many different resources and you will waste time by looking at the wrong one.

Many different types of resources are used in a geography examination.

> **Tip**
> Maps, graphs and diagrams contain valuable information. Do not ignore them.

Examples of types of resources used in Alternative to Coursework examinations

Map	Large-scale map such as a town plan or map to show river fieldwork sites
	Isoline map to show pedestrian flow
	Land use map of an industrial area
Graph	Line graph to show river velocity at different sites
	Bar graph to show height of vegetation
	Wind rose
	Dispersion graph to show the results of an environmental quality survey
	Pie chart to show types of shops and services in a village
	Scatter graph to show the relationship between wind direction and rainfall
Photograph	Fieldwork equipment such as a flowmeter
	Feature such as a coastal groyne
	Aerial view of an industrial area
Table	Data such as results from a traffic survey
	Results of river measurements
	Information such as results of a questionnaire
Diagram	Fieldwork equipment such as a flowmeter
	Recording sheet of fieldwork measurements
	Field sketch such as sand dunes
Information	Questionnaire used in a tourist survey
	Factfile of information about a topic such as acid rain

Remember that resources may be included in an examination paper itself or in a separate resource booklet. In an examination you may be required to put information onto a resource or read and interpret information from the resource. This is shown in the following examples.

Example 1

The students recorded their results in a summary table. Use these results to complete the scatter graph and draw in a best-fit line.

The students accepted the hypothesis: Rainfall is more acidic after a period of dry weather. Do you agree with them? Support your answer with evidence from the completed scatter graph.

> **Tip**
>
> Use data accurately, both for plotting and interpreting.
>
> Include the correct units of measurement where required.

Example 2

Use the data from the results table to draw in the flow lines on the map to show the number of vehicles travelling along Station Road at 17.00.

Use the information on the two maps to describe the variation in traffic at the two survey times of 08.00 and 17.00 along Independence Way.

It is important that you take care when plotting data because marks will only be awarded for accurate answers. Look at the two answers (A and B) to each task below and decide which answer is correct.

Task 1: Use the results in the table below to complete Fig. 4, to show the average height of vegetation at points 8, 9, 10 and 11 across the transect at Site A.

sample point	1	2	3	4	5	6	7	8	9	10	11
average height of vegetation (cm)	14	11	7	4	2	0	3	4	5	12	17

Average height of vegetation at Site A

Fig. 4

(Adapted from Cambridge IGCSE Geography 0460 Paper 4 Q1a (iii) November 2009)

Answer A

Average height of vegetation at Site A

Fig. 4

Section 5.4: Preparing for your Geography examinations

Answer B

Average height of vegetation at Site A

Fig. 4

Task 2: On Fig. 3 shade in the land valued above 60 thousand US$/m^2.
(Adapted from Cambridge IGCSE Geography 0460 Paper 4 Q1f (ii) June 2007)

Key
— 60 — isoline of land value (thousand US$/m^2)
minor road

Fig. 3

356 Exam preparation

Answer A

Fig. 3

Key
— 60 — isoline of land value (thousand US$/m²)
▬ minor road

Answer B

Fig. 3

Key
— 60 — isoline of land value (thousand US$/m²)
▬ minor road

Section 5.4: Preparing for your Geography examinations

Make sure you are prepared for your examinations

To do well in this type of examination it is important to have experience of carrying out real fieldwork assignments. The best way to prepare is to do simple geographical investigations where appropriate during your geography course. The fieldwork can be carried out:

- Around the school site, for example conducting a questionnaire survey with other students to investigate the catchment area of the school.
- In the local area, for example measuring river velocity or drawing a simple land use transect through the town.

In your fieldwork investigation you should follow the 'route to geographical enquiry' which has five steps:

1. Create a hypothesis.
2. Collect relevant data.
3. Present the data in maps and graphs.
4. Analyse the data that you have collected.
5. Make a conclusion about the hypothesis and evaluate the investigation.

You might think that you cannot revise for the IGCSE Alternative to Coursework and O Level Geographical Investigations examinations. There are no case studies to learn and you don't know which themes the two questions will focus on. However, you can still revise very effectively for this type of examination by:

- looking through any fieldwork investigations you have done during the course
- practising the map and graph skills which are used in an examination paper
- understanding the principle of hypothesis testing
- learning details of fieldwork methodology such as sampling
- knowing how you could evaluate an investigation and suggest improvements.

> **Skills link**
>
> You can find out more about the route to geographical enquiry in Section 5.3 on pages 329–330.

> **Tip**
>
> Make realistic suggestions for improvement to an investigation.

Examples of two answers

You have now found out more about the IGCSE Alternative to Coursework and O Level Geographical Investigations examinations and how to improve your skills to be successful. Next you have the opportunity to look in detail at examination questions from a past paper. In this section you will find the questions and resources from one examination question. There are two example answers – one answer should achieve a high mark and the other answer should achieve a medium level mark. Each example answer is followed by a suggestion of how the answer may be marked and possibly improved.

Read the questions and look at the resources, then study the two example answers. Can you understand how the marks may be awarded and the answer might be improved?

Fig. 1 for Question 1

Section 5.4: Preparing for your Geography examinations

Key to shops and services

Number on map	Type of shop or service
1	Gift shop
2	Food takeaway
3	Gift shop
4	Tourist information
5	Sweet shop
6	Public house
7	Restaurant
8	Gift shop
9	Book shop
10	Café
11	Bank
12	Post office
13	Butcher
14	Food store
15	Baker
16	Sweet shop
17	Public house
18	Hairdresser
19	Food store
20	Flower shop

Number on map	Type of shop or service
21	Chemist
22	Restaurant
23	Gift shop
24	Café
25	Book shop
26	Gift shop
27	Book shop
28	Gift shop
29	Gift shop
30	Café
31	Public house
32	Museum shop
33	Restaurant
34	Food takeaway
35	Flower shop
36	Restaurant
37	Food store
38	Gift shop
39	Café
40	Art gallery

Fig. 3 for Question 1

Scoring sheet for the survey of the impacts of tourism

Site:

	-2	-1	0	1	2	
Lots of litter						No litter
Noisy						Quiet
Crowded						Few people
Many tourist signs and adverts						No tourist signs and adverts
Lots of tourist buildings						No tourist buildings

Table 2 for Question 1

Classification of shops and services

Customers

Used mainly by tourists	Number	Used mainly by local residents	Number	Used by both tourists & local residents	Number
Art gallery	1	Baker	1	Flower shop	2
Book shop	3	Bank	1	Food takeaway	2
Café	4	Butcher	1	Public house	3
Gift shop	8	Chemist	1	Sweet shop	2
Museum shop	1	Food store	3		
Restaurant		Hairdresser	1		
Tourist information	1	Post office	1		
Total	**22**	**Total**	**9**	**Total**	**9**

Table 3 for Question 1

Results of the survey of the impacts of tourism

	Site A	Site B	Site C	Site D
Litter	-1	-2	-1	0
Noise	-1	-2	-1	2
Crowding	-2	-2	0	2
Tourist signs and adverts	-1	-2	-1	2
Tourist buildings	-1	-2	0	1
Total score	**-6**	**-10**	**-3**	**7**

Table 1

Details of shops and services

Type of shop or service	Tally	Total	Percentage of total number of shops
Art gallery	/	1	2.5
Baker	/	1	2.5
Bank	/	1	2.5
Book shop	///	3	7.5
Butcher	/	1	2.5
Café	////	4	10.0
Chemist	/	1	2.5
Flower shop	//	2	5.0
Food store	///	3	7.5
Gift shop	⊬⊬ ///	8	
Hairdresser	/	1	2.5
Museum shop	/	1	2.5
Post office	/	1	2.5
Public house	///	3	7.5
Restaurant			10.0
Sweet shop	//	2	5.0
Food takeaway	//	2	5.0
Tourist information	/	1	2.5
Total		**40**	**100**

Students wanted to investigate the possible impacts of tourism on a village visited by many people. They wanted to find out if there were both positive and negative effects. To do this they decided to test the following hypotheses:

Hypothesis 1: Tourism has a major impact on the shops and services in the village.

Hypothesis 2: The impact of tourism decreases away from the main car park.

5.4

To investigate the importance of tourism, the students mapped different types of shops and services, as shown on Fig. 1, to see if they were mainly used by tourists or local people.

Question (a) (i)
How many hotels are shown on Fig. 1? [1 mark]

(Adapted from Cambridge IGCSE Geography 0460 Paper 41 Q1a(i) November 2010)

Answer 1
3 (✓)

Teacher's comment
The hotels are counted accurately.

Answer 2
3 (✓)

Teacher's comment
The hotels are counted accurately.

Question (a) (ii)
Look at Fig. 1 and complete the tally and total number of restaurants on Table 1. [1 mark]

(Adapted from Cambridge IGCSE Geography 0460 Paper 41 Q1a(ii) November 2010)

Answer 1
4 (✓)

Teacher's comment
Tally and total are completed accurately.

Answer 2
5

Teacher's comment
Tally and total are completed inaccurately, due to miscounting. You should always check tasks like this to make sure that you have not made a simple error.

Question (a) (iii)
Calculate and write in the missing percentage for gift shops on Table 1. [1 mark]

(Adapted from Cambridge IGCSE Geography 0460 Paper 41 Q1a(iii) November 2010)

Answer 1
20% (✓)

Teacher's comment
The answer correctly calculates 8/40 to be 20%.

Answer 2
No response

Teacher's comment

This answer does not address the question. This may be because the question does not have any answer lines and the answer had to be written in a table. Always read through the question paper again before the end of the examination to make sure you have not missed out any questions.

To test Hypothesis 1, the students classified the shops and services into three groups just by looking at them:

- used mainly by tourists;
- used mainly by local residents;
- used by both tourists and local residents.

The results of the decisions the students made about this classification are shown on Table 2.

Question (b) (i)
Why would the students have found it difficult to classify some shops and services? [2 marks]

(Adapted from Cambridge IGCSE Geography 0460 Paper 41 Q1b(i) November 2010)

Answer 1

> Because some shops might fall into two categories (✓) and it is difficult to decide which type a shop is. Also because just looking at them you do not know if it is certain that only one type of customer visits them (✓).

Teacher's comment

The answer makes two valid points: that some shops are difficult to classify because categories overlap, and the student who is doing the fieldwork cannot distinguish between residents and tourists just by looking at them.

Answer 2

> Because they don't really know exactly what services would tourists and local people use, they didn't know who were tourists and who were local people (✓).

Teacher's comment

The answer makes one valid point: that it is not possible to distinguish between residents and tourists just by looking at them.

Question (b) (ii)
How could the students be more certain that the customers of each shop were tourists or local residents? [2 marks]

(Adapted from Cambridge IGCSE Geography 0460 Paper 41 Q1b(ii) November 2010)

Answer 1

> By interviewing customers and asking where they came from (✓). Also by asking the shop owner if the customers were local people or tourists (✓).

Teacher's comment

Credit is given for the suggestions of interviewing customers and the shop owners.

Answer 2

> By asking them through a survey if they are tourists or local people (✓).

Teacher's comment

The answer is credited for the suggestion of interviewing customers. The answer needs a second idea such as asking the shop owner about the different types of customer. Remember that if there are 2 marks to be scored in a question you will need to suggest two ideas or develop one suggestion.

Question (b) (iii)

Use the results in Table 2 to complete the pie graph shown in Fig. 2. [2 marks]

(Adapted from Cambridge IGCSE Geography 0460 Paper 41 Q1b(iii) November 2010)

> **Skills link**
>
> You will find out more about how to complete a pie chart on page 255 of Section 4 Geographical Skills.

Answer 1

Teacher's comment

The line is plotted accurately at 31 and both segments are shaded.

Section 5.4: Preparing for your Geography examinations

Answer 2

Pie graph of classification of shops and services

Number of shops and services

Key:
- ■ Used mainly by tourists
- ╱ Used mainly by local residents
- ⊠ Used both by tourists and local residents

Teacher's comment
The line is inaccurately plotted at 32. Credit would be awarded for shading both segments correctly.

Question (b) (iv)
The students accepted **Hypothesis** 1 that tourism has a major impact on the shops and services in the village.

Do you agree with them? Support your answer with evidence from Table 1 and Fig. 2. [2 marks]

(Adapted from Cambridge IGCSE Geography 0460 Paper 41 Q1b(iv) November 2010)

Answer 1

The hypothesis was correct (✓) because 55% of the total number of shops was used mainly by tourists (✓). This shows that tourism has a major impact on shops and services.

Teacher's comment
A correct decision is made about the hypothesis (that it is correct) and there is appropriate supporting evidence (55% of shops used mainly by tourists).

Answer 2

I agree with them (✓) because the number of shops and services used mainly by tourists are much more than that used by local people (✓).

Teacher's comment
An appropriate decision is made (to agree with the hypothesis) and there is appropriate supporting evidence (number of tourist shops is greater than those used mainly by local people). The evidence does not have to include percentage figures.

Next the students tested Hypothesis 2: The impact of tourism decreases away from the main car park. They devised a scoring system to measure the impacts of tourism at four survey sites in the village. These survey sites are labelled **A** to **D** on Fig. 1. Fig. 3 shows the final scoring sheet after the students completed a pilot study.

Question (c) (i)
What is a pilot study and why is it important in an investigation? [2 marks]

(Adapted from Cambridge IGCSE Geography 0460 Paper 41 Q1c(i) November 2010)

Answer 1

> A pilot study is an investigation done before an actual test (✓) to see if the survey sites are good for the study. It is important in the investigation because it helps the people to be sure of the information they collect (✓).

Teacher's comment
This is a high level answer which shows good knowledge and understanding of the term 'pilot study'.

Answer 1

> A pilot study is a practice study (✓). It is where the students write the results of the survey before putting it on the final scoring sheet.

Teacher's comment
The answer understands the basic idea of a 'pilot study', but the second idea is irrelevant.

Question (c) (ii)
What decisions would the students have to make in organising and carrying out the main survey? [3 marks]

(Adapted from Cambridge IGCSE Geography 0460 Paper 41 Q1c(ii) November 2010)

Answer 1

> The students would need to decide where would be the survey sites (✓) and how many there would be (✓). Also they would have to decide what impacts they wanted to investigate (✓).

Teacher's comment
There are many possible answers to this type of question. This answer identifies three possible decisions: where to locate the survey sites and how many sites to choose. A third decision is what impacts to measure in the survey.

Answer 2

> What they will test in the survey (✓) and at what points in the village they will do the survey (✓).

Section 5.4: Preparing for your Geography examinations

Teacher's comment

This answer identifies two possible decisions. The first suggestion ('What they will test in the survey') is rather weak but would just be credited. The answer would have been better if 'characteristic', 'feature' or 'criteria' was used rather than just 'what'. The second idea of where to locate survey points is appropriate.

The results of the main survey of the impacts of tourism are shown on Table 3.

Question (d) (i)

Complete Fig. 4 by plotting the results for tourist buildings for sites B and D from information given in Table 3. [2 marks]

(Adapted from Cambridge IGCSE Geography 0460 Paper 41 Q1d(i) November 2010)

Results of the survey of the impacts of tourism

Fig. 4

368 Exam preparation

Answer 1

Results of the survey of the impacts of tourism

Site A, Site B, Site C, Site D bar charts showing scales from −2 to +2 with categories: lots of litter / no litter, noisy / quiet, crowded / few people, many tourist signs and adverts / no tourist signs and adverts, lots of tourist buildings / no tourist buildings.

Fig. 4

Teacher's comment

Both bars are plotted accurately and shading is done correctly.

Answer 2

Results of the survey of the impacts of tourism

Site A, Site B, Site C, Site D bar charts with the same categories and scale as above.

Skills link

You will find out more about how to draw a bar graph on page 252 of Section 4 Geographical Skills.

Section 5.4: Preparing for your Geography examinations

Teacher's comment

Site B is completely accurate, but no credit would be awarded for site D because the bar is not shaded.

Question (d) (ii)

Identify **one** similarity and **one** difference between the results for sites A and C. [2 marks]

(Adapted from Cambridge IGCSE Geography 0460 Paper 41 Q1d(ii) November 2010)

Answer 1

Similarity: Litter scored –1 at both sites A and C. (✓)

Difference: Crowding is –2 at site A and 0 at site C. (✓)

Teacher's comment

Both similarity and difference are interpreted from the graph accurately. Although the difference is not comparative, such as using a phrase like 'more crowded at site A', the answer would be credited because it includes figures taken from the graph.

Answer 2

Similarity: Both sites are noisy.

Difference: Site A is more crowded than site C. (✓)

Teacher's comment

The similarity is too vague to be credited. The answer needs to state that the score for noise is the same at both sites. The difference would be credited because the answer is comparative, even though measurements are not included.

Question (d) (iii)

To what extent do these results support **Hypothesis 2** that the impact of tourism decreases away from the main car park? [2 marks]

(Adapted from Cambridge IGCSE Geography 0460 Paper 41 Q1d(iii) November 2010)

Answer 1

The hypothesis is correct (✓) because the sites that are further away are the ones with less signs of the impact of tourism. However, site A (the one which is closer to the car park) presents less impacts than site B which is further away (✓).

Teacher's comment

A correct decision is made about the hypothesis (that it is correct). The answer also takes account of the question asking 'to what extent' by identifying an anomaly in the results (site A has less evidence of impact even though it is closer to the car park than site B).

Answer 2

I support the hypothesis (✓) because if you do a survey near the main car park you will get a lot of litter, noise, crowded by people, but far away from the car park less litter and noise will be found (✓).

Teacher's comment

A correct decision is made about the hypothesis. The answer also gives evidence to support the hypothesis (this is an alternative to identifying an anomaly).

Question (d) (iv)

Suggest reasons for the results of the survey of the impacts of tourism. Refer back to Fig. 1.   [4 marks]

(Adapted from Cambridge IGCSE Geography 0460 Paper 41 Q1d(iv) November 2010)

Tip

If a question asks for your opinion about a hypothesis you will gain credit for giving a correct opinion, such as 'I agree with the hypothesis' or 'The hypothesis is correct'.

Answer 1

Site B has most impacts because it is closer to the hotels (✓), the majority of the shops and the car park (✓). Site D has least impacts because it is located near a residential area (✓) and is far away from the car park. So the places where tourist attractions are clustered are the places with the most impacts of tourism.

Teacher's comment

The answer suggests three reasons for the varying impacts. These reasons relate to evidence from the map, as required. The answer could have been improved by identifying the shops as 'tourist shops' because the investigation is about tourism.

Answer 2

Site A is more crowded, some litter, a bit noisy and some buildings. Site B has a lot of litter, is very noisy, very crowded, has many signs and lots of buildings. Site D has some litter, very quiet, few people, no tourist signs and very few buildings. This is because sites A and B are nearer to the car park (✓).

Teacher's comment

The answer does not answer the question until the last sentence. The question asks for possible reasons for differing impacts of tourism at the survey sites, but the answer focuses on the varying levels of impact. This is an example of how it is possible to misinterpret a question. You should always think carefully, 'Am I answering the question that has been set?'

Question (e)

Suggest one other issue the students could have investigated in the village. Briefly describe how they could have done their investigation.   [4 marks]

(Cambridge IGCSE Geography 0460 Paper 41 Q1e November 2010)

Section 5.4: Preparing for your Geography examinations   371

Answer 1

They could have investigated how traffic varies between different sites (✓). They could have done this by counting how many cars, lorries, motor bikes etc. pass in a certain time (✓), for example five minutes (✓). They could count by filling in a tally chart (✓) and then putting all their results into a table to compare them (✓).

Teacher's comment

This is a high level answer. An investigation issue is clearly stated – how traffic amounts vary in the village. The answer gives details of methodology to be used in an investigation. Note that this question does not require a specific hypothesis to be identified.

Answer 1

They could have investigated the number of pedestrians in a certain amount of time at specific places. They could visit different sites and with a stopwatch record the time. As pedestrians pass by they make a line on the tally results (✓), and when the time is finished they count and get a total (✓).

Teacher's comment

The answer suggests a possible issue for investigation – variation in pedestrian flow – but it would be too vague to credit. A better issue would be to investigate if pedestrian flow varies between different places in the village, or if pedestrian flow varies at different times in the village. However, the methodology of a pedestrian survey is described in some detail.

Glossary

Accessibility the ease with which a place may be reached

Acid rain rainfall that damages the environment because it has been made acidic by pollution in the atmosphere

Adaptation the way in which plants and animals change to survive the environmental conditions where they live

Age dependency the link between the number of adult people who create wealth and the young and elderly population which depends on them for support

Age/sex pyramid a diagram which uses horizontal bar graphs to show the age-gender characteristics of a population

Agribusiness large companies involved in agriculture, often with many different farms

Algae simple, plant-like organisms

Alluvium the material deposited by a river

Altitude the height above sea level

Anemometer an instrument used to measure wind speed

Annual temperature range difference between the highest and lowest average monthly temperature

Anti-natalist policies strategies designed to limit a country's population growth

Aquifer a layer of porous rock which stores underground water

Arch rocky opening through a headland

Aspect the direction that land faces

Atmospheric pressure the pressure at a point on the Earth's surface due to the weight of the air above that place

Attrition when boulders and large stones carried by the river bash into each other and break up into smaller pieces

Avalanche a sudden downhill movement of snow that occurs as a result of a natural trigger, for example an earthquake, or human activity

Backwash the movement of water back down a beach towards the sea

Bar ridge of sand or shingle across the entrance to a bay or river estuary

Bar graph shows data that fits into categories

Barometer an instrument used to measure atmospheric (air) pressure

Bay indentation in coastline where wave action erodes softer rock

Beaufort scale measure, in 12 steps, of a guide to wind strength

Bed the bottom of a large expanse of water such as a river or the sea

Bedload the load found on the bottom of the river

Biodiversity the range of species within an ecosystem

Biofuel fuel made from plants

Biogas power from rotting plants and animal matter

Birth rate the average number of live births in a year (for every 1000 people)

Blue Revolution the increase in growing fish as a source of food

Bore hole a shaft in the ground containing a pipe to allow the extraction of water

Calories the unit used to measure the energy we get from food

Capital money used to invest in industry or business

Cash crop a crop grown to sell for profit

Catchment area/sphere of influence the area served by the shops and other facilities in an urban settlement

Cave area at the base of a cliff that has been hollowed out by wave action

Census a count of a country or region's population

Central Business District (CBD) the central and most accessible zone within a large settlement, which has many offices, large shops and public buildings

Choropleth map a map that uses colour shading to show a distribution pattern

Cliff steep rock outcrop

Climate average weather conditions over a period of at least 30 years

Climate change changes to global climate and weather patterns caused by the increase in greenhouse gases (global warming)

Collision margins where two pieces of continental crust move towards each other

Comparison goods items such as cars which are expensive and bought only very occasionally

Condensation the change of state of a gas (water vapour) to a liquid (water droplets) as a result of cooling

Confluence the point where two rivers join

Congestion charges a charge imposed on vehicles entering a central urban zone to reduce its traffic congestion and level of air pollution

Conservation the protection of the Earth and its natural resources

Conservative margins an area where two plates slide past each other

Constructive margins where two plates move away from each other

Constructive waves low-frequency waves of low height, with a strong swash but weak backwash; the waves therefore build up material on a beach

Contamination when pollutants are added to the natural environment

Contour line a line on a map joining points of equal height above sea level

Conurbation a very large built-up area formed by urban sprawl

Convectional rainfall precipitation formed by rising currents of warm, moist air

Converging plate boundary an area where tectonic plates move towards each other

Coral bleaching the whitening of coral due to expulsion or death of their symbiotic algae, usually as a result of changing environmental conditions

Coral reef underwater structures made from calcium carbonate secreted by polyps

Core the extremely hot centre of the Earth

Corrasion/abrasion when sand and stones carried by the river rub against the bank and bed and knock off other particles

Corrosion/solution when acids in the river dissolve the rocks that make up the bank and bed

Counter-urbanisation the movement of people from cities to the countryside

Crater a bowl-shaped depression with steep sides formed by a volcanic eruption

Cross-section a drawing to show changes in relief between two points on a map

Crust the top layer of the Earth; it can be either continental (with land on top) or oceanic

Currency money used in a specific country

Death rate the average number of deaths in a year (for every 1000 people)

Deforestation the removal of tree cover in an area for farming or other activities

Delta the area where silt is deposited as a river enters the sea (or a lake)

Densely populated describes an area where a lot of people live (often a number of people per 1 km²)

Deposition the laying down of material that has been transported (by water, ice, sea, rivers, wind)

Desertification the process in which semi-arid environments change to become more desert-like

Desire line map a map which uses straight lines to show movements between places

Destructive margins where an oceanic plate slides under a continental plate

Destructive waves high-frequency, steep waves which have little swash and so move little material up a beach; however, they have strong backwash and so drag material down the beach into the sea

Dipterocarp a family of 500 species of tropical lowland rainforest plants, most of which are tall tree species that are important for essential oils, balsam, resins and as a source of plywood

Dispersed describes the way that isolated farms or houses are scattered over an area, far apart from each other

Distributaries separate water channels created by sediment blocking rivers at a delta

Diurnal temperature range the difference between the highest and the lowest temperature in a 24-hour period

Dormancy non-growing period for plants and seeds

Eastings grid lines running vertically over a large-scale map

Economic activity the ways in which people make money for themselves and for their country

Economic migrants people who migrate to find work

Ecosystem a community of plants and animals that live within a physical area

Ecotourist a tourist who particularly wants to experience the natural environment

Emigrants people leaving a country

Energy security when a country has enough sources of power to cover most, if not all, of its energy needs

Epicentre point on the Earth's surface directly above where an earthquake occurs

Erosion the wearing away of the land by an agent of erosion

Estuary the tidal mouth of a river

Evaporation the change of state from water droplets (liquid) to water vapour (gas) caused by heating

Evapotranspiration loss of water into the atmosphere from plants (transpiration) and water surfaces (evaporation)

Exclusion zone an area where people are not allowed to go

Exploit to use, usually to try to make money

Exports the goods that a country sells overseas

Factor anything which influences where a place is, what it is like or what function(s) it fulfils

Fault a fracture in rock caused by earth movements

Fertility rate the average number of children people in a country or region have in their lifetime

Fetch the distance across open sea or ocean over which the wind blows to create waves; the longer the fetch, the greater the possibility of large waves

Flash floods dangerous flow of surface water following unusually heavy rainfall

Flood plain the area to the sides of a river channel which floods when the river overflows its banks

Flow diagram generally shows movement plotted on a base map

Flow line map a map which uses straight lines whose thickness is proportional to the volume of traffic along routes between places

Focus the point within the Earth's crust where an earthquake originates

Fold mountains the types of mountains that are formed by the squeezing of rock at converging plate boundaries

Footloose an industry that is not tied to specific location factors

Forced migration when people are made to leave a country, for example because of war or natural disaster

Formal sector regular employment providing people with taxable earnings

Fossil fuels energy resources such as oil, gas and coal

Fuelwood wood (twigs, branches etc.) used as an energy source for cooking and heating

Function the way that a place provides employment and services for the people who live in or visit it

Geographic Information System (GIS) a computer system which can store and analyse 'layers' of different types of spatial information

Geothermal power power from magma, hot rocks and hot water within the Earth

Global Positioning System (GPS) a high-tech mapping system that uses satellites to locate places on the Earth's surface with great accuracy

Gradient how steep a slope is

Green belt a rural area in which new residential and industrial developments are strictly limited; green belts control urban sprawl and maintain the historical character of villages

Greenhouse gases gases in the atmosphere that act like a blanket and reflect heat

Grey water water which has already been used but not been 'treated' (cleaned)

Grid lines numbered parallel lines drawn over a map to make it possible to locate features and places accurately

Grid references a system for locating places and features accurately using numbered grid lines

Grid square the space bounded by two adjacent northings and eastings

Gross domestic product (GDP) the total annual value of the goods manufactured and services provided by a country

Gross national product (GNP) measures a country's total ecomonic activity, taking GDP plus income earned by domestic residents from foreign investments, minus income earned by foreign investors in the country's domestic market

Groundwater underground water supplies

Groyne barrier of wood or stone built down a beach to stop beach materials from being washed away

Gullies channels in the soil caused by water erosion

Habitat the 'home' of a plant or animal

Halophyte plant that has adapted to live in salty conditions

Headland point along a coast where harder rock juts out into the sea

Histogram graph showing data that is continuous in some way

HIV/AIDS viral infection (Human Immunodeficiency Virus) which leads to AIDS

Human Development Index (HDI) a system of ranking countries based on their GDP (gross domestic product) per capita and rates of adult literacy and life expectancy

Humus soil material rich in nutrients due to the decomposition of animal and vegetable material

Hydraulic action when the force of the water knocks particles off the sides (banks) and the bed of the river

Hygrometer an instrument used to measure relative humidity

Illegal immigrants people entering a new country without the permission of the authorities

Immigrants people arriving in a new country

Impervious does not let water through

Imports the goods that a country buys from overseas

Indicators of development show a country's progress economically as well as in other social aspects

Industrial location where a factory or business is found

Infant mortality rate the proportion of children dying at birth or before their first birthday

Infiltration the downward movement of water into the soil

Informal sector employment which has no set hours or employment benefits; its low, irregular earnings are not taxed

Glossary

Infrastructure the network of services needed for industry and services to run efficiently – transport, communications, energy supplies, water and sanitation systems

Insolation solar energy which reaches the Earth's surface

In situ in the same place

Irrigation artificially diverting water to fields to grow crops

Isoline any line on a map which joins places having the same value

Labour workers

Lagoon area of salt water separated from the sea by a bar or reef

Lahar highly dangerous, fast-flowing mixture of rainwater and ejected volcanic materials

Land use zones urban areas which have different functions and characteristics to other nearby areas

Landslide a sudden downward movement of a section of hillside or cliff face

Leaching the removal of nutrients and other minerals from the soil as rainwater washes the minerals downwards through the soil

Leaf litter dead plant material that falls to the ground, releasing nutrients as it decomposes

Least developed countries (LDCs) the poorest countries in the world

Less economically developed country (LEDC) one of the poorer countries in the world

Levee naturally formed ridges on the edges of a river channel

Levels of consumption the amount of energy used

Linear describes long, narrow-shaped settlements, often built along a road

Line graph shows data that changes continuously over time

Load all the material carried by a river

Long profile the appearance of a river from beginning to end

Longshore drift the transportation of material along a coastline

Low pressure the result of air rising; the weight of the air pressing down on the Earth's surface is reduced and so is lower than average

Magma liquid rock found beneath the Earth's crust

Magnitude the strength of an earthquake

Malnutrition the condition that results when the body does not get enough vitamins, minerals or other nutrients

Mangrove swamp a muddy swamp found on tropical coasts and estuaries where mangrove trees have adapted to live in salt water

Mantle the part of the Earth between the core and the crust

Marram grass species of grass able to survive on the dry habitat of shifting sand

Maximum-minimum thermometer an instrument used to measure both the highest and lowest temperatures within a 24-hour period

Meander winding bends found along a river's course

Megacity a city with more than 10 million inhabitants

Meteorologist a person who is able to forecast (predict) future weather by referring to previous, similar atmospheric conditions

Migration the movement of people from one place to another

Monoculture growing only one type of crop, usually in large amounts

Monsoon season of very heavy rainfall resulting from the seasonal shift of pressure belts

More economically developed country (MEDC) one of the wealthier, more industrialised countries in the world

Mouth where a river enters the sea

Multiplier effect the additional economic effects experienced when money is spread throughout a community

New town a planned, self-contained settlement usually built to re-house people from a large urban area

Newly industrialised countries (NICs) countries that are developing their economies through rapid expansion of secondary industries

Nomadic a lifestyle that involves moving around with no permanent home

Non-renewable energy which is used once and cannot be used again

Northings grid lines running horizontally over a large-scale map

Nucleated describes a 'compact' settlement, about the same width in most directions, built around a central point such as a road junction or river crossing

Okta the unit used to measure and record cloud cover; describes the proportion of the sky which is covered by cloud

Optimum population the number of people needed to make the best possible economic use of a country's natural resources

Over-population when a country does not have the resources to give all its people an adequate standard of living

Oxbow lake a curved lake found on the flood plain of a river where a meander has been cut off

Pandemic an outbreak of an infectious disease on such a large scale that it results in millions of deaths across large parts of the world

Permaculture people growing their own food in local garden areas

Photosynthesis the process where plants convert carbon dioxide into oxygen

Pie chart (pie graph) a circular diagram with sectors which show the different size of parts of a data set

Plate boundaries (margins) the edges of tectonic plates

Pollutants substances that have harmful or hazardous effects

Pollution what happens when the environment is harmed; its four types are air, noise, visual and water pollution

Population density the number of people living in a 1 km² area

Population distribution the way in which a population is spread out over an area

Population explosion the dramatic rise in world population which took place during the last two centuries

Population replacement level the number of children per couple required to maintain a stable population

Population structure the way a population is composed of different age-gender groups

Pothole a small hollow in the rock bed of a river

Poverty line the minimum income needed to provide an adequate standard of living

Primary industry industries that take something from the ground or sea

Pro-natalist policies strategies designed to stimulate a country's population growth by increasing its fertility rate

Pyroclastic flow flow of materials such as ash ejected during a volcanic eruption

Quaternary industry high-technology or research-based industries

Radial graph (also called a rose diagram) a circular diagram which uses different sized sectors to show how often a particular type of data occurs

Rain gauge an instrument used to measure the amount of rain that falls

Rainshadow the sheltered side of a range of mountains which receives little rain, also known as the leeward side; air is descending and warming, therefore moisture evaporates and rainfall is unlikely

Rapid transit systems a transport network, such as an underground railway, designed to carry large numbers of people within an urban area

Rapids areas of turbulent water found along a river

Raw materials the things that are used to make something else

Reactor the machine that produces electricity in a nuclear power station

Recycle to turn waste into something that can be used again

Redevelopment raising housing standards by demolishing and then replacing existing accommodation

Refugees people who are forced to move, often by war or natural disaster

Relative humidity the ratio between the actual amount of water vapour in the air and the total amount of water the air could hold if it was saturated at a particular temperature

Remote sensing the technology of using satellites to obtain images of the Earth's surface

Renewable energy sources of power that can be used over and over again

Renovation raising housing standards by improving peoples' accommodation, not demolishing and replacing it

Revenue the money earned (by a country, for example)

Richter Scale the scale used to measure the magnitude (or intensity) of an earthquake

Salinity the amount of salt that something (for example soil) contains

Salt marsh wet, low-lying area near to the coast that is regularly flooded by the sea

Sand dune ridge of sand created by the wind; found in deserts, near lakes and the sea

Satellite image an image captured by remote sensing, using satellites able to detect electromagnetic radiation from the Earth's surface

Scale the relationship between the actual size of an area on the ground, and the representation of the same area on a map

Scatter graph a diagram used to show the strength of a relationship between two sets of data

Sea-floor spreading the bottom of the ocean growing wider at a constructive margin

Secondary industry industries that make products from raw materials

Sedentary settled and permanent

Sediment any material, regardless of size, which has been transported by an agent of erosion

Seismograph (seismometer) a machine used to measure the strength of an earthquake

Self-help scheme a way of raising housing conditions for squatters by providing them with some land and the basic materials needed to build and improve their own homes

Settlement any place, ranging in size from a hamlet to a mega-city, where people live and work

Settlement hierarchy arranging settlements according to their population size

Shield volcano a low gently-sloping volcano formed from thin, runny lava and frequent gentle eruptions

Shifting cultivation a type of rainforest agriculture which involves moving on from one plot of cultivated land to another

Site a small area of land on which the first part of a settlement was built

Site and service scheme a way of raising housing conditions for squatters by providing them with basic accommodation and facilities such as water supply and sewage disposal

Situation the location of a settlement in relation to the wider area around it

Slumping weathered material moves down-slope due to lubrication by rainwater

Smog air pollution due to a combination of smoke and fog

Soil degradation the process of soil becoming less fertile

Soil exhaustion when soils can no longer support plants and crops

Solar power power from the sun

Source the start of a river

Sparsely populated describes an area (usually 1 km²) where few people live

Spit ridge of sand or shingle attached to the land at only one end

Spot height a point on a map measured to its exact height (in metres or feet) above sea level; spot heights are marked with a small dot on a map at the exact location, with the height alongside

Squatter settlement/shanty town an area of poorly built, low-cost housing on land not owned or rented by its inhabitants

Stack pillar of rock surrounded by sea and separated from the mainland

Stevenson screen a wooden box on legs used to house weather recording equipment

Storm surge a significant increase in sea level due to sudden, very low air pressure

Strato-volcano also known as a composite volcano, made up of alternate ash and lava layers and often has very violent eruptions

Stump the remains of a stack that has been eroded almost to sea level

Subduction zone where oceanic crust is forced under continental crust

Subsidies payments given to farmers, usually by governments

Subsistence crop a crop grown to feed a farmer and his family

Sunshine recorder records the hours of sunshine by using a glass sphere that focuses the Sun's rays to burn a track on a paper strip

Surface runoff the movement of water over the ground surface following precipitation – also known as overland flow

Sustainable something that can be used on a long-term basis with very little effect on the environment

Swash the body of water rushing up a beach after a wave has broken

Tectonic plates the Earth's crust, divided into large pieces called plates

Temperate a region characterised by mild temperatures

Tertiary industry industries that provide a service

Textile industry industries concerned with making clothes and fabric

Thematic map a map which displays information on a particular theme

Threshold population the minimum number of people needed to support a facility or service

Tombolo ridge of sand linking an offshore island to the mainland

Topographical map a map that shows accurate, large-scale representation of relief, usually by using contour lines, and other features in the landscape

Tornado narrow column of air that rotates rapidly around an area of very low air pressure, causing widespread devastation in its path

Tourism the industry associated with people going on holiday; can be either national or international

Toxic poisonous

Traffic congestion occurs when roads cannot cope with their volume of traffic

Transect a section which shows how features change across an area

Transnational corporation a very large business operating in many countries

Transpiration loss of water from vegetation into the atmosphere

Transportation the removal of weathered material

Triangular graph a type of diagram which allows three sets of data to be plotted against each other

Tributary a small river that joins a larger one

Tropical depression area of low atmospheric pressure that forms in tropical regions

Tropical revolving storm intense spinning storm with high winds and torrential rain around a calm centre (the eye); at a certain point of intensity it becomes a cyclone or hurricane

Tsunami huge sea wave created as a result of a major earthquake or volcanic eruption

Under-populated describes an area where the population is well below that which can be supported by its natural resources

Uninhabited describes an area where very few, if any, people live

Urban sprawl the outward growth of a built-up area into nearby rural areas

Urbanisation an increase in the percentage of people living in urban areas

Velocity the speed at which the river flows

Vent the part of a volcano where magama, steam, ash and dust emerge from under the ground

Water deficit a situation where available water supplies do not meet all the needs of local people

Waterfall a cascade of water where the level of a river or stream changes due to softer rock downstream being eroded more rapidly than the resistant rock at the cascade

Watershed the boundary, often a ridge of high ground, between two drainage basins

Water table the upper edge of the saturated zone in porous rocks

Water transfer the movement of water from an area of surplus to one having a shortage

Water vapour water held in the atmosphere in the form of a gas

Wave-cut notch indentation along the base of a cliff where wave action is strongest

Wave-cut platform gently sloping surface of rock that is the result of cliff retreat and is exposed at low tide

Weather short-term, changeable, atmospheric conditions which include air temperature, cloud cover, precipitation and wind direction and speed

Well a structure, which is dug or drilled to access groundwater that is brought to the surface using a pump or a container

Where-to-be-born Index (formerly Quality of Life Index) an indicator of how people assess their lifestyle based on criteria which include GDP per capita and life expectancy

Wilderness an uncultivated, uninhabited and inhospitable region

Wildfire forest fire that rages out of control

Wind rose graph a diagram showing the proportion of winds that blow from each compass direction at a given place

Wind vane an instrument used to indicate the direction of the wind

Index

6th of October City, Cairo 69

'ABC' slogan 14
abortion, sex-specific 17
abrasion 83, 85, 93, 95
accessibility 39
acid rain 192, 221
acquired immune deficiency syndrome (AIDS) 12, 13–15
add value 141
Adivasi tribe 43
adoption 16, 17
adventure tourism 182, 218
aerial photography 264–5
Africa
    and AIDS/HIV 14–15
    and desertification 38
    and drought 248–9
    and food shortages 165–6, 248–9
    North 36–7
    and population growth 9, 11
    and tourism 187–8
    see also specific countries
age dependency 17, 30
age/sex pyramids 27, 29–30, 254, 262
Agenda for Sustainable Development 2030 140
agribusinesses 156, 158, 168–70
agricultural labour 9, 168
agricultural land 161, 162, 164, 168
agriculture
    and anti-natalist policies 16
    Brazilian 146–7
    Canadian 12
    commercial 213–14
    and deforestation 120, 146, 147
    and environmental damage 4, 158–9, 216, 220–2, 226
    and life expectancy 4–5
    and pollution 4, 216
    and river flood plains 90
    and water use 205, 206, 208, 210
    see also farming
agrochemicals 156
aid 134, 165–6
AIDS (acquired immune deficiency syndrome) 12, 13–15
air pollution 57, 220–1
    and coal power stations 59
    and global warming 222–3
    and quarrying 60
    reduction measures 71
    and squatter settlements 67
    and traffic congestion 64
air pressure *see* atmospheric pressure
air temperature 111, 116–17, 119, 155
air travel 182
algae 101
alluvial 128

alluvium 87, 135
altitude 111, 256
    and air temperature 116
    and climate 116
    and clouds 113
    and maps 237
Amazon rainforest 146–7, 225, 287
Amazon River 83
Amu Darya river 215, 216
anaemia 165
analytic skills 247–8, 330, 334, 339–40, 344–6
andesite 80
anemometers 109, 111
Angel Falls, Venezuela 85
animal life 43
    extinction 223, 232
    hot desert 127
    rainforest 120
annotation 238
annual temperature 115, 119
annual temperature range 115
annuals 124–5
Antarctica 32, 217–18
anti-natalist population policies 16–18
anti-social behaviour 68
aquifers 208, 210
Arabat Tongue, Sea of Azov 97
Aral Sea disaster 215–17
arches 95
Arctic 217–18
arid environments 121, 122, 127
ash 75, 79, 80
aspect 155
Aswan High Dam 211
Atacama Desert, Chile 121
atmospheric pressure (air pressure) 256
    and climate 116
    and deserts 122
    high 122
    low 116, 132
    measurement 111
attrition 83, 93
Australia
    and age/sex pyramids 29
    and coastal areas 103–5
    and coastal erosion 95–6
    and the Great Barrier Reef Marine Park 229–32
avalanches 129

baby booms 16
backwash 93, 277
Bangladesh 133–5, 161–2, 176–7
bar graphs 110, 247–8, 251–2, 260, 292
    divided 144
barometers 109, 111

barriadas 66
bars 97
bays 94, 97
beaches 93, 95, 96–7
    beach material analysis 277
    beach profiles 277
    as hazards 330
    and longshore drift 277–8
    width 94
bearings 236
Beaufort Scale 111–12
bedload 84, 85, 86
beef 146, 147
benefit systems 16
bidonvilles 66
bilharzia 57
biodiversity 117
biofuels 146, 168, 197
biogas 197
biomass 58
Biopolis, Singapore 179
birth control 5
birth rates 5, 6, 19, 29
Black Death 13
Blue Revolution 166
Bolivia 168–70
bore holes 208
Borneo 119–21, 225–6, 287–8
Botswana 14, 15
Brandt report 139
Brazil 69, 71–2, 139, 146–7
BRIC (Brazil, Russia, India, China) 139
buildings 68, 156
Burgess urban land use model 53
Burkina Faso 29
buses 65, 72
bustees 66

calories 163
Cambridge, UK 318–20
Canada 11–12
capital cities 50–1
capital (money) 156, 174, 179
car ownership 64
car-sharing 65
carbon dioxide emissions 58, 192, 225
carbon-neutral 58
careers, women's 5
Carte Familles Nombreuses ('Large Family Card') 19
Carteret Islands 224
cartoons 267
case studies vi, 1
    Aral Sea 215–17
    Bangladesh 161–2, 176–7
    Bolivia 168–70
    Borneo 119–21, 225–6
    Carteret Islands 224
    command words 291

examinations 286–90, 291
focus 286–7
Great Barrier Reef 103–4
Great Barrier Reef Marine Park 229–32
India 210
Isle of Wight 48–9
Liberia 9
location 286–7
marking 288–9
Mekong delta, Vietnam 87–8
Mississippi river, USA 89–91
Mumbai 67
Namib Desert 126–8
the Sahel 36–8
Sarawak, Malaysia 158–60
Senegal-Europe migration 25–6
topics 286–7
cash crops 36–7, 43, 158, 169
catchment areas (spheres of influence) 47, 48
cattle 37, 43, 147, 164
caves 95
census 27
Central Business District (CBD) 53, 54–5, 64, 316
CFCs *see* chlorofluorocarbons
Chembakolli, India 43–4
Chernobyl, Ukraine 200–1
child labour 4, 66
childcare, state-funded 19
children
  causes of death 6–7
  economic value of 4, 6
China
  and the '4-2-1' problem 17
  and Brazil 146–7
  and coal 192–3
  and dam building 88
  and energy use 191–3
  and environmental damage 221
  and Nike 151–2
  and the 'one-child policy' 16–18, 151
  and rural–urban migration 23
  and tourism 182–3
  and the 'two-child policy' 17
chlorofluorocarbons (CFCs) 223
choropleth maps 260
cholera 57, 134
cities 50
  capital 50–1
  centres 22
  changing urban land use 52, 53–4
  green 57–8, 71–2
  inner city areas 53
  megacities 45
  and population density 34
  problems caused by the growth of 64–6
  settlement hierarchies 45–6
  site 50
  situation 50, 51

smallest 45
sustainable 70–2
urban zones 54–6
citizens, global v
civil war 9, 164
cliffs 94–5, 240
climate 34, 106–7, 115–35
  equatorial 115–21
  and farming 155, 161, 164, 168
  and food shortages 164
  of hot deserts 121–8
  and industrial location 176
  and natural vegetation 117–19, 124–5, 127
  of the Sahel 36–7
climate change 10, 129
  and coral reefs 103–4
  and desertification 38
  effects of 223–4
  and fossil fuels 192, 195
  and global warming 221, 222–4
  and the Great Barrier Reef Marine Park 230–1
  human factors 37
  and the Mekong delta 88
  natural factors 37
climate graphs 107, 261, 292
climatic events 129
clinometers 277
clothing 10
clouds 112, 113–14, 326–7
  absence 122, 123
  condensation 113
  cumulus 113
  stratus 113
coal 189, 191–3, 198–9, 222
coastal deposition 93, 96–100
coastal erosion 93, 94–6, 278
coastal fog 127
coasts 34, 92–105
  changing coastlines 92–4
  coastal measurements 276–8
  coastal processes 92–4
  and coral reefs 101–5
  and mangrove swamps 101–3
  mapping 311–17
  and settlement sites 40
Colorado river, USA 203
command words 290–1, 303, 308–9
communities 48
  remote 29
commuting 21, 55, 58, 64–5
comparison goods 55
compasses 235, 236, 241
compound graphs 260
concave 239
condensation 113
conflict 223
  and food production 165–6, 168
  and population 7
  and water supplies 211
  see also war
confluence 40, 85, 241

congestion charges 65
conservation management 232–4
construction 68
consumers 227
contamination 220
contour lines 237–8, 240–1, 256
contraception 14, 16
conurbations 50, 51
convection 115, 116
convection currents 74
convex 239
cooling systems 91
  green 58
Copenhagen, Denmark 57–8
coral bleaching 103–4
coral reefs 101–5, 223, 229–31
  atoll 101–2
  barrier 101–2
  fringing 101–2
corrasion 83
corrosion 83
cost of living 5
cotton 176–7, 216
counter-urbanisation 22–3, 59
coursework assignments 328–47
  analysis and interpretation 330, 334, 339–40, 344–6
  conclusion and evaluation 334–5, 340–1, 346–7
  definition 328–9
  examples 335–47
  fieldwork 329–47
  'knowledge with understanding' 333, 335–6, 342
  marking schemes 332
  observation and collection of data 333, 336–7, 343
  organisation and presentation of data 333–4, 337–9, 343–4
  preparation for 335
  river study example 335–41
  'route to geographical enquiry' 329–30
  skills 333–5
  tourism study example 342–7
crime 68
Croatia 45
crop yields 4–5, 170
crops
  cash 36–7, 43, 158, 169
  damage to 60
  dry-land 36
  genetically modified (GM) 167
  Green Revolution 166
  subsistence 43
cross-sections 238–9, 260, 274–5, 313–14
  annotation 238
  interpretation 238–9
crown-of-thorns starfish 104, 105
crust 73, 74
  continental 74, 76, 80
  oceanic 74, 76, 80

culture, and tourism 182, 183–4
cumulus clouds 113
Curitiba, Brazil 71–2
currency 183
currents 97, 123
customers 3
cycle lanes 58
cycling 65
cyclones 230
    Cyclone Aila 134–5

dams 88, 91, 167, 197, 202–3, 208–11, 217
data
    capture 279, 281
    collection 329, 331, 333, 336–8, 343
    graphing 251–5
    interpretation 144
    mapping 256–7
    observation 333, 336–7, 343
    organisation 333–4, 337–9, 343–4
    presentation 144, 333–4, 337–9, 343–4
    primary 329
    recording 330, 331
    secondary 329
data tables 310
death rates 5, 6, 13, 29
deforestation 10, 43, 120, 224–6
    and agriculture 120, 146, 147
    examination questions on 287–8
    and fuelwood 193, 194–5
    and global warming 222, 225
    and immigrants 194–5
deformation monitoring 81
deltas 87–8
demand 156, 176, 207–9
demographic crises 17
Demographic Transition Model 30
densely populated 8, 32, 34–5, 213
dependency, age 17, 30
dependent variables 253
deposition
    coastal 93, 96–100
    rivers and 83–7
deprivation 66
desalination plants 208
desert tourism 214
desertification 38, 193, 217
deserts (cold) 121, 217–19
deserts (hot)
    climate 121–8
    life in 126–8
    seasons 122–3
    vegetation 124–5, 127
development 136–70
    changing stages of 29–31
    and employment in less economically developed countries 143–5
    environmental risks 213–34

examination questions 283, 285–6
and food production 153–70
and globalisation 147–52
goals 140
indicators of 138
and industry classification 141–2
and inequalities 139–40
measurement 138–9
and Newly Industrialised Countries 139, 145–7
and quality of life 136–7
Dharavi, India 67
diamond mining 127, 128
diarrhoea 44, 210
dipterocarp forests 120
disease 165
    see also infectious diseases
displaced persons 70
distributaries 87, 91
diurnal temperature range 115, 116–17, 122, 124
Docklands, London 62
domestic waste 58
dormancy 124–5
drainage 240–2
drainage basin processes 82–3
Drakensberg Mountains 127
drought 10, 88, 121, 164, 248–9
dry points 40
Dual Citizen Inc. 58
Dubai 281

Earth, structure of the 73–4
earthquakes 7, 10, 73–81, 93, 129, 130
    epicentre 78
    examination questions 307–8
    focus 78, 307–8
    intensity 77
    Japan 2011 77–9
East End, London 61–3
eastings 236
economic crises 25
economic development see development
economic factors 3, 4
economic growth 146
economic inputs 156, 158, 160
economic opportunities
    and population growth 3
    and rivers 89–91
    and volcanoes 79–80
ecosystems 92, 117–18, 127, 225
ecotourism 182, 218
Edinburgh, Scotland 22–3
education 12, 45, 47–9, 66, 68
Egypt 69–70, 211
Eiffel Tower, Paris, France 57, 185
elder care 4, 17
elderly people 27, 29
electricity generation 198–202, 208, 305–6

emigration 23, 26, 295–6
employment 3, 143
    and career choice 171–3
    figures 144
    formal sector 66
    and industrial development 143–5
    informal sector 67, 143
    pressures of 30
    and under-population 136
    see also underemployment; unemployment
endangered species 225
energy 12, 189–204
    electricity generation 198–9
    exports 192
    and fossil fuels 189–93
    and the fuelwood crisis 193–5
    geothermal 196, 198
    global consumption 190–1
    hydroelectric 197, 199, 202
    imports 192
    and industrial location 174, 175–6
    levels of consumption 189, 190–1
    non-renewable 190
    nuclear power 198, 200–2
    renewable 190, 195–8, 202–4, 305–6
    and rivers 83
    solar 167, 189, 197
    sources 189–91
    tidal 196–7, 199
    water power 196–7, 199, 202–4, 208
    wind 196, 199, 306
energy conservation 58
energy production maps 247, 250
energy security 192, 195
enhanced greenhouse effect 222–3
entrepreneurs 175, 177, 188
environment
    exploitation 215–19
    extreme 33
    good places to live 213–14
    harsh 214
    human impact on 103–4, 127–8, 152, 278
    impact of pollution on 57–8
    and industrial location 175
    tropical rainforest 119–21
    see also natural environment
environmental conservation 227–34
environmental damage 57–8, 152, 215–17, 220–2, 278
    and deforestation 287–8
    and habitat destruction 127, 128, 158–9, 225
    and tourism 103–4, 221, 229, 231, 233
environmental hazard maps 247
environmental monitoring 81
environmental protection 127, 152
environmental quality surveys 273–4

384 Index

environmental risks 213–34
epicentres 78
Equatorial climate 115–21
erosion 83
    coastal 93, 94–6, 278
    lateral 85
    and rivers 83–5
    vertical 85
    see also soil erosion
escarpments 240
estuaries 87, 97
Europe, migration to 25–6
evaporation 82, 110
evapotranspiration 124
examinations 283–347
    case studies 286–90, 291
    command words 290–1, 303, 308–9
    coursework assignments 328–47
    example answers 293–300, 310–27
    Geographical Investigations examination 328
    Geographical Skills examination 301–27
    Geographical Themes examination 283–300
    illustrations 320–4
    marking schemes 293
    past papers 285–6, 292, 303–8, 310–27, 335–47
    question choices 284
    question understanding 284, 302
    resources 291–2, 309–10
    skills 301, 303
    themes 283, 284, 293
    time management skills 283–4, 301–2
exclusion zones 80
exploitation 215–19
exports 141, 143, 149, 192
extinction 223, 232
extreme environments 33
eye of the storm 132

factories 143, 151–2
    and environmental damage 220, 221
    and industrial location 174
    jobs in 172
    textile 177
Falls of St Anthony 89, 90
family planning advice 16
family size 2–3, 6
    restrictions 16
famine 6, 24, 36–7, 248–9
farmers
    and conflict 60
    and decision-making 154–5
    nomadic 37, 128, 154
farming 43, 153–5
    arable 153
    and climate 155, 161, 164, 168
    and climate change 223, 224
    commercial 153, 157–60
    and deforestation 120
    extensive 153, 154, 157
    inputs 154–61
    intensive 153, 161, 216, 290
    labour-intensive 290
    mixed 153
    outputs 154
    pastoral 153
    processes 154
    and river sediment 88
    in the Sahel 36–7
    sedentary 154
    subsistence 43, 143, 153–4, 160–2, 166, 289–90, 305
    systems diagram models 154–60
    types of 153–4, 157
    and volcanoes 79–80
    see also agriculture
faults 95
favelas 66, 69
feedback 154
fertilisers 105, 156, 216, 222, 226
fertility, soil 34, 37–8, 79, 90
fertility rate 5
    China 17
    France 19
    Western Europe 18–19
    world's 5, 18
fetch 93
fieldwork 329–34, 329–47
    common techniques 333
    and data collection 329, 331, 333, 336–8, 343
    equipment 331
    examples 335–47
    fieldwork skills 269–78
    planning 331
    politeness 331–2
    practical hints 330–2
    practice/pilot investigation 331
    precautions 330–1
    recoding data 330, 331
    'route to geographical enquiry' 329–30
    safety issues 330
financial services 49
fire 68, 120, 129, 225
fishing 34, 215, 216, 217
    see also overfishing
floats 278
flood plains 85, 87, 89–90, 91, 134
    mapping 242
floods 10, 87, 128–30, 230
    Bangladeshi 133–5
    coastal 224
    flash 133
    and land fertility 34, 90
    mapping 242
    and the Mekong delta 88
    and the Mississippi 91
    and tropical storms 132
flow diagrams 257
flow meters 275
focus 78, 307–8
fog, coastal 127
food aid 165–6
food chains 104
food distribution 163, 168
food needs 10
food prices 164, 169, 170
food production 8, 153–70
    local 153–5
food shortages 163–70
    causes of 164
    and food distribution 163
    health effects 165
    tackling 165–70
    see also famine
food supplies 50
footloose industries 178
forest fires 120, 225
forests 43, 120
    dipterocarp 120
    swamp 158–9
    see also deforestation; rainforests
fossil fuels 34, 189–93, 195, 198–9
    and global warming 222
    maps 248
    sustainability 71
France 19–20, 50–1, 184–6
free trade 145, 151
friction 84, 86
fuelwood 43, 193–5
Fukushima Daiichi nuclear power plant 78, 79
functions (site) 39, 47, 53

garimpeiros 220
gas *see* natural gas
GDP *see* gross domestic product
GDP per capita 11, 137
gender
    age/sex pyramids 27, 29–30, 254, 262
    imbalance 17
genetically modified (GM) crops 167, 170
Geographic Information System (GIS) v, 279–82
geological events 129
    see also earthquakes; volcanoes
geology 94
geothermal energy 196, 198
Germany 19, 27, 300
Gha grass 127
Ghana 205
giant triton 104
ginger 43
GIS *see* Geographic Information System
glaciers 223
global citizens v

Index **385**

Global Green Economy Index 58
Global Positioning System (GPS) 279
global warming 164, 221, 222–5
globalisation 147–52
    causes of 148
    definition 147
    future of 149–50
    and transnational corporations 148–9
GM (genetically modified) crops 167, 170
GNP per capita 138, 140
gold 218, 220
'good life' 136–7
goods 3
    comparison 55
    high order 48
    locally made 136
    low order 48
governments
    and farming 156
    and food shortages 168–70
    and industrial location 175
GPS see Global Positioning System
gradients 238, 239, 276
grain production 163
graphs 251–5, 338–9
    age/sex pyramids 254, 262, 292
    bar graphs 110, 144, 247–8, 251–2, 260, 292
    climate graphs 107, 261, 292
    compound graphs 260
    and examinations 292, 309
    histograms 110, 251–2, 254, 260
    interpretation 260–1
    line graphs 251, 260, 292
    pie graphs (pie charts/circle graphs) 144, 255, 261, 292
    radial graphs 255
    scatter graphs 253–4, 292
    simple graphs 251–3
    triangular graphs 144, 254
    wind rose graphs (rose diagrams) 255
grazing see overgrazing
Great Barrier Reef, Australia 103–5
    Great Barrier Reef Marine Park 229–32
green belts 59
green cities 57–8, 71–2
Green Revolution 166
greenhouse effect, enhanced 222–3
greenhouse gases 222–3
Greenland 218–19
grey water 205
grid lines 236
grid references 236–7
grid squares 237
grid systems 55, 81
gross domestic product (GDP) 137
    see also GDP per capita
groundwater 83, 162, 220

groynes 96, 278
Gudalur, India 44
gullies 226

habitat destruction 127, 128, 158–9, 225
habitats 43, 117
    coastal 92
    rainforest 120
Haiti 27
halocarbons 223
halophytic species 97, 102, 125
hamlets 45, 50
harsh environments 214
hazard maps 247
hazards 330
    see also natural hazards
HDI see Human Development Index
headlands 94
health 165
health and safety 177
HEP see hydroelectric power
herbicides 156
high pressure 122
high-rise flats 70
high-technology industry 178–80
    global distribution 178
    and industry location 178–9
    and research and development 178–9
histograms 110, 251–2, 254, 260
HIV (human immunodeficiency virus) 13–15
Holderness 95
Hoover Dam 203
Horn of Africa 164
hot springs 196
housing
    in the Central Business District 55
    inner zone 55
    near volcanoes 79–81
    outer zone (suburbs) 55–6
    in the rural-urban fringe 59
    self-help schemes 68–9
    site and service schemes 68, 69–70
    upgrading 68–70
Hoyt urban land use model 53
Hsinchu Science Park, Taiwan 179–80
Hum, Croatia 45
human activity
    and climatic events 129
    and deserts 127–8
    environmental risks of 213–34
    mapping 242, 244
Human Development Index (HDI) 136, 137, 138–9
Human Development Report 138–9
human features 242–4, 264–5
human immunodeficiency virus (HIV) 13–15
human impact, environmental 103–4, 127–8, 152, 278

human inputs, and agriculture 156, 157, 160, 161
humidity
    equatorial 115, 119
    relative 110–11
humus 124
hurricanes 131–3
    Hurricane Katrina 132–3
hydraulic action 83, 85, 93, 95
hydroelectric power (HEP) 197, 199, 202
hydrological events 129
hygrometers 109, 110–11
hypotheses 329, 330, 333, 336–47

ice caps 223
ice sheets 218, 223
illegal immigrants 24
illiteracy 66
illustrations 263–8, 292, 310, 320–4
immigrants 23, 24, 194–5
immigration 19, 295–6
impervious rock 203
imports 136, 141, 192
income
    children and 4
    disposable 59, 182
    in rural areas 43
    and transnational corporations 149
independent variable 253
India 52
    and car ownership 64
    and deforestation 194–5
    and the fuelwood crisis 194–5
    and rice farming 289–90
    and rural areas 43–4
    and squatter settlements 67
    and water use 210
Indonesia 151, 152
industrial development 143–5
industrial location 52–3, 174–5
Industrial Revolution 55, 69
industrialised countries 4
industry 12, 88, 171–80
    classification 141–2
    and environmental damage 221
    high-technology 178–80
    local manufacturing 173
    primary (extractive) 141, 145
    quaternary (knowledge and information) 142
    secondary (processing/manufacturing) 3, 141, 145, 149, 171–80
    tertiary (service) 142, 145
    and water use 2–6
industry sectors 141
inequalities
    between country 139, 140
    and development 139–40
    in life expectancy 140

386   Index

regional 139
wealth 139–40, 147
infant mortality rate 4, 6, 12, 13
infectious diseases 6, 13–15
and food shortages 164
in rural areas 44
in squatter settlements 67
tropical 223
water-borne 10, 57, 134
infiltration 82, 124
infiltration rates 278
information resources 292, 310
infrastructure 53
and food production 168
and mining 127
and tourism 183
and water supply 210
inner city areas 53
inner core 73
inner zones 54, 55, 69–70
inputs
and farming 154–61
and secondary industry 174, 175–6, 178
insolation 116
interception 82
Internet users 148
interviews 269–72, 343
investment
in farming 168
foreign 145, 146, 149
government 146, 168
iodine deficiency 165
irrigation 135, 155, 205, 210–11
and the Aral Sea disaster 216
and hydroelectric power 203
and rice farming 161–2
solar-powered 167
and water conservation 209
islands 95
Isle of Wight 48–9
isobars 256
isogons 256
isohyets 256
isolines 256
isotachs 256
isotherms 256

Japan
age/sex pyramid 30
earthquake 2011 77–9
nuclear programmes 78, 79
tsunami 2011 77–8, 281
jobs
and counter-urbanisation 22
loss of 10
and under-population 136
see also employment

karoshi (working yourself to death) 30
Kazakhstan 216, 217

Kenya 187–8
keys, map 235, 258
knolls 240
Kolkata, India 52
kwashiorkor 165

labour 156
agricultural 9, 168
cheap 151
child 4, 66
and industrial location 174, 176
migrant 66, 68, 136
lagoons 97
lahars 80, 129
lakes 208
land
agricultural 161, 162, 164, 168
fertility 34, 37–8, 79, 90
flat 40, 200
and industrial location 174, 179, 200
and nuclear power stations 200
sites 39
land shape 237–9
land use maps 258–60
land use zones 53
landforms 240–2
landscapes, sketching 266–7
landslides 132
lava 74, 75, 80
lava domes 80
leaching 38, 118
leaf adaptations 125
leaf litter 118
LEDCs *see* less economically developed countries
leisure industry 181–8
leisure time 59
see also recreation
less economically developed countries (LEDCs) 139
age/sex pyramids of 27, 29
and cities 46, 54, 55
and development 139, 143, 145
and energy use 197, 198
and environmental damage 220
and food shortages 165, 167, 168
and fuelwood 194
and globalisation 148
and the impact of natural hazards 130, 131
and industrial development 143
main causes of death in 14
and manufacturing 176–7
and squatter settlements 66–8
and tourism 182, 183, 186–8
and water supplies 209, 210
levees 87, 91
Liberia 9
life expectancy 137
inequalities in 140
Japanese 30

and population explosion 4–5
and under-population 12
line of best-fit 254
line graphs 251, 260, 292
literacy rates 12, 137
load
rivers 83–7, 89, 275–6
of the sea 93
see also bedload
location
of hydroelectric power stations 202–3
industrial 174–6, 178–9
of nuclear power stations 200–1
of retail parks 59
locusts 6
London 61–3
London Docklands Development Corporation 63
longshore drift 96–7, 98, 277–8
low pressure 116, 132
Lyon, France 51

machinery 156
magma (molten rock) 74, 76, 196
magnitude 76
malaria 13, 14
Malaysia 158–60
malnutrition 164, 165, 216
mangrove swamps 101–3
Manila, Philippines 22
mantle 73, 74, 76
manufacturing *see* secondary industry (manufacturing)
maps
analysis 247–8
comparing 248–9
contour lines 237–8, 240–1, 256
conventions 235
cross-sections 313–14
data mapping 256–7
describing 245–6
desire line maps (rose/ray diagrams) 257
digitised maps 280, 281
and direction giving 235–6
and distance 236
drainage maps 240–2
and examinations 292, 302–3, 309, 311–20
flow line maps 257
and Geographic Information Systems 280
and gradients 239
and grid references 236–7
and grid systems 81
and human landscapes 242–4
and isolines 256
keys 235, 258
and land shape 237–9
land use maps 258–60
and landforms 240–2

Index **387**

map skills 235–44, 246–7
Ordnance Survey maps 41–2
and scale 236
sketching from 265–6
thematic maps 247–8, 260
topographical maps 236, 237–8
using 245–50
marasmus 165
markets 156, 175
marram grass 97
marshes, salt 97
mean annual rainfall 155
meanders 40, 85–7, 89
'swan's neck' 86
MEDCs see more economically developed countries
medicine 12, 49
and death rates 13
and life expectancy 4, 5
in rural areas 44
mega-dams 208
megacities 45
Mekong delta, Vietnam 87–8
mercury contamination 221
meteorologists 111, 113
methane 222
Mexican migrants 299
Mexico 29
mid-Atlantic trench 76
migrant labour 66, 68, 136
migrants, economic 24, 126, 293–300
migration 21–6
definition 21
examination questions on 293–300
forced 24
from one country to another 23–6
from Poland 293–8
international 6, 12
major migration routes 24
motivations for 21–3
and population growth 6
rural–urban 21–2, 23, 34
voluntary 24
military activity 233
mineral deposits 34, 218
mineral production maps 247
mining 127–8, 172, 192, 218–19, 221
Mississippi river, USA 89–91
MNCs see Multinational Corporations
monocultures 158
monsoon rains 43, 52, 119, 133
Montserrat 80–1
more economically developed countries (MEDCs) 145–6, 176
and age/sex pyramids 27, 29
and cities 53–4
and development 139
and energy use 191, 198, 200
and environmental damage 220
and high-technology industry 179

and the impact of natural hazards 130, 131
main causes of death in 14
and tourism 184–6
and transnational corporations 149
mosquitoes 13, 14
mountains, fold 73, 76
multinational corporations (MNCs) 145, 148
see also transnational corporations
multiplier effects 149, 183
Mumbai, India 67

Namib Desert, Namibia 126–8
Nasser, Lake 211
National Parks 95–6, 120, 187, 232–4, 270
see also Great Barrier Reef Marine Park
natural disasters 128–35
and farming 164
and migration 24
and over-population 10
natural environment 71, 283
natural gas 189, 191–2, 198, 222
natural gas-fired power stations 199
natural hazards 73–81, 128–35, 330
climatic and weather events 129
geological events 129
hydrological events 129
natural hazard maps 247
and population 6, 7
prediction 130
preparation 130
protection from 130
see also earthquakes; storms; volcanoes
natural inputs 155–7, 160–1
natural population growth (NPG) 9, 16
natural resources 71, 136, 213, 227–9
needs, basic 10, 213
New Zealand 99–100
Newly Industrialised Countries (NICs) 139, 145–7
and globalisation 148
and high-technology industry 179
and tourism 182
Nike 150–2
Nile basin 211
Nile River 83, 211
nitrous oxides 222
noise levels 58
noise pollution 57, 60, 67
nomads 37, 154, 164
nomadic herding 128
North Africa 36–7
northings 236
NPG see natural population growth

nuclear power 78, 79, 198, 200–2, 250
nuclear reactors 200
nutrient leaching 38, 118
nutrient recycling 118

oases 124
ocean currents 123
oil 189, 191–2, 198, 222
oil-fired power stations 199
prices 191
oktas 113–14
Olympic Games (Summer), London 2012 62, 63
Olympic Village, Stratford 62
Omara Spit, New Zealand 99–100
online shopping 47
optimum population 136
orangutan 120, 225
Ordnance Survey (OS) 41–2, 280
outer core 73
outer zones (suburbs) 54, 55–6
outputs
and farming 154
and secondary industry 174
over-population 3, 8–13, 136
overfishing 104, 230
overgrazing 37, 128
overland flow 82
overtime 30
oxbow lakes 85, 86

palm oil 119–20, 158–60, 225
pandemics 13
PARC acronym 243
Paris, France 50–1
Paris Basin 50
park-and-ride facilities 65
parks 71, 72
see also National Parks
pass (gap) 240
pedestrianisation 65
perennial plants 125
permaculture 167
pesticides 156, 216
pests 164
photographs 263–5, 292, 310
aerial 264–5
photosynthesis 225
Pico Hydro plants 204
pie graphs (pie charts/circle graphs) 144, 255, 261, 292
plantations 158–60
plate boundaries/margins 73–6, 250, 320–4
collision 76
conservative 76, 77
constructive 76
destructive 76, 80
plate tectonics 73–4
plateaus 240
plunge pools 85

388   Index

Poland 293–8
polar regions 217–19, 223
political factors 175
political maps 247
pollutants 220
pollution
   environmental impact 57–8
   'haze' 225
   noise 57, 60, 67
   nuclear 79, 200–1
   reduction measures 71
   and transnational corporations 149, 152
   visual 57, 60
   water 57, 104–5, 220–1, 230, 285
   see also air pollution
polyps (coral) 101, 104, 105
poor, the 139–40, 169
   see also poverty
population dynamics 2–20
   and anti-natalist population policies 16–18
   densely populated areas 8, 32, 34–5, 213
   examination questions on 283, 304
   and family size 2–3
   and infectious diseases 13–15
   and migration 21–6
   optimum populations 136
   over-population 3, 8–13, 136
   and population control policies 5, 16–18
   population density 8, 32–8, 213
   population distribution 32–8
   population explosions 2, 4–6
   population size and settlement hierarchies 45
   and pro-natalist population policies 18–20
   and replacement levels 16, 30
   and resources 3, 8–10, 11, 12, 25, 34
   sparsely populated 8, 32–4, 36–8
   and threshold populations 47–8
   total population 7
   under-population 8, 9, 11–13, 136
   urban populations 51
population growth 2–3, 223
   control 5, 16–18
   declining rates of 5
   and densely populated areas 35
   different rates of 6–7
   economic benefits of 3
   effects on people 3
   and food shortages 163, 164
   and migration 19, 25
   natural 9, 16
   negative 30
   and over-population 10, 12
   and population explosions 2, 4–6
   population growth-resource link 8–10

   and pro-natalist population policies 18–20
   rapid 10, 12, 25
   and water demands 207
population structure 27–31
   unbalanced 17
Port Campbell National Park, Victoria 95–6
Port Castries, St Lucia 41–2, 45
ports 34, 61–2, 314–16
potholes 84, 85
poverty 24, 137, 139–40, 147
   see also poor, the
poverty line 136
power stations 91, 196, 198–202
   coal-burning 59, 192, 199
   hydroelectric 202–4
   natural gas-fired 199
   nuclear 200–2
   oil-fired 199
   thermal 199
primary data 329
primary (extractive) industry 141, 145
prison 30
pro-natalist population policies 18–20
processes
   farming 154
   rivers 83–4
   secondary industry 174
protractors 235, 236, 277
public transport 65, 72, 320
pull factors (migration) 21
push factors (migration) 21
pyroclastic flows 75, 80, 129

quadrats 277
quality of life 55, 68, 136–7, 138
quarrying/quarries 60, 233
quaternary (knowledge and information) industry 142
questionnaires 269–70, 331–2, 343

R&D see research and development
radial graphs 255
rain gauges 109, 110
rainfall 88
   convectional 115, 116
   and desertification 38
   equatorial 115, 116, 119
   extreme 106, 132
   and farming 155
   global 208
   and hot deserts 121, 122–4, 126, 127
   mean annual 155
   measurement 109, 110
   monsoon 43, 52, 119, 133
   rainfall maps 256
   and the Sahel 36–7
   and soil erosion 226
   and tropical storms 132

rainforests 146–7, 225, 287
   and deforestation 146, 147, 287–8
   environment 119–21
   and vegetation 117–19
rainshadow effects 123, 127
rainwater harvesting
   large-scale 208
   small-scale 209–10
Rajasthan, India 210
Rana Plaza disaster 2013 177
rapid transit systems 65
rapids 84, 85
raw materials 34, 151, 214
   and industrial location 174–6, 178
   and nuclear power 200–1
   and primary industry 141
re-use 228
recreation 91
   see also leisure time
recycling 58, 71, 72, 174, 228
redevelopment 55, 70
reduce 228
redundancy 149
refugees 24, 62, 134, 164
relative humidity 110–11
relief 155, 237–8, 240, 243, 259–60, 317
remote communities 29
remote sensing 281
renovation 69–70
rent 55
replacement level 16, 30
research and development (R&D) 175, 178–9
reservoirs 202, 208, 211
residential areas
   upgrading 68–70
   see also housing
resources
   and population 3, 8–12, 25, 34
   see also natural resources
retail parks 59
revenue 184
rice production 153, 161–3, 166, 289–90
rich, the 139–40
Richter Scale 76, 77
ridges 240, 241
risks, environmental 213–34
river basins 89
river beds 83, 85
river bridging points 40
river deltas 102
river mouths 83, 87–8, 97
rivers 82–91, 208
   confluence 40, 85, 241
   courses 84–7
   cross-sections 274–5
   and deposition 83–4, 85, 86, 87
   depth of 274
   describing on maps 241–2

Index **389**

and drainage basin processes 82–3
energy of 83
and erosion 83–5
features 84–9
gradients of 276
as hazards 330
load of 83–7, 89, 275–6
long profile of 82, 83, 276
and meanders 40, 85–7, 89
measurements 274–6
and pollution 285
processes of 83–4
and settlement sites 40
sources of 83
and transportation 84, 86
velocity of 83–5, 87, 275, 336–7, 340–1
wetted perimeters of 275, 339–40
width of 274
world's greatest 89–91
roads 52–3, 60, 64–5, 318–20
Roçinha, Rio de Janeiro 69
rock, impervious 203
Romans 61–2
'route to geographical enquiry' 329–30
rural areas 39–49
and aerial photography 265
and anti-natalist population policies 16
attractions of 22, 39–40
hardships of 21
life in 39–40, 43–7
on Ordnance Survey maps 41–2
in St Lucia 41–2
and urbanisation 59
rural land use maps 260
rural–urban fringe 54–6, 59–61
rural–urban migration 21–2, 23, 34
rush hours 64
Ryde, Isle of Wight 48–9

safety issues 330
Sahara desert 36, 37, 123, 193, 226
Sahel 36–8, 210
St Helens, Mount 323–4
St Lucia 41–2, 45
salinisation 37
salinity
  soil 124, 125
  water 216, 217
salt marshes 97
sampling 271–2
  random 272
  stratified 272
  systematic 272
San Andreas Fault, California 76
sand dunes 95, 97–8, 125–7
Sarawak, Malaysia 158–60
satellite images 258, 279–82
Saudi Arabia 139–40, 191
scatter graphs 253–4, 292
school runs 64

science parks 178–80
Scotland 22–3
sea 92–3, 208
sea bed gradients 93
sea temperature rises 104, 223, 230
sea-floor spreading 76
sea-level rises 132, 223, 224
secondary data 329
secondary industry (manufacturing) 3, 141, 145, 149, 171–80
  and career choices 171–3
  and feedback 174
  high-technology industry 178–80
  and industrial location 174–6, 178–9
  and inputs 174, 175–6, 178
  local 173
  and outputs 174
  and processes 174
  systems diagram of 173
  and waste 174
sediment 87–8, 91, 93, 96–7, 276, 278
sedimentation 97
seismic activity 76, 80–1
seismic monitoring 76, 81
seismographs (seismometers) 76
semi-arid environments 38
Senegal 25–6, 228
service provision 45–9
settlements 39–49
  deciding where to build 39
  linear 244
  mapping patterns of 242–4
  nucleated 244
  rural 39–49
  settlement hierarchies 45–8, 50
  shape 244
  sites 50, 243
  situation 50, 243
  squatter 52, 54–5, 66–9, 71
  urban 50–63
sewage 210
sexually transmitted infections (STIs) 13
shanty towns 66
  see also squatter settlements
shape 244
SHAWL acronym 243
shelter 10
shifting cultivation 160–1
shipping industry 35, 104
shopping facilities 45, 47, 48, 49
silt 89–90, 135
Singapore 11, 34, 70, 179
sites 39
  and industrial location 174
  mapping 243
  settlement 50, 243
  site factors 39–40
  site functions 39, 47, 53
situation 50–1, 243
sketching 265–7
slopes 155, 238–41, 277

slumping 95
slums 70
  see also squatter settlements
smog 57
smoke 225
soil
  desert 124
  and farming 155, 161
  fertility 34, 37–8, 79, 90
  leaching 38
  rainforest 118
  salinity 124, 125
  topsoil 124
soil degradation 37–8
soil erosion 37, 118, 164
  and deforestation 193, 225, 226
  desert 124, 128
  environmental effects 226
  protection measures 167
soil exhaustion 164
soil fertility 37–8, 79, 118, 135, 155
solar energy 167, 189, 197
solution 83, 93
Soufriere Hills volcano, Montserrat 80–1
Soviet Union 216
soybeans 146, 147
Spanish Flu 13
sparsely populated 8, 32–4, 36–8
spits 97, 99–100
sports tourism 182
spot heights 237–8
spurs 240
squatter settlements 52, 54–5, 66–9, 71
stacks 95
standard of living 3, 8, 136–7
  Canadian 12
  and migration 25
  suburban 55–6
  and transnational corporations 149
  and water demands 207
starvation 164
Stevenson, Thomas 108
Stevenson screens 108, 109
STIs see sexually transmitted infections
storm surges 132, 133, 134, 224
storms 129
  eye of the 132
  tropical 129, 131–3
stratus clouds 113
street patterns 55
stumps 95
Sub-Saharan Africa 14
subduction zones 76
subsidies 156
subsistence crops 43
subsistence farming 43, 143, 153–4, 160–2, 166, 289–90, 305
suburbanisation 59
suburbs (outer zones) 54, 55–6

390 Index

Sudan 211
suicide 30
sulphur dioxide 57
sunshine levels 110
surface runoff 124
surveys, environmental quality 273–4
suspension 276
sustainability issues
   and coral reefs 104
   and energy sources 195
   and environmental conservation 227
   and environmental exploitation 217–19
   and natural resources 71, 227–9
   sustainable cities 70–2
   and water supplies 206–7, 211
swamp forests 158–9
swash 93, 277
systems diagram models 154–60

Tanzania 11, 12
taxation 149
tea 43
technology
   and farming 156
   and food production 167
   high-technology industry 178–80
   and industrial location 175
tectonic plates 73–4, 320–4
temperate 213
temperature
   air 108, 111, 116–17, 119, 155
   measurement 108
   sea 104, 223, 230
   temperature maps 256
temperature ranges
   annual 115
   diurnal 115, 116–17, 122, 124
terrorism, Kenyan 187, 188
tertiary (service) industry 142, 145
textile workers 66, 67, 176–7
thermometers 108
   maximum-minimum 108, 109
   wet and dry bulb (hygrometers) 109, 110–11
threshold populations 47–8
throughflow 82
tidal creeks 97
tidal energy 196–7, 199
tides, high 92
tiger economies 145
time management skills 283–4, 301–2
tombolos 98
topsoil 124
tornadoes 129
total population 7
tourism 181–8
   activity 128
   adventure 182, 218
   coastal 96
   and coral reefs 103, 104, 229, 231

coursework assignments 342–7
desert 214
ecotourism 182, 218
and environmental damage 103–4, 221, 229, 231, 233
global 182, 183–6
jobs in 172
in less economically developed countries 182, 183, 186–8
in more economically developed countries 184–6
revenue 184
and rivers 88, 91
speciality 182
sports 182
and volcanoes 80
towns 44, 50
   changing urban land use 53
   new 39, 59, 69, 70
   and population density 34, 35
   and settlement hierarchies 45
   town centres 330
toxic chemicals 220, 221
trade 12
   free 145, 151
trade barriers 148
traffic congestion 60, 64–5, 318–20
traffic exhaust fumes 57
traffic light systems 65
trains 65
transects 259, 260
transnational corporations (TNCs) 66
   definition 148
   and globalisation 148–9
   negative effects on economic development 149
   Nike 150–2
   organisation 148
   positive effects on economic development 149
   see also multinational corporations
transpiration 110
transport
   costs 169, 170
   and environmental damage 221
   and farming 156, 169, 170
   and industrial location 174, 175–6
   international 148
   links 45, 50, 59, 90, 174
   and rivers 90
   and the rural-urban fringe 59
   and settlement hierarchies 45
   and tourism 182
transport of materials 83
   coastal 93, 96–8, 278
   and rivers 83, 84, 86
travel 64
tree re-planting schemes 225
triangular graphs 144, 254
tributaries 85
tropical cyclones 230

tropical depressions 132
tropical storms 129, 131–3
tsunami 7, 129
   Japan 2011 77–8, 281
turbines 198–9, 202, 208
Turkish migrants 300
typhoid 44, 57

Ukraine 200–1
under-population 8, 9, 11–13, 136
underemployment 143
unemployment 3
   in less economically developed countries 143
   Liberian 9
   and migration 25
   and transnational corporations 149
   and under-population 12
uninhabited 32, 33
United Kingdom (UK)
   National Parks 232–4
   new towns 70
   renewable energy sources 305–6
United Nations (UN) 24, 140, 164
   Climate Change Conference 2009 58
   Human Development Index 137
   Human Development Report 138–9
United States 89–91, 137, 203, 205, 299
Upper Ddwli Falls, South Wales 85
uranium 200
urban areas 50–63, 264–5
urban change 61–3
urban land use 52–4, 259
urban sprawl 59, 71
urban zones 54–6
urbanisation 21–3, 34–5, 52, 64–72
   effect on the rural-urban fringe 59–61
   global rate 53
   maps 247
   problems caused by 64–6
   rapid 59–61
   and sustainable cities 70–2
Uzbekistan 216

valleys 40, 240–2
   V-shaped 84
value added 141
variables, dependent/independent 253
vegetation 115–35
   dormancy 124–5
   and farming 155
   of hot deserts 124–5, 127
   of tropical rainforests 117–19
velocity, rivers 83–5, 87, 275, 336–7, 340–1
Vietnam 87–8, 151, 152, 204

villages 43–4
- dispersed 41
- global population density 43
- linear 41
- nucleated 41, 44
- shapes and patterns 41, 44
- sites 50
- situations 50
- suburbanisation 59

viruses 13
visual pollution 57, 60
vitamin A deficiency 165
volcanoes 73–81, 128
- active 74, 79
- composite (strato-volcanoes) 74–5
- dormant 74
- and economic opportunity 79–80
- extinct 74
- and geothermal energy 196
- housing near 79–81
- mapping 250, 320–4
- shield 74
- sites 75–6
- structure 76
- and tourism 182
- types of 74–5

volcanological monitoring 81

wages
- low 66, 169
- minimum 177
- and transnational corporations 149, 151–2

warfare
- civil war 9, 164
- and migration 24
- and population 7

waste
- domestic 58
- energy production from 174, 175
- recycling 58, 71

water 12, 44, 205–212
- access to safe 207, 208–9
- collection 125
- contamination 134
- demand for 207–9
- lack of clean 10
- and population density 34
- salinity 216, 217
- and settlement sites 40
- and squatter settlements 67
- supply issues 209–10
- sustainable use 206–7
- and upgrading residential areas 69

water conservation 167
water deficit 206, 207
water pollution 57, 104–5, 220–1, 230, 285
water power 196–7, 199, 202–4, 208
water retention 125
water table 124
water transfer 207
water vapour 110
water-borne diseases 10, 57, 134
watercourses, damage to 220, 221
waterfalls 84, 85, 89
wave energy 196–7
wave frequency 276
wave-cut notches 95
wave-cut platforms 95
waves 92–5
- breaking 93
- constructive 93, 94, 276
- destructive 93, 94, 276
- measurement 276

wealth 48, 147
- inequality 139–40, 147
- and natural hazards 130
- and natural resources 218–19
- and tourism 182
- and transnational corporations 149

wealth distribution maps 247
weather 106–14
- digital recording equipment 112
- extreme 106, 129, 131–3, 223, 230
- investigation 108–10
- measurement 108–12
- typical/average (climate) 106–7
- see also rainfall; wind

weather events 129
weather stations 108, 109, 112, 261, 324–7
weathering processes 93, 95
wells 44, 210
West Bengal, India 194–5
Westminster, London 61–3
Where-to-be-born Index 12, 136, 137
wilderness areas 232
wildfire 129
wind
- direction 111
- dry 122, 123
- equatorial 115
- observation and measurement 111–12
- prevailing 122, 123, 127
- and sand dunes 97
- and soil erosion 226
- of tropical storms 131–2
- and waves 92–3

wind direction maps 256
wind energy 196, 199, 306
wind rose graphs (rose diagrams) 255
wind speed 111–12, 325
- maps 256
wind vanes 109, 111
woodlands 40
work, and rivers 83
working conditions 149, 152
'working-space levies' 65

x axis 251, 254

y axis 251, 254
Yorkshire Dales National Park, England 233–4
young people 27, 29

zones of activity 76

Acknowledgements

The publishers wish to thank the following for permission to reproduce photographs. Every effort has been made to trace copyright holders and to obtain permission for the use of copyright materials. The publishers will gladly receive any information enabling them to rectify any error or omission at the first opportunity.

Key: t = top, c = centre, b = bottom, r = right, l = left.

Cover illustration: Maria Herbert-Liew

2A: Monkey Business Images/Shutterstock
2B: VikramRaghuvanshi/iStockphoto
4B: Tomasz Otap/Shutterstock
4C: Dmitry Kalinovsky/Shutterstock
7C: Hideo Kurihara/Alamy
7D: Friedrich Stark/Alamy
12B: gary yim/Shutterstock
15D: Stephen Ford/Alamy
22B: Thomas Cockrem/Alamy
23: alanf/Shutterstock
24B: Sadik Gulec/Shutterstock
32A: Komar/Shutterstock
32B: Giancarlo Liguori/Shutterstock
33D: oksana.perkins/Shutterstock
33E: Andre Nantel/Shutterstock
33F: Hung Chung Chih/Shutterstock
33G: Vitalii Nesterchuk/Shutterstock
34A: Pakmor/Shutterstock
34B: Maria Gioberti/Shutterstock
35C: Graham Norris/iStockphoto
39A: ziggysofi/Shutterstock
39B: Evgeny Murtola/Shutterstock
41B: Sam Strickler/Shutterstock
42C: Map sourced from Exam Extract No 717/St Lucia © Government of Saint Lucia
43B: N Vasuki Rao/iStockphoto
44E: Jon Arnold Images Ltd/Alamy
45C: Justin Kase z04z/Alamy
49C: London Aerial Photo Library/Alamy
50A: David R. Frazier Photolibrary, Inc./Alamy
50B: Ruslana Iurchenko/Shutterstock
51D: Samot/Shutterstock
52A: Aman Khan/iStockphoto
54A: Hung Chung Chih/Shutterstock
55B: Baloncici/Shutterstock
55C: Paulo Pampolin/Shutterstock
56D: iofoto/Shutterstock
56E: Ulrike Stein/Shutterstock
57B: Ella Hanochi/Shutterstock
58D: Rodrigo Riestra/Shutterstock
59A: Andrew Holt/Alamy
59B: stocker1970/Shutterstock
60C: xtrekx/Shutterstock
62B: Greg Balfour Evans/Alamy
62C: s duffett/Shutterstock
62D: r.nagy/Shutterstock
65D: Petronilo G. Dangoy Jr./Shutterstock
67B: Holger Mette/iStockphoto
68C: Holger Mette/iStockphoto
69A: Peter Treanor/Alamy
69B: Bojan Brecelj/Corbis via Getty Images
69C: Terraxplorer/iStockphoto
70D: toonman/Shutterstock
71A: Marcelo Rudini/Alamy
72B: Wesley Jenkins/iStockphoto
72C: Hervé Collart/Sygma/Getty Images
78B: Miyako City Officer/REX/Shutterstock
78C: NOAA
78D: Propaganda/Alamy
80A: Justin Kase zsixz / Alamy
81B: Andrew Woodley/Alamy
82B: MarArt/Shutterstock
83D: Doug McCutcheon/LGPL/Alamy
85C t: Melodia plus photos/Shutterstock
85C b: The Photolibrary Wales/Alamy
84B: Karel Gallas/Shutterstock:
88B: NASA
88C: beboy/Shutterstock:
88D: Kees Metselaar/Alamy
90C l: Robert N. Dennis collection
90C r: Angela/CC by SA 3.0
90D: NASA Goddard Space Flight Center
92A tl: MartiniDry/Shutterstock
92A tr: Piotr Wawrzyniuk/Shutterstock
92A bl : Iakov Kalinin/Shutterstock
92A br: Thierry Maffeis/Shutterstock
96D (i): Philiphist/CC by 3.0
96D (ii): Kaspars Grinvalds/Shutterstock
97B: donsimon/Shutterstock
98C: Adam Gregor/Shutterstock
98D: David Wall/Alamy
98F: Sarah Pettegree/Shutterstock
99A: David Wall/Alamy
100B: Map sourced from NZTopo50-BA35 Whitianga. Crown Copyright Reserved
101A t: Specta/Shutterstock
101A b: Soren Egeberg Photography/Shutterstock
102C (a): Wolfgang Steiner/iStockphoto
102C (b): LordDimwit
102C (c) : ISS Astronaut Photography of Earth, Expedition 24 crew
102D: Matt Tilghman/Shutterstock
104C (a): Images & Stories/Alamy
104C (b): Khoroshunova Olga/Shutterstock
106A tl: B747/Shutterstock
106A tr: Asianet-Pakistan/Shutterstock
106A br: Gregory Gerber/Shutterstock
106A br: Brykaylo Yuriy/Shutterstock
109A bl: Caroline Green
109A b: Caroline Green
109A br: donvictorio@o2.pl/Shutterstock
109A bl: Artur Synenko/Shutterstock
109A b: ID1974/Shutterstock
109A br: VVO/Shutterstock
109A c: Pablo Paul/Alamy
110C: 501room/Shutterstock
112D: Malinovskyy Kostyantyn/Shutterstock
114C l: iofoto/Shutterstock
114C c: Serg64/Shutterstock
114C r: paul prescott/Shutterstock
118C: Vitaly Titov & Maria Sidelnikova/Shutterstock
120C: Eric Gevaert/Shutterstock
122B: Alexander Yu. Zotov/Shutterstock
124B: Patrick Poendl/Shutterstock
125C: Pichugin Dmitry/Shutterstock
125D: Katherine James
125E: Jens Peermann/Shutterstock
126B: NASA
126C l: Katherine James
126C c: Katherine James
126C r: Katherine James
128A: Sascha Burkard/Shutterstock
129B b: Asianet-Pakistan/Shutterstock
129B c: Martin Haas/Shutterstock
129B b: Darrenp/Shutterstock
132C: Jeff Schmaltz/MODIS/NASA
134C b: Mike Goldwater/Alamy
134C b: Koustav2007

136A: guentermanaus/Shutterstock
137D: Alan Gordine/Shutterstock
140G: UNMDC
141A: Jason Duggan/Shutterstock
141B: SDBCHINA/Alamy :
142C: wavebreakmedia ltd/Shutterstock
143D: Hans Martens/iStockphoto
146B: David R. Frazier Photolibrary, Inc./Alamy:
149E: arindambanerjee/Shutterstock
150A: Peter Charlesworth/LightRocket via Getty Images
152D: Nike
153A: kataleewan intarachote/Shutterstock
156A: Marko5/Shutterstock
156B: Ryan Rodrick Beiler/Shutterstock
156C: Daniele Silva/Shutterstock
159B: Eky Studio/Shutterstock
162B: gallimaufry/Shutterstock
163A: Reuters/David Mercado
164C: Mike Goldwater/Alamy
165B: AFP/Getty Images
167C: Riderfoot /Shutterstock.com
169C: Matthi/Shutterstock
171A bl: Catalin Petolea/Shutterstock
171A br: wavebreakmedia ltd/Shutterstock
171A bl: Zurijeta/Shutterstock
171A br: Nomad_Soul/Shutterstock
172B b: Image Source/Alamy
172B c: Werner Buchel/Shutterstock
172B b: JJM Stock Photography/Alamy
173B: arek_malang/Shutterstock
173A b: Sapsiwai/Shutterstock
173A b: Shamleen/Shutterstock
175C: nostal6ie/Shutterstock
176A: Chris Schmidt/iStockphoto:
177 D: rijans/CC by SA 2.0
178A br: 3d brained/Shutterstock
178A b: vovan/Shutterstock
178A bl: Jon Le-Bon/Shutterstock:
179D: Peellden/CC by SA 3.0
179E: Henry Leong Him Who/CC by SA 2.0
181A l: Dianne Maire/Shutterstock
181A br: Pincasso/Shutterstock
181A br: l i g h t p o e t/Shutterstock
185B: Andrea Paggiaro/Shutterstock
185C bl: Julia Zakharova/Shutterstock
185C bc: StockLite/Shutterstock

185C bl: mangostock/Shutterstock
185C bc: iofoto/Shutterstock
185C bl: doglikehorse/Shutterstock
188D: Eric Isselée/Shutterstock
188E: Irene Abdou/Alamy
189A bl: Image Source/Alamy
189A bl: Phil Date/Shutterstock
189A br: iordani/Shutterstock
189A br: RamonaS/Shutterstock
192C r: Aurora Photos/Alamy
192C l: loong/Shutterstock
193A: Geralda van der Es/iStockphoto
193B: Patrik Dietrich/Shutterstock
195F: Kailash K Soni/Shutterstock:
196D: Eugene Suslo/Shutterstock
197E: lafoto/Shutterstock
197F: Darren Baker/Shutterstock
197G: Joerg Boethling/Alamy
199C: VLADJ55/Shutterstock
199D: Clynt Garnham Energy/Alamy
199E: Yury Zakharov/Shutterstock
201B: Vlade Shestakov/Shutterstock
201C: Bullwinkle/Shutterstock
202A: Belinda Pretorius/Shutterstock
203D: iofoto/Shutterstock
204E: wesley bakker/Shutterstock
205A: PT Images/Shutterstock
205B: Olivier Asselin/Alamy
206C l: Ken Brown/iStockphoto
206C c: Photographee.eu/Shutterstock
206C br: newphotoservice/Shutterstock
206C br: Ilya Andriyanov/Shutterstock
208C: gopixgo/Shutterstock
210A: Randy Plett/iStockphoto
211C: ostill/Shutterstock
213A: LiTn/Shutterstock
214C: hipproductions/Shutterstock
216C: NASA
218B: Anders Peter Photography/Shutterstock
219C: Corepics VOF/Shutterstock
220B: grynold/Shutterstock
221C l: Worldwide Picture Library/Alamy
221C r: Sue Cunningham Photographic/Alamy
224D: jeremy sutton-hibbert/Alamy
226C: Yuri Kravchenko/Shutterstock
226D: NASA image by Jeff Schmaltz, LANCE/EOSDIS Rapid Response.
227B l: Andresr/Shutterstock

227B c: Mario Savoia/Shutterstock
227B r: photoflorenzo/Shutterstock
228D: Photononstop/Alamy
229 b: Pete Niesen/Shutterstock
231D: Robin Jeffries
233C b: Richard Bowden/Shutterstock
233C b: Stephen Meese/Shutterstock
234C: chris2766/Shutterstock
240A cl: Sky Light Pictures/Shutterstock
240a b: Studio 37/Shutterstock
240A cr: wildzero/shutterstock
240A bl: Peter Wey/Shutterstock
240A br: Valuykin Sergey/Shutterstock
242A: Martin Lehmann/Shutterstock
243B: Jorg Hackemann/Shutterstock
258A: NASA
263A: NASA/GSFC/METI/ERSDAC/JAROS and U.S./Japan ASTER Science Team
263B: allensima/Shutterstock
264C: Pakmor/Shutterstock
267B: Brian Granger/Van Rhijn Aerial Photography
267C: Kirena Barka/Shutterstock
269A: Bubbles Photolibrary/Alamy
271A: kret87/Shutterstock
273B: Chee-Onn Leong/Shutterstock
273C: Roman Mahmutoff/Shutterstock
275B: Graham Bool Photography/courtesy of Geopacks
275C: Ashley Cooper pics/Alamy
276D: Martin Shields/Alamy
276A: Royal Geographical Society (with IBG)
278C: Sue Robinson/Shutterstock
279A: Mechanik/Shutterstock
280C: Goodluz/Shutterstock
281A: NASA/GSFC/METI/ERSDAC/JAROS and U.S./Japan ASTER Science Team:
281B t: NASA/Landsat Project Science Office
281B c and b: NASA/GSFC/METI/ERSDAC/JAROS and U.S./Japan ASTER Science Team
282C: National Snow and Ice Data Center, Colorado, USA
312: Map sourced from Extract No 1544/Port Louis © Government of Mauritius